Year 2B

A Guide to Teaching for Mastery

Series Editor: Tony Staneff

Contents

Introduction

Foreword by the series editor and author, Tony Staneff

For far too long in the UK, maths has been feared by learners – and by many teachers, too. As a result, most learners consistently underachieve. More crucially, negative beliefs about ability, aptitude and the nature of maths are entrenched in children's thinking from an early age.

Yet, as someone who has loved maths all my life, I've always believed that every child has the capacity to succeed in maths. I've also had the great pleasure of leading teams and departments who share that belief and passion. Teaching for mastery, as practised in China and other South-East Asian jurisdictions since the 1980s, has confirmed my conviction that maths really is for everyone and not just those who have a special talent. In recent years my team and I at Trinity Academy, Halifax, have had the privilege of researching with and working with some of the finest mastery practitioners from the UK and beyond, whose impact on learners' confidence, achievement and attitude is an inspiration.

The mastery approach recognises the value of developing the power to think rather than just do. It also recognises the value of making a coherent journey in which whole-class groups tackle concepts in very small steps, one by one. You cannot build securely on loose foundations – and it is just the same with maths: by creating a solid foundation of deep understanding, our children's skills and confidence will be strong and secure. What's more, the mindset of learner and teacher alike is fundamental: everyone can do maths… EVERYONE CAN!

I am proud to have been part of the extensive team responsible for turning the best of the world's practice, research, insights, and shared experiences into *Power Maths*, a unique teaching and learning resource developed especially for UK classrooms. *Power Maths* embodies our vision to help and support primary maths teachers to transform every child's mathematical and personal development. 'Everyone can!' has become our mantra and our passion, and we hope it will be yours, too.

Now, explore and enjoy all the resources you need to teach for mastery, and please get back to us with your *Power Maths* experiences and stories!

What is *Power Maths*?

Created especially for UK primary schools, and aligned with the new National Curriculum, *Power Maths* is a whole-class, textbook-based mastery resource that empowers every child to understand and succeed. *Power Maths* rejects the notion that some people simply 'can't do' maths. Instead, it develops growth mindsets and encourages hard work, practice and a willingness to see mistakes as learning tools.

Best practice consistently shows that mastery of small, cumulative steps builds a solid foundation of deep mathematical understanding. *Power Maths* combines interactive teaching tools, high-quality textbooks and continuing professional development (CPD) to help you equip children with a deep and long lasting understanding. Based on extensive evidence, and developed in partnership with practising teachers, *Power Maths* ensures that it meets the needs of children in the UK.

Power Maths and Mastery

Power Maths makes mastery practical and achievable by providing the structures, pathways, content, tools and support you need to make it happen in your classroom.

To develop mastery in maths children must be enabled to acquire a deep understanding of maths concepts, structures and procedures, step by step. Complex mathematical concepts are built on simpler conceptual components and when children understand every step in the learning sequence, maths becomes transparent and makes logical sense. Interactive lessons establish deep understanding in small steps, as well as effortless fluency in key facts such as tables and number bonds. The whole class works on the same content and no child is left behind.

Power Maths

- Builds every concept in small, progressive steps
- Is built with interactive, whole-class teaching in mind
- Provides the tools you need to develop growth mindsets
- Helps you check understanding and ensure that every child is keeping up
- Establishes core elements such as intelligent practice and reflection

The *Power Maths* approach

Everyone can!

Founded on the conviction that every child can achieve, *Power Maths* enables children to build number fluency, confidence and understanding, step by step.

Child-centred learning

Children master concepts one step at a time in lessons that embrace a concrete-pictorial-abstract (C-P-A) approach, avoid overload, build on prior learning and help them see patterns and connections. Same-day intervention ensures sustained progress.

Continuing professional development

Embedded teacher support and development offer every teacher the opportunity to continually improve their subject knowledge and manage whole-class teaching for mastery.

Whole-class teaching

An interactive, whole-class teaching model encourages thinking and precise mathematical language and allows children to deepen their understanding as far as they can.

Introduction to the author team

Power Maths arises from the work of maths mastery experts who are committed to proving that, given the right mastery mindset and approach, **everyone can do maths**. Based on robust research and best practice from around the world, *Power Maths* was developed in partnership with a group of UK teachers to make sure that it not only meets our children's wide-ranging needs but also aligns with the National Curriculum in England.

Tony Staneff, Series Editor and author

Vice Principal at Trinity Academy, Halifax, Tony also leads a team of mastery experts who help schools across the UK to develop teaching for mastery via nationally recognised CPD courses, problem-solving and reasoning resources, schemes of work, assessment materials and other tools.

✚ A team of experienced authors, including:

- ⚡ **Josh Lury** – a specialist maths teacher, author and maths consultant with a passion for innovative and effective maths education

- ⚡ **Jenny Lewis, Stephen Monaghan, Beth Smith and Kelsey Brown** – skilled maths teachers and mastery experts

- ⚡ **Cherri Moseley** – a maths author, former teacher and professional development provider

- ⚡ **Paul Wrangles** – a maths author and former teacher, Paul's goal is to "ignite creative thought in teachers and pupils by providing creative teaching resources".

✚ Professor Liu Jian, Series Consultant and author, and his team of mastery expert authors:

⚡ **Hou Huiying, Huang Lihua, Wang Mingming, Yin Lili, Zhang Dan, Zhang Hong and Zhou Da**

Used by over 20 million children, Professor Liu Jian's textbook programme is one of the most popular in China. He and his author team are highly experienced in intelligent practice and in embedding key maths concepts using a C-P-A approach.

✚ A group of 15 teachers and maths co-ordinators

We have consulted our teacher group throughout the development of *Power Maths* to ensure we are meeting their real needs in the classroom.

Your *Power Maths* resources

To help you teach for mastery, *Power Maths* comprises a variety of high-quality resources.

Pupil Textbooks

Discover, Share, and Think together sections promote discussion and introduce mathematical ideas logically, so that children understand more easily.

Using a Concrete-Pictorial-Abstract approach, clear mathematical models help children to make connections and grasp concepts.

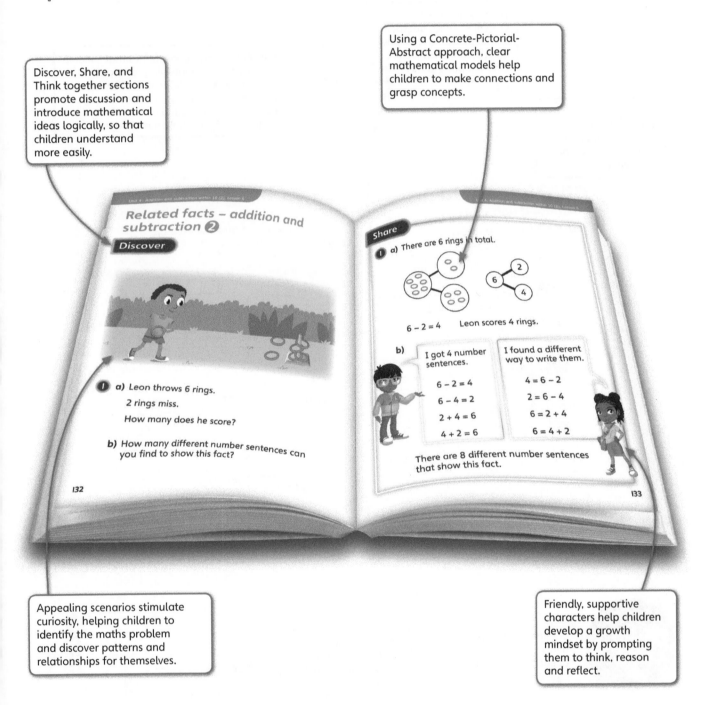

Appealing scenarios stimulate curiosity, helping children to identify the maths problem and discover patterns and relationships for themselves.

Friendly, supportive characters help children develop a growth mindset by prompting them to think, reason and reflect.

The coherent *Power Maths* lesson structure carries through into the vibrant, high-quality textbooks. Setting out the core learning objectives for each class, the lesson structure follows a carefully mapped journey through the curriculum and supports children on their journey to deeper understanding.

Pupil Practice Books

The Practice Books offer just the right amount of intelligent practice for children to complete independently in the final section of each lesson.

The practice questions are for everyone – each question varies one small element to move children on in their thinking. Look at the different parts in question ❶!

Calculations are connected so that children think about the underlying concept. In question ❸, children have to write out the calculation to find the answer. Concepts are presented differently again in question ❹ to challenge children.

Practice questions are finely tuned to move children forward in their thinking and to reveal misconceptions.

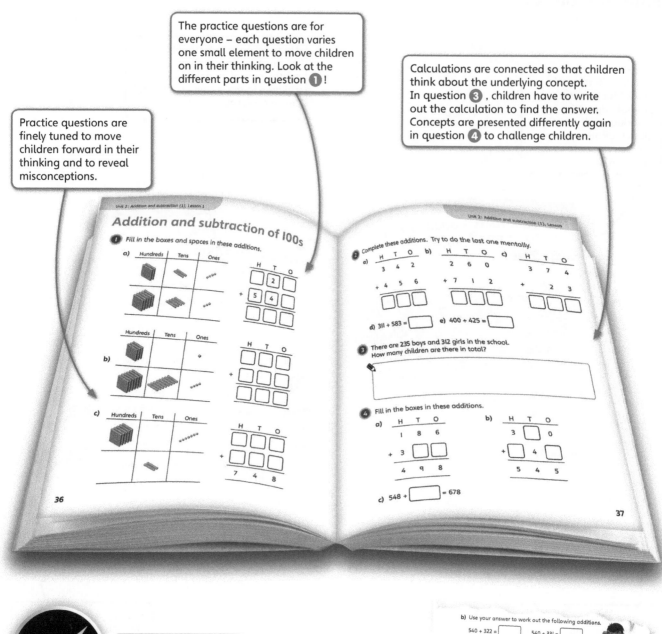

Challenge questions allow children to delve deeper into a concept.

Reflect questions reveal the depth of each child's understanding before they move on.

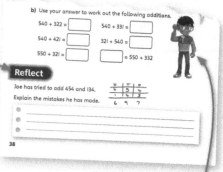

The *Power Maths* characters support and encourage children to think and work in different ways.

Online subscriptions

The online subscription will give you access to additional resources.

eTextbooks

Digital versions of *Power Maths* Textbooks allow class groups to share and discuss questions, solutions and strategies. They allow you to project key structures and representations at the front of the class, to ensure all children are focusing on the same concept.

Teaching tools

Here you will find interactive versions of key *Power Maths* structures and representations.

Power Ups

Use this series of daily activities to promote and check number fluency.

Online versions of Teacher Guide pages

PDF pages give support at both unit and lesson levels. You will also find help with key strategies and templates for tracking progress.

Unit videos

Watch the professional development videos at the start of each unit to help you teach with confidence. The videos explore common misconceptions in the unit, and include intervention suggestions as well as suggestions on what to look out for when assessing mastery in your students.

End of unit Strengthen and Deepen materials

Each Strengthen activity at the end of every unit addresses a key misconception and can be used to support children who need it. The Deepen activities are designed to be low ceiling / high threshold and will challenge those children who can understand more deeply. These resources will help you ensure that every child understands and will help you keep the class moving forward together. These printable activities provide an optional resource bank for use after the assessment stage.

Underpinning all of these resources, *Power Maths* is infused throughout with continual professional development, supporting you at every step.

The *Power Maths* teaching model

At the heart of *Power Maths* is a clearly structured teaching and learning process that helps you make certain that every child masters each maths concept securely and deeply. For each year group, the curriculum is broken down into core concepts, taught in units. A unit divides into smaller learning steps – lessons. Step by step, strong foundations of cumulative knowledge and understanding are built.

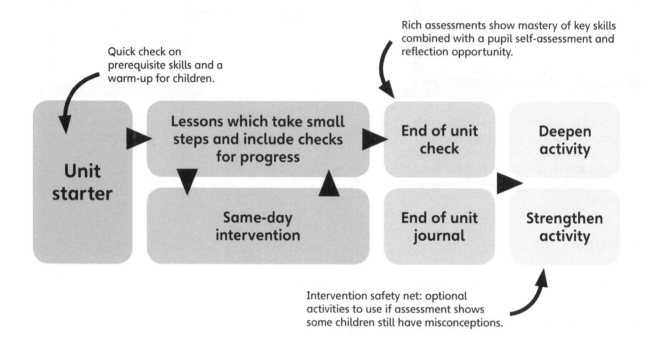

Quick check on prerequisite skills and a warm-up for children.

Rich assessments show mastery of key skills combined with a pupil self-assessment and reflection opportunity.

Intervention safety net: optional activities to use if assessment shows some children still have misconceptions.

Unit starter

Each unit begins with a unit starter, which introduces the learning context along with key mathematical vocabulary and structures and representations.

- The Pupil Textbooks include a check on readiness and a warm-up task for children to complete.

- Your Teacher Guide gives support right from the start on important structures and representations, mathematical language, common misconceptions and intervention strategies.

- Unit-specific videos develop your subject knowledge and insights so you feel confident and fully equipped to teach each new unit. These are available via the online subscription.

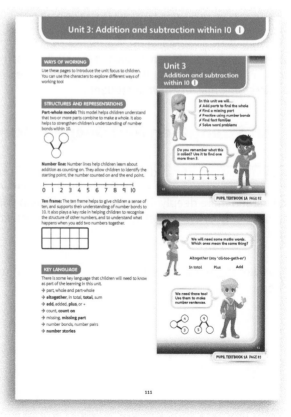

Lesson

Once a unit has been introduced, it is time to start teaching the series of lessons.

- Each lesson is scaffolded with Pupil Textbook and Practice Book activities and always begins with a Power Up activity (available via online subscription).

- *Power Maths* identifies lesson by lesson what concepts are to be taught.

- Your Teacher Guide offers lots of support for you to get the most from every child in every lesson. As well as highlighting key points, tricky areas and how to handle them, you will also find question prompts to check on understanding and clarification on why particular activities and questions are used.

Same-day intervention

Same-day interventions are vital in order to keep the class progressing together. Therefore, *Power Maths* provides plenty of support throughout the journey.

- Intervention is focused on keeping up now, not catching up later, so interventions should happen as soon as they are needed.

- Practice section questions are designed to bring misconceptions to the surface, allowing you to identify these easily as you circulate during independent practice time.

- Child-friendly assessment questions in the Teacher Guide help you identify easily which children need to strengthen their understanding.

End of unit check and journal

At the end of a unit, summative assessment tasks reveal essential information on each child's understanding. An End of unit check in the Pupil Textbook lets you see which children have mastered the key concepts, which children have not and where their misconceptions lie. The Practice Book also includes an End of unit journal in which children can reflect on what they have learned. Each unit also offers Strengthen and Deepen activities, available via the online subscription.

The Teacher Guide offers different ways of managing the End of unit assessments as well as giving support with handling misconceptions.

The End of unit check presents four multiple-choice questions. Children think about their answer, decide on a solution and explain their choice.

Unit 1: Numbers to 10 — → Textbook 1A p56

End of unit check

My journal

Bea has 5 red ◯ and 1 yellow ◯. Colour them in.

◯◯◯◯◯◯

Seth has 3 red ◯ and 3 yellow ◯. Colour them in.

◯◯◯◯◯◯

What is the same? _____

_____

What is different? _____

_____

These words might help you.

balloon	1	one
less	3	three
more	5	five

42

The End of unit journal is an opportunity for children to test out their learning and reflect on how they feel about it. Tackling the 'journal' problem reveals whether a child understands the concept deeply enough to move on to the next unit.

Unit 1: Numbers to 10

End of unit check

Your teacher will ask you these questions.

① What is the missing number?

____ 1   2   3

A 4   B 1   C 0   D 5

② What is the number?

A 3   B 4   C 5   D 7

③ Demi is counting from 1 to 10. She says, 'four'.
What numbers come next?

A 3, 2, 1   C 5, 6, 7
B 5, 7, 6   D 4, 5, 6

56

11

The *Power Maths* lesson sequence

At the heart of *Power Maths* is a unique lesson sequence designed to empower children to understand core concepts and grow in confidence. Embracing the National Centre for Excellence in the Teaching of Mathematics' (NCETM's) definition of mastery, the sequence guides and shapes every *Power Maths* lesson you teach.

Flexibility is built into the *Power Maths* programme so there is no one-to-one mapping of lessons and concepts meaning you can pace your teaching according to your class. While some children will need to spend longer on a particular concept (through interventions or additional lessons), others will reach deeper levels of understanding. However, it is important that the class moves forward together through the termly schedules.

Power Up ⏱ 5 minutes

Each lesson begins with a Power Up activity (available via the online subscription) which supports fluency in key number facts.

The whole-class approach depends on fluency, so the Power Up is a powerful and essential activity.

TOP TIP
If the class is struggling with the task, revisit it later and check understanding.

Power Ups reinforce the two key things that are essential for success: times-tables and number bonds.

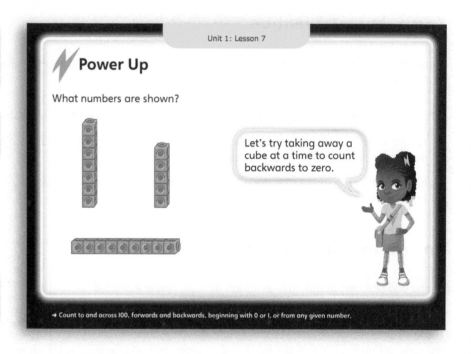

Discover ⏱ 10 minutes

A practical, real-life problem arouses curiosity. Children find the maths through story-telling.

TOP TIP
Discover works best when run at tables, in pairs with concrete objects.

Question ❶ a) tackles the key concept and question ❶ b) digs a little deeper. Children have time to explore, play and discuss possible strategies.

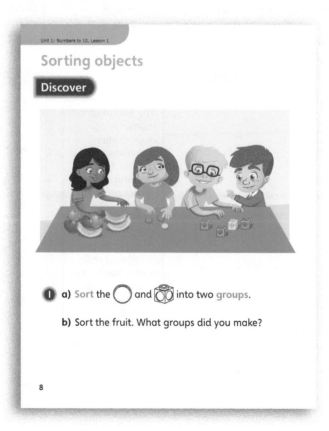

Share 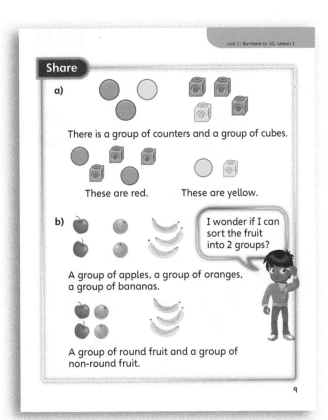 10 minutes

Teacher-led, this interactive section follows the Discover activity and highlights the variety of methods that can be used to solve a single problem.

TOP TIP
Bring children to the front or onto the carpet to discuss their methods. Pairs sharing a textbook is a great format for this!

Your Teacher Guide gives target questions for children. The online toolkit provides interactive structures and representations to link concrete and pictorial to abstract concepts.

Bring children to the front to share and celebrate their solutions and strategies.

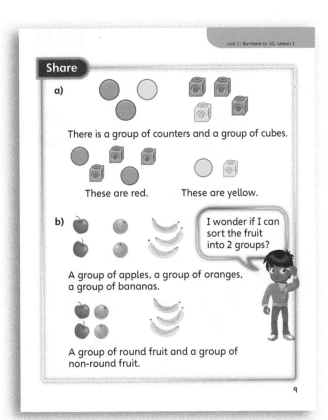

Share

a) There is a group of counters and a group of cubes.

These are red.   These are yellow.

b) A group of apples, a group of oranges, a group of bananas.

I wonder if I can sort the fruit into 2 groups?

A group of round fruit and a group of non-round fruit.

9

Think together

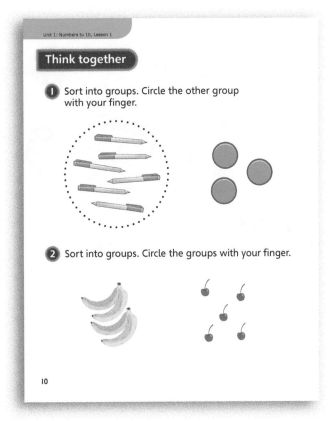 10 minutes

Children work in groups on the carpet or at tables, using their textbooks or eBooks.

TOP TIP
Make sure children have mini whiteboards or pads to write on if they are not at their tables.

Using the Teacher Guide, model question ❶ for your class.

Question ❷ is less structured. Children will need to think together in their groups, then discuss their methods and solutions as a class.

Question ❸ – the openness of the Challenge question helps to check depth of understanding.

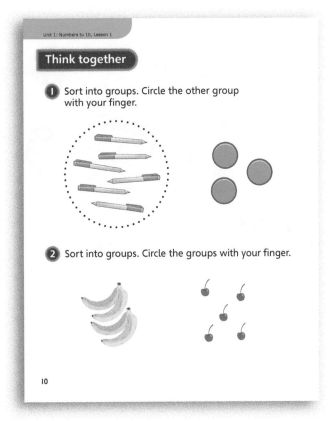

Think together

❶ Sort into groups. Circle the other group with your finger.

❷ Sort into groups. Circle the groups with your finger.

10

Practice ⏱ 15 minutes

Using their Practice Books, children work independently while you circulate and check on progress.

Questions follow small steps of progression to deepen learning.

TOP TIP
Some children could work separately with a teacher or assistant.

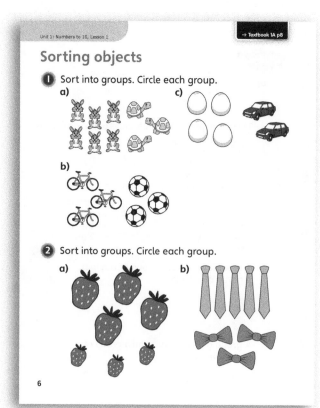

Are some children struggling? If so, work with them as a group, using mathematical structures and representations to support understanding as necessary.

There are no set routines: for real understanding, children need to think about the problem in different ways.

Reflect ⏱ 5 minutes

'Spot the mistake' questions are great for checking misconceptions.

The Reflect section is your opportunity to check how deeply children understand the target concept.

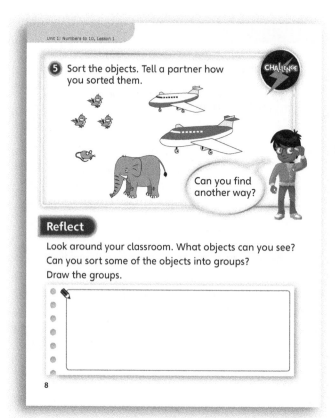

The Practice Books use various approaches to check that children have fully understood each concept.

Looking like they understand is not enough! It is essential that children can show they have grasped the concept.

Using the *Power Maths* Teacher Guide

Think of your Teacher Guides as *Power Maths* handbooks that will guide, support and inspire your day-to-day teaching. Clear and concise, and illustrated with helpful examples, your Teacher Guides will help you make the best possible use of every individual lesson. They also provide wrap-around professional development, enhancing your own subject knowledge and helping you to grow in confidence about moving your children forward together.

There is a Teacher Guide per year group for every term with unit and lesson level guidance and support.

Tips and advice on key elements such as C-P-A approaches, misconceptions, language, modelling growth mindsets and same-day intervention.

Annotations for every Pupil Textbook and Practice Book page, providing prompts for key questions to ask to expose understanding and explanations as to why key questions have been chosen.

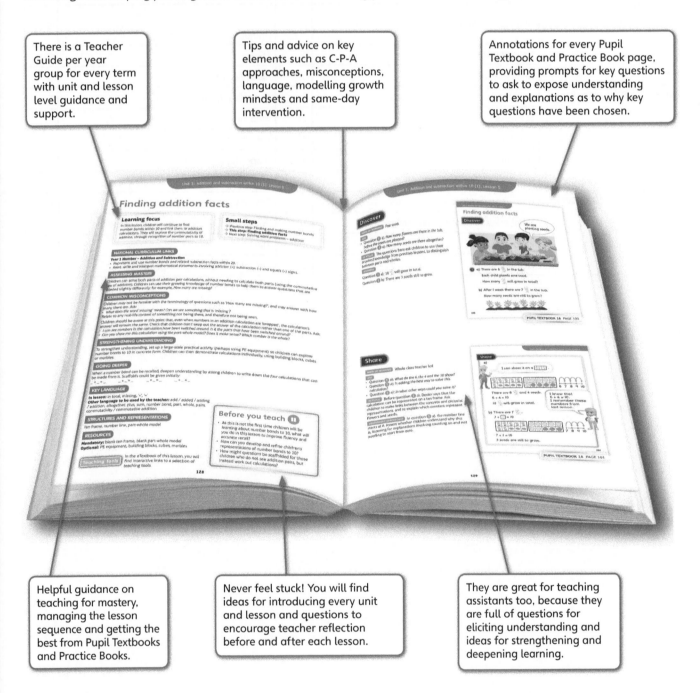

Helpful guidance on teaching for mastery, managing the lesson sequence and getting the best from Pupil Textbooks and Practice Books.

Never feel stuck! You will find ideas for introducing every unit and lesson and questions to encourage teacher reflection before and after each lesson.

They are great for teaching assistants too, because they are full of questions for eliciting understanding and ideas for strengthening and deepening learning.

At the end of each unit, your Teacher Guide helps you identify who has fully grasped the concept, who has not and how to move every child forward. This is covered later in the Assessment strategies section.

Power Maths Year 2, yearly overview

Textbook	Strand	Unit	Number of Lessons	
Textbook A / Practice Book A (Term 1)	Number – number and place value	1	Numbers to 100	10
	Number – addition and subtraction	2	Addition and subtraction (1)	12
	Number – addition and subtraction	3	Addition and subtraction (2)	9
	Measurement	4	Money	9
	Number – multiplication and division	5	Multiplication and division (1)	9
Textbook B / Practice Book B (Term 2)	Number – multiplication and division	6	Multiplication and division (2)	9
	Statistics	7	Statistics	7
	Measurement	8	Length and height	5
	Geometry – properties of shape	9	Properties of shapes	12
	Number – fractions	10	Fractions	14
Textbook C / Practice Book C (Term 3)	Geometry – position and direction	11	Position and direction	4
	Number – addition and subtraction	12	Problem-solving and efficient methods	12
	Measurement	13	Time	9
	Measurement	14	Weight, volume and temperature	10

Power Maths Year 2, Textbook 2B (Term 2) overview

Strand 1	Strand 2	Unit		Lesson number	Lesson title	NC Objective 1	NC Objective 2	NC Objective 3
Number – multiplication and division		Unit 6	Multiplication and division (2)	1	Making equal groups	Solve problems involving multiplication and division, using materials, arrays, repeated addition, mental methods, and multiplication and division facts, including problems in contexts	Calculate mathematical statements for multiplication and division within the multiplication tables and write them using the multiplication (×), division (÷) and equals (=) signs	
Number – multiplication and division		Unit 6	Multiplication and division (2)	2	Sharing and grouping	Solve problems involving multiplication and division, using materials, arrays, repeated addition, mental methods, and multiplication and division facts, including problems in contexts	Calculate mathematical statements for multiplication and division within the multiplication tables and write them using the multiplication (×), division (÷) and equals (=) signs	
Number – multiplication and division		Unit 6	Multiplication and division (2)	3	Dividing by 2	Solve problems involving multiplication and division, using materials, arrays, repeated addition, mental methods, and multiplication and division facts, including problems in contexts	Recall and use multiplication and division facts for the 2, 5 and 10 multiplication tables, including recognising odd and even numbers	
Number – multiplication and division		Unit 6	Multiplication and division (2)	4	Odd and even numbers	Recall and use multiplication and division facts for the 2, 5 and 10 multiplication tables, including recognising odd and even numbers		
Number – multiplication and division		Unit 6	Multiplication and division (2)	5	Dividing by 5	Recall and use multiplication and division facts for the 2, 5 and 10 multiplication tables, including recognising odd and even numbers		
Number – multiplication and division		Unit 6	Multiplication and division (2)	6	Dividing by 10	Recall and use multiplication and division facts for the 2, 5 and 10 multiplication tables, including recognising odd and even numbers		
Number – multiplication and division		Unit 6	Multiplication and division (2)	7	Bar modelling – grouping	Solve problems involving multiplication and division, using materials, arrays, repeated addition, mental methods, and multiplication and division facts, including problems in contexts		
Number – multiplication and division		Unit 6	Multiplication and division (2)	8	Bar modelling – sharing	Solve problems involving multiplication and division, using materials, arrays, repeated addition, mental methods, and multiplication and division facts, including problems in contexts		
Number – multiplication and division		Unit 6	Multiplication and division (2)	9	Solving word problems – division	Solve problems involving multiplication and division, using materials, arrays, repeated addition, mental methods, and multiplication and division facts, including problems in contexts		
Statistics		Unit 7	Statistics	1	Making tally charts	Interpret and construct simple pictograms, tally charts, block diagrams and simple tables		
Statistics		Unit 7	Statistics	2	Creating pictograms (1)	Interpret and construct simple pictograms, tally charts, block diagrams and simple tables		
Statistics		Unit 7	Statistics	3	Creating pictograms (2)	Interpret and construct simple pictograms, tally charts, block diagrams and simple tables		

Strand 1	Strand 2	Unit		Lesson number	Lesson title	NC Objective 1	NC Objective 2	NC Objective 3
Statistics		Unit 7	Statistics	4	Interpreting pictograms (1)	Interpret and construct simple pictograms, tally charts, block diagrams and simple tables	Ask and answer simple questions by counting the number of objects in each category and sorting the categories by quantity	Ask and answer questions about totalling and comparing categorical data
Statistics		Unit 7	Statistics	5	Interpreting pictograms (2)	Interpret and construct simple pictograms, tally charts, block diagrams and simple tables	Ask and answer simple questions by counting the number of objects in each category and sorting the categories by quantity	Ask and answer questions about totalling and comparing categorical data
Statistics		Unit 7	Statistics	6	Block diagrams	Interpret and construct simple pictograms, tally charts, block diagrams and simple tables	Ask and answer simple questions by counting the number of objects in each category and sorting the categories by quantity	Ask and answer questions about totalling and comparing categorical data
Statistics		Unit 7	Statistics	7	Solving word problems	Ask and answer simple questions by counting the number of objects in each category and sorting the categories by quantity	Ask and answer questions about totalling and comparing categorical data	
Measurement		Unit 8	Length and height	1	Measuring in centimetres	Choose and use appropriate standard units to estimate and measure length/height in any direction (m/cm); mass (kg/g); temperature (°C); capacity (litres/ml) to the nearest appropriate unit, using rulers, scales, thermometers and measuring vessels		
Measurement		Unit 8	Length and height	2	Measuring in metres	Choose and use appropriate standard units to estimate and measure length/height in any direction (m/cm); mass (kg/g); temperature (°C); capacity (litres/ml) to the nearest appropriate unit, using rulers, scales, thermometers and measuring vessels		
Measurement		Unit 8	Length and height	3	Comparing lengths	Compare and order lengths, mass, volume/capacity and record the results using >, < and =		
Measurement		Unit 8	Length and height	4	Ordering lengths	Compare and order lengths, mass, volume/capacity and record the results using >, < and =		
Number – addition and subtraction		Unit 8	Length and height	5	Solving word problems – length	Solve problems with addition and subtraction: using concrete objects and pictorial representations, including those involving numbers, quantities and measures		
Geometry – properties of shape		Unit 9	Properties of shapes	1	Recognising 2D and 3D shapes	Compare and sort common 2D and 3D shapes and everyday objects		
Geometry – properties of shape		Unit 9	Properties of shapes	2	Drawing 2D shapes	Identify and describe the properties of 2D shapes, including the number of sides and line symmetry in a vertical line		
Geometry – properties of shape		Unit 9	Properties of shapes	3	Counting sides on 2D shapes	Identify and describe the properties of 2D shapes, including the number of sides and line symmetry in a vertical line		
Geometry – properties of shape		Unit 9	Properties of shapes	4	Counting vertices on 2D shapes	Identify and describe the properties of 2D shapes, including the number of sides and line symmetry in a vertical line		
Geometry – properties of shape		Unit 9	Properties of shapes	5	Finding lines of symmetry	Identify and describe the properties of 2D shapes, including the number of sides and line symmetry in a vertical line		
Geometry – properties of shape		Unit 9	Properties of shapes	6	Sorting 2D shapes	Compare and sort common 2D and 3D shapes and everyday objects		

Strand 1	Strand 2	Unit		Lesson number	Lesson title	NC Objective 1	NC Objective 2	NC Objective 3
Geometry – position and direction		Unit 9	Properties of shapes	7	Making patterns with 2D shapes	Order and arrange combinations of mathematical objects in patterns and sequences		
Geometry – properties of shape		Unit 9	Properties of shapes	8	Counting faces on 3D shapes	Identify and describe the properties of 3D shapes, including the number of edges, vertices and faces		
Geometry – properties of shape		Unit 9	Properties of shapes	9	Counting edges on 3D shapes	Identify and describe the properties of 3D shapes, including the number of edges, vertices and faces		
Geometry – properties of shape		Unit 9	Properties of shapes	10	Counting vertices on 3D shapes	Identify and describe the properties of 3D shapes, including the number of edges, vertices and faces		
Geometry – properties of shape		Unit 9	Properties of shapes	11	Sorting 3D shapes	Compare and sort common 2D and 3D shapes and everyday objects		
Geometry – position and direction		Unit 9	Properties of shapes	12	Making patterns with 3D shapes	Order and arrange combinations of mathematical objects in patterns and sequences		
Number – fractions		Unit 10	Fractions	1	Introducing whole and parts	(Year 1) recognise, find and name a half as one of two equal parts of an object, shape or quantity		
Number – fractions		Unit 10	Fractions	2	Making equal parts	(Year 1) recognise, find and name a half as one of two equal parts of an object, shape or quantity		
Number – fractions		Unit 10	Fractions	3	Recognising a half ($\frac{1}{2}$)	(Year 1) recognise, find and name a half as one of two equal parts of an object, shape or quantity		
Number – fractions		Unit 10	Fractions	4	Finding a half	(Year 1) recognise, find and name a half as one of two equal parts of an object, shape or quantity		
Number – fractions		Unit 10	Fractions	5	Recognising a quarter ($\frac{1}{4}$)	(Year 1) recognise, find and name a quarter as one of four equal parts of an object, shape or quantity	Recognise, find, name and write fractions $\frac{1}{3}$, $\frac{1}{4}$, $\frac{2}{4}$ and $\frac{3}{4}$ of a length, shape, set of objects or quantity	
Number – fractions		Unit 10	Fractions	6	Finding a quarter	(Year 1) recognise, find and name a quarter as one of four equal parts of an object, shape or quantity	Recognise, find, name and write fractions $\frac{1}{3}$, $\frac{1}{4}$, $\frac{2}{4}$ and $\frac{3}{4}$ of a length, shape, set of objects or quantity	
Number – fractions		Unit 10	Fractions	7	Unit fractions	Recognise, find, name and write fractions $\frac{1}{3}$, $\frac{1}{4}$, $\frac{2}{4}$ and $\frac{3}{4}$ of a length, shape, set of objects or quantity		
Number – fractions		Unit 10	Fractions	8	Understanding other fractions	Write simple fractions for example, $\frac{1}{2}$ of 6 = 3 and recognise the equivalence of $\frac{2}{4}$ and $\frac{1}{2}$		
Number – fractions		Unit 10	Fractions	9	$\frac{1}{2}$ and $\frac{2}{4}$	Write simple fractions for example, $\frac{1}{2}$ of 6 = 3 and recognise the equivalence of $\frac{2}{4}$ and $\frac{1}{2}$		
Number – fractions		Unit 10	Fractions	10	Finding $\frac{3}{4}$	Recognise, find, name and write fractions $\frac{1}{3}$, $\frac{1}{4}$, $\frac{2}{4}$ and $\frac{3}{4}$ of a length, shape, set of objects or quantity		
Number – fractions		Unit 10	Fractions	11	Understanding a whole	Recognise, find, name and write fractions $\frac{1}{3}$, $\frac{1}{4}$, $\frac{2}{4}$ and $\frac{3}{4}$ of a length, shape, set of objects or quantity		
Number – fractions		Unit 10	Fractions	12	Understanding whole and parts	Recognise, find, name and write fractions $\frac{1}{3}$, $\frac{1}{4}$, $\frac{2}{4}$ and $\frac{3}{4}$ of a length, shape, set of objects or quantity		
Number – fractions		Unit 10	Fractions	13	Counting in halves	Non-statutory guidelines: Pupils should count in fractions up to 10, starting from any number		
Number – fractions		Unit 10	Fractions	14	Counting in quarters	Non-statutory guidelines: Pupils should count in fractions up to 10, starting from any number		

Mindset: an introduction

Global research and best practice deliver the same message: learning is greatly affected by what learners perceive they can or cannot do. What is more, it is also shaped by what their parents, carers and teachers perceive they can do. Mindset – the thinking that determines our beliefs and behaviours – therefore has a fundamental impact on teaching and learning.

Everyone can!

Power Maths and mastery methods focus on the distinction between 'fixed' and 'growth' mindsets (Dweck, 2007).[1] Those with a fixed mindset believe that their basic qualities (for example, intelligence, talent and ability to learn) are pre-wired or fixed: 'If you have a talent for maths, you will succeed at it. If not, too bad!' By contrast, those with a growth mindset believe that hard work, effort and commitment drive success and that 'smart' is not something you are or are not, but something you become. In short, everyone can do maths!

Key mindset strategies

A growth mindset needs to be actively nurtured and developed. *Power Maths* offers some key strategies for fostering healthy growth mindsets in your classroom.

It is okay to get it wrong

Mistakes are valuable opportunities to re-think and understand more deeply. Learning is richer when children and teachers alike focus on spotting and sharing mistakes as well as solutions.

Praise hard work

Praise is a great motivator, and by focusing on praising effort and learning rather than success, children will be more willing to try harder, take risks and persist for longer.

Mind your language!

The language we use around learners has a profound effect on their mindsets. Make a habit of using growth phrases, such as, 'Everyone can!', 'Mistakes can help you learn' and 'Just try for a little longer'. The king of them all is one little word, 'yet... I can't solve this...yet!' Encourage parents and carers to use the right language too.

Build in opportunities for success

The step-by-small-step approach enables children to enjoy the experience of success. In addition, avoid ability grouping and encourage every child to answer questions and explain or demonstrate their methods to others.

[1]Dweck, C (2007) The New Psychology of Success, Ballantine Books: New York

The *Power Maths* characters

The *Power Maths* characters model the traits of growth mindset learners and encourage resilience by prompting and questioning children as they work. Appearing frequently in the Textbooks and Practice Books, they are your allies in teaching and discussion, helping to model methods, alternatives and misconceptions, and to pose questions. They encourage and support your children, too: they are all hardworking, enthusiastic and unafraid of making and talking about mistakes.

Meet the team!

Creative Flo is open-minded and sometimes indecisive. She likes to think differently and come up with a variety of methods or ideas.

Determined Dexter is resolute, resilient and systematic. He concentrates hard, always tries his best and he'll never give up – even though he doesn't always choose the most efficient methods!

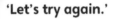

'Let's try again.'

'Mistakes are cool!'

'Have I found all of the solutions?'

'Let's try it this way…'

'Can we do it differently?'

'I've got another way of doing this!'

'I'm going to try this!'

'I know how to do that!'

'Want to share my ideas?'

Curious Ash is eager, interested and inquisitive, and he loves solving puzzles and problems. Ash asks lots of questions but sometimes gets distracted.

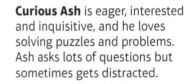

'What if we tried this…?'

'I wonder…'

'Is there a pattern here?'

Sparks the Cat

Miaow!

Brave Astrid is confident, willing to take risks and unafraid of failure. She's never scared to jump straight into a problem or question, and although she often makes simple mistakes she's happy to talk them through with others.

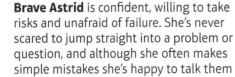

Mathematical language

Traditionally, we in the UK have tended to try simplifying mathematical language to make it easier for young children to understand. By contrast, evidence and experience show that by diluting the correct language, we actually mask concepts and meanings for children. We then wonder why they are confused by new and different terminology later down the line! *Power Maths* is not afraid of 'hard' words and avoids placing any barriers between children and their understanding of mathematical concepts. As a result, we need to be planned, precise and thorough in building every child's understanding of the language of maths. Throughout the Teacher Guides you will find support and guidance on how to deliver this, as well as individual explanations throughout the Pupil Textbooks.

Use the following key strategies to build children's mathematical vocabulary, understanding and confidence.

Precise and consistent

Everyone in the classroom should use the correct mathematical terms in full, every time. For example, refer to 'equal parts', not 'parts'. Used consistently, precise maths language will be a familiar and non-threatening part of children's everyday experience.

Full sentences

Teachers and children alike need to use full sentences to explain or respond. When children use complete sentences, it both reveals their understanding and embeds their knowledge.

Stem sentences

These important sentences help children express mathematical concepts accurately, and are used throughout the *Power Maths* books. Encourage children to repeat them frequently, whether working independently or with others. Examples of stem sentences are:

'4 is a part, 5 is a part, 9 is the whole.'

'There are … groups. There are … in each group.'

Key vocabulary

The unit starters highlight essential vocabulary for every lesson. In the Pupil Textbooks, characters flag new terminology and the Teacher Guide lists important mathematical language for every unit and lesson. New terms are never introduced without a clear explanation.

Symbolic language

Symbols are used early on so that children quickly become familiar with them and their meaning. Often, the *Power Maths* characters will highlight the connection between language and particular symbols.

The role of talk and discussion

When children learn to talk purposefully together about maths, barriers of fear and anxiety are broken down and they grow in confidence, skills and understanding. Building a healthy culture of 'maths talk' empowers their learning from day one.

Explanation and discussion are integral to the *Power Maths* structure, so by simply following the books your lessons will stimulate structured talk. The following key 'maths talk' strategies will help you strengthen that culture and ensure that every child is included.

Sentences, not words

Encourage children to use full sentences when reasoning, explaining or discussing maths. This helps both speaker and listeners to clarify their own understanding. It also reveals whether or not the speaker truly understands, enabling you to address misconceptions as they arise.

Working together

Working with others in pairs, groups or as a whole class is a great way to support maths talk and discussion. Use different group structures to add variety and challenge. For example, children could take timed turns for talking, work independently alongside a 'discussion buddy', or perhaps play different *Power Maths* character roles within their group.

Think first – then talk

Provide clear opportunities within each lesson for children to think and reflect, so that their talk is purposeful, relevant and focused.

Give every child a voice

Where the 'hands up' model allows only the more confident child to shine, *Power Maths* involves everyone. Make sure that no child dominates and that even the shyest child is encouraged to contribute – and praised when they do.

Assessment strategies

Teaching for mastery demands that you are confident about what each child knows and where their misconceptions lie: therefore, practical and effective assessment is vitally important.

Formative assessment within lessons

The **Think together** section will often reveal any confusions or insecurities: try ironing these out by doing the first Think together question as a class. For children who continue to struggle, you or your teaching assistant should provide support and enable them to move on. ▶ Performance in **Practice** can be very revealing: check Practice Books and listen out both during and after practice to identify misconceptions. ▶ The **Reflect** section is designed to check on the all-important depth of understanding. Be sure to review how the children performed in this final stage before you teach the next lesson.

End of unit check – Textbook

Each unit concludes with a summative check to help you assess quickly and clearly each child's understanding, fluency, reasoning and problem-solving skills. Your Teacher Guide will suggest ideal ways of organising a given activity and offer advice and commentary on what children's responses mean. For example, 'What misconception does this reveal?'; 'How can you reinforce this particular concept?'

For Year 1 and Year 2 children, assess in small, teacher-led groups, giving each child time to think and respond while also consolidating correct mathematical language. Assessment with young children should always be an enjoyable activity, so avoid one-to-one individual assessments, which they may find threatening or scary. If you prefer, the End of unit check can be carried out as a whole-class group using whiteboards and Practice Books.

End of unit check – Practice Book

The Practice Book contains further opportunities for assessment, and can be completed by children independently whilst you are carrying out diagnostic assessment with small groups. Your Teacher Guide will advise you on what to do if children struggle to articulate an explanation – or perhaps encourage you to write down something they have explained well. It will also offer insights into children's answers and their implications for next learning steps. It is split into three main sections, outlined below.

My journal and Think!

My journal is designed to allow children to show their depth of understanding of the unit. It can also serve as a way of checking that children have grasped key mathematical vocabulary. The question children should answer is first presented in the Pupil Textbook in the Think! section. This provides an opportunity for you to discuss the question first as a class to ensure children have understood their task. Children should have some time to think about how they want to answer the question, and you could ask them to talk to a partner about their ideas. Then children should write their answer in their Practice Book, using the word bank provided to help them with vocabulary.

Power check

The Power check allows pupils to self-assess their level of confidence on the topic by colouring in different smiley faces. You may want to introduce the faces as follows:

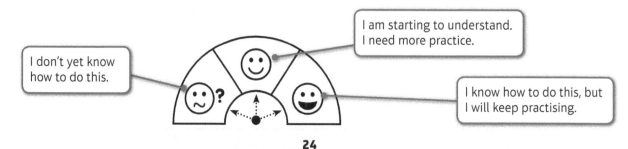

I am starting to understand. I need more practice.

I don't yet know how to do this.

I know how to do this, but I will keep practising.

Power play or Power puzzle

Each unit ends with either a Power play or a Power puzzle. This is an activity, puzzle or game that allows children to use their new knowledge in a fun, informal way.

How to ask diagnostic questions

The diagnostic questions provided in children's Practice Books are carefully structured to identify both understanding and misconceptions (if children answer in a particular way, you will know why). The simple procedure below may be helpful:

Ask the question, offering the selection of answers provided.

▼

Children take time to think about their response.

▼

Each child selects an answer and shares their reasoning with the group.

▼

Give minimal and neutral feedback (for example, 'That's interesting', or 'Okay').

▼

Ask, 'Why did you choose that answer?', then offer an opportunity to change their mind by providing one correct and one incorrect answer.

▼

Note which children responded and reasoned correctly first time and everyone's final choices.

▼

Reflect that together, we can get the right answer.

▼

Record outcomes on the assessment grid (on the next page).

Power Maths unit assessment grid

Year ___   **Unit** ___ _____

Record only as much information as you judge appropriate for your assessment of each child's mastery of the unit and any steps needed for intervention.

Name	Q1	Q2	Q3	Q4	Q5	My journal	Power check	Power play/puzzle	Mastery	Intervention/ Strengthen

Keeping the class together

Traditionally, children who learn quickly have been accelerated through the curriculum. As a consequence, their learning may be superficial and will lack the many benefits of enabling children to learn with and from each other.

By contrast, *Power Maths'* mastery approach values real understanding and richer, deeper learning above speed. It sees all children learning the same concept in small, cumulative steps, each finding and mastering challenge at their own level. Remember that when you teach for mastery, EVERYONE can do maths! Those who grasp a concept easily have time to explore and understand that concept at a deeper level. The whole class therefore moves through the curriculum at broadly the same pace via individual learning journeys.

For some teachers, the idea that a whole class can move forward together is revolutionary and challenging. However, the evidence of global good practice clearly shows that this approach drives engagement, confidence, motivation and success for all learners, and not just the high flyers. The strategies below will help you keep your class together on their maths journey.

Mix it up

Do not stick to set groups at each table. Every child should be working on the same concept, and mixing up the groupings widens children's opportunities for exploring, discussing and sharing their understanding with others.

Recycling questions

Reuse the Pupil Textbook and Practice Book questions with concrete materials to allow children to explore concepts and relationships and deepen their understanding. This strategy is especially useful for reinforcing learning in same-day interventions.

Strengthen at every opportunity

The next lesson in a *Power Maths* sequence always revises and builds on the previous step to help embed learning. These activities provide golden opportunities for individual children to strengthen their learning with the support of teaching assistants.

Prepare to be surprised!

Children may grasp a concept quickly or more slowly. The 'fast graspers' won't always be the same individuals, nor does the speed at which a child understands a concept predict their success in maths. Are they struggling or just working more slowly?

Depth and breadth

Just as prescribed in the National Curriculum, the goal of *Power Maths* is never to accelerate through a topic but rather to gain a clear, deep and broad understanding.

"Pupils who grasp concepts rapidly should be challenged through being offered rich and sophisticated problems before any acceleration through new content. Those who are not sufficiently fluent with earlier material should consolidate their understanding, including through additional practice, before moving on."

National Curriculum: Mathematics programmes of study: KS1 & 2, 2013

The lesson sequence offers many opportunities for you to deepen and broaden children's learning, some of which are suggested below.

Discover

As well as using the questions in the Teacher Guide, check that children are really delving into why something is true. It is not enough to simply recite facts, such as '6 + 3 = 9'. They need to be able to see why, explain it, and to demonstrate the solution in several ways.

Share

Make sure that every child is given chances to offer answers and expand their knowledge and not just those with the greatest confidence.

Think together

Encourage children to think about how they solved the problem and explain it to their partner. Be sure to make concrete materials available on group tables throughout the lesson to support and reinforce learning.

Practice

Avoid any temptation to select questions according to your assessment of ability: practice questions are presented in a logical sequence and it is important that each child works through every question.

Reflect

Open-ended questions allow children to deepen their understanding as far as they can by finding new ways of finding answers. For example, *Give me another way of working out how high the wall is… And another way?*

My friends and I often ask questions that make children think more deeply!

Have I found all of the solutions?

Is that always true?

Online materials

For each unit you will find additional strengthening activities to support those children who need it and to deepen the understanding of those who need the additional challenge.

Same-day intervention

Since maths competence depends on mastering concepts one by one in a logical progression, it is important that no gaps in understanding are ever left unfilled. Same-day interventions – either within or after a lesson – are a crucial safety net for any child who has not fully made the small step covered that day. In other words, intervention is always about keeping up, not catching up, so that every child has the skills and understanding they need to tackle the next lesson. That means presenting the same problems used in the lesson, with a variety of concrete materials to help children model their solutions.

We offer two intervention strategies below, but you should feel free to choose others if they work better for your class.

Within-lesson intervention

The Think together activity will reveal those who are struggling, so when it is time for Practice, bring these children together to work with you on the first practice questions. Observe these children carefully, ask questions, encourage them to use concrete models and check that they reach and can demonstrate their understanding.

After-lesson intervention

You might like to use Think together before an assembly, giving you or teaching assistants time to recap and expand with slow graspers during assembly time. Teaching assistants could also work with strugglers at other convenient points in the school day.

The role of practice

Practice plays a pivotal role in the *Power Maths* approach. It takes place in class groups, smaller groups, pairs, and independently, so that children always have the opportunities for thinking as well as the models and support they need to practise meaningfully and with understanding.

Intelligent practice

In *Power Maths*, practice never equates to the simple repetition of a process. Instead we embrace the concept of intelligent practice, in which all children become fluent in maths through varied, frequent and thoughtful practice that deepens and embeds conceptual understanding in a logical, planned sequence. To see the difference, take a look at the following examples.

Traditional practice

- Repetition can be rote – no need for a child to think hard about what they are doing

- Praise may be misplaced

- Does this prove understanding?

Intelligent practice

- Varied methods – concrete, pictorial and abstract

- Calculations expressed in different ways, requiring thought and understanding

- Constructive feedback

All practice questions are designed to move children on and reveal misconceptions.

Simple, logical steps build onto earlier learning.

C-P-A runs throughout – different ways of modelling and understanding the same concept.

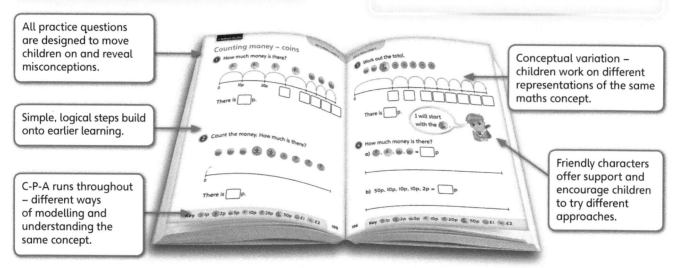

Conceptual variation – children work on different representations of the same maths concept.

Friendly characters offer support and encourage children to try different approaches.

A carefully designed progression

The Pupil Practice Books provide just the right amount of intelligent practice for children to complete independently in the final sections of each lesson. It is really important that all children are exposed to the practice questions, and that children are not directed to complete different sections. That is because each question is different and has been designed to challenge children to think about the maths they are doing. The questions become more challenging so children grasping concepts more quickly will start to slow down as they progress. Meanwhile, you have the chance to circulate and spot any misconceptions before they become barriers to further learning.

Homework and the role of carers

While *Power Maths* does not prescribe any particular homework structure, we acknowledge the potential value of practice at home. For example, practising fluency in key facts, such as number bonds and times tables, is an ideal homework task for Key Stage 1 children, and carers could work through uncompleted Practice Book questions with children at either primary stage.

However, it is important to recognise that many parents and carers may themselves lack confidence in maths, and few, if any, will be familiar with mastery methods. A Parents' and Carers' Evening that helps them understand the basics of mindsets, mastery and mathematical language is a great way to ensure that children benefit from their homework. It could be a fun opportunity for children to teach their families that everyone can do maths!

Structures and representations

Unlike most other subjects, maths comprises a wide array of abstract concepts – and that is why children and adults so often find it difficult. By taking a concrete-pictorial-abstract (C-P-A) approach, *Power Maths* allows children to tackle concepts in a tangible and more comfortable way.

Non-linear stages

Concrete

Replacing the traditional approach of a teacher working through a problem in front of the class, the concrete stage introduces real objects that children can use to 'do' the maths – any familiar object that a child can manipulate and move to help bring the maths to life. It is important to appreciate, however, that children must always understand the link between models and the objects they represent. For example, children need to first understand that three cakes could be represented by three pretend cakes, and then by three counters or bricks. Frequent practice helps consolidate this essential insight. Although they can be used at any time, good concrete models are an essential first step in understanding.

Pictorial

This stage uses pictorial representations of objects to let children 'see' what particular maths problems look like. It helps them make connections between the concrete and pictorial representations and the abstract maths concept. Children can also create or view a pictorial representation together, enabling discussion and comparisons. The *Power Maths* teaching tools are fantastic for this learning stage, and bar modelling is invaluable for problem solving throughout the primary curriculum.

Abstract

Our ultimate goal is for children to understand abstract mathematical concepts, symbols and notation and, of course, some children will reach this stage far more quickly than others. To work with abstract concepts, a child must be comfortable with the meaning of and relationships between concrete, pictorial and abstract models and representations. The C-P-A approach is not linear, and children may need different types of models at different times. However, when a child demonstrates with concrete models and pictorial representations that they have grasped a concept, we can be confident that they are ready to explore or model it with abstract symbols such as numbers and notation.

Use at any time and with any age to support understanding

Variation helps visualisation

Children find it much easier to visualise and grasp concepts if they see them presented in a number of ways, so be prepared to offer and encourage many different representations.

For example, the number six could be represented in various ways:

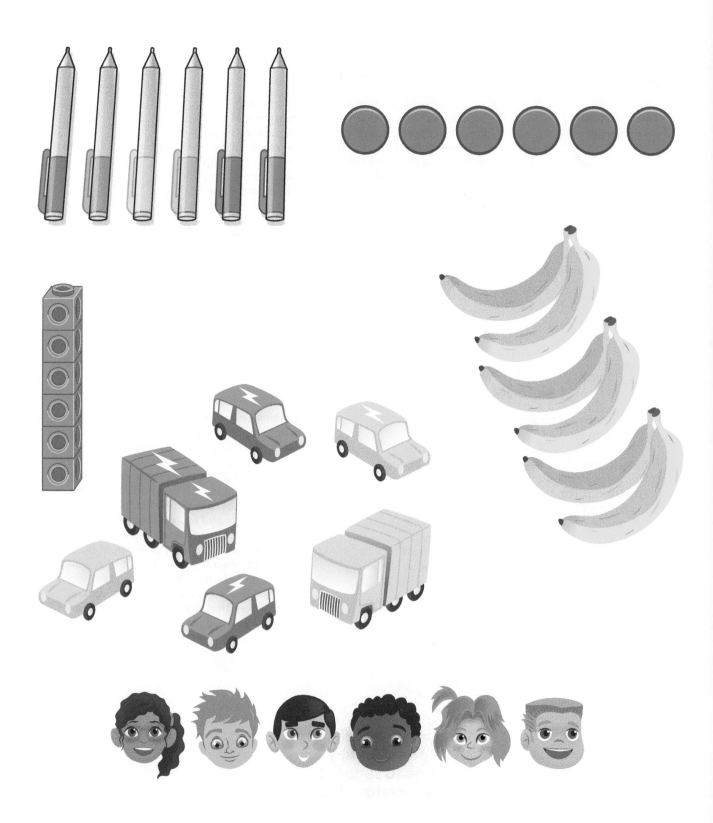

Getting started with *Power Maths*

As you prepare to put *Power Maths* into action, you might find the tips and advice below helpful.

STEP 1: Train up!

A practical, up-front full-day professional development course will give you and your team a brilliant head-start as you begin your *Power Maths* journey. You will learn more about the ethos, how it works and why.

STEP 2: Check out the progression

Take a look at the yearly and termly overviews. Next take a look at the unit overview for the unit you are about to teach in your Teacher Guide, remembering that you can match your lessons and pacing to your class.

STEP 3: Explore the context

Take a little time to look at the context for this unit: what are the implications for the unit ahead? (Think about key language, common misunderstandings and intervention strategies, for example.) If you have the online subscription, don't forget to watch the corresponding unit video.

STEP 4: Prepare for your first lesson

Familiarise yourself with the objectives, essential questions to ask and the resources you will need. The Teacher Guide offers tips, ideas and guidance on individual lessons to help you anticipate children's misconceptions and challenge those who are ready to think more deeply.

STEP 5: Teach and reflect

Deliver your lesson – and enjoy!

Afterwards, reflect on how it went… Did you cover all five stages? Does the lesson need more time? How could you improve it?

Unit 6
Multiplication and division ❷

Mastery Expert tip! "Number lines and 100 squares will be used a lot throughout this unit. It would be useful to have giant class versions up at the front to refer to when teaching. If laminated, they can be drawn on or highlighted numerous times and wiped away at the end of each lesson."

Don't forget to watch the Unit 6 video!

WHY THIS UNIT IS IMPORTANT

This unit focuses on two methods of division (grouping and sharing), and how to calculate using these two different strategies. Children will be introduced to the division sign (÷). Children will learn the importance of equal groups when dividing, and how to distinguish between the number of equal groups and the number in one group. Children will be introduced to the bar model to represent both grouping and sharing problems.

Within this unit, children will also make the link between division and multiplication facts. They will be asked to match a multiplication sentence to the inverse division sentence, and to work out missing numbers based on facts from one of the operations.

Children will use a 100 square to spot patterns for numbers that can be divided by 2, 5 and 10. They will make generalisations between different division facts and fact families, for example, all numbers that can be divided by 5 end in 0 or 5. Children will also build on their knowledge of dividing by 2 to explore what it means for a number to be even and odd. They will start to recognise when numbers are odd by considering the ones digit.

WHERE THIS UNIT FITS

→ Unit 5: Multiplication and division (1)
→ **Unit 6: Multiplication and division (2)**
→ Unit 7: Statistics

This unit builds on equal groups as a key idea in multiplication and division. Children have been exposed to repeated addition as a strategy for multiplication and will apply this knowledge to use repeated subtraction as a strategy for division. Unit 6 looks at division facts within the context of other multiplication facts that have been learned previously. The primary method that we are looking at is sharing and most examples are sharing, however we want children to see the difference between sharing and grouping. It is important that teachers discuss this difference with children. Following this unit, children will move on to using tallies and creating tally charts.

Before they start this unit, it is expected that children:
- know how to count backwards in equal groups on a number line
- understand how to use an array for multiplication (or repeated addition).

ASSESSING MASTERY

Children who have mastered this unit will be able to use a range of strategies for working out a division sentence. They will know when to apply a particular strategy based on the numbers in the division sentence. Children will be confident counting backwards on a number line, sharing into equal groups, grouping a number into equal groups, and using a bar model to represent a problem. Importantly, children will also recognise when they do not need to calculate a division fact because they already know a multiplication fact that can help them.

COMMON MISCONCEPTIONS	STRENGTHENING UNDERSTANDING	GOING DEEPER
Children may not understand that division is not commutative and might switch numbers round in a division number sentence.	Ask children to act out a division sentence using both a sharing and a grouping strategy.	Sometimes, a division sentence has the same number of equal groups as numbers in a group such as $25 \div 5 = 5$. Get children to come up with a context to show that the numbers represent different things.
Children may repeat the number of equal groups in a division sentence instead of writing the number in one group.	Ask children which division sentences they do not have to calculate because they can use multiplication facts to help them.	Give three numbers (for example 2, 5, 10) and get children to write as many multiplication and division facts as they can.

WAYS OF WORKING

Use these pages to highlight that children will be continuing learning from the previous unit and will need to remember their times-table facts. Ask children where they have seen equal sharing before and tell them they will be learning about it in new contexts.

STRUCTURES AND REPRESENTATIONS

Number line: This model helps children visualise the repeated subtraction strategy to work out a division fact. Show a number line with equal jumps going back to 0. The number of jumps is the missing part of the division sentence.

0 5 10 15 20 25 30 35

100 square: Once highlighted, this model helps make generalisations about which numbers are divisible by which numbers. It also highlights odd and even numbers.

1	2	3	4	5	6	7	8	9	10
11	12	13	14	15	16	17	18	19	20
21	22	23	24	25	26	27	28	29	30
31	32	33	34	35	36	37	38	39	40
41	42	43	44	45	46	47	48	49	50
51	52	53	54	55	56	57	58	59	60
61	62	63	64	65	66	67	68	69	70
71	72	73	74	75	76	77	78	79	80
81	82	83	84	85	86	87	88	89	90
91	92	93	94	95	96	97	98	99	100

Bar model: To represent equal groups, the parts of the bar model must be an equal width and labelled the same amount. The total should be written on top.

40			
10	10	10	10

KEY LANGUAGE

There is some key language that children will need to know as part of the learning in this unit:

➜ divide, division, the division sign (÷)

➜ share

➜ group

➜ odd, even

➜ times-tables

➜ equal groups, number of equal groups

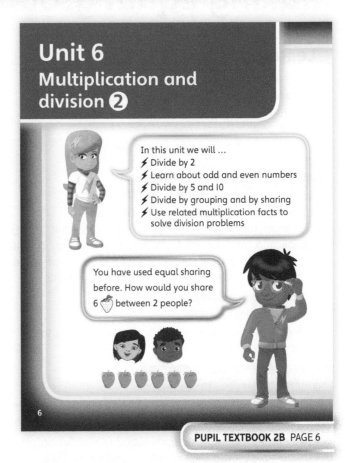

PUPIL TEXTBOOK 2B PAGE 6

PUPIL TEXTBOOK 2B PAGE 7

Making equal groups

Learning focus

In this lesson, children will use repeated subtraction to model division calculations. They will put numbers into equal groups using counters and show this on a number line.

Small steps

→ Previous step: Solving word problems – multiplication
→ **This step: Making equal groups**
→ Next step: Sharing and grouping

NATIONAL CURRICULUM LINKS

Year 2 Number – Multiplication and Division
- Solve problems involving multiplication and division, using materials, arrays, repeated addition, mental methods, and multiplication and division facts, including problems in contexts.
- Calculate mathematical statements for multiplication and division within the multiplication tables and write them using the multiplication (×), division (÷) and equals (=) signs.

ASSESSING MASTERY

Children can model repeated subtraction and link this to the '÷' sign. Children will be secure with the idea of splitting a number into *equal* groups.

COMMON MISCONCEPTIONS

It is common to mix up the number in a group and the number of groups. Children may not understand how to to fill in a blank division number sentence such as 12 ÷ ? = ? using the information provided.

The two different division methods may cause confusion: grouping and sharing. This lesson models the grouping method but children may revert back to sharing and have difficulty assimilating grouping models. Ask:
- *Look at the problem. How many equal groups are you trying to make? What will this look like?*

STRENGTHENING UNDERSTANDING

The **Pupil Textbook** models how to use and circle counters to group them into a certain number. Use another physical resource such as cubes to demonstrate grouping. The cubes can be joined together and become one group that is fixed. These groups can be shown as stacks next to each other as well as lying flat horizontally.

GOING DEEPER

Children who are secure at sharing into equal groups and modelling on a number line can write a division number sentence from workings on a number line, understanding that the number at the end is the starting number, the number in one jump is what is being divided by, and the number of jumps back is the 'answer'.

KEY LANGUAGE

In lesson: ÷, divide, division, groups, share

Other language to be used by the teacher: equal groups, repeated subtraction

STRUCTURES AND REPRESENTATIONS

Number line, groups of counters

RESOURCES

Mandatory: counters, blank number lines

Optional: cubes

 In the eTextbook of this lesson, you will find interactive links to a selection of teaching tools.

Before you teach

- Have children been exposed to '÷' before?
- What real-life contexts can you give for sharing?

Discover

Whole class teacher led

ASK

- *How many children are there in total?*
- *Will the groups always be the same size?*

IN FOCUS In the image, the 12 children dancing can be modelled with actual children in the class. When children get into groups of 4, ask them to stand together or hold hands to show that they are one group. When they move back to a group of 12, and then into groups of 3, reinforce the idea that the group sizes have to be equal, but there can be any number of groups.

ANSWERS

Question ① a): There are 3 groups of 4.

Question ① b): There are 4 groups of 3 now.

Making equal groups

Discover

① a) 12 children want to dance in groups of 4.
   How many groups are there?

b) The 12 children now dance in groups of 3.
   How many groups are there now?

8

PUPIL TEXTBOOK 2B PAGE 8

Share

Whole class teacher led

ASK

- *Question ① a): What does Flo say about the counters? How is grouping the counters like taking them away?*
- *Question ① b): What does the number line show?*
- *How is the working out in question ① a) different from question ① b)?*

IN FOCUS In this section children should have their own 12 counters to put into different groups. They need to lay the counters in a horizontal line and separate them into groups of 4 and then 3.

Children should remove 4 counters at a time, repeating the subtraction until they have used all the counters. Children might get confused and share counters into 4 groups instead of putting the counters into groups of 4. Make sure children count how many counters are in each group and then count how many groups they have made.

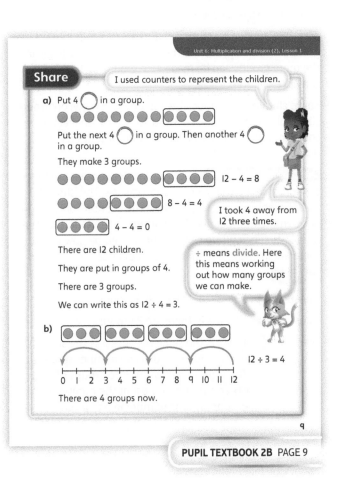

Share

I used counters to represent the children.

a) Put 4 ◯ in a group.

Put the next 4 ◯ in a group. Then another 4 ◯ in a group.
They make 3 groups.

$12 - 4 = 8$

$8 - 4 = 4$

$4 - 4 = 0$

I took 4 away from 12 three times.

There are 12 children.
They are put in groups of 4.
There are 3 groups.
We can write this as $12 \div 4 = 3$.

÷ means **divide**. Here this means working out how many groups we can make.

b)

0 1 2 3 4 5 6 7 8 9 10 11 12

$12 \div 3 = 4$

There are 4 groups now.

9

PUPIL TEXTBOOK 2B PAGE 9

Think together

WAYS OF WORKING Whole class teacher led (I do, We do, You do)

ASK

- Question **1** : *How does what you are doing with the children match what is happening on the number line?*
- Question **2** : *Will there be more or fewer groups this time?*
- Question **3** : *Has the total number of counters changed?*

IN FOCUS Question **1** shows drawings of the children alongside counters to represent them on top of the number line. Children can circle the number of children and counters every time a jump back of 2 is made on the number line to embed understanding. In question **2** children need to use their understanding of the method and how to put numbers in the division scaffold onto the number line. Question **3** leads children to two different conclusions; what the '÷' sign means as it is shown in many different number sentences, and that the fewer there are in each group, the larger the number of groups – draw children's attention to Ash's comment on this.

STRENGTHEN In question **3** , 12 children have been grouped using counters. Get children to represent each division calculation by drawing groups of children, using cubes or even showing it on a number line if they have enough understanding. Children should see each time that the total number of objects or starting point on the number line always stays at 12. Also, there are never any left over and '0' is always reached on the number line.

DEEPEN The deeper truth is that the same quantity can be grouped in different ways. The fewer dancers in the group, the more groups can be made. Use groups of 1 and of 12 to convince children.

Some children may notice the relationship between group sizes, for example, 12 ÷ 4 = 3 and 12 ÷ 3 = 4. Challenge children to find other pairs of division calculations at the disco.

ASSESSMENT CHECKPOINT Look out for clear understanding that division is making equal sized groups. This should be apparent in how children circle the counters and jump back on the number line. Do children understand that the number in each group will be represented by how many there are in each jump on the number line?

ANSWERS

Question **1** : 12 ÷ 2 = 6. There are 6 groups.

Question **2** : 12 ÷ 6 = 2. There are 2 groups.

Question **3** : 12 stays the same because it is the same total number for each division number sentence. The sign '÷' means 'put into groups of'. The other numbers represent the number of equal groups and the number in one group.

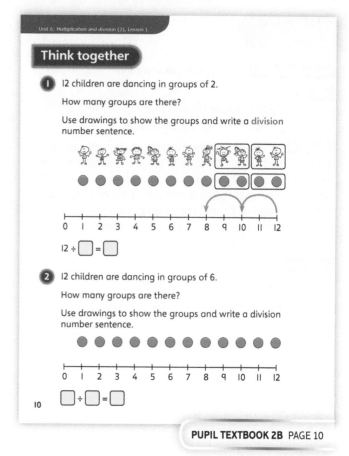

PUPIL TEXTBOOK 2B PAGE 10

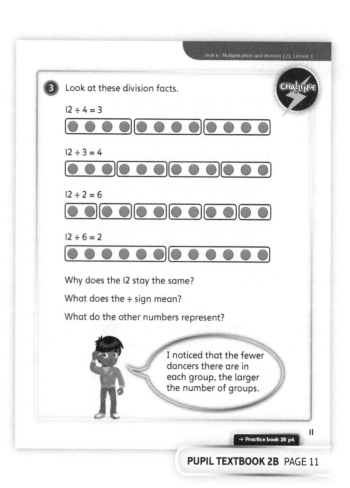

PUPIL TEXTBOOK 2B PAGE 11

Practice

WAYS OF WORKING Independent working

IN FOCUS Question ❶ gives children a chance to practise jumping back on the number line independently to work out division number sentences. The number line has the first jump already completed so children can compare and check their own jumps are the right size.

STRENGTHEN Get children to represent each division number sentence in question ❹ with cubes and put them into stacks to compare. This gives children an alternative way of comparing how many are in one group rather than just looking at the number line. This may also help children answer the question of which makes the most groups and why.

DEEPEN Question ❸ shows a common misconception of mixing up the number of equal groups with the number in one group. Give a real-life context to this question. Can children think of scenarios where they would want the most groups of something? Maybe sharing something out between as many friends as possible?

ASSESSMENT CHECKPOINT In question ❸ can children spot what Astrid did incorrectly? Can they explain it with the number line? Do children understand that if the number in a group is smaller, the number of groups will be bigger?

ANSWERS Answers for the **Practice** part of the lesson appear in the separate **Practice and Reflect answer guide**.

Reflect

WAYS OF WORKING Independent thinking

IN FOCUS This section gives a context for children to write their own division number sentence (without making the mistake from question ❸). The number line has not been numbered or given a start or end number.

ASSESSMENT CHECKPOINT Do children understand that 5 cups on one tray will be represented as '÷ 5' in the number sentence? Do children know that the start and end points of the number line should be 0 and 15? Do they mark on each interval or do they just mark the numbers where the jumps going backwards land?

ANSWERS Answers for the **Reflect** part of the lesson appear in the separate **Practice and Reflect answer guide**.

After the lesson ⏸

- Did children relate repeated subtraction to division?
- Could children explain what the '÷' sign means?
- Did children make the common mistake of mixing up the number in one group with the number of groups?

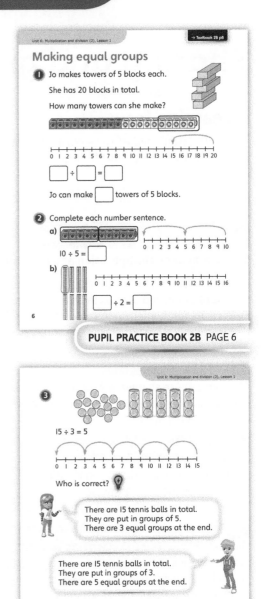

PUPIL PRACTICE BOOK 2B PAGE 6

PUPIL PRACTICE BOOK 2B PAGE 7

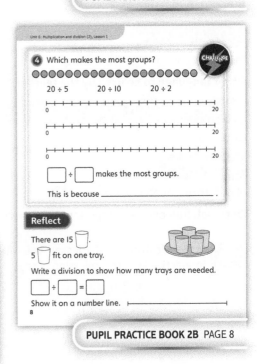

PUPIL PRACTICE BOOK 2B PAGE 8

Sharing and grouping

Learning focus

In this lesson, children will learn another strategy for dividing by sharing a number equally into groups.

Small steps

→ Previous step: Making equal groups
→ **This step: Sharing and grouping**
→ Next step: Dividing by 2

NATIONAL CURRICULUM LINKS

Year 2 Number – Multiplication and Division

- Solve problems involving multiplication and division, using materials, arrays, repeated addition, mental methods, and multiplication and division facts, including problems in contexts.
- Calculate mathematical statements for multiplication and division within the multiplication tables and write them using the multiplication (×), division (÷) and equals (=) signs.

ASSESSING MASTERY

Children can use sharing as a method to work out a division sentence. Children can understand each group receives one object until there are no more left to hand out and know that each group must have been shared an equal number of objects and that there have to be none left over.

COMMON MISCONCEPTIONS

Children can become distracted by other differences when sharing. For example, with a mixture of red and green apples, children may focus on giving one person all green and another all red rather than focusing on how many they get. Ask:
- *Does each item or object still represent one even if it looks different?*

STRENGTHENING UNDERSTANDING

Act out sharing with children using real objects in class by means of a 'one for you, one for me' approach. This will reinforce several key ideas: there has to be an equal amount given to each person otherwise it is not 'fair' and the number cannot be shared equally if there is something left over at the end.

GOING DEEPER

Sharing between more people results in fewer for each person. Once children have practised sharing, discuss this idea using a specific context. Would children rather share something they liked between more or less people? What about something they do not like, such as chores?

KEY LANGUAGE

In lesson: division sign (÷), sharing

Other language to be used by the teacher: fair, division sentence

STRUCTURES AND REPRESENTATIONS

Groups of counters

RESOURCES

Mandatory: counters, cubes

Optional: fruit or objects representing the word problems

 In the eTextbook of this lesson, you will find interactive links to a selection of teaching tools.

Before you teach

- Can children explain what the ÷ sign means?
- Do children know the difference between the number in a group and the number of groups?

Discover

WAYS OF WORKING Pair work

ASK

• *What does 'share equally' mean?*
• *Does every child have to have the same number at the end?*

IN FOCUS In this question, the same number of friends share different numbers of pieces of fruit. This is easy to act out in the class using children and fruit. This would also reinforce that the number '3' (the number the objects are being shared into) does not change in either of these questions: only the number of pieces of fruit does.

ANSWERS

Question **1** a): Each friend gets 2 🍎.

Question **1** b): Each friend gets 3 🍐.

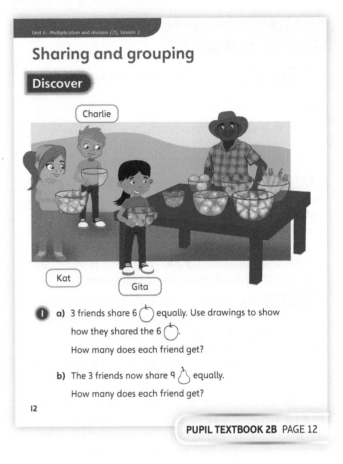

PUPIL TEXTBOOK 2B PAGE 12

Share

WAYS OF WORKING Whole class teacher led

ASK

• *What is the same in each question? What is different?*
• *Which division sentence matches which problem?*

IN FOCUS Children can act out the situations at their table. They can use one counter or cube to represent one apple (or other fruit), so that they are using one-to-one correspondence to help them model the situation. Children will also need to draw three circles to share the cubes into, to represent the three children in the question. Flo and Dexter give two different methods for working this out. Flo takes three and gives everyone one. This links closely with the last lesson on grouping. Dexter takes an apple and gives it to the next person, until he has no apples left. The division sentences are also shown alongside visual representations of the workings out.

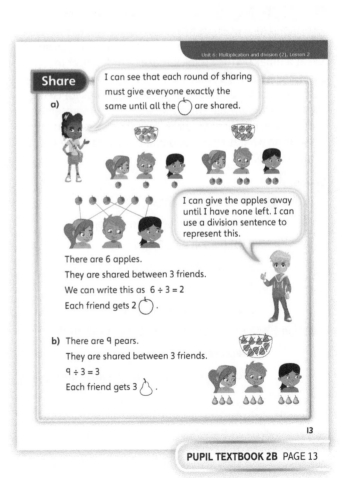

PUPIL TEXTBOOK 2B PAGE 13

Think together

Whole class teacher led (I do, We do, You do)

ASK

- *What could you use to represent what you are sharing in your drawings and workings out?*
- *What does '÷' mean now that you are sharing?*

IN FOCUS In question ❶ and question ❷, children have to work out what the division sentence looks like for the new problem and how to draw a picture to represent it. Question ❶ looks at taking two at a time, and giving each person one. Question ❷ looks at giving the apples away one at a time. Question ❸ asks children to examine what each number in a division sentence represents.

STRENGTHEN Ask children to use resources to model the difference between grouping and sharing. For example, to model sharing in question ❶, children could draw two circles and share six counters between the circles. Then to model grouping, children could join cubes into groups of 2 and count the groups.

DEEPEN Get children to compare the division sentence 6 ÷ 2 = 3 in question ❶, and the division sentence 6 ÷ 3 = 2. Ask: *What is the same or different about them. Do they show the same answer? How did you work them out differently?* Can children use this to write another division sentence for question ❷, such as 10 ÷ 2 = 5?

ASSESSMENT CHECKPOINT Do children use one-to-one correspondence when using resources to model a problem? Do children always share one at a time or sometimes do two at a time? Do they think it makes a difference? In questions ❶ and ❷, do children put the correct numbers into the division sentence? In question ❸, look for clear understanding of what the number sentence represents. Compare the number sentences for grouping and sharing, recognising what is known and unknown before any action is undertaken.

ANSWERS

Question ❶ : There are 6 oranges.

We share them between 2 people.

Each person gets 3 each.

So 6 ÷ 2 = 3.

Question ❷ : 10 ÷ 5 = 2

Each child gets 2 strawberries.

Question ❸ : 8 represents the number to be shared.

2 represents the number to be shared into.

4 represents the number in each equal group.

PUPIL TEXTBOOK 2B PAGE 14

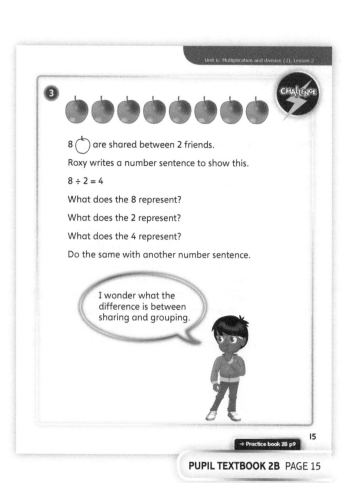

PUPIL TEXTBOOK 2B PAGE 15

Practice

WAYS OF WORKING Independent thinking

IN FOCUS Questions ❶ and ❷ give children an opportunity to work out a sharing problem independently as modelled previously. Each question uses the same starting number to share out. In question ❸, the number used to divide by is kept equal. Each time children will be dividing by 4. A visual representation of resources is given each time. Question ❹ requires children to explain what each number represents in a division story. Question ❺ asks children to solve a written division story, and then to use numbers and the division sign to represent the story as a division sentence.

STRENGTHEN In question ❺, ask children to act out the first part of each sentence to help them match it up. They will require 20 cubes to start with and can see the sentences like an instruction: 'I shared between 4 people' becomes 'share between 4 people'.

DEEPEN For question ❺, if children have spotted this pattern previously, ask them to rearrange the numbers in the division sentences to form different division sentences. For example, 20 ÷ 4 = 5 becomes 20 ÷ 5 = 4.

ASSESSMENT CHECKPOINT Do children notice in questions ❶ and ❷ that the numbers have been 'switched'? Can they correctly write numbers into the division sentences? In question ❹, do children count the carrots and rabbits to know which number is which, or can they tell there are more carrots by looking?

ANSWERS Answers for the **Practice** part of the lesson appear in the separate **Practice and Reflect answer guide**.

Reflect

WAYS OF WORKING Pair work

IN FOCUS With partners, children need to come up with their own way of drawing 10 ÷ 5 = 2. Children can choose their own context if they like, as long as 10 is the number of objects being shared.

ASSESSMENT CHECKPOINT You can use the **Reflect** question to assess the methods children use. Do they draw 10 objects and draw circles around them (grouping)? Do they draw 5 people with a tally underneath showing how many marbles are shared out? Do children draw 2 sharing circles (in which case they are misunderstanding the question)?

ANSWERS Answers for the **Reflect** part of the lesson appear in the separate **Practice and Reflect answer guide**.

After the lesson

- Are children confident using a sharing strategy for division?
- Can children compare a grouping and sharing strategy?
- Can children create a division sentence from a certain context or story?

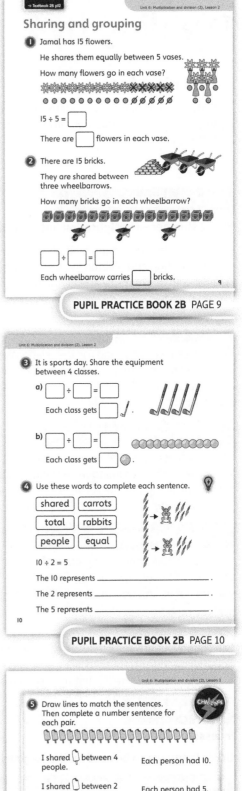

PUPIL PRACTICE BOOK 2B PAGE 9

PUPIL PRACTICE BOOK 2B PAGE 10

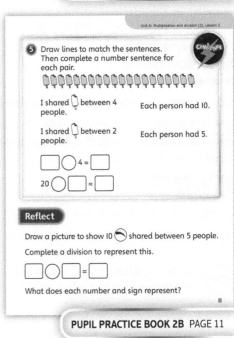

PUPIL PRACTICE BOOK 2B PAGE 11

Dividing by 2

Learning focus

In this lesson, children will relate 2 times-table facts to dividing by 2. Children will say how many 'groups of 2' there are.

Small steps

→ Previous step: Sharing and grouping
→ **This step: Dividing by 2**
→ Next step: Odd and even numbers

NATIONAL CURRICULUM LINKS

Year 2 Number – Multiplication and Division

- Solve problems involving multiplication and division, using materials, arrays, repeated addition, mental methods, and multiplication and division facts, including problems in contexts.
- Recall and use multiplication and division facts for the 2, 5 and 10 multiplication tables, including recognising odd and even numbers.

ASSESSING MASTERY

Children can recognise and use the relationship between dividing by 2 and the 2 times-table (understanding the inverse) and can model this by grouping objects into 2s and jumping back 2 on a number line. Children can understand that how many 'groups of 2' is not the total number of objects or number of objects in a group, but the number of groups; they will also link grouping to multiplication facts.

COMMON MISCONCEPTIONS

When writing multiplication and division calculations alongside each other, children may get confused about what number goes where. When trying to write inverse facts, children may become unsure of what each number represents and may write something along the lines of '4 ÷ 2 = 8' from 4 × 2 = 8. Ask:
- *Are you multiplying or dividing? Can you act out your number sentence? Does it make sense?*

STRENGTHENING UNDERSTANDING

This lesson asks how many 'groups of 2' there are. Use real-life objects that come in 2s to reword this question if children are unsure, or to reinforce learning. For example, how many pairs of socks, shoes, gloves. Children will make the distinction that you are not asking how many individual socks, but how many *pairs*.

GOING DEEPER

Can children relate what they are doing with dividing something by 2 to 'halving'? This may be a word they have heard but not understood. Introduce 'halving' and explain it means dividing into 2. Can children reword division sentences from '8 ÷ 2 = 4' to 'half of 8 is 4'? The 2 is not represented as a number, but as the word 'half'.

KEY LANGUAGE

In lesson: dividing, division

Other language to be used by the teacher: equal, pairs

STRUCTURES AND REPRESENTATIONS

Number line, 100 square

RESOURCES

Mandatory: blank number line, cubes, counters, 100 square

Optional: objects that come in pairs such as socks, shoes, gloves

 In the eTextbook of this lesson, you will find interactive links to a selection of teaching tools.

Before you teach

- Do children know their 2 times-table?
- Are children confident grouping and sharing?

Discover

WAYS OF WORKING Pair work

ASK

• *How have you worked out division sentences before?*
• *Is there another known fact like the one Flo says you can use to work this answer out?*

IN FOCUS Question ❶ a) shows a half-filled division sentence as children have seen previously. However, it now includes the phrase 'how many groups of 2 are there?'. Children will be grouping to find the answer. In question ❶ b), children will link grouping to known multiplication facts.

ANSWERS

Question ❶ a): 8 ÷ 2 = 4; there are 4 groups of 2.

Question ❶ b): Flo used that number fact because it is the inverse; 4 × 2 = 8, so 8 ÷ 2 = 4.

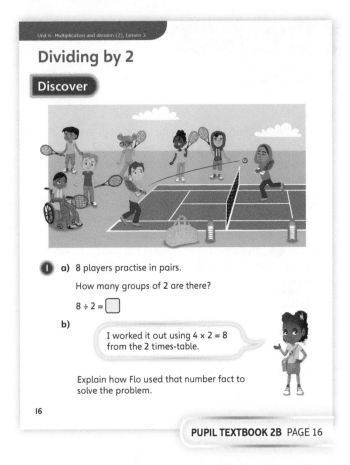

PUPIL TEXTBOOK 2B PAGE 16

Share

WAYS OF WORKING Whole class teacher led

ASK

• *When have you counted in 2s previously?*
• *How will these 2 times-table facts help you?*

IN FOCUS Link with counting in 2s to 8, asking children how they have recorded counting in 2s before. Give eight children tennis racquets and ask them to find a partner to play tennis with. Do this outside so that you can give children the opportunity to play the game briefly. Ask what other games are played in pairs. Represent putting eight players into groups of 2 for different games, for example, table tennis, chess, snap. Play some of the games, indoors or outdoors as appropriate. Children know that 4 × 2 = 8 and should start to see the connection with 8 ÷ 2 = 4. They may then practise this with other numbers in the 2 times-table.

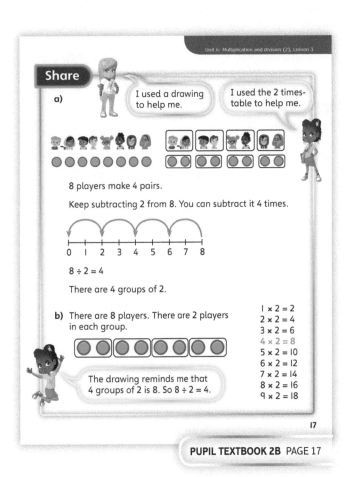

PUPIL TEXTBOOK 2B PAGE 17

Think together

WAYS OF WORKING Whole class teacher led (I do, We do, You do)

ASK

- *What multiplication facts can you use to help work this out? How do you know this particular one will help?*
- *If one more group of 2 has been added, how many more have been added? 1 or 2?*

IN FOCUS In question **2**, one more group of 2 has been added. Children need to relate this to the extra group of 2 counters and extra jump of 2 on the number line. For question **3**, give children their own 100 square to work out and draw the pattern of numbers that can be divided by 2.

STRENGTHEN For question **2**, can children write their own multiplication and division sentences that are linked for 14, 16 and 18 players? Children can use the same structure and multiplication sentences as in question **2**.

DEEPEN If children are confident in which numbers can be divided by 2, ask them to generate their own general statement, for example, 'numbers that end in 2, 4, 6, and 8 can be divided by 2'. Do children miss out 0 or are they sure that multiples of 10 can also be divided by 2? Do children also include 100 in that generalisation?

ASSESSMENT CHECKPOINT In question **1**, do children think 1 or 2 is being added if one more *group* of 2 is added? In question **2**, are children able to choose the correct fact to help them work out the division fact based on the numbers in the sentences? In question **3** with the 100 square, do children have to count 2 and colour it in every time or, alternatively, can they spot the pattern quickly or do they know it already? Do children hesitate in colouring in 100 as being a number able to be divided by 2?

ANSWERS

Question **1** : 10 ÷ 2 = 5; 5 groups of 2 can be made now.

Question **2** : 6 × 2 = 12 so 12 ÷ 2 = 6; 6 groups of 2 players.

> If there were 14 players, there would be 7 groups of 2.
>
> If there were 16 players, there would be 8 groups of 2.
>
> If there were 18 players, there would be 9 groups of 2.

Question **3** : All the even numbers on the 100 square are coloured in, as they can be divided by 2.

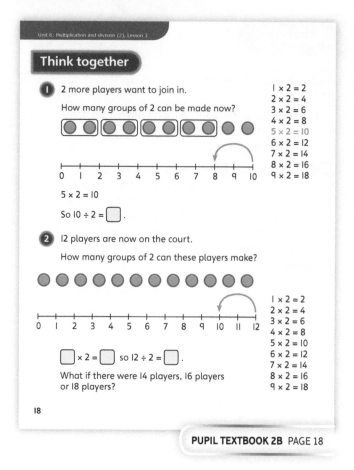

PUPIL TEXTBOOK 2B PAGE 18

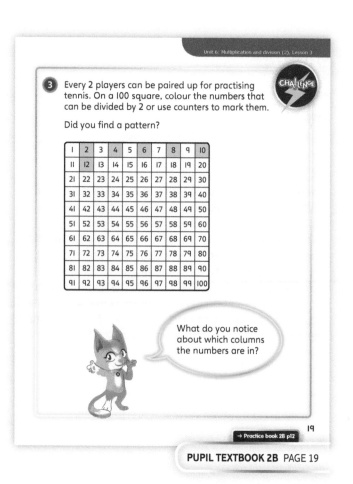

PUPIL TEXTBOOK 2B PAGE 19

Practice

WAYS OF WORKING Independent thinking

IN FOCUS Questions ❶ and ❷ give children a chance to practise counting back in 2s independently. Question ❸ shows arrays where children can derive both multiplication and division facts. The first array gives a prompt of grouping objects into 2 groups. In question ❺, children may have to work out each division sentence before being able to match them to their corresponding multiplication sentence.

STRENGTHEN For question ❸, get children to make each array using cubes or counters. Children can then physically group the objects into 2s to help them work out what each number is and where it goes in the multiplication scaffold.

DEEPEN In question ❺, ask children to draw arrays to show each of the corresponding multiplication and division sentences. They can do it in order, adding two counters or cubes in a different colour each time.

ASSESSMENT CHECKPOINT In questions ❸ and ❹, do children get the right numbers in the right order in the multiplication and division calculations or do they get the numbers mixed up? In question ❹, do children spot that every time the first number in the calculation goes up by one, the answer goes up by two?

ANSWERS Answers for the **Practice** part of the lesson appear in the separate **Practice and Reflect answer guide**.

Reflect

WAYS OF WORKING Pair work, Whole class

IN FOCUS Children work in pairs to fill in the missing number. Each pair should then think of a story or a context to help them explain how the calculations are related. Compare stories between pairs, discussing what is the same about them and what is different about them.

ASSESSMENT CHECKPOINT Assess what strategy children use to work out 10 ÷ 2; do they use known multiplication facts to help them? In their story, do children use objects that naturally come in groups of 2 or do they just choose two objects that need to be counted in 2s? Do children use the word 'pair' in their story?

ANSWERS Answers for the **Reflect** part of the lesson appear in the separate **Practice and Reflect answer guide**.

After the lesson ⏸

- Are children aware of the link between multiplication and division?
- Could children use previous facts to work out a 'one more group of 2 is added' question?
- Could children recall any division facts? Do they work answers out by drawing dots or on a number line?

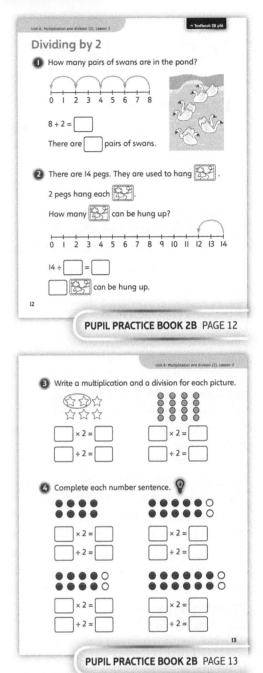

PUPIL PRACTICE BOOK 2B PAGE 12

PUPIL PRACTICE BOOK 2B PAGE 13

PUPIL PRACTICE BOOK 2B PAGE 14

Odd and even numbers

Learning focus

In this lesson, children will understand the difference between odd and even. They will tell if a number is odd or even by grouping it in 2s.

Small steps

→ Previous step: Dividing by 2
→ **This step: Odd and even numbers**
→ Next step: Dividing by 5

NATIONAL CURRICULUM LINKS

Year 2 Number – Multiplication and Division

Recall and use multiplication and division facts for the 2, 5 and 10 multiplication tables, including recognising odd and even numbers.

ASSESSING MASTERY

Children can identify which numbers are odd and even. Children know that even numbers can be divided equally into 2 and odd numbers will have one left over. They will know that it is only the ones digit that needs to be looked at when deciding whether it is odd or even, and that the amount of tens is irrelevant.

COMMON MISCONCEPTIONS

Children may not understand that there is always one left over when an odd number is sorted into 2s. They may try to 'fit' that extra one into the other groups or think they have made a mistake when one does not fit. Ask:
• *Is every group equal? Can you put that extra one into any group and still have equal groups?*

STRENGTHENING UNDERSTANDING

Encourage children to first take the relevant number of counters and see if they can share them equally between themselves and their partner. What do they notice? Do they sometimes have one left over?

In a similar way to their work in the previous lesson, get children to mark on a fresh 100 square where odd and even numbers are and ask them if there are any patterns they spot. Do children automatically know to colour in each column when highlighting odd and even numbers? Can they make general statements about what even and odd numbers end in?

GOING DEEPER

Once children are confident with what odd and even numbers end in, show them odd numbers with an even number of tens and even numbers with an odd number of tens. Ask children what the tricky part might be with these numbers in deciding whether they are odd or even. What about numbers that go above 100? Can they apply their knowledge to 101, 102 and so on?

KEY LANGUAGE

In lesson: even, odd

Other language to be used by the teacher: equal groups, dividing by 2, one left over

STRUCTURES AND REPRESENTATIONS

Groups of counters, 100 square, number line

RESOURCES

Mandatory: counters

Optional: pairs of items such as socks or shoes that come in 2s, 100 square

 In the eTextbook of this lesson, you will find interactive links to a selection of teaching tools.

Before you teach ⏸

• Were children confident dividing by 2 in the previous lesson?
• Do children know what the word 'pair' means in a mathematical context?

Discover

WAYS OF WORKING Pair work

ASK

- *How many socks are in a pair?*
- *If one row can be sorted into pairs and one more sock is added, can you work out whether that row can be put into pairs without grouping into 2s?*

IN FOCUS Socks come in pairs so it is logical to group them into 2s. Children can group each row into 2s to see whether any socks are left over. The socks must be grouped into *equal* groups with no more or less in each group. As children work their way through the rows, do they notice a pattern? In question ① b) do children have to draw the socks to work it out or can they use the previous pattern to help them?

ANSWERS

Question ① a): The plain yellow socks can be sorted into pairs. The red stripy socks cannot be sorted into pairs.

Question ① b):

8		yes
9		no
10		yes
11		no
12		yes

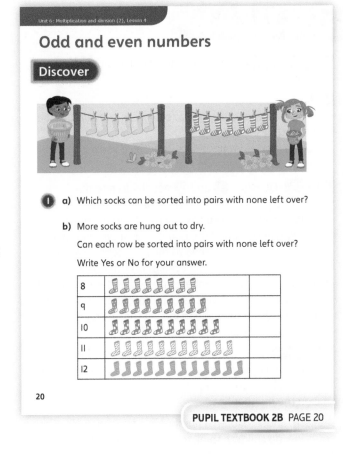

Odd and even numbers

Discover

1. a) Which socks can be sorted into pairs with none left over?

   b) More socks are hung out to dry.

   Can each row be sorted into pairs with none left over?

   Write Yes or No for your answer.

8		
9		
10		
11		
12		

20

PUPIL TEXTBOOK 2B PAGE 20

Share

WAYS OF WORKING Whole class teacher led

ASK

- *What does 'odd' mean? What does 'even' mean?*
- *What pattern do you spot with the numbers?*

IN FOCUS Refer to what Flo is saying about there sometimes being one left over. Look at the row of 7 socks with 3 pairs and one left over and ask children if that left over sock can be put into a pair? What if another sock is added to make 8 socks, does that mean 2 socks will be left over? Show children that those 2 remaining socks will be made into their own pair so there can only be one sock left over. Say to children that when we have one left over, we call this an odd number. When a number divides by 2 equally then it is an even number.

Refer to the box at the bottom and ask: *Where have you seen the even numbers before?* Link this to the last lesson and when children looked at multiplying by 2.

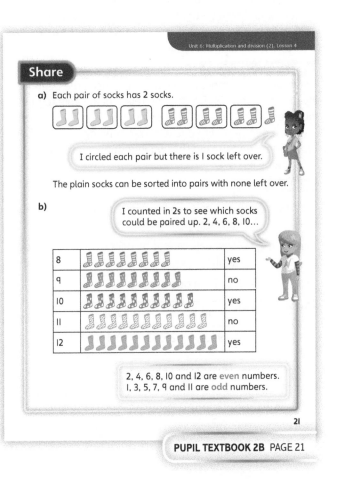

Share

a) Each pair of socks has 2 socks.

I circled each pair but there is 1 sock left over.

The plain socks can be sorted into pairs with none left over.

b)

I counted in 2s to see which socks could be paired up. 2, 4, 6, 8, 10...

8		yes
9		no
10		yes
11		no
12		yes

2, 4, 6, 8, 10 and 12 are **even** numbers.
1, 3, 5, 7, 9 and 11 are **odd** numbers.

21

PUPIL TEXTBOOK 2B PAGE 21

Think together

Whole class teacher led (I do, We do, You do)

ASK

- *Can even numbers be put into pairs? Can odd numbers be put into pairs?*
- *Did you have to group 15 into 2s or could you base your answer on what you found with 14?*

IN FOCUS Question ① and ② get children to put wheels into pairs to see if there are any left over. For both questions, children need to copy the diagram and show that they have grouped the number of wheels into pairs correctly. Children then need to fill in sentence scaffolds about those numbers being even or odd. In question ③ b) children need to sort numbers into odd and even without seeing them grouped. Use Ash's prompt to help children realise that they only need to look at the last digit of these numbers to sort them as even or odd.

STRENGTHEN Get children to draw pictures of wheels and counters onto a number line to reinforce how many there are. Ask children to circle the objects as well as doing jumps of 2 on the number line.

DEEPEN Show children a number line marked 1–10. Without counting, do children think they could work out *how many* even and odd numbers there would be? Would there be the same number? What about a number line starting at 11 and ending in 20? Do children notice a pattern with the amount of numbers shown on the number line and the amount of odd and even numbers? (There will always be the same amount of odd and even numbers.)

ASSESSMENT CHECKPOINT Do children have to work out whether each number can be paired up from the beginning by grouping into 2s? Do children relate being able to put numbers into groups of 2s as being even numbers as well as those numbers with one left over as being odd numbers? Do children understand that when grouping into 2s only one can be left over?

ANSWERS

Question ① : 14 wheels can be paired up. 14 is an even number.

Question ② : 15 wheels cannot be paired up. 15 is an odd number.

Question ③ a): 17 is an odd number.

Question ③ b):

Odd	Even
9, 11, 17, 25, 33	10, 16, 20, 32

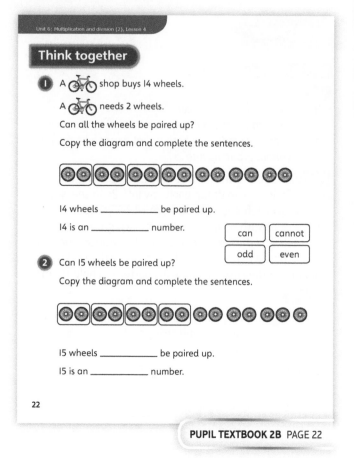

Practice

WAYS OF WORKING Independent thinking

IN FOCUS In question ①, children will relate 'one left over' to 'one child on their own', giving it a physical context. Question ③ helps children with the link to the 2 times-table. If the number appears as an answer in the 2 times-table, it is even, if not then it is odd. In question ④, children must find two numbers that are 5 apart. They might use trial and error or pick a number and work out what is 5 more or less and see if any number matches.

STRENGTHEN Demonstrate question ① by getting the same number of children to stand up as in the image and hold hands in pairs. It will make it more obvious when one is left over as they will have no hand to hold. In question ②, ask children to get the resource that is pictured (bead string, ten frame, coins) and represent what is being shown.

DEEPEN In a similar way to question ④, tell children Rani has chosen an even number. James chooses a number that is 2 away (more or less). Ask: *Could James's number ever be an odd number? Why?*

ASSESSMENT CHECKPOINT In question ①, do children write '0' or 'no' to how many children will be left over when it is an even number? In question ③, check if children can link the images to a times-table fact.

In question ④, do children show awareness that if two numbers are 5 apart, they cannot be even and even, or odd and odd?

ANSWERS Answers for the **Practice** part of the lesson appear in the separate **Practice and Reflect answer guide**.

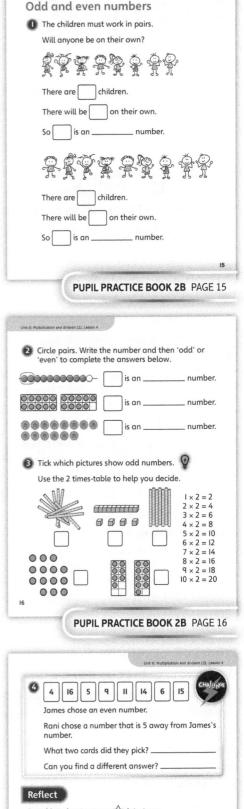

PUPIL PRACTICE BOOK 2B PAGE 15

PUPIL PRACTICE BOOK 2B PAGE 16

Reflect

WAYS OF WORKING Pair work

IN FOCUS In this **Reflect** question, Jamal is trying to group an odd number into 2s and has tried many different ways. A different star keeps being left over each time a different formation of 2s is attempted. Children explain why Jamal cannot find a way.

ASSESSMENT CHECKPOINT Assess whether children count the number of stars to check whether it is odd or even. Do children try to find their own way of grouping the stars into 2? Do children make a mistake such as trying to put the left over star into a group of 2 to make it a group of 3?

ANSWERS Answers for the **Reflect** part of the lesson appear in the separate **Practice and Reflect answer guide**.

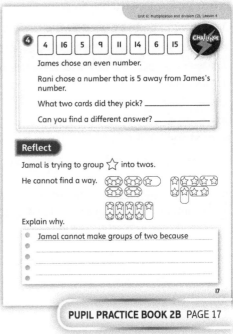

PUPIL PRACTICE BOOK 2B PAGE 17

After the lesson

- Do children recognise that even numbers can be grouped into 2 and odd numbers have one left over?
- Could children name different odd and even numbers?
- Can children generalise about what odd and even numbers always end in?

Dividing by 5

Learning focus

In this lesson, children will divide numbers by 5 by grouping and on a number line. They will link division facts to times-tables.

Small steps

→ Previous step: Odd and even numbers
→ **This step: Dividing by 5**
→ Next step: Dividing by 10

NATIONAL CURRICULUM LINKS

Year 2 Number – Multiplication and Division

Recall and use multiplication and division facts for the 2, 5 and 10 multiplication tables, including recognising odd and even numbers.

ASSESSING MASTERY

Children can divide a number by 5 and can link grouping to multiplication facts and those multiplication facts to division facts. Children can recognise that they can divide numbers that end in 0 or 5 by 5.

COMMON MISCONCEPTIONS

When filling in their own division sentences such as 45 ÷ 5 = 9, children may write 45 ÷ 9 = 5 instead. While this is not inaccurate, it does not link to the 5 times-table fact. They would have to group the objects into 9 instead of 5, which would give the idea of commutativity, but this is not dividing by 5. Ask:
• *What number are you trying to divide by? You are trying to make groups of what number?*

STRENGTHENING UNDERSTANDING

The idea of flowers needing 5 petals has been used in this lesson. Use other ideas of objects that naturally come in 5s such as gloves, fingers, toes, points on a star and so on, to give a different context.

GOING DEEPER

If children have been confident dividing by 5 and linking to multiplication facts, give them another investigation. Ask them to work out how many fingers and hands there are in the room (always a multiple of 5). Working out how many hands there are will give the number that needs to be multiplied by 5. Finding the total amount of fingers is finding the multiple of 5. Both numbers can be put into a multiplication and division sentence with 5.

KEY LANGUAGE

In lesson: five times-table, divide by five

Other language to be used by the teacher: equal groups, multiplication facts, division facts

STRUCTURES AND REPRESENTATIONS

Number line

RESOURCES

Mandatory: blank number line, cubes and counters, 100 square

Optional: straws to make houses, objects that come in 5s such as pictures of fingers and gloves

 In the eTextbook of this lesson, you will find interactive links to a selection of teaching tools.

Before you teach ⏸

• Were children able to link multiplication and division facts in the last lesson?
• Are children already aware of the patterns in the 5 times-table?

Discover

WAYS OF WORKING Pair work

ASK

- How could you work out 20 ÷ 5?
- How could you use the multiplication fact 4 × 5 = 20 to help you?

IN FOCUS In this section, the context of using 5 petals to make one flower helps children to link multiplication and division facts about the 5 times-table. Children may have different strategies for dividing by 5, some being used from the previous lesson. Flo mentions a 5 times-table fact: draw attention to this and ask if children can spot any similarities between the number sentences.

ANSWERS

Question ① a): You can make 4 flowers with 20 ◯ because each flower needs 5 ◯.

Question ① b): 20 ÷ 5 = 4. The multiplication fact is the opposite (inverse) of the division fact. The numbers are the same but the operation has changed.

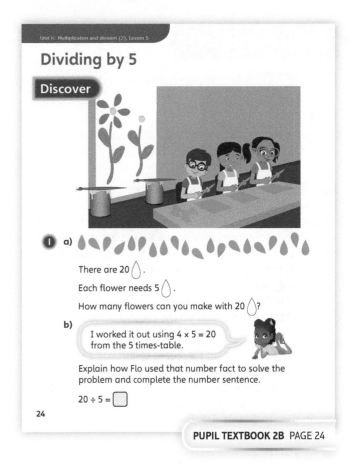

PUPIL TEXTBOOK 2B PAGE 24

Share

WAYS OF WORKING Whole class teacher led

ASK

- Where is the 5 represented on the number line and on the drawing?
- Where can you see the groups of 5?

IN FOCUS The number line shows groups of 5 being continually subtracted from 20. Teachers may link this with repeated subtraction. Children must count the number of jumps back to know how many 5s have been counted back. There is also a drawing of 4 groups of 5 next to the multiplication fact. Also look with children at how the times-table is another way of expressing the multiplication table and counting in 5s. Children may like to predict what comes next and continue the patterns, but without recognising what this means in the situation under consideration.

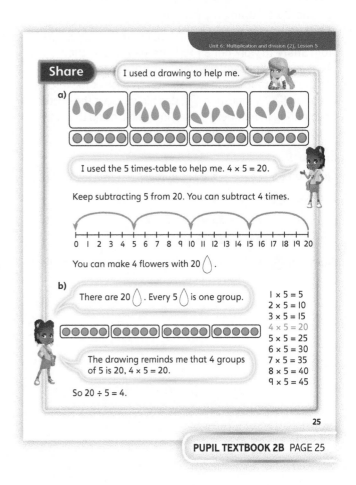

PUPIL TEXTBOOK 2B PAGE 25

Think together

WAYS OF WORKING Whole class teacher led (I do, We do, You do)

ASK

• *Why have intervals of 5 been used on the number line?*
• *Do you notice a pattern on the 100 square? What do the numbers always end in?*

IN FOCUS Question ❶ shows a number line to 25 with intervals of 5, and 5 jumps to be made backwards. Check children understand the difference between the two 5s in the number sentences. Question ❷ gives a number line to work out multiplication and division facts and gets children to complete related multiplication and division sentences. Question ❸ shows a 100 square partially filled in with multiples of 5. Children must continue the pattern. This leads children to comment on the pattern across and the pattern down.

STRENGTHEN In question ❷ , could children use a blank number line instead of one with given intervals of 5 to work out the missing numbers? Children would have to be able to count up in 5s and keep track of how many 5s they have counted up to do this. Ask: *Do you notice anything about the ones digit?*

DEEPEN If children are confident with the pattern on the 100 square that is made when counting in 5s, ask them to tell you the multiple of 5 either side of a given multiple of 5. For example, if you said '15' to them, could children tell you '10' and '20' following the pattern?

ASSESSMENT CHECKPOINT Do children use the previous fact from **Share** to work out 25 ÷ 5? Alternatively, do they see it as a distinct and new fact to work out? Do children require the number line to make jumps back or forwards in question ❷ ? In question ❸ , do children spot the pattern of colouring in numbers ending in 5 and 0 or do they have to count 5 on from each number?

ANSWERS

Question ❶ : 25 ÷ 5 = 5; you can make 5 flowers with 25 ◌.

Question ❷ : 6 × 5 = **30** so 30 ÷ 5 = **6**.

7 × 5 = 35 so 35 ÷ 5 = **7**.

8 × 5 = 40 so 40 ÷ 5 = **8**.

Question ❸ : All numbers ending in 5 or 0 are coloured on the 100 square.

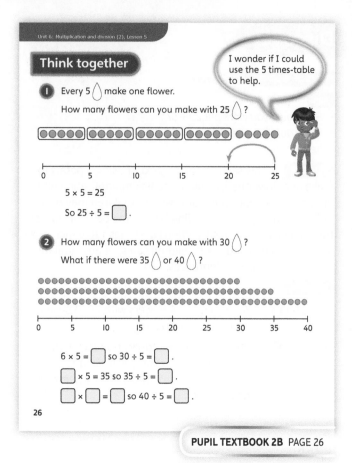

PUPIL TEXTBOOK 2B PAGE 26

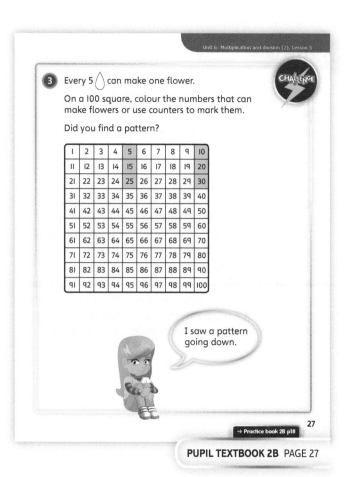

PUPIL TEXTBOOK 2B PAGE 27

Practice

WAYS OF WORKING Independent thinking

IN FOCUS Questions ❶ and ❷ let children independently count back 5 on a number line. The number lines have multiples of 5 labelled so children just need to keep track of how many 5s they are jumping back. Question ❸ shows the 5 times-table visually, children fill in the missing numbers in the multiplication and division sentences underneath.

STRENGTHEN For question ❷, give out counters to make the groups. Get children to predict how many counters they need to make a certain number of groups. Also, give children an amount of counters and ask how many groups they can make. This is practising multiplication and division facts in context and with practical resources.

DEEPEN Question ❺ looks at whether multiples of 5 were multiplied by an odd or even number. Children may work out each fact separately to sort them. Can children make generalisations such as 'if you multiply 5 by an even number you get an even number' and 'if you multiply 5 by an odd number you get an odd number'? Can children discuss why that might be? Talk about 'one left over' in odd numbers but two joining up to make an even number.

ASSESSMENT CHECKPOINT Are children making the link between repeated subtraction and division? Are they confident that counting the number of jumps back is counting the number of 5s? In question ❸, can children link the total number in the division sentences to the multiplication fact pictures? For example, do they see '10 ÷ 5 = ?' is linked to '2 × 5'?

ANSWERS Answers for the **Practice** part of the lesson appear in the separate **Practice and Reflect answer guide**.

Reflect

WAYS OF WORKING Pair work then whole class

IN FOCUS Use the **Reflect** question as the basis for discussion. Many different ways of working out are valid. Ask children in pairs to decide which method they would use and draw a picture to represent it. In the class there should be a varied response to how different pairs would work it out – get children to compare and contrast their methods.

ASSESSMENT CHECKPOINT Is there a certain method that is more prevalent in the class? Which one is it and why might that be? Do children make the link between division and times-tables? Alternatively, do they still see division as a separate operation?

ANSWERS Answers for the **Reflect** part of the lesson appear in the separate **Practice and Reflect answer guide**.

After the lesson ⏸

- Could children say if a given number was in the 5 times-table based on its last digit?
- Did children spot any similarities between 5 times-table facts and 2 times-table facts, for example, 2 × 5 = 10?
- Was there a particular method children particularly struggled with? Why is that?

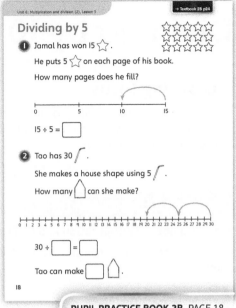

PUPIL PRACTICE BOOK 2B PAGE 18

PUPIL PRACTICE BOOK 2B PAGE 19

PUPIL PRACTICE BOOK 2B PAGE 20

Dividing by 10

Learning focus

In this lesson, children will divide numbers by 10. They will link 10 times-table facts to dividing by 10 and show this on a number line.

Small steps

→ Previous step: Dividing by 5
→ **This step: Dividing by 10**
→ Next step: Bar modelling – grouping

NATIONAL CURRICULUM LINKS

Year 2 Number – Multiplication and Division

Recall and use multiplication and division facts for the 2, 5 and 10 multiplication tables, including recognising odd and even numbers.

ASSESSING MASTERY

Children can divide a number by 10 and can link grouping to multiplication facts and link multiplication facts to division facts. Children can recognise that they can divide numbers that end in 0 by 10.

COMMON MISCONCEPTIONS

Multiplying and dividing by 10 is linked to place value. Children may see multiplying by 10 as 'adding a 0' and dividing by 10 as 'taking off a 0' but it needs to be discussed in terms of digits moving up the place value columns. Show T and O place value headings and put a digit in the ones column. Model dividing by 10 and the digit going up to the tens column or back to the ones column. Ask:

• *What happens to the digit each time? Why is the '0' needed or not needed?*

STRENGTHENING UNDERSTANDING

Children each have ten fingers which can give a real-life context to multiplying and dividing by 10. *If you know the number of children (for example, 2) you can multiply by 10 to find out how many fingers. If you know the number of fingers (for example, 30) you can divide by 10 to work out how many children they belong to.*

GOING DEEPER

Linked to previous lessons, ask children whether multiplying by 10 gives you an odd or even number. Ask: *Does it matter if the number you are multiplying is odd or even to start with?* Get children to generate some examples to help their answer. Discuss why there is always an even number when multiplying by 10. Talk about 'one being left over' in odd numbers but being able to 'pair up' once multiplied.

KEY LANGUAGE

In lesson: 10 times-table, divide by 10

Other language to be used by the teacher: place value, equal groups, multiplication facts, division facts

STRUCTURES AND REPRESENTATIONS

Number line

RESOURCES

Mandatory: blank number line, cubes and counters, 100 square

Optional: packs of objects in 10s such as pens or pencils, pictures of ten fingers or ten toes

 In the eTextbook of this lesson, you will find interactive links to a selection of teaching tools.

Before you teach

• Are children already able to skip count up in 10s?
• Can children recall that numbers in the 5 times-table sometimes end in 0?

Discover

WAYS OF WORKING **WAYS OF WORKING** Pair work

ASK

- *How many pencils are there altogether?*
- *How many pencils are in each packet?*

IN FOCUS This image shows three packs of 10 pencils but tells children that there are 30 pencils. Children have to work out how many *packs* of 10 there are. This is like working out how many *groups* of a number there are, which is similar to what children have done in previous lessons. Children could theoretically count the packs in the picture, but ask them to look at the numbers in the division sentence.

ANSWERS

Question ① a): 30 − 20 = 10

20 − 10 = 10

10 − 10 = 0

There are 3 packs of 10 ‖.

Question ① b): 3 × 10 = 30. Flo used this times-table fact to work it out because it is the opposite of the division fact. If you know that 3 × 10 = 30 then you know that 30 ÷ 10 must be 3.

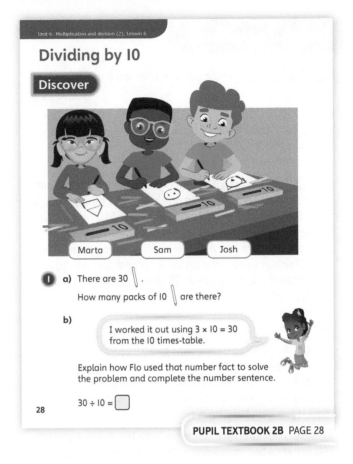

Dividing by 10

Discover

① a) There are 30 ‖.

How many packs of 10 ‖ are there?

b) I worked it out using 3 × 10 = 30 from the 10 times-table.

Explain how Flo used that number fact to solve the problem and complete the number sentence.

30 ÷ 10 = ☐

28

PUPIL TEXTBOOK 2B PAGE 28

Share

WAYS OF WORKING Whole class teacher led

ASK

- *How many jumps back are made on the number line?*
- *How many tens do you subtract until you get to 0?*

IN FOCUS Flo shows the multiplication fact 3 × 10 = 30 alongside a visual representation of 10 pencils in three packs. It has 10 counters to represent each pencil. This also shows the 10 times-table that is linked to the division sentence as well as showing that three groups of 10 is 30.

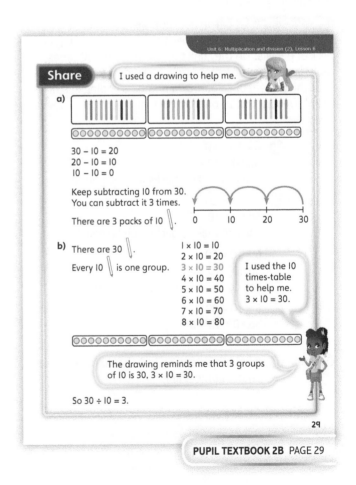

Share I used a drawing to help me.

a)

30 − 10 = 20
20 − 10 = 10
10 − 10 = 0

Keep subtracting 10 from 30. You can subtract it 3 times.

There are 3 packs of 10 ‖.

b) There are 30 ‖.

Every 10 ‖ is one group.

1 × 10 = 10
2 × 10 = 20
3 × 10 = 30
4 × 10 = 40
5 × 10 = 50
6 × 10 = 60
7 × 10 = 70
8 × 10 = 80

I used the 10 times-table to help me. 3 × 10 = 30.

The drawing reminds me that 3 groups of 10 is 30, 3 × 10 = 30.

So 30 ÷ 10 = 3.

29

PUPIL TEXTBOOK 2B PAGE 29

Think together

WAYS OF WORKING Whole class teacher led (I do, We do, You do)

ASK

• *Why have intervals of 10 been used on the number line?*
• *Do you notice a pattern on the 100 square? What do the numbers always end in?*

IN FOCUS Question ❶ asks how many **packs** can be made (not how many pencils are in one pack). The number line has intervals of 10 and gives a starting jump of 10 backwards. In question ❷, different numbers of packs are laid out against a number line with one more 10 being added each time. Children can label each pack 10, or label each 10 more than the last. Question ❸ shows a 100 square with multiples of 10 coloured. Children continue the colouring in, looking for patterns.

STRENGTHEN In question ❶, can children use a blank number line instead of one with given intervals of 10 to work out the missing numbers? Children would need to be able to count down in 10s and keep track of how many 10s they have subtracted. They would also have to work out which number to start jumping back from on the number line.

DEEPEN If children are confident with the pattern on the 100 square when counting in 10s, could they tell you the multiple of 10 either side of a given multiple of 10? For example, if you said '20' to them, could they tell you '10' and '30' following the pattern?

ASSESSMENT CHECKPOINT In question ❶, do children understand that each jump back of 10 is representing one *pack* of pencils? Do they link this question to a 10 times-table fact without prompting? In question ❸, do children spot the pattern of colouring in numbers ending in 0 or do they have to count 10 on from each number?

ANSWERS

Question ❶ : 4 × 10 = 40
So 40 ÷ 10 = 4.
You can make 4 packs with 40 pencils.

Question ❷ : 5 × 10 = 50
So 50 ÷ 10 = 5.
You can make 5 packs with 50 pencils.

6 × 10 = 60
So 60 ÷ 10 = 6.
You can make 6 packs with 60 pencils.

8 × 10 = 80
So 80 ÷ 10 = 8.
You can make 8 packs with 80 pencils.

Question ❸ : All numbers ending in 0 should be coloured on the number line.

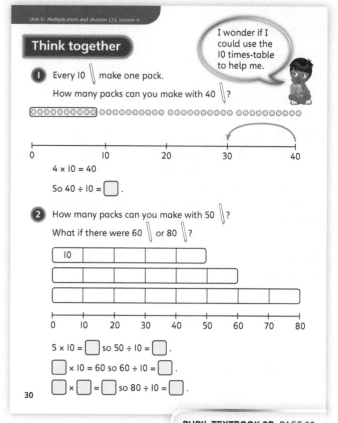

PUPIL TEXTBOOK 2B PAGE 30

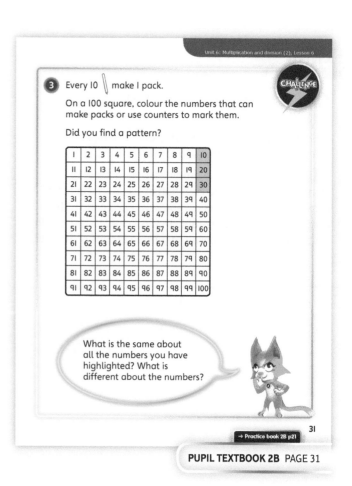

PUPIL TEXTBOOK 2B PAGE 31

58

Practice

WAYS OF WORKING Independent work

IN FOCUS Question ❶ lets children practise dividing by 10 on a number line. Intervals of 10 are marked and the first jump has been done. Question ❷ shows ten frames above a number line. Each frame can be seen as one group of 10. In question ❸, children link multiplication facts to division facts. The number 10 is the only consistent number across the number sentences so they need to fill in the missing numbers.

STRENGTHEN Help children understand question ❺, where a shape represents a number by getting them to take it in turns to create and solve their own questions. Ask children to write a series of number sentences using the same number such as 3 × 10 = 30 and 30 ÷ 10 = 3, then choose a number to be a shape, for example '3' is a square. Children then rewrite the number sentences using this shape, ☐ × 10 = 30 and 30 ÷ 10 = ☐.

DEEPEN Can children work out what a multiplication and division sentence would be if 10 more or less was added or taken away? For example, give children 4 × 10 = 40 and 40 ÷ 10 = 4. What would the number facts be if 10 more was added? (5 × 10 = 50 and 50 ÷ 10 = 5). What would the number facts be if 10 was taken away?

ASSESSMENT CHECKPOINT In question ❷, do children use the ten frames to count up how many groups of 10 there are? Do they work it out by jumping back on a number line? In question ❸, can children match the sentences based on the answers of one side only? Do they spot a pattern in the digits that helps them match them up?

ANSWERS Answers for the **Practice** part of the lesson appear in the separate **Practice and Reflect answer guide**.

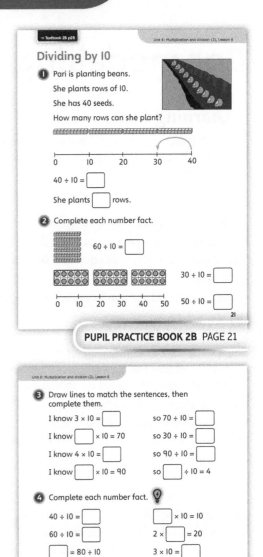

PUPIL PRACTICE BOOK 2B PAGE 21

PUPIL PRACTICE BOOK 2B PAGE 22

Reflect

WAYS OF WORKING Independent work

IN FOCUS Children need to write division sentences based on the 10 times-table multiplication facts. They need to use the numbers given and rearrange them correctly around the ÷ sign.

ASSESSMENT CHECKPOINT Are children writing correct division sentences? Do they write them in order? Do they use the multiplication sentences to help them or do they work out separately?

ANSWERS Answers for the **Reflect** part of the lesson appear in the separate **Practice and Reflect answer guide**.

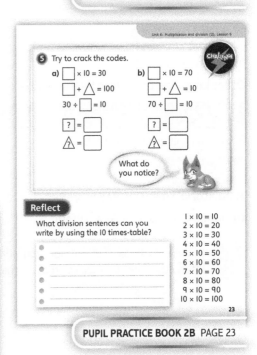

PUPIL PRACTICE BOOK 2B PAGE 23

After the lesson ⏸

- Do children know the 10 times-table pattern? Can they identify numbers not in the 10 times-table?
- Can children answer division questions using their 10 times-table knowledge?
- Are children aware of the link of multiplying and dividing by 10 and place value?

Bar modelling – grouping

Learning focus

In this lesson, children will be able to represent division calculations using a bar model and using grouping.

Small steps

→ Previous step: Dividing by 10
→ **This step: Bar modelling – grouping**
→ Next step: Bar modelling – sharing

NATIONAL CURRICULUM LINKS

Year 2 Number – Multiplication and Division

Solve problems involving multiplication and division, using materials, arrays, repeated addition, mental methods, and multiplication and division facts, including problems in contexts.

ASSESSING MASTERY

Children can use a bar model to represent a division problem involving grouping and they will be able to label the whole, each part and how many equal parts there are. Children can see that the number of equal jumps on a number line and number of equal parts in the bar model are representing the same component of a number sentence.

COMMON MISCONCEPTIONS

Children may misinterpret the number of equal parts in a bar model for the number each part is worth. For example, they may represent $20 \div 4 = 5$ as:

Ask:

• *What does each number represent in the division calculation? Is that what you have shown?*

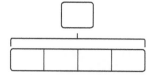

STRENGTHENING UNDERSTANDING

Ask children which methods they have used before when thinking about equal sized groups (skip counting, multiplication table, array, bar model and so on). Challenge them to represent the problem in a different way, a way they have not used for a while. Children could use ten frames as trays or something else. The key idea is how many groups of a given size can be made with the given amount. The focus is on grouping, not sharing.

GOING DEEPER

Could children use the same bar model outline to write different division sentences, recognising that the number being divided by remains the same? For example, this bar model could make $8 \div 4 = 2$, $12 \div 4 = 3$, $16 \div 4 = 4$, $20 \div 4 = 5$, and so on.

KEY LANGUAGE

In lesson: bar model

Other language to be used by the teacher: equal parts, number of equal parts, whole

STRUCTURES AND REPRESENTATIONS

Bar model split into equal parts

RESOURCES

Mandatory: cubes and counters, empty bar model scaffolds

Optional: buttons to make a pattern

 In the eTextbook of this lesson, you will find interactive links to a selection of teaching tools.

Before you teach

• Are children confident with grouping as a method for division?
• Have they seen the bar model before? How could you draw on this in your teaching?

Discover

Unit 6: Multiplication and division (2), Lesson 7

WAYS OF WORKING Pair work

ASK

• *What strategy will you use to work these out?*
• *Can you use times-table facts?*

IN FOCUS This section shows a division by 10 question and division by 5 question. The image shows the drinks which can be circled into groups of 10 and 5 to show how many trays are needed.

ANSWERS

Question ❶ a): 40 ÷ 10 = 4; 4 trays are needed for 40 🥤.

Question ❶ b): 35 ÷ 5 = 7; 7 trays are needed for 35 🥤.

Bar modelling – grouping

Discover

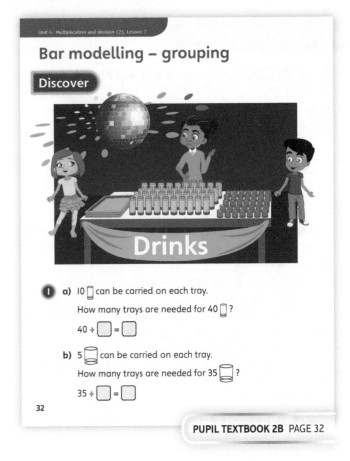

❶ a) 10 🥤 can be carried on each tray.
   How many trays are needed for 40 🥤?
   40 ÷ ☐ = ☐

b) 5 🥤 can be carried on each tray.
   How many trays are needed for 35 🥤?
   35 ÷ ☐ = ☐

32

PUPIL TEXTBOOK 2B PAGE 32

Share

WAYS OF WORKING Whole class teacher led

ASK

• *What is the same or different about the number line and the bar model?*
• *What is each bar worth? Are they equal?*
• *Where is the 4 and 7 represented on the bar model?*

IN FOCUS The bar model is introduced alongside the number line and visual representations of the drinks. Sparks asks how many equal parts of 10 there are. Children may know the answer from the previous lesson, but get them to show you where it is on the bar model. The number '4' is not written anywhere; it has to be calculated from the number of equal parts. Show how the bar model builds up one by one. Start with the first bar of 10 (there are 30 left using the number line). Then add on next bar of 10. At the beginning of the question, children do not know that 4 trays are required. Flo explains this, but it is important that this is modelled correctly.

Share

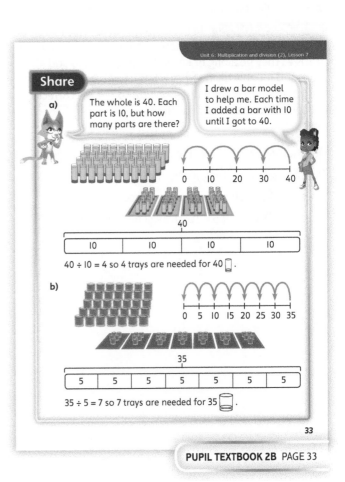

a) The whole is 40. Each part is 10, but how many parts are there?

I drew a bar model to help me. Each time I added a bar with 10 until I got to 40.

40 ÷ 10 = 4 so 4 trays are needed for 40 🥤.

b) 35 ÷ 5 = 7 so 7 trays are needed for 35 🥤.

33

PUPIL TEXTBOOK 2B PAGE 33

Think together

WAYS OF WORKING Whole class teacher led (I do, We do, You do)

ASK

- *How many bars are needed in total?*
- *How many more bars need to be drawn on?*

IN FOCUS Questions ❶ and ❷ show a part-drawn bar model that must be completed. The whole is written on, as are two equal parts, but not enough parts have been drawn on. Children have to work out how many more bars need to be drawn on. Sparks gives a helpful reminder that each tray can hold 10 drinks so each bar must be worth 10. Children write the division sentence each time.

STRENGTHEN In question ❸, can children draw their own bar model to represent each problem? Check they can label the total correctly, have the right number of equal parts and label each part correctly. Do children draw the bar models the same width as they both have the same total, or is the bar model that has 10 equal parts made wider because the parts are the same width even though they are worth a different amount?

DEEPEN In question ❸, the number of equal parts and value of each part switch over. This gives a different meaning to the word problem as a different number of boxes are required. Can children think of other division sentences where those two values are switched? What do these look like on a bar model? Can children draw them?

ASSESSMENT CHECKPOINT In question ❶, do children attempt to draw the bars an equal length? Do they count up or down in 10s as they go along or know that they need to add 40 more and roughly divide what is left into 4? Do children use the information in the word problems to put the correct numbers into the division scaffolds?

ANSWERS

Question ❶ : 60 ÷ 10 = 6; there are 6 more trays needed.

Question ❷ : 21 ÷ 3 = 7; Joe will need 7 trays.

Question ❸ a): 50 ÷ 10 = 5; she will need 5 boxes.

Question ❸ b): 50 ÷ 5 = 10; she will need 10 boxes.

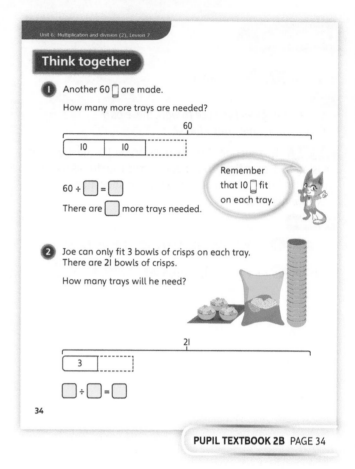

Think together

❶ Another 60 ▯ are made.

How many more trays are needed?

60 ÷ ▢ = ▢

There are ▢ more trays needed.

Remember that 10 ▯ fit on each tray.

❷ Joe can only fit 3 bowls of crisps on each tray. There are 21 bowls of crisps.

How many trays will he need?

21

▢ ÷ ▢ = ▢

34

PUPIL TEXTBOOK 2B PAGE 34

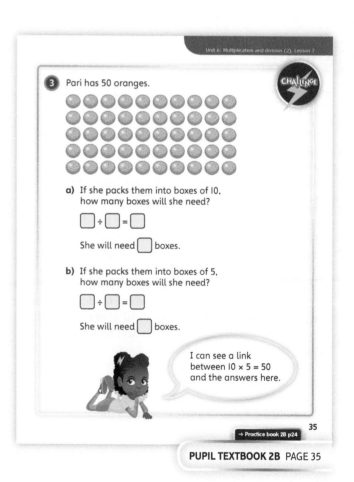

❸ Pari has 50 oranges.

CHALLENGE

a) If she packs them into boxes of 10, how many boxes will she need?

▢ ÷ ▢ = ▢

She will need ▢ boxes.

b) If she packs them into boxes of 5, how many boxes will she need?

▢ ÷ ▢ = ▢

She will need ▢ boxes.

I can see a link between 10 × 5 = 50 and the answers here.

35

→ Practice book 2B p24

PUPIL TEXTBOOK 2B PAGE 35

Practice

IN FOCUS Questions ❶ and ❷ require children to fill in the missing parts of a division calculation, bar model and number line by identifying the whole, the number of equal parts and the value of one part. Question ❸ shows a partial bar model from which to construct division sentences by adding all the parts to find the total and counting how many parts there are. Question ❹ requires matching pictures to bar models and number sentences. Children need to count the number in one group in the picture and match it to the number in one part of the bar model.

STRENGTHEN In question ❷, give children buttons to make the pattern shown. Give them 40 buttons to act out the problem of how many patterns Jamal can make. In question ❸, can children label the whole above each bar model?

DEEPEN Question ❺ gives a partially filled-in bar model with different possible answers. Get children to redraw their bar models with their potential possibilities, this time ensuring that the bars are an equal width.

ASSESSMENT CHECKPOINT Do children count the number of equal parts, as well as looking at the value of one part? Can children find the three pieces of information in question ❸? In question ❺, do children add more bars? Are they an equal width?

ANSWERS Answers for the **Practice** part of the lesson appear in the separate **Practice and Reflect answer guide**.

Reflect

WAYS OF WORKING Pair work then whole class

IN FOCUS In pairs, children can think up their own division story to match the bar model. They need to count up the total to know what is going to be grouped. Children can share and compare their stories with other pairs and discuss what is the same and what is different. They should all have 20 objects that need to be put into groups of 5.

ASSESSMENT CHECKPOINT Do children know to count up the total number of parts to get the total number of objects? Does their story make sense – do they have 20 objects that *can* be grouped? For example, if their problem is to do with people in cars for a trip, does 20 represent the people and the 5 represent the number that can fit in one car?

ANSWERS Answers for the **Reflect** part of the lesson appear in the separate **Practice and Reflect answer guide**.

After the lesson ⏸

- Do children understand the three different parts of a bar model?
- Do children see the link between the bar model and division?
- Have children had the opportunity to draw or fill in their own bar model to show grouping?

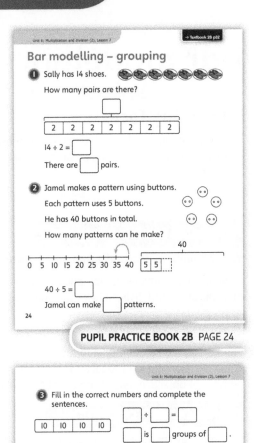

PUPIL PRACTICE BOOK 2B PAGE 24

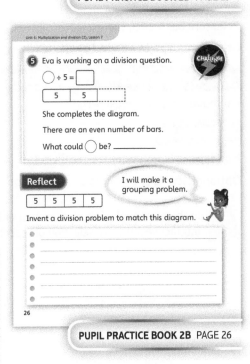

PUPIL PRACTICE BOOK 2B PAGE 25

PUPIL PRACTICE BOOK 2B PAGE 26

Bar modelling – sharing

Learning focus

In this lesson, children will be able to represent division calculations using a bar model and a sharing method.

Small steps

→ Previous step: Bar modelling – grouping
→ **This step: Bar modelling – sharing**
→ Next step: Solving word problems – division

NATIONAL CURRICULUM LINKS

Year 2 Number – Multiplication and division

Solve problems involving multiplication and division, using materials, arrays, repeated addition, mental methods, and multiplication and division facts, including problems in contexts.

ASSESSING MASTERY

Children can use a bar model to represent a division problem involving sharing. Children can draw the correct number of equal parts on the bar model and share a number equally between them and they will know that their answer will be the number of objects in one of the equal parts in the bar model.

COMMON MISCONCEPTIONS

Children may try to use a grouping method when solving sharing problems, and have an equal part worth 2 instead of 2 equal parts. Remind children of the context of the division story and that you are sharing between the amount given. Ask:
• *What does [2] represent, 2 [pirates] or 2 [jewels]?* Change wording and number depending on context.

STRENGTHENING UNDERSTANDING

Sharing can be acted out physically as has been done previously. This time, the outline of the bar model can be drawn out and children share the number of objects into pre-drawn bars or represent them with dots.

GOING DEEPER

Can children look at a completed bar model and make up their own division story? Can they do this within the context of sharing? Look out for children correctly labelling the number of equal parts as the number of groups that it is being shared into. The total number of dots in the bar model is the total number of objects being shared, and the number in one of the bars is the number each group in their story gets.

KEY LANGUAGE

In lesson: bar model, sharing

Other language to be used by the teacher: equal parts, value of each equal part

STRUCTURES AND REPRESENTATIONS

Bar model split into equal parts

RESOURCES

Mandatory: blank bar models to fill in, lots of small objects to share out into them (buttons, coins, cubes)

Optional: jewels or similar to act out division situations

 In the eTextbook of this lesson, you will find interactive links to a selection of teaching tools.

Before you teach

- Were children confident using a sharing strategy for division problems before?
- Are children confident using the bar model for grouping division problems?
- Were there any misconceptions when using the bar model that need to be addressed?

Discover

WAYS OF WORKING Pair work

ASK

- *Does it make a difference if you share one jewel or two jewels at a time?*
- *What changes between each question?* (Both the amount of jewels and the amount of pirates)

IN FOCUS In this division problem, children will need to use the 'one for you, one for you' strategy, sharing one jewel at a time. Some children may be able to share two at a time, which links to grouping. Clarify each time how many pirates are being shared to and how many jewels are being shared.

ANSWERS

Question ❶ a): 12 ÷ 2 = 6; the pirates get 6 jewels each.

Question ❶ b): 15 ÷ 3 = 5; the pirates get 5 diamonds each.

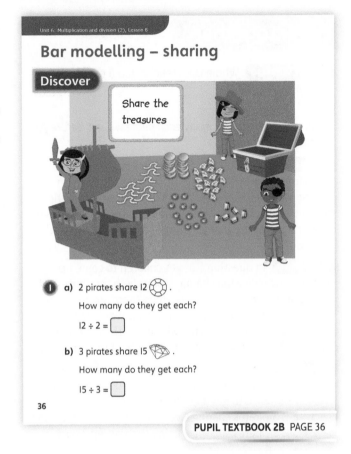

Bar modelling – sharing

Discover

Share the treasures

❶ a) 2 pirates share 12 ⬡.
How many do they get each?

12 ÷ 2 = ☐

b) 3 pirates share 15 ◈.
How many do they get each?

15 ÷ 3 = ☐

36

PUPIL TEXTBOOK 2B PAGE 36

Share

WAYS OF WORKING Whole class teacher led

ASK

- Question ❶ a): *What do the equal parts on the bar model represent?*
- Question ❶ b): *Does it matter if you share one at a time or three at a time?*

IN FOCUS Question ❶ a) shows a sharing strategy of sharing one-by-one between two pirates. The bar model has been split into two equal parts to show the two pirates (as Astrid points out) and the jewels have been shared equally between them. Demonstrate this using a blank bar model and dragging objects into each equal part. In question ❶ b), Flo suggests a quicker strategy of sharing 3 at a time. Model this into a blank bar model and compare it with sharing one-by-one. Ask children if it makes a difference.

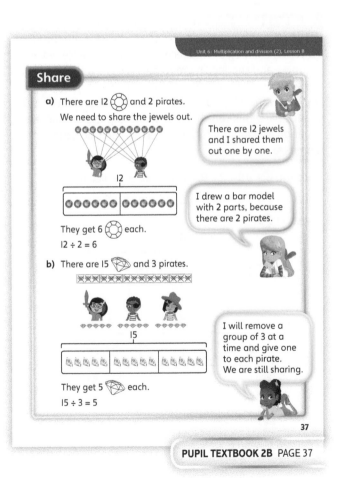

Share

a) There are 12 ⬡ and 2 pirates.
We need to share the jewels out.

There are 12 jewels and I shared them out one by one.

12

I drew a bar model with 2 parts, because there are 2 pirates.

They get 6 ⬡ each.
12 ÷ 2 = 6

b) There are 15 ◈ and 3 pirates.

15

I will remove a group of 3 at a time and give one to each pirate. We are still sharing.

They get 5 ◈ each.
15 ÷ 3 = 5

37

PUPIL TEXTBOOK 2B PAGE 37

Think together

Whole class teacher led (I do, We do, You do)

ASK

- Can you work out how many each pirate will get, before you have finished sharing?

IN FOCUS In question **2**, there is an empty bar model for children to use. This builds upon the scaffolding in question **1** where 18 dots have been placed above the bar model to help children and the number 18 has been filled in on the top of the model. Physical objects can be used instead of dots.

STRENGTHEN In question **3**, get children to come up with their own division sharing stories with the context of pirates and jewels. 6 ÷ 3 = 2 becomes 'there are 3 pirates who each share 6 coins. How many coins would they each get?' Children may mix up the whole and think it reflects the number of pirates. Acting it out will highlight the mistake.

DEEPEN If children are confident making up their own division sharing stories, can they switch numbers in the division sentence to get a different answer and bar model? 6 ÷ 3 = 2 is 3 pirates sharing 6 coins and getting 2 each and 6 ÷ 2 = 3 is 2 pirates sharing 6 coins and getting 3 each.

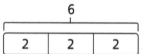
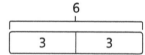

ASSESSMENT CHECKPOINT Assess whether children can say what each number represents in a division number sentence. Children should recognise the difference between grouping and sharing: in grouping, they know the whole and the size of each part, but not how many parts. In sharing, they know the whole and how many parts, but not the size of each part. Children should begin to express the same situation as a multiplication and a division calculation.

ANSWERS

Question **1** : 18 ÷ 2 = 9; each pirate gets 9 coins.

Question **2** : 20 ÷ 4 = 5; each pirate gets 5 coins.

Question **3** : 6 ÷ 3 = 2

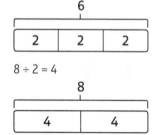

8 ÷ 2 = 4

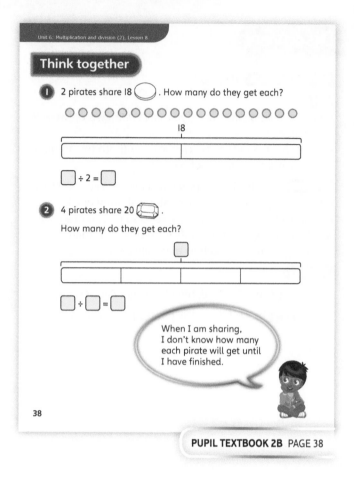

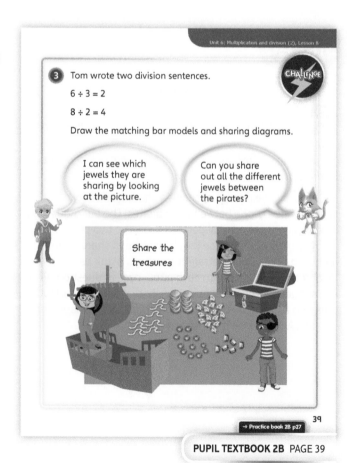

Practice

IN FOCUS Questions ❶ and ❷ give division sharing stories and scaffolded bar models for children to show their workings. Question ❶ represents 15 books with 15 dots so children can cross them off as they go. Questions ❷ and ❸ do not provide this so children need to have an alternate strategy or draw the brushes and pets themselves. Question ❸ starts with the same total but is shared into a different number of equal parts. Question ❹ requires knowledge of how many minutes there are in half an hour and for that to be the total when sharing out minutes.

STRENGTHEN Question ❹ is very abstract. Five children are sharing out a specific amount of time. In order to work this out, children need to know that there are 30 minutes in half an hour. A minute is not a physical object that can be shared out. Talk about how children could represent each minute – perhaps a tally line or cube for each minute.

DEEPEN Give children three numbers. Ask them to make up a division sharing story around the three numbers and draw their own bar model to match their problem. For example, '2, 6, and 12' or '3, 5 and 15'.

ASSESSMENT CHECKPOINT In question ❶, do children cross the dots off as they go? Do they try to share more than one at a time? If so, are they consistent with sharing 2 or 3 across each equal groups? In question ❸, do children realise it is the same total each time being shared into a different number of equal parts? Do they link this to times-table facts?

ANSWERS Answers for the **Practice** part of the lesson appear in the separate **Practice and Reflect answer guide**.

Reflect

IN FOCUS This question asks children to compare sharing and grouping with the bar model. Get children to draw each bar model, showing sharing as a strategy and then grouping. Are children able to give contexts to each type of problem from previous lessons? Get them to answer and draw this in pairs and then talk to the class about what they did. Discuss how each bar model looks different and what is being done differently each time.

ASSESSMENT CHECKPOINT Do children realise that the answer is the same in each question, but its meaning is different in a sharing and a grouping problem? Do children realise that 6 is the number in one group when sharing and that 5 is the number of groups when grouping? Can children give a correct context to each type of problem?

ANSWERS Answers for the **Reflect** part of the lesson appear in the separate **Practice and Reflect answer guide**.

After the lesson ⏸

- Were children able to apply their knowledge of a sharing strategy to the bar model?
- Are children able to explain the difference between sharing and grouping using the bar model?
- Were children able to use previous contexts for sharing and grouping or could they think up their own?

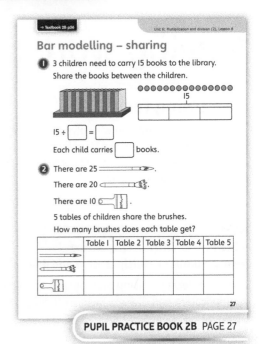

PUPIL PRACTICE BOOK 2B PAGE 27

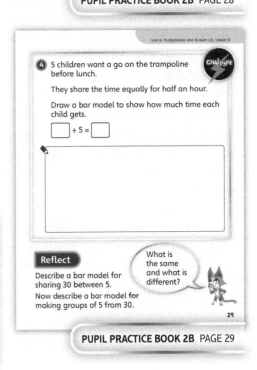

PUPIL PRACTICE BOOK 2B PAGE 28

PUPIL PRACTICE BOOK 2B PAGE 29

Solving word problems – division

Learning focus

In this lesson, children will solve a range of division problems using all of the visual representations they have learned about. They will come up with their own division problems.

Small steps

→ Previous step: Bar modelling – sharing
→ **This step: Solving word problems – division**
→ Next step: Making tally charts

NATIONAL CURRICULUM LINKS

Year 2 Number – Multiplication and division

Solve problems involving multiplication and division, using materials, arrays, repeated addition, mental methods, and multiplication and division facts, including problems in contexts.

ASSESSING MASTERY

Children can understand different contexts and situations where division is required and can interpret word problems accurately and put the numbers into a division sentence to calculate with. Children can make up their own division problems for a friend to solve.

COMMON MISCONCEPTIONS

Word problems provide an additional language barrier and can sometimes use unfamiliar contexts that children do not understand. Therefore it is important to give children plenty of practice with these types of question, across a variety of contexts. Get children to draw pictures of what they think the question is asking them. Draw pictures of key objects in the text and label them with numbers if this information is given. Let children have a go at making up their own questions to get an idea of how these word problems are constructed. Ask:

· *What information does the question give you? What are you trying to find out?*

STRENGTHENING UNDERSTANDING

Get children to draw each problem or act out each situation they are trying to work out. If they use drawings, ask them to label what each part of the drawing represents. If they are acting it out, get them to explain to you what they are doing and what their chosen objects represent.

GOING DEEPER

The **Think together** section gives children a context to base their division word problem on. Get children to come up with their own context for division. What objects would they like to divide? (pens, pencils, eggs, cakes). What would they like them to be divided into? (pots, boxes, crates). Children can be creative and use inspiration from around the classroom and at home.

KEY LANGUAGE

In lesson: word problems, division, sharing, grouping

Other language to be used by the teacher: equal groups, number of groups

STRUCTURES AND REPRESENTATIONS

Bar model split into equal parts, number line going up in equal jumps

RESOURCES

Mandatory: blank number lines and bar models to fill in

Optional: the football uniform price image displayed somewhere in the classroom, plastic £1 coins or counters, objects to model different division situations (objects that can be shared out, like pens, and objects they can be shared into, like pots.)

 In the eTextbook of this lesson, you will find interactive links to a selection of teaching tools.

Before you teach

· Has the context of a division question previously caused problems for children?
· Are children confident using different representations to model division questions?
· Are children relying on times-table knowledge and not working everything out from scratch?

Discover

Unit 6: Multiplication and division (2), Lesson 9

WAYS OF WORKING Pair work

ASK

• *How much is each item?*
• *How many children are there?*

IN FOCUS There is a lot of information in this image. Spend some time discussing it with children to check they understand what each part is showing before looking at the questions. Children should recognise that the division calculation is the same in question ① b) as it was in question ① a). They simply need to decide what each player can do with £8. Drawing the bar model with £1 coins and highlighting £6 for shorts and £2 for socks shows that the £8 can be spent in this way. Children could also explore £6 × 5 = £30 and £2 × 5 = £10, so £30 + £10 = 40. Children may approach the question in two, equally valid, ways. £40 ÷ 5 to work out how much each person can have, or £40 ÷ £8 to work out how many shirts can be bought for £40. These questions give children the opportunity to use and link division, multiplication and addition. For question ① b) misconceptions could arise if children try to divide 40 by 6 or 2, the price of each item. Remind them that there are 5 players and they must share the £40 between them.

ANSWERS

Question ① a): £40 ÷ 5 = £8. Yes, they have enough money to buy a 👕 for everyone.

Question ① b): £6 + £2 = £8   £40 ÷ £8 = 5
They have enough money to buy 🩳 and 🧦 for everyone.

Share

WAYS OF WORKING Whole class teacher led

ASK

• *How has the array been drawn? How will you make your array?*
• *Can the children buy everything? Why not?*

IN FOCUS Give children £40 in plastic £1 coins (or use counters to represent each £1) to arrange in an array. Do they arrange in coins/counters rows of 8 or 10? Arrange the coins or counters on a whiteboard to draw around the groups. Can children share the £40 if they draw a bar with 5 parts? Challenge children to use multiplication to find the cost of 5 of each item and the total cost of the five-a-side strip for 5 players. Remind children that they have £80. Focus on the fact that the same problem can be solved with multiplication and addition, or with division and addition.

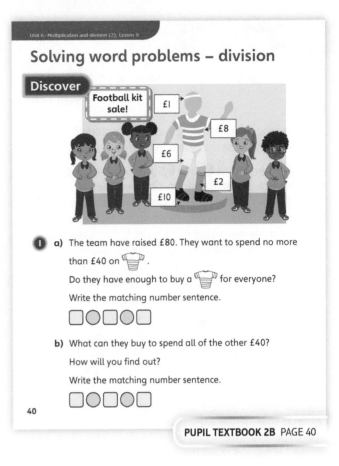

Solving word problems – division

Discover

Football kit sale!

① **a)** The team have raised £80. They want to spend no more than £40 on 👕.
Do they have enough to buy a 👕 for everyone?
Write the matching number sentence.
⬜⭕⬜⭕⬜

b) What can they buy to spend all of the other £40?
How will you find out?
Write the matching number sentence.
⬜⭕⬜⭕⬜

40

PUPIL TEXTBOOK 2B PAGE 40

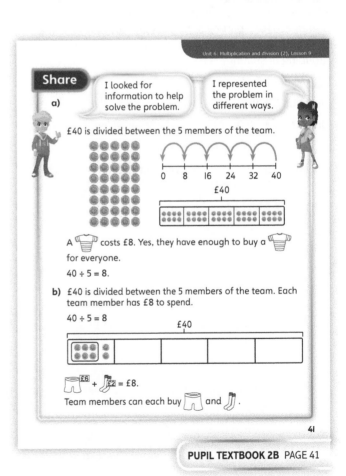

Share

a) "I looked for information to help solve the problem."   "I represented the problem in different ways."

£40 is divided between the 5 members of the team.

0 8 16 24 32 40
£40

A 👕 costs £8. Yes, they have enough to buy a 👕 for everyone.
40 ÷ 5 = 8.

b) £40 is divided between the 5 members of the team. Each team member has £8 to spend.
40 ÷ 5 = 8
£40

🩳 £6 + 🧦 £2 = £8.
Team members can each buy 🩳 and 🧦.

41

PUPIL TEXTBOOK 2B PAGE 41

Think together

Whole class teacher led (I do, We do, You do)

ASK

• *Are you sharing or grouping onto the bar model?*
• *How could you use multiplication to help you?*

IN FOCUS Questions ❶ and ❷ give two further problems related to the football uniform. Children need to fill in the rest of the bar model and complete the jumps back on the number line. They may also be using multiplication facts to work out the answer. Explain that the football team spent the £80 from the **Discover** section, so for question ❷, they now have only £50. In question ❸, children have the opportunity to write a division problem based on some images given.

STRENGTHEN Question ❶ can be acted out by cutting a piece of string to 25 cm. Children can mark on 5 cm intervals to see if they would have enough. For question ❷, children could have five printed £10 notes that they share between five pairs of shoes.

DEEPEN In question ❸, there are different images and contexts to generate a division question from. Are children able to generate a division question if you give them a set answer? If you tell them their answer must be 2, they could generate $10 ÷ 5 = 2$, or $20 ÷ 10 = 2$, or $16 ÷ 8 = 2$, for example.

ASSESSMENT CHECKPOINT Are children able to link division sentences to multiplication facts? Do they show a preference for a particular model (bar model or jumping back on a number line)? Are children aware if they are grouping or sharing?

ANSWERS

Question ❶ a): $25 ÷ 5 = 5$; they can make 5 🛡.

Question ❷: $£50 ÷ £10 = 5$; yes, they have enough to buy 👟 for everyone.

Question ❸ a): $£12 ÷ 3 = £4$; you can spend £4 on each friend.

Question ❸ b): $£10 ÷ £2 = 5$; you can buy 5 ◇.

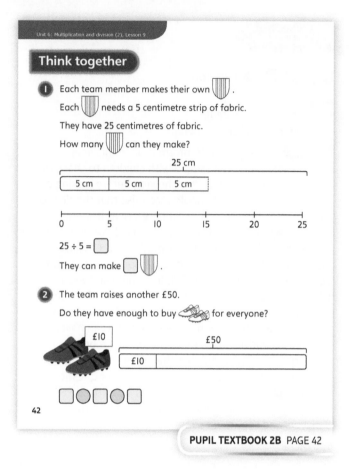

PUPIL TEXTBOOK 2B PAGE 42

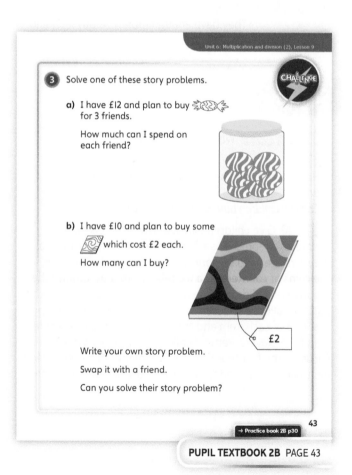

PUPIL TEXTBOOK 2B PAGE 43

Practice

WAYS OF WORKING Independent thinking

IN FOCUS In question ❸, give different amounts of money for children to share between 8 people. Question ❹ is a problem-solving question with multiple layers. Each sentence can be broken down and modelled on a 100 square. First, cross out numbers over 60, then highlight numbers that can be divided by 5 and 10. Children may use trial and error to find a number that fills the criteria, crossing numbers off on the 100 square as they go.

STRENGTHEN In question ❷, get children to act out making each man, tallying the number of sticks and counters with the headings being number of men; number of counters; number of sticks. They should spot that the number of men and counters is the same, as each man has one head. The number of sticks goes up by 5 each time. It is the 5 times-table. Can children work out how many sticks are needed for any number of men, by multiplying it by 5?

DEEPEN Can children explain why certain numbers fill the criteria in question ❹? Can they articulate that it has to be a multiple of 10 with an odd number of tens? Change the wording of the question so that it is the opposite: if the sweets were shared between 5 people, everyone would have an ODD number. If the sweets were shared between 10 people, everyone would have an EVEN number. Discuss if this criteria works. Why not?

ASSESSMENT CHECKPOINT In question ❸, do children realise it is not the £20 note that should be cut in half, but that each should be exchanged for two £10 so that they can be shared between 8? Do children want to swap all of the notes for pound coins and work it out by sharing?

ANSWERS Answers for the **Practice** part of the lesson appear in the separate **Practice and Reflect answer guide**.

Reflect

WAYS OF WORKING Pair work then whole class

IN FOCUS This **Reflect** question gives children a number sentence to create a question around. There must be 35 objects in their question that have to be shared or grouped into 5 objects. Get children to write a question in pairs then draw a picture and a bar model to represent it. Choose two pairs who have each done a sharing problem and a grouping problem. Ask the class what is different about their problem and how they would solve it differently.

ASSESSMENT CHECKPOINT Do children's problems match the question? Can they use abstract thinking, such as sharing time?

ANSWERS Answers for the **Reflect** part of the lesson appear in the separate **Practice and Reflect answer guide**.

After the lesson ⏸

- Were children able to use other operations when working out a division problem?
- Could children apply their knowledge of division and times-table facts across this wide range of contexts?
- Could children come up with contexts for division or did they create subtraction questions instead?

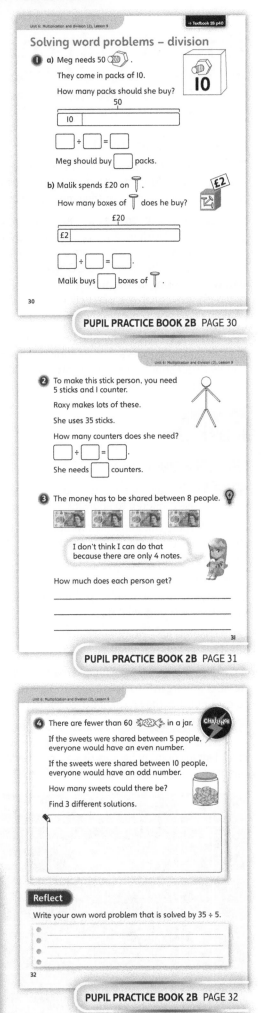

End of unit check

> Don't forget the *Power Maths* unit assessment grid on p26.

WAYS OF WORKING Group work – adult led

IN FOCUS In question ❶ , the same digits have been used in the division sentences so children need to look carefully at where the numbers are in the division sentence and what they mean in relation to each other.

In question ❷ , children need to understand what is being asked in the division sentence and relate it to different visual models. The question is asking for 30 to be divided into 5 equal parts. There are 5 equal parts in C and D but they have the incorrect number in each part. Diagram C may further confuse children as they will be looking for the number '5'. The correct answer is B which can be grouped into 5 equal rows of 6. Children will need to work out the total and the amount of rows and columns themselves.

In question ❹ , children may be tempted to circle the sentences which use the same numbers as the multiplication sentence. They may select answer C, but should notice that this is a multiplication, not a division, and is therefore incorrect.

Think!

WAYS OF WORKING Pair work

IN FOCUS This question brings together knowledge of 5 and 10 times-table facts and asks children to apply it.

Before starting, children will draw upon their knowledge of times-tables and the numbers that times-tables end in. This will help children to decide what to start dividing by.

Children can make a table or a list of numbers they are dividing by and what their answers are. This will help children see what does *not* give them an odd or even answer and what does.

Once children have numbers that fit, get them to colour the 100 square to see a pattern and generalise.

If children think they have found a pattern, for example 'it has to be a number ending in 5 to divide by 5 and get an odd number' encourage them to try a number they have not tried yet to test their theory.

ANSWERS AND COMMENTARY Children who have mastered this unit will be able to utilise a range of strategies for working out a division sentence and know when to apply a particular strategy based on the numbers in the division sentence. They will be confident in counting backwards on a number line, sharing into equal groups, grouping a number into equal groups, and using a bar model to represent a problem. Children will also recognise when they already know a multiplication fact that can help them.

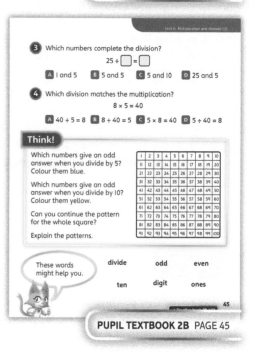

PUPIL TEXTBOOK 2B PAGE 44

PUPIL TEXTBOOK 2B PAGE 45

Q	A	WRONG ANSWERS AND MISCONCEPTIONS	STRENGTHENING UNDERSTANDING
1	B	Children will not look for the number of rows and numbers of column separately and may just look for the numbers they know.	Children may be confused with commutativity of multiplication and try to apply it to division. Any questions children are unsure about, they should make using physical resources or use a representation to prove that it cannot be correct to put numbers anywhere in a division sentence.
2	B	Children may be confused by the fact that A and C have numbers from the question in them and B does not.	
3	B	Children have been looking for numbers they recognise that relate to 25 in the 5 times-table.	
4	A	D has the same numbers but in the wrong places which may confuse children who are just looking for the numbers in the question. C is a multiplication, not a division.	

My journal

WAYS OF WORKING Independent thinking

ANSWERS AND COMMENTARY

Children should articulate that numbers ending in 0 are even and numbers ending in 5 are odd, using words from the word bank. Children may articulate that the pattern for blue is numbers that end in 5 because they are odd already so give an odd answer. For the next pattern, children should realise that all multiples of 10 are even. However, these numbers have either an odd or even number of tens. If the multiple of 10 has an odd number of tens and is divided by 10, the answer will be odd. Look for children's explanations to include phrases such as the tens have to be odd so the answer will be odd. If the tens are even the answer will be even.

If children are struggling, get them to look at the differences in numbers that do give an odd or even answer and those that do not. Can children look for patters in odd and even digits between the two groups?

Power check

WAYS OF WORKING Independent thinking

ASK

- *Do you think division is linked to multiplication?*
- *Can you work out division facts from multiplication facts?*
- *Do you like using the bar model to show division?*

Power puzzle

WAYS OF WORKING Pair work or small groups

IN FOCUS This question is best answered in pairs or groups with cubes to model children's thinking. It brings in knowledge of different times-tables and remainders. Talk about what the remainders mean in each context. *If there are groups of 3 and 1 left over, could the number be odd or even?* Do children realise it could be both because odd and even numbers are in the 3 times-table? However, if you ask the same question about groups of 4 and 1 left over, the 4 times-table is always even so the number must be odd. Draw these conclusions out before children tackle each sentence as a whole.

ANSWERS AND COMMENTARY If children are struggling, get them to choose any amount of cubes to start with. They should work their way through each sentence to see if their number fills the criteria. If it does not, how will they change their start number? Will they need to add more or take some away? Children may come across a number of cubes that satisfies one sentence but not the other. Remind them that all criteria must be met for the answer to be correct.

If children quickly find an answer, can they find any more? Can they make generalisations about the cubes James has? Get children to prove their theories with different examples.

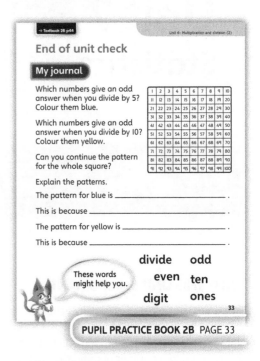

PUPIL PRACTICE BOOK 2B PAGE 33

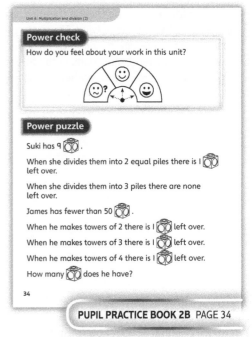

PUPIL PRACTICE BOOK 2B PAGE 34

After the unit ⏸

- Were children able to subtract repeatedly in order to divide?
- Did children understand how different representations yield the answer to a division sentence (such as the *number* of jumps back on a number line, and the *amount* in each equal part in a bar model)?
- Did children apply their knowledge of times-table facts in this unit?
- Were children able to use an array to spot division facts as well as multiplication facts from previous units?

Strengthen and **Deepen** activities for this unit can be found in the *Power Maths* online subscription.

Unit 7
Statistics

Mastery Expert tip! "My class frequently used resources such as cubes and counters to represent pictograms and block diagrams. It certainly reinforced their understanding of the unit."

Don't forget to watch the Unit 7 video!

WHY THIS UNIT IS IMPORTANT

This unit is important because it is the first time children will have been introduced to statistics. The unit shows children how data can be collected effectively and then represented in a number of different ways. The unit will require children to use a range of different skills such as calculating and problem solving. These are great ways to consolidate prior learning. Children will be introduced to several different representations in the form of charts and diagrams and to some new mathematical language.

WHERE THIS UNIT FITS

→ Unit 6: Multiplication and division (2)
→ **Unit 7: Statistics**
→ Unit 8: Length and height

In this unit, children will build on their learning from a number of previous units. To interpret charts and diagrams, children must use their knowledge of addition and subtraction, counting and multiplication involving 2s, 5s and 10s. They will be introduced to symbols representing one or more pieces of data and to tally marks which they will need to be able to count. Finally, previous units on problem solving will need to be called upon. Following this unit, children will go on to learn about length and height.

Before they start this unit, it is expected that children:
• can count in 2s, 5s and 10s
• can add and subtract 2-digit numbers
• can compare numbers to 100
• understand the language associated with problem solving.

ASSESSING MASTERY

In this unit, children will show mastery by being able to read charts and diagrams with ease and come to accurate conclusions. They will be able to confidently explain their methodology as well as their answer. Children will be able to independently collect data, construct an appropriate chart or diagram and then interpret it (writing down useful statements using the correct terminology). Finally, problems and puzzles will be solved efficiently.

COMMON MISCONCEPTIONS	STRENGTHENING UNDERSTANDING	GOING DEEPER
Children may miscount symbols or tallies.	Use apparatus to reinforce understanding.	Ask children to think of more questions they could ask about a chart or diagram.
Children may assume one symbol always represents one item.	Practise counting totals in pictograms in which a symbol represents more than one item.	Challenge children to think about where each chart or diagram would be used in real-life situations.

Unit 7: Statistics

WAYS OF WORKING

Give children a few minutes to read the unit starter pages of the **Pupil Textbook**. Then read it together as a class. Ask children:

- *What puzzled you?*
- *Which of the key words did you understand?*
- *What do they mean?*

STRUCTURES AND REPRESENTATIONS

Tally charts

Tariq	Amy
ЖТ ЖТ ЖТ III	ЖТ ЖТ ЖТ ЖТ IIII

ЖТ means 5

Pictograms

Name	Number
Tariq 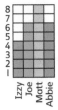	🍎🍎🍎🍎🍎🍎🍎🍎🍎
Amy	🍎🍎🍎🍎🍎🍎

Block diagrams

```
8
7
6
5
4
3
2
1
  Izzy Joe Matt Abbie
```

Representations such as number lines, apparatus and bar models may be used to support the interpretation of data or solving problems.

KEY LANGUAGE

There is some key language that children will need to know as part of the learning in this unit:

→ tally chart, tally
→ pictogram
→ block diagram
→ table
→ more, less, most, least
→ favourite, popular
→ equal
→ represent, symbol, key, information
→ total, altogether
→ compare

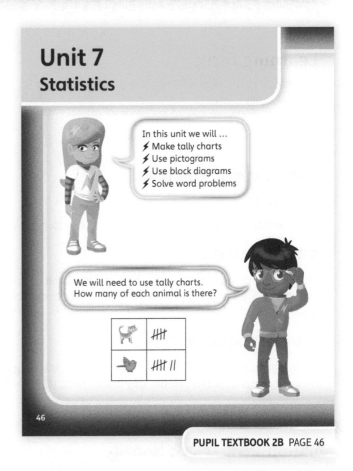

PUPIL TEXTBOOK 2B PAGE 46

PUPIL TEXTBOOK 2B PAGE 47

Making tally charts

Learning focus

In this lesson, children will learn how to read and construct tally charts.

Small steps

→ Previous step: Solving word problems – division
→ **This step: Making tally charts**
→ Next step: Creating pictograms (1)

NATIONAL CURRICULUM LINKS

Year 2 Statistics

Interpret and construct simple pictograms, tally charts, block diagrams and simple tables.

ASSESSING MASTERY

Children can confidently read a tally chart and explain it clearly, using the correct vocabulary. They can construct tally charts independently from a given set of data. Children understand why tally charts are useful and can say where they could be used in real-life situations.

COMMON MISCONCEPTIONS

Children may count a tally of 5 as 4 (due to not understanding that the oblique mark counts as 1). Ask:
• *What does the sloping mark mean? Why is it useful to tally like this?*

Be careful of children counting two tally marks as 11. Ask:
• *Is it eleven? If I put three marks, would it mean one hundred and eleven?*

STRENGTHENING UNDERSTANDING

This lesson is a great opportunity to do some extra counting practice, including counting in 5s and grouping in 5s (you could start with counters and move on to tallies). Children could practise recording numbers up to 20 as a tally and reading numbers to 40 given as a tally before working with actual tally charts.

GOING DEEPER

To deepen learning, ask children why tally charts are used. *Why are they useful? Where could they be used in real-life situations? Why is it useful to record in 5s instead of 1s?*

KEY LANGUAGE

In lesson: tally chart, marks, table, count, fifth, total, tallied, groups of 5, greater than, choice, how many?, more, most, least, create, results

Other language to be used by the teacher: favourite, record

STRUCTURES AND REPRESENTATIONS

Tally charts and tables, number lines

RESOURCES

Mandatory: number lines, counters, ruler

Optional: counting in 5s number line

 In the eTextbook of this lesson, you will find interactive links to a selection of teaching tools.

Before you teach

• Do children need counting support?
• Can children count in 5s?
• Could you make a small display to reinforce tally charts and tallying?

Discover

Pair work

ASK

- *How is the first table different to the second table?*
- *Whose tally is easier to count? Why?*

IN FOCUS In question ① a), children may be unfamiliar with tallies of 5, so let children practise recording numbers up to 20 as a '5' tally and reading numbers to 40 given as a tally before moving on to look at this question closely.

ANSWERS

Question ① a): Tariq won 18 games; Amy won 24 games.

Question ① b): 24 is greater than 18. Amy won overall.

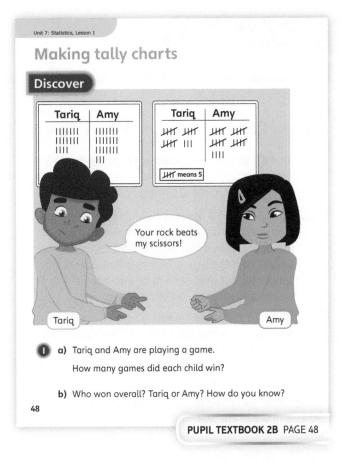

Share

Whole class teacher led

ASK

- *Question ① b): Which mathematical sign could you use to explain your answer?*
- *Why is it useful to arrange the marks in groups of 5?*
- *Without counting, how can you see from the tally marks that Amy scored more than Tariq?*

IN FOCUS In question ① b), link back to prior learning of comparing numbers. Explain the vocabulary to children and remind them of the signs they can use. Can children use the signs in their answers? Children could work in pairs, one recording a score on a number line showing jumps of 5 and some extra ones, and one child recording a score as tally. Children swap to each get a chance to record the number line score as a tally and to show the tally on a number line.

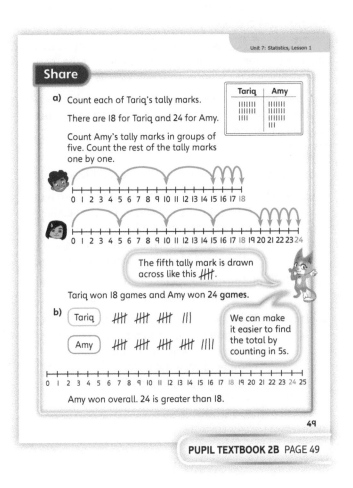

77

Think together

WAYS OF WORKING Whole class teacher led (I do, We do, You do)

ASK

- Question ❷ a): *Look at the question. What should you do first?*
- Question ❷ a): *How many rows and columns should the table have?*
- Question ❷ a): *Should you use any equipment?*

IN FOCUS Question ❷ requires children to create a tally chart from the given data. Support children carefully with this. Some children may need a table template and adult support with the layout. Others will be able to do it independently, but may need to be reminded of key features such as headings and using a ruler.

STRENGTHEN To strengthen learning here, check if any children are still counting the tallies of 5 individually. Run some intervention groups in which children are shown that it is more efficient to count in 5s. Afterwards, practise counting in 5s to make sure children are secure with this.

Furthermore, you could run some extra intervention sessions in which children practise constructing tally charts from data.

DEEPEN Children could create more tally charts from their own collected data, such as tallying the colours of pencils in their pencil case. Children could also create a simple survey on, for example, eye colour, favourite snack, sandwich or fruit from 3–4 choices.

ASSESSMENT CHECKPOINT Question ❶ will allow you to assess whether children can count tally marks and find the total numerical value.

Question ❷ is an excellent opportunity to see whether children can apply what they have learned, and construct a tally chart from data.

ANSWERS

Question ❶ : 13 rocks, 14 pieces of paper and 12 scissors

Question ❷ a): Check that children have constructed a table of 3 columns and 4 rows. Ensure headings are included and a ruler has been used. The tallies within the table should show 15 rocks, 12 pieces of paper and 18 scissors.

Question ❷ b): The most popular choice was 'scissors' and the least popular choice was 'paper'.

Question ❸ : The table shows the results from option A. This group is represented in the tally chart because the tallies in the table match the number of each choice for rock, paper and scissors shown in option A.

Think together

❶ These choices have been tallied in a **tally chart**.

Write the tally number for each choice.

Choice	Tally	Number
✊	卌 卌 |||	
🖐	卌 卌 ||||	
✌	卌 卌 ||	

❷ More children play the game. Here are the results.

a) Create a tally chart to show how many of each is shown.

b) Which choice was the most popular?

Which choice was the least popular?

50

PUPIL TEXTBOOK 2B PAGE 50

CHALLENGE

❸ Tariq and Amy play another game of 'Rock, Paper, Scissors'.

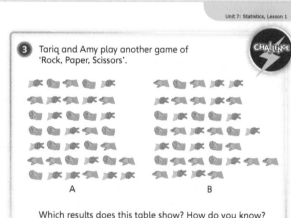

A   B

Which results does this table show? How do you know?

Choice	Tally	Number
✊	卌 卌 |||	13
🖐	卌 卌	10
✌	卌 卌 ||||	14

→ Practice book 2B p35

51

PUPIL TEXTBOOK 2B PAGE 51

Practice

IN FOCUS Question ❸ requires children to complete a tally chart where they have already been given some of the information. They are then asked to interpret the results. Children will need to write a tally as a number and a number as a tally. Then they will need to use the information to make statements about what the table shows.

STRENGTHEN Give children extra support when interpreting a tally chart. Discuss how you can tell if something is more popular than something else just by looking. There will certainly be a discussion about how one of them 'looks more'. This is a good opportunity to show the importance of making tally marks of similar size – so we can see results clearly.

DEEPEN After making some statements about what the chart shows in question ❸, ask children to write questions relating to the chart for a partner to answer. Can they write questions that will involve addition or subtraction to answer them?

ASSESSMENT CHECKPOINT Question ❶ a) will assess whether children can count in 5s to complete the tally chart. Question ❶ b) will allow you to assess which children can interpret a tally chart to identify the most and the least popular animal.

ANSWERS Answers for the **Practice** part of the lesson appear in the separate **Practice and Reflect answer guide**.

Reflect

IN FOCUS Create a group tally chart, choosing just five school subjects. You may want to have a template on the board and choose a child to be the scribe. Start by discussing the best way to create the tally chart – a useful way to assess how children will go about collecting data as a whole class. Complete the chart and ask children to think of some questions they might ask such as: *Which subject was the most popular? Which subject was the least popular? Can you think of a question that will need subtraction to answer it? How many more children liked maths than PE?*

ASSESSMENT CHECKPOINT This activity will allow you to assess which children can use efficient strategies to collect data and construct a tally chart. You will also be able to assess their interpretation of the tally chart by the questions they ask.

ANSWERS Answers for the **Reflect** part of the lesson appear in the separate **Practice and Reflect answer guide**.

After the lesson ⏸

- Do children need support with counting or recording scores in 5s?
- Can children construct a tally chart independently and discuss what the chart shows?
- How can you link this lesson to the following one (pictograms)?

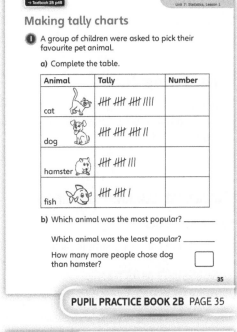

PUPIL PRACTICE BOOK 2B PAGE 35

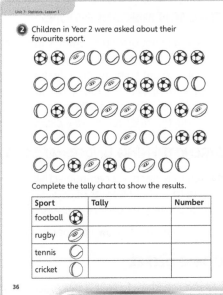

PUPIL PRACTICE BOOK 2B PAGE 36

PUPIL PRACTICE BOOK 2B PAGE 37

Creating pictograms

Learning focus

In this lesson, children will read pictograms, linking them to tally charts. They will also construct them from given data.

Small steps

→ Previous step: Making tally charts
→ **This step: Creating pictograms (1)**
→ Next step: Creating pictograms (2)

NATIONAL CURRICULUM LINKS

Year 2 Statistics

Interpret and construct simple pictograms, tally charts, block diagrams and simple tables.

ASSESSING MASTERY

Children can create accurate pictograms and explain them in detail using the correct mathematical vocabulary. Children can also use symbols and keys to represent more than one object.

COMMON MISCONCEPTIONS

Children may not draw the symbols in a neat or organised manner. They may space them out or make some larger than others. This could mean that children think that the row that is more spaced out or the symbol that is larger is the greater in value. Sketch out some incorrectly drawn symbols and discuss why they are not right. Ask:

• *What is wrong with this row of symbols?* (spaced out more than the other rows)
• *What mistake have I made in this row?* (symbols are not the same size)
• *What are the 'rules' for drawing pictograms?* (same size, same spacing)

STRENGTHENING UNDERSTANDING

Children may need intervention activities in which pictograms are created from sets of data. They should focus on reading the data (this could be sets of objects or a tally chart), then creating symbols, a key, the outline table (using a ruler) and finally inputting the correct symbols.

If children create their own pictograms for a class survey, some children may need an outline template for support.

GOING DEEPER

Challenge children to collect data such as eye colour or favourite ice cream flavour, presenting it first as a tally chart and then as a pictogram. Children may need advice for choosing a suitable symbol relating to the data (simple oval for an eye and lolly shape for ice cream) and they may also need reminding that there should be a limited choice of no more than five items. Alternatively, provide a class data list or quickly record choices on the board from a hand count.

KEY LANGUAGE

In lesson: represent, **pictogram**, symbol, tally chart, draw, make, count, **key**, result, compare

Other language to be used by the teacher: accurate, data, row, survey, favourite, rules, solve, strategy

STRUCTURES AND REPRESENTATIONS

Pictograms, tally charts

RESOURCES

Mandatory: rulers, some children may need pictogram outline templates

Optional: counters

 In the eTextbook of this lesson, you will find interactive links to a selection of teaching tools.

Before you teach

• Have children mastered tally charts from the previous lesson?
• How can children be supported when converting a tally chart to a pictogram?
• Will you do a whole-class data collection and representation activity?

Discover

Pair work

ASK

- *Why is it important to arrange the symbols in a neat way?*
- *Question ❶ b) : Look at the question. How can you solve this? What strategy will you use?*

IN FOCUS Question ❶ a) focuses children on thinking about the layout of the symbols in the pictogram. You could show neatly arranged counters next to erratically placed counters on the children's desks. This will reinforce the fact that arrangements of the symbols are important for displaying information and interpreting said information easily.

ANSWERS

Question ❶ a): Table 2 has the most points. To make the points easier to count, you could order them neatly in a pictogram or tally chart.

Question ❶ b): The children on table 3 will now have 9 stickers.

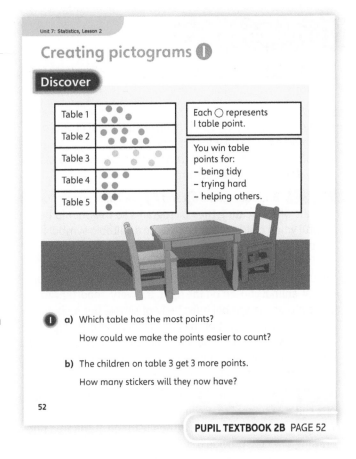

Share

Whole class teacher led

ASK

- *Look back to the Discover section. Which pictogram is easier to read? Why?*
- *Why have different colours been used for each row?*

IN FOCUS Question ❶ a) provides a good opportunity to talk about using different colours and different symbols for each row. Explain that the clearer you can make information, the easier it is to read. Ensure that children notice the equal sizing and spacing of the counters.

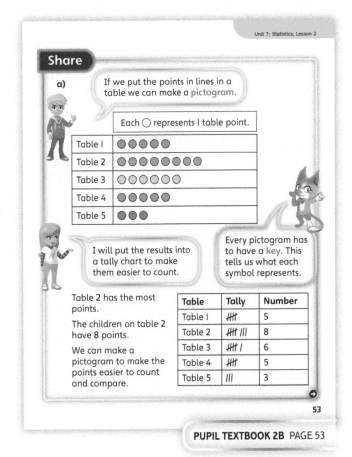

81

Think together

WAYS OF WORKING Whole class teacher led (I do, We do, You do)

ASK

• *We need a symbol to represent an animal. What do lots of animals have?* (a paw, for example)
• *Could you draw that complicated symbol 20 times – could you draw it the same each time?*

IN FOCUS Both questions ❶ and ❷ ask children to choose animals when creating their pictograms so this should be helpful when children come to create a suitable symbol for the pictogram. The name of the animal will be written in the left-hand side of the table (or possibly a cut and stick picture if available), with symbols to represent the number of that animal chosen on the right. It is very important to explain that the symbol must be kept simple but it should also reflect the subject of the data. Model some examples of animal symbols. Discuss why children should not spend a long time drawing a beautiful picture and why the symbols are all the same for different animals.

STRENGTHEN Questions ❷ and ❸ require children to think of a suitable symbol to use in the pictogram and in the key. This is a good chance to strengthen learning. If children find drawing difficult, provide a small 2D shape for them to draw around or suggest a very simple design for them to use. Check that their symbols are all roughly the same size and equally spaced.

DEEPEN Give children a choice of four 'favourite sports', then say: *12 children took part in a survey of their favourite sport.* Ask the children to make as many different pictograms as possible. Can they work methodically?

Alternatively, get children to compare the effectiveness of tally charts and pictograms. Ask: *What is the same? What is different? Which one is easier to read? Which one is more interesting to look at?*

ASSESSMENT CHECKPOINT Question ❶ will allow you to assess whether children can collect data accurately and tally it. Question ❷ will allow you to assess whether children can convert the data into a pictogram.

ANSWERS

Question ❶ : This question depends on children's choices. Check that they have chosen five animals, tallied accurately, and found the totals with appropriate symbols or names.

Question ❷ : This question also depends on children's choices. Check for a carefully-constructed pictogram – symbols should be all the same, ordered neatly and the same size.

Question ❸ : An exemplary title could be: A pictogram to show the favourite animals in Mr Jarrett's class.

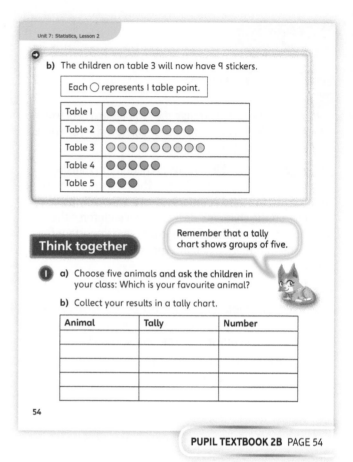

Practice

WAYS OF WORKING Pair work

IN FOCUS Question **4** will make children think carefully. They will first have to find the total amount of children who like rugby and football. Then they will have to find the difference between that total (18) and the overall pictogram total (25). This problem may require you to break it down into the two steps for some children.

STRENGTHEN In questions **1** and **2**, children will find it easier to read the pictograms if they work out the totals first and write these next to each row. If they do not, they might have to keep counting rows – this may mean they lose their train of thought.

DEEPEN Give children some data which has all even totals. See if they can use a key to represent each symbol as two items. Repeat with data with totals that are all multiples of 5.

Alternatively, give children a similar challenge to question **4**. Could they then make up their own problem relating to the number of children in the class?

ASSESSMENT CHECKPOINT Question **4** will give you a clear indication of which children can confidently read and interpret pictograms, whilst question **2** will assess their understanding of the connection between tally charts and pictograms.

ANSWERS Answers for the **Practice** part of the lesson appear in the separate **Practice and Reflect answer guide**.

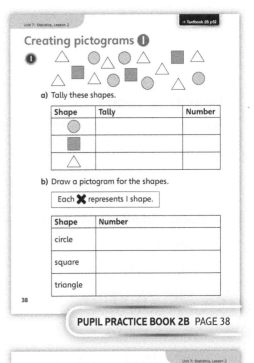

PUPIL PRACTICE BOOK 2B PAGE 38

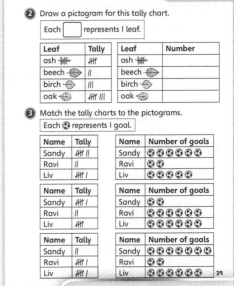

PUPIL PRACTICE BOOK 2B PAGE 39

Reflect

WAYS OF WORKING Pair work

IN FOCUS This is an excellent opportunity to reinforce the vocabulary associated with the lesson. Start the reflection off by having children individually working then encourage them to discuss their answers with the person sitting next to them. Try asking children what each word means if they are finding it challenging.

ASSESSMENT CHECKPOINT This reflective exercise will allow you to assess children's understanding of the lesson's vocabulary. Check if they can explain what each word means.

ANSWERS Answers for the **Reflect** part of the lesson appear in the separate **Practice and Reflect answer guide**.

After the lesson ⏸

- What went well in the lesson?
- Could you display the key words somewhere in the classroom?
- What home-learning activity would fit in well with this lesson?

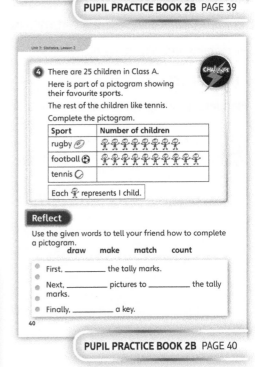

PUPIL PRACTICE BOOK 2B PAGE 40

Creating pictograms ②

Learning focus

In this lesson, children will read and construct pictograms in which symbols represent more than one item.

Small steps

→ Previous step: Creating pictograms (1)
→ **This step: Creating pictograms (2)**
→ Next step: Interpreting pictograms (1)

NATIONAL CURRICULUM LINKS

Year 2 Statistics

Interpret and construct simple pictograms, tally charts, block diagrams and simple tables.

ASSESSING MASTERY

Children can confidently construct pictograms to display data effectively by choosing the most appropriate key (for example, choosing one symbol to represent two, five or ten items as appropriate).

COMMON MISCONCEPTIONS

Children may not realise that a symbol can represent more than one object. Ask:
· *What does the key say? How many objects does each symbol represent?*

STRENGTHENING UNDERSTANDING

There is a lot of counting in this lesson. Children may need counting intervention, in particular practising counting on in 2s, 5s and 10s. Support children with printed number lines in intervals of 2, 5 or 10.

GOING DEEPER

Deepen learning by asking children to create keys for data sets. For instance, give children: 35, 0, 5, 10, 30, 20, 40 and ask them what the key should be. Then ask them to explain why they have chosen the key they have.

KEY LANGUAGE

In lesson: pictogram, symbol, how many?, key, equal, =, results, tally chart, represent, difference, most, least, popular, key, title, odd number

Other language to be used by the teacher: collect, survey, even number, multiple, number line, data, data set

STRUCTURES AND REPRESENTATIONS

Pictograms and tally charts, number lines

RESOURCES

Mandatory: pictogram templates, number lines

 In the eTextbook of this lesson, you will find interactive links to a selection of teaching tools.

Before you teach

· Do children need to recap prior learning of halving shapes?
· How will you give children extra counting support?
· Can children construct a 1-1 pictogram?

Discover

Pair work

ASK

- *Why are five hot dinners represented by one plate?*
- *If you have 50 plates, why not just draw all 50?*
- *Would you change the key if you needed to represent 100 hot dinners? What would each plate represent?*

IN FOCUS Question **1** a) requires children to read the key and realise that each plate represents five hot dinners. This may be difficult for some children to understand. Explain that when you are working with higher numbers, it would be difficult to draw so many plates. So instead we represent five things with just one symbol.

ANSWERS

Question **1** a): 25 hot dinners were made on Tuesday.

Question **1** b): You need to draw 7 ◎.

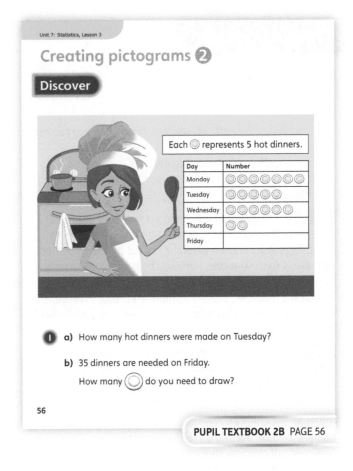

Share

WAYS OF WORKING Whole class teacher led

ASK

- *What is an efficient strategy to work out question **1** b)?*
- *Could Monday's amount help you answer question **1** b)?*
- *Can you explain your answer?*

IN FOCUS For question **1** b), focus children on the strategies they used to find the answer. Some may have drawn the 35 dinners and then made 7 groups; others may have used their knowledge of counting in 5s. It is good practice here to link the long-winded way with the efficient method. Making connections is important for achieving mastery.

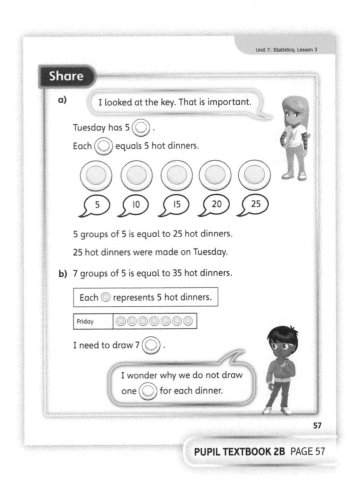

Think together

WAYS OF WORKING Whole class teacher led (I do, We do, You do)

ASK

- *If a symbol represents two children, how would you represent one child?*
- *Can you explain your results to me?*
- *What did you find out in this survey? How do most children get to school?*

IN FOCUS For question ❷ , children may find it difficult to represent an odd number when a symbol represents two things. Ask children what they could do with a symbol to make it represent one. Remind them of prior learning of halving shapes because half of 2 is 1. Discuss how it is important that they choose a suitable symbol to represent two (or four) things, so that the thing can easily be halved (or quartered).

STRENGTHEN Some children may need intervention in halving regular shapes and in representing odd numbers. Discuss how to show odd numbers such as 3, 5 and 7 using whole symbols and one half symbol.

DEEPEN Set children the challenge of creating a pictogram using the same data collected in question ❶ a). This time, however, tell children that one smiley face represents four children. How would they represent one, two and three children here?

ASSESSMENT CHECKPOINT Question ❷ should help you decide whether children can create a pictogram in which a symbol represents two children. Look carefully to see if they managed to represent an odd number accurately.

ANSWERS

Question ❶ a): Results will depend on your class. Check for accurate tallying.

Question ❶ b): Results will depend on your class.

Question ❷ : An accurate pictogram should be constructed. Look for smiley faces being the same size and with the correct amount shown. An exemplary title would read: A pictogram to show how Mr Jarrett's class travel to school.

Question ❸ a): Children should notice that the difference between the most and least popular ways of getting to school will be the number of ☺.
The least popular way will have fewer ☺.

Question ❸ b): Results will depend on your class.

Think together

❶ Ask the children in your class: How do you travel to school?

a) Collect your results in a tally chart.

Transport	Tally	Number
car		
bus		
bike		
walk		
other		

b) Which way of travelling to school was the most popular?
Which way of travelling to school was the least popular?

I wonder if I could use a pictogram instead of a tally chart.

58

PUPIL TEXTBOOK 2B PAGE 58

---

❷ Now complete a pictogram to show your results.
Use a ☺ to represent the children.
Give your pictogram a title and a key.

This is a pictogram to show _____

_____ .

Each ☺ represents 2 children.

Transport	Number
car	
bus	
bike	
walk	
other	

❸ a) What is the difference between the most and least popular way of getting to school?

b) How many children travel in a car or walk to school altogether?

CHALLENGE

→ Practice book 2B p41

59

PUPIL TEXTBOOK 2B PAGE 59

Practice

WAYS OF WORKING Independent thinking

IN FOCUS When on question **2**, children must look carefully at the keys as they are all different. Children may also need support in understanding that the sun icon represents a way of counting all types of days (whatever the weather) and that the half-sun icon represents half as many days as the whole icon.

STRENGTHEN Work with children who require support with question **3**. The problem may need to be broken down into bitesize chunks. Start by asking children to read the statements aloud, then ask them what they already know. Finally, explore which clue helps first, second and last. Discuss how to represent 5 when the key shows that the symbol represents 10.

DEEPEN Present children with a pictogram without a key, including some half symbols. Ask them what the data could have been. Can they show it in a table? They will probably start by counting the symbols one-by-one. Ask: *But, what if each symbol represents 2?* Children will realise there are different options.

ASSESSMENT CHECKPOINT Question **2** will allow you to assess children's progress towards mastery of reading pictograms in which symbols represent more than one thing.

Question **3** presents a good opportunity to assess children's reasoning skills when completing a pictogram from the clues given.

ANSWERS Answers for the **Practice** part of the lesson appear in the separate **Practice and Reflect answer guide**.

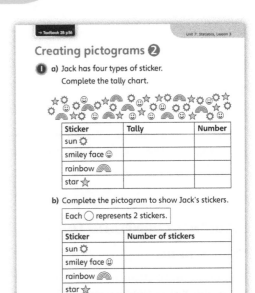

PUPIL PRACTICE BOOK 2B PAGE 41

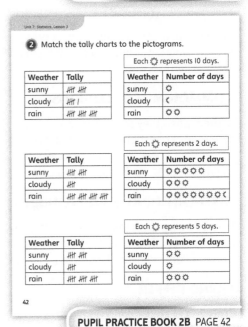

PUPIL PRACTICE BOOK 2B PAGE 42

Reflect

WAYS OF WORKING Independent thinking, Whole class

IN FOCUS This question will generate some deep thinking and group discussion. Children may choose 10 because it is a factor of 100 – however, they may realise that it may be difficult to represent one child. They may then explore lower numbers (some children may share 100 between the 5 authors to find out an average for if the results are fairly spread).

ASSESSMENT CHECKPOINT This activity is an excellent way to assess group problem-solving skills, observe language used, and assess which children use effective reasoning.

ANSWERS Answers for the **Reflect** part of the lesson appear in the separate **Practice and Reflect answer guide**.

After the lesson ⏸

- Have children mastered reading and constructing pictograms?
- Can children represent more than one item with just one symbol?
- Are children ready for interpreting pictograms?

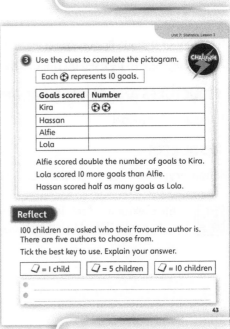

PUPIL PRACTICE BOOK 2B PAGE 43

Interpreting pictograms

Learning focus

In this lesson, children will read and interpret pictograms. They will find totals and compare amounts.

Small steps

→ Previous step: Creating pictograms (2)
→ **This step: Interpreting pictograms (1)**
→ Next step: Interpreting pictograms (2)

NATIONAL CURRICULUM LINKS

Year 2 Statistics

- Interpret and construct simple pictograms, tally charts, block diagrams and simple tables.
- Ask and answer simple questions by counting the number of objects in each category and sorting the categories by quantity.
- Ask and answer questions about totalling and comparing categorical data.

ASSESSING MASTERY

Children can understand and have a strong grasp of the vocabulary associated with interpreting data and pictograms. Children can answer questions relating to pictograms accurately and in detail, including where one symbol represents more than one item.

COMMON MISCONCEPTIONS

Children, when they see the word 'more' in a word problem, often assume it means they need to add. Practise answering these type of questions using counters to illustrate the problem. Ask:
- *If you have 1 sweet and I have 4 sweets, how many more do I have? The picture shows there are 4 crabs and 8 sea snails. How many more sea snails than crabs are there?*

STRENGTHENING UNDERSTANDING

Understanding mathematical vocabulary will be very important in this lesson. Children may need extra support with key words – especially understanding the meaning when used in context. Make flashcards and highlight key words in problems to help children explain the problem, not just the answer.

GOING DEEPER

In this lesson, to deepen learning, challenge children to think of their own questions for a given pictogram.

KEY LANGUAGE

In lesson: pictogram, how many?, most, least, count, represent, fewer, more, amount, tally chart, altogether, bar model

Other language to be used by the teacher: table, diagram, check, answers, opposite, symbol

STRUCTURES AND REPRESENTATIONS

Pictograms, bar model

RESOURCES

Mandatory: counters, number lines, extra pictograms

 In the eTextbook of this lesson, you will find interactive links to a selection of teaching tools.

Before you teach ⏸

- Are children secure with reading pictograms?
- Have you prepared resources for extension activities?

Discover

Pair work

ASK

- *What is the name of this table? How do you know that it is a pictogram?*
- *What do you need to do to answer this question? Could you count the creatures in 2s?*
- *How does a pictogram show which creatures were found the most?*

IN FOCUS For question ① a), encourage children to check their answers. *Which creatures are easiest to count first?* Draw attention to the fact that the information they need is in the large picture at the top of the page and that the pictogram shows clearly which creature there is most or least of.

ANSWERS

Question ① a): In order: crab, sea snail, shrimp, razor shell, starfish.

Question ① b): The creature the children found the most of was the ⭐ .

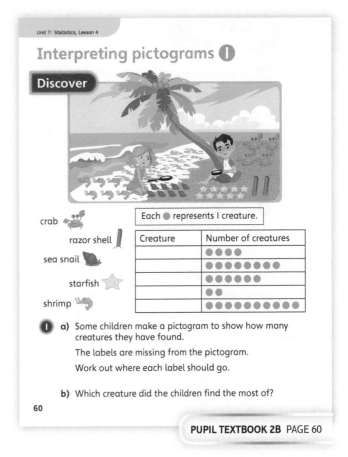

PUPIL TEXTBOOK 2B PAGE 60

Share

Whole class teacher led

ASK

- *Can you repeat the steps to make the pictogram without looking at the page?*
- *Was there the same amount of any creature? How do you know?*
- *What makes this pictogram easy to read?*

IN FOCUS In question ① b), focus on the word 'most'. Discuss what it means with children. Ask children if they know the opposite word ('least'). You could deepen learning here, by asking the children if they found ten crabs and ten starfish – which would be the most? Neither? Both?

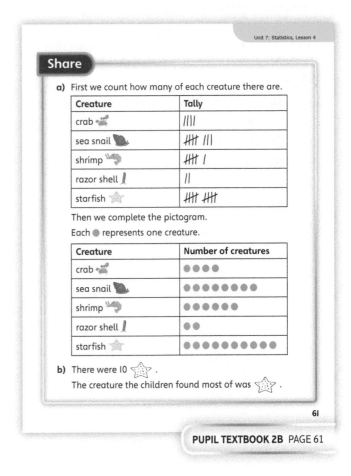

PUPIL TEXTBOOK 2B PAGE 61

Think together

WAYS OF WORKING Whole class teacher led (I do, We do, You do)

ASK

- Question **1** : *Do you have to count all the symbols or is there another way to tell which creature was found the least?*
- Question **2** : *How could you use the way the circles are arranged in the pictogram to find out how many fewer crabs than sea snails there are?*
- Question **4** : *How does the bar model help? Could you use counters for the extra shrimps and then count them all by adding on?*

IN FOCUS Question **2** provides support for children to turn a word problem into a number sentence. Encourage children to think up more word problems using 'fewer than' or 'more than' with other pairs of creatures from the pictogram.

STRENGTHEN Question **4** supports children by using a bar model to compare amounts on a pictogram. Encourage children to show questions **2** and **3** with bar models first and ask similar questions relating to the data on the pictogram before tackling question **4** . Repeat question **4** with other creatures, for example: *Two more starfish and some more sea snails were seen on the beach. There is now the same amount of both. How many more sea snails were seen? Draw a bar model to answer the question.*

DEEPEN Ask children to use the pictogram to write three more questions using the words: more than, total, 4 less.

ASSESSMENT CHECKPOINT Question **3** will give you a useful insight into whether children can understand the word problem and subsequently interpret the data. Look carefully at any markings or strategies the children use.

ANSWERS

Question **1** : The creature the children found the least of was razor shell.

Question **2** : 8 – 4 = 4; there are 4 fewer crab .

Question **3** : There are 6 more sea snail than razor shell .

There are 2 fewer sea snails than star .

Question **4** : 8 more razor shell were seen.

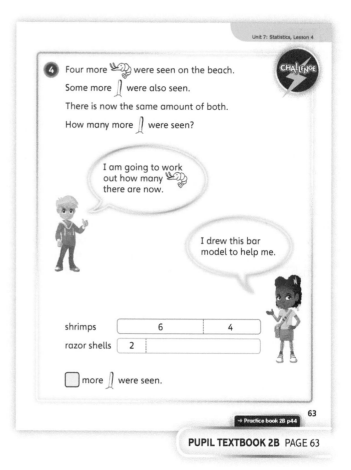

Practice

WAYS OF WORKING Independent thinking

IN FOCUS Question ❶ is a useful way to recap tally charts. The children will have to read the pictogram and convert it.

STRENGTHEN In question ❷, encourage children not to count all of the flowers individually. Show children how to count on or back using the actual symbols rather than the total for each flower. Ask: *Do you need to know how many of each flower there are before you can work out how many more or fewer there are?* It may help some children to write totals of each flower on the pictogram.

DEEPEN Challenge children to create a pictogram based on the following information:
There are 7 cows.
There are more sheep than cows.
The total number of animals is 24.
There are 2 fewer cats than cows.
There are fewer chickens than cows.
There are more dogs than chickens but fewer dogs than cows.

Then ask: *Are there any other solutions?*

ASSESSMENT CHECKPOINT Can children read the amounts on pictograms and use their knowledge of number bonds to 20 to solve the problem?

ANSWERS Answers for the **Practice** part of the lesson appear in the separate **Practice and Reflect answer guide**.

Reflect

WAYS OF WORKING Pair work

IN FOCUS This **Reflect** exercise will stimulate discussion about pictograms. You should find children discussing that, although the quantity of ice creams could be correct, the size of the symbols are not. Children should also notice that the key is missing from this pictogram, and might also notice that it is missing a title. Ask children why the size of the ice creams is a problem. You should hear answers like, 'It is difficult to read the pictogram'.

ASSESSMENT CHECKPOINT Can children read pictograms accurately? Can children explain why the symbols should be the same size and equally spaced so that the pictogram can be read accurately? Can children explain why a key is always needed?

ANSWERS Answers for the **Reflect** part of the lesson appear in the separate **Practice and Reflect answer guide**.

After the lesson ⏸

- Do children understand the key vocabulary relating to pictograms?
- How well did the prompts and questions promote learning and what were children's responses to them?
- Could children be given an opportunity to create pictograms from other areas of the curriculum?

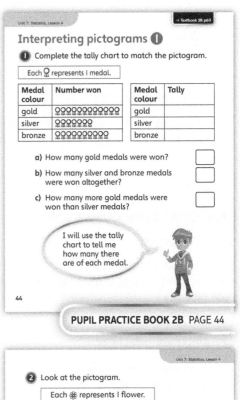

PUPIL PRACTICE BOOK 2B PAGE 44

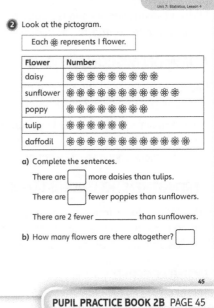

PUPIL PRACTICE BOOK 2B PAGE 45

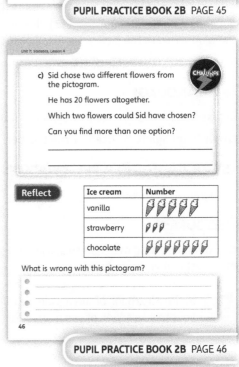

PUPIL PRACTICE BOOK 2B PAGE 46

Interpreting pictograms ❷

Learning focus

In this lesson, children will read and interpret pictograms that have symbols representing more than one item.

Small steps

→ Previous step: Interpreting pictograms (1)
→ **This step: Interpreting pictograms (2)**
→ Next step: Block diagrams

NATIONAL CURRICULUM LINKS

Year 2 Statistics

- Interpret and construct simple pictograms, tally charts, block diagrams and simple tables.
- Ask and answer simple questions by counting the number of objects in each category and sorting the categories by quantity.
- Ask and answer questions about totalling and comparing categorical data.

ASSESSING MASTERY

Children can answer questions about given pictograms confidently and in detail. Children can think of appropriate questions which show deeper interrogation of data.

COMMON MISCONCEPTIONS

Children may not read the key and may count each symbol as one item. Ask:
- *How can you find out what each symbol represents?*

Children may forget about the key midway through counting. For example, with five symbols, they may count: 2, 4, 6, 7, 8. Ask:
- *Can you check your answer? What are you counting in? Are you counting in 1s, 2s, 5s?*

STRENGTHENING UNDERSTANDING

In this lesson, extra intervention may be needed, in which children study a pictogram and then answer questions about it. Guiding their answers is important to ensure they use the correct terminology. Children may need support in counting in 2s, 5s or 10s and in interpreting half symbols for symbols representing 2 and 10.

GOING DEEPER

Arrange for a traffic survey with your class. Collect the data, create pictograms (emphasise the need for an appropriate key depending on the amount of traffic), then interpret the data. Children could write questions about the pictogram and answer them underneath the pictogram. Finally, ask children: *Who might find these statistics useful?*

If a traffic survey is not possible, an alternative might be to collect data of books on the class bookshelf.

KEY LANGUAGE

In lesson: pictogram, represent, symbol, groups, multiplication, how many?, worth, equals, count, more, less

Other language to be used by the teacher: most, least, total, altogether, check, answer, data, statistics, survey

STRUCTURES AND REPRESENTATIONS

Pictograms, bar model

RESOURCES

Optional: Counting materials such as number lines, 100 squares, multiplication grids (2s, 5s, 10s)

 In the eTextbook of this lesson, you will find interactive links to a selection of teaching tools.

Before you teach ⏸

- How will you make links to the previous lesson?
- Are children confident with the language that will be used in this lesson?
- Are there any misconceptions that need addressing?

Discover

ASK

- *Do you need to count in 1s to answer this question?*
- *What does the key tell you? What do you need to count in?*
- *Can you count in 5s?*

IN FOCUS Listen to the answers given in question ① b). Note whether any children have still not grasped why a symbol sometimes represents more than one thing.

ANSWERS

Question ① a): There were 15 blackbirds, 10 robins, 5 sparrows and 20 blue tits seen.

Question ① b): Each 🐦 being worth 5 birds makes it easier to count and quicker to draw. The key tells how many birds one symbol is worth.

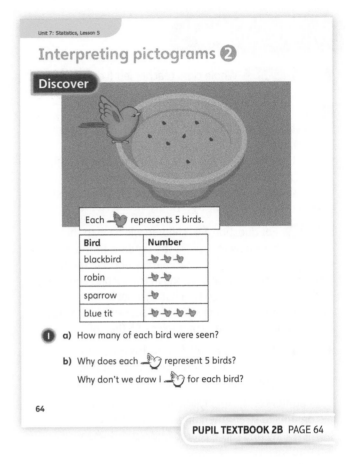

Share

ASK

- *What is 3 × 5?*
- *Look at the robins. What multiplication fact can help you here?*
- *How many birds would four symbols represent?*

IN FOCUS Question ① a) links to times-table facts. This is a good opportunity to revise these with the class. Children should be able to recall quickly 2, 5 and 10 times-table facts. Children need to understand that if there is a lot of data then using a symbol to represent more than one piece of data is a helpful way of displaying the data so that it is easy to read.

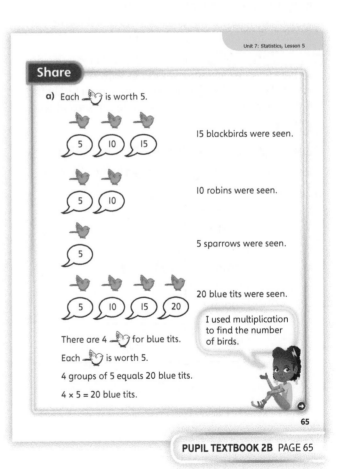

Think together

Whole class teacher led (I do, We do, You do)

ASK

- Question ❶ and ❷ : *What do you need to do to answer a 'how many more' question with pictograms?*
- Question ❸ : *Why do you use half a symbol in pictograms? What is half a symbol worth in this pictogram?*
- *How should we go about solving question ❸ ? What steps should we take?*

IN FOCUS For question ❸ , children will have to think carefully about how to convert the symbols for the different keys. Discuss that for every two bird symbols in the first pictogram, there will only be one in the second and that 5 birds will be represented by a half symbol because 5 is half of 10. Children could circle them for support. This pictogram can still only show clearly multiples of 5 (half of 10).

STRENGTHEN Counting in 2s, 5s and 10s is a good way to strengthen learning. If children cannot count fluently, they will find interpretation of data much more difficult.

Use counters to make physical representations of the pictograms to strengthen understanding. Kinaesthetic learners may find this easier to understand when interpreting.

DEEPEN Get children to create two pictograms from the same set of data but with different keys. Once complete, ask children to evaluate which one is the most effective. You may need to suggest that one key is double the other so that a half symbol has a definite value.

ASSESSMENT CHECKPOINT Question ❷ will help you decide whether children can represent things with symbols correctly. For question ❸ , assess how children tackle the task to translate the first pictogram into the second one.

ANSWERS

Question ❶ : 15 − 5 = 10; there are 10 more blackbirds.

Question ❷ : 2 more 🐦 are needed in the pictogram.

Question ❸ :

Bird	Number
blackbird	🐦 🐦
robin	🐦 🐦
sparrow	🐦
blue tit	🐦 🐦

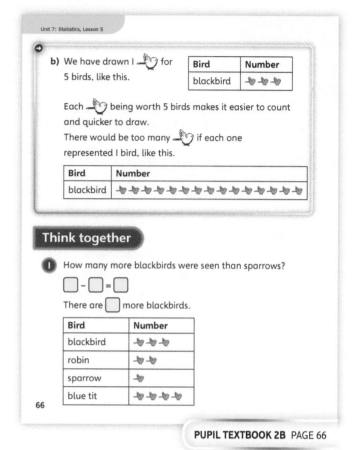

PUPIL TEXTBOOK 2B PAGE 66

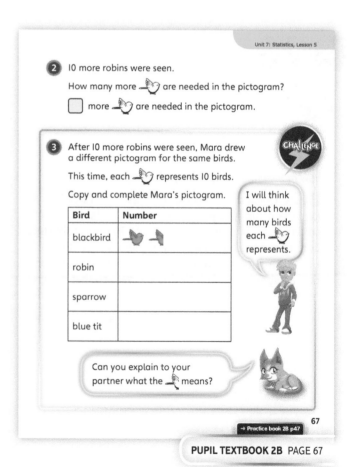

PUPIL TEXTBOOK 2B PAGE 67

Practice

WAYS OF WORKING Independent thinking

IN FOCUS Question **2** c) asks children to find the total number of boys in both classes. Children will have to use the information from both pictograms. Discuss useful strategies with them.

STRENGTHEN Can children spot any patterns that will help them count in 2s, 5s or 10s? For question **3**, ask children to write the total amounts at the end of each row in the first table, so they do not have to keep recounting.

DEEPEN Ask children to write some rules which help to decide what a key should be.

ASSESSMENT CHECKPOINT Question **2** will give you an opportunity to assess whether children can interpret data from two related pictograms. Question **3** will allow you to assess whether children can convert data from one pictogram to another when a different key is used.

ANSWERS Answers for the **Practice** part of the lesson appear in the separate **Practice and Reflect answer guide**.

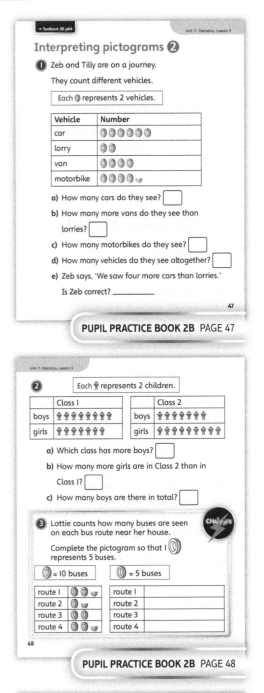

PUPIL PRACTICE BOOK 2B PAGE 47

PUPIL PRACTICE BOOK 2B PAGE 48

Reflect

WAYS OF WORKING Pair work

IN FOCUS Children should come up with some clear, concise statements for this **Reflect** question such as 'the first pictogram is much easier to read'; 'the second pictogram took a lot longer to count'.

ASSESSMENT CHECKPOINT This activity will let you see which children have fully understood the importance of having an appropriate key and easily countable symbols.

ANSWERS Answers for the **Reflect** part of the lesson appear in the separate **Practice and Reflect answer guide**.

After the lesson

- What opportunities can you identify to reinforce and apply this lesson's learning?
- Are children ready to move on to block diagrams?
- Did children understand the issues with using keys representing more than one item?

PUPIL PRACTICE BOOK 2B PAGE 49

Block diagrams

Learning focus

In this lesson, children will read, construct and interpret block diagrams.

Small steps

→ Previous step: Interpreting pictograms (2)
→ **This step: Block diagrams**
→ Next step: Solving word problems

NATIONAL CURRICULUM LINKS

Year 2 Statistics

- Interpret and construct simple pictograms, tally charts, block diagrams and simple tables.
- Ask and answer simple questions by counting the number of objects in each category and sorting the categories by quantity.
- Ask and answer questions about totalling and comparing categorical data.

ASSESSING MASTERY

Children can accurately construct a block diagram and then interpret it effectively. Children can spot mistakes and recognise when it is not useful to use a block diagram.

COMMON MISCONCEPTIONS

Following on from the previous lesson, children may assume that a block could represent more than one thing. Ask:
- *Look through the* **Pupil Textbook** *– are there any block diagrams where each block represents more than one block?*

Children may forget to label all parts of the block diagram when constructing it. Ask:
- *Did you remember the scale? Have you labelled the scale correctly? Have you missed any numbers?*

STRENGTHENING UNDERSTANDING

Using cubes to make 3D block diagrams (graphs) will strengthen understanding. Children could then lay the towers on squared paper with squares matching the size of the cubes to make a 3D block diagram before labelling it and then colouring squares to replace the cubes. A checklist may be useful for them such as: *Did you use a ruler? Have you included a scale? Did you label what the blocks* (cubes) *represent?*

GOING DEEPER

Children could think about when it is appropriate to use a block diagram, and when it would not be appropriate. Ask them if it would represent high numbers effectively.

KEY LANGUAGE

In lesson: block diagram, most, least, same, amount, count, compare, scale, height, score, more, less, fewer, popular, prefer

Other language to be used by the teacher: block graph, label, labelled, construct, represent, strategy

STRUCTURES AND REPRESENTATIONS

Block diagrams, cubes

RESOURCES

Mandatory: interlocking cubes, ruler

Optional: 1 cm or 2 cm squared paper (same size as interlocking cubes)

 In the eTextbook of this lesson, you will find interactive links to a selection of teaching tools.

Before you teach ⏸

- Do you have apparatus (cubes, squared paper) ready to reinforce learning in this lesson?
- How will you link block diagrams to pictograms?
- How will you link block diagrams to tally charts?

Discover

Discover

Unit 7: Statistics, Lesson 6

Block diagrams

WAYS OF WORKING Pair work

ASK

- *How do you know those two towers show the same amounts?*
- *What strategies did you use to work out the answers?*

IN FOCUS Counting the blocks out loud is an effective strategy; it will make the questions easier to answer. Children may also be able to see, as with the length of pictograms, the tallest tower shows the greatest amount; the shortest tower shows the least amount.

ANSWERS

Question ❶ a): Matt has the most points. You can tell visually from the block diagram (it is the tallest) and also from counting the towers.

Question ❶ b): Joe and Abbie have the same number of points. You can tell visually from the graph (they are both the same height) and also from counting the towers.

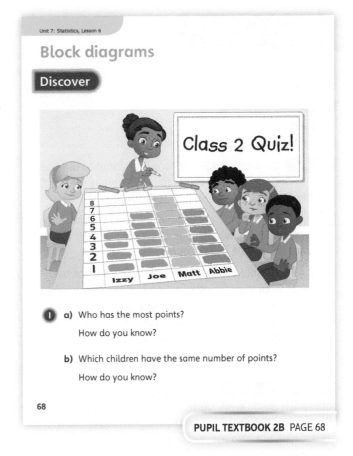

❶ a) Who has the most points?

How do you know?

b) Which children have the same number of points?

How do you know?

68

Share

WAYS OF WORKING Whole class teacher led

ASK

- *Can you explain what you did to answer the question?*
- *Did anyone use a different way?*
- *Can you show me how to make the block diagram with cubes?*

IN FOCUS For question ❶ , have cubes ready for your class to make the block diagrams. This will reinforce learning and understanding. Encourage children to line up the towers of cubes next to each other vertically so that children can easily see which tower is the tallest and therefore who has the most. Then lay the towers out horizontally so that it looks like a block diagram, ensuring children understand that the bottom of each tower needs to be level with the bottom of all the other towers.

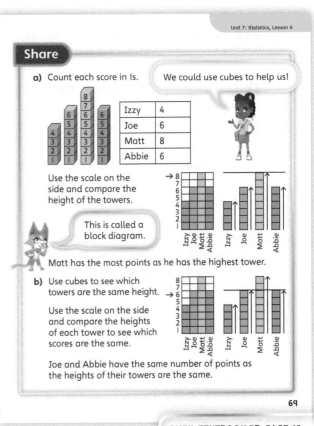

Share

Unit 7: Statistics, Lesson 6

a) Count each score in 1s.

We could use cubes to help us!

Izzy	4
Joe	6
Matt	8
Abbie	6

Use the scale on the side and compare the height of the towers.

This is called a block diagram.

Matt has the most points as he has the highest tower.

b) Use cubes to see which towers are the same height.

Use the scale on the side and compare the heights of each tower to see which scores are the same.

Joe and Abbie have the same number of points as the heights of their towers are the same.

69

Think together

WAYS OF WORKING Whole class teacher led (I do, We do, You do)

ASK

- *How does having a scale help?*
- *Why are the towers different colours?*

IN FOCUS In question **1**, encourage children to use the scale to find the answers more quickly. You may find that children are counting the blocks individually.

STRENGTHEN Continue to support children by providing apparatus (blocks). When reading the scale, a ruler can be useful to ensure the correct number is read.

DEEPEN Can children construct a block diagram of the vowels in 10 of their friends' first names or surnames? Ask them to write three statements about what they found and write these under the block diagram. Children could compare results for first names and surnames if they do them separately. Which vowels are used the most and which are used the least?

ASSESSMENT CHECKPOINT Question **3** will give you an insight into which children are mastering interpretation of block diagrams as they have to use the diagrams to check the statements but also use reasoning skills to make up their own questions.

ANSWERS

Question **1** a): Team D scored the most points. The tallest tower is D. This shows the greatest amount of points.

Question **1** b): Team E scored the least points. The smallest tower is E. This shows the smallest amount of points.

Question **2** : Check that the correct number of blocks have been used.

Question **3** a): The most popular animal is the tiger – correct.

5 fewer children prefer the elephant to the tiger – incorrect.

8 more children prefer the monkey to the rhino – correct.

Question **3** b): Look for accurate use of mathematical vocabulary and correct sense in the context of the block diagram.

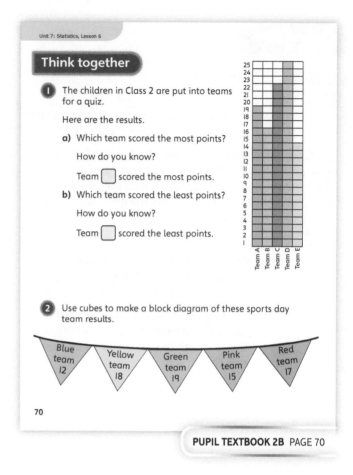

PUPIL TEXTBOOK 2B PAGE 70

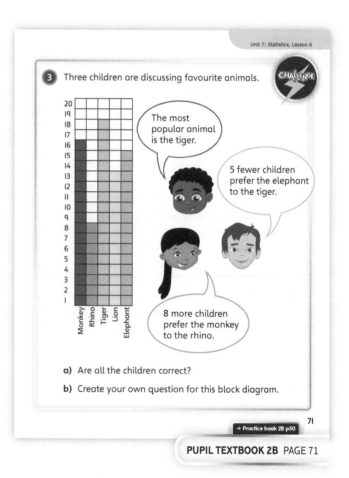

PUPIL TEXTBOOK 2B PAGE 71

Practice

WAYS OF WORKING Independent thinking

IN FOCUS Question **4** will promote some deep thinking about block diagrams. Children should spot that the block sizes are unequal, 11 is missing from the scale and the towers are not labelled.

STRENGTHEN Questions **1** and **3** : When comparing towers, ask children to place their finger on the top of the shorter tower and count on in 1s to the taller tower to find the difference.

DEEPEN Children have now covered tally charts, pictograms and block diagrams. Ask children to discuss each one: where they may be used in real life, and the pros and cons of each.

ASSESSMENT CHECKPOINT Question **2** will provide you with evidence of whether children can complete a block diagram.

Question **3** will provide you with evidence of whether children can interpret a block diagram.

Question **4** will assess whether children understand how a block diagram must be constructed.

ANSWERS Answers for the **Practice** part of the lesson appear in the separate **Practice and Reflect answer guide**.

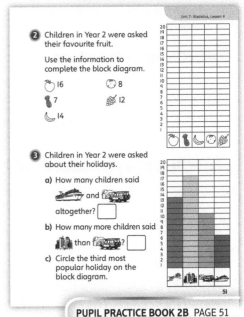

PUPIL PRACTICE BOOK 2B PAGE 50

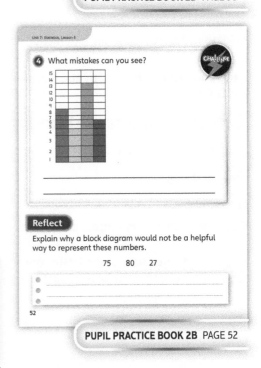

PUPIL PRACTICE BOOK 2B PAGE 51

Reflect

WAYS OF WORKING Pair work

IN FOCUS This question will get children thinking about the practical use of block diagrams and their limitations. Children will realise that the numbers are high and it would have to be a very large diagram to fit the blocks on.

ASSESSMENT CHECKPOINT Assess whether children are able to explain their answers and reason why it would not be a good idea.

ANSWERS Answers for the **Reflect** part of the lesson appear in the separate **Practice and Reflect answer guide**.

After the lesson ⏸

- Can you give children an opportunity to collect some data and construct a block diagram independently?
- Did children master block diagrams?

PUPIL PRACTICE BOOK 2B PAGE 52

Solving word problems

Learning focus

In this lesson, children will draw upon all of the learning throughout the unit, and use it to solve word problems.

Small steps

→ Previous step: Block diagrams
→ **This step: Solving word problems**
→ Next step: Measuring in centimetres

NATIONAL CURRICULUM LINKS

Year 2 Statistics

- Ask and answer simple questions by counting the number of objects in each category and sorting the categories by quantity.
- Ask and answer questions about totalling and comparing categorical data.

ASSESSING MASTERY

Children can use effective strategies to solve word problems. Children can think deeply and explain their answers as well as their methods.

COMMON MISCONCEPTIONS

Children may not read the question properly and make mistakes. Ask:
- *Do you need to add or subtract the amounts in this question?*

Children may not understand the key vocabulary or what the question means. Ask:
- *Which diagram is a pictogram? What does a block graph look like? How do you show five in a tally?*

STRENGTHENING UNDERSTANDING

If children are struggling, ask them to draw the objects or use apparatus. Bar models may be useful here.

GOING DEEPER

Asking children to prove their answers would work well. This could be through a written explanation or by using a structure or representation.

To deepen learning further, ask children to construct a tally chart, pictogram and block diagram from some data. Then ask children to think of their own word problems and write them down.

KEY LANGUAGE

In lesson: diagram, represent, information, tally chart, pictogram, block diagram, represent, match, =, how many?, more, less, altogether

Other language to be used by the teacher: equal, key, scale, solve, word problem, amount, bar model, explain, strategy, add, subtract

STRUCTURES AND REPRESENTATIONS

Pictograms, tally charts, block diagrams, number lines, cubes, bar models

RESOURCES

Mandatory: cubes, ruler

Optional: 1 cm or 2 cm squared paper

 In the eTextbook of this lesson, you will find interactive links to a selection of teaching tools.

Before you teach ⏸

- Are children secure with reading and interpreting tally charts, pictograms and block diagrams?
- Are children ready to solve problems?
- Do you need to provide children vocabulary support?

Discover

WAYS OF WORKING Pair work

ASK

- *What is the question asking you to do? How do you work out the totals for this diagram?*
- *How do you know your answer is correct?*

IN FOCUS Point out which symbol represents each item – in case children are not sure what a cotton reel is for instance.

For question ① b), children might not immediately see something is missing from the pictogram as all sections are present. Encourage them to count the dots and use the key to check their knowledge of how many of each item is needed.

ANSWERS

Question ① a): The block graph represents the model robot.

Question ① b): 2 paper clips and 1 straw are missing.

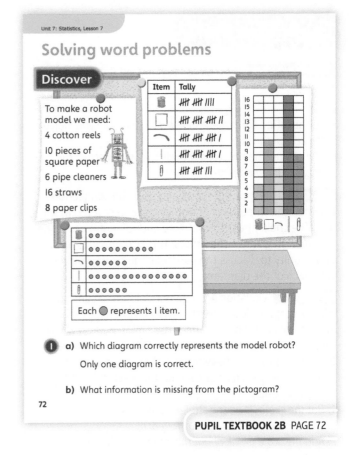

Share

WAYS OF WORKING Whole class teacher led

ASK

- *Look at the tally chart. Is the number of cotton reels correct? Do you need to check the rest of the tally chart?*
- *Look at the pictogram. Do you count the symbol in the first column to find the answer?*

IN FOCUS For question ① a), children may think they need to check all of the totals in the tally chart even though the total for the cotton reels is incorrect, and therefore rules out the tally chart as the correct diagram. If children identify the block graph as correct before checking the pictogram, encourage them to spot where the incorrect information is. For question ① b), children may make the mistake of counting the symbol in the first column of the pictogram. Explain that the table helps separate them.

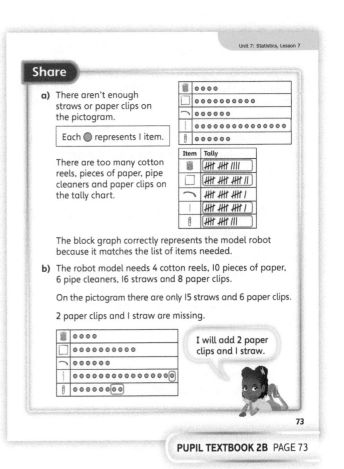

Think together

Whole class teacher led (I do, We do, You do)

ASK

• For question ❸ : *Where should you start? Did you look at the key for the pictogram?*
• *Can you tell me the steps you will take to construct the block diagram independently?*

IN FOCUS Question ❸ shows and uses the connections between the three ways of displaying data covered in this unit. The challenge is to complete each diagram using the information given in the others. This also provides a useful opportunity to discuss the particular merits or problems with each of the diagrams.

STRENGTHEN Question ❷ requires children to construct a block graph independently. Giving children a list of instructions to follow may help. Ask children to draw the horizontal and vertical axis (note, children have not yet been introduced to these terms so ensure you refer to them in another way such as 'the straight line across' and 'the straight line up'). Say:
1) Put the symbols on the straight line along the bottom (remember to only use one box for each).
2) Add the scale (think about the largest number you will need to go to).
3) Use different colours to shade in the results.

DEEPEN Question ❸ is an excellent way to promote deep thinking about statistics. Children will have to use the different charts to fill in the missing parts. This is made trickier, because the pictogram represents two items per symbol.

ASSESSMENT CHECKPOINT Question ❷ will allow you to assess whether children can construct an accurate block diagram independently.

Question ❸ will give you an insight into whether children can read and make connections between the different chart types.

ANSWERS

Question ❶ a): 12 – 5 = 7; 7 more ✐ are needed than ▯ .

Question ❶ b): 48 pieces are needed altogether.

Question ❷ : Children need to construct a block graph independently. Check for an accurate scale, same-sized blocks, use of a ruler and correct numbers of blocks for each.

Question ❸ : Check that:
Cotton reel = 8
Paper = 4
Straws = 6
Pipe cleaners = 10
Paper clips = 6

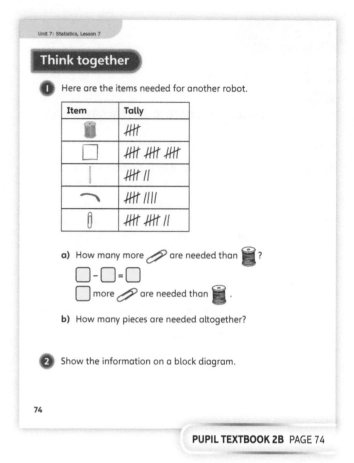

PUPIL TEXTBOOK 2B PAGE 74

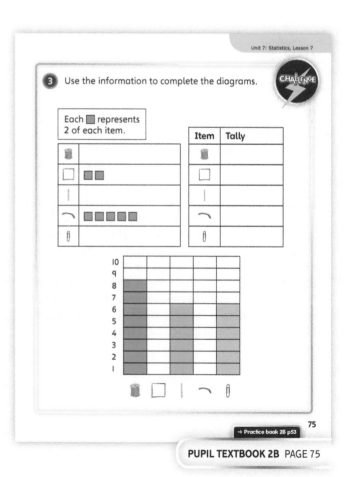

PUPIL TEXTBOOK 2B PAGE 75

Practice

WAYS OF WORKING Pair work

IN FOCUS In question **1** c), remind children that symbols should be roughly the same size. Also remind them of the key. Ask: *How will you represent one child?*

STRENGTHEN Help children to achieve success with question **3** by asking key questions and guiding them through the process: *How can you work out the key for the pictogram? Which data is shown in both the pictogram and the block diagram? How many blue shirts are there in the block graph? How many blue shirts in the pictogram? What must each shirt symbol represent? Which colour shirt is only given in the tally chart?*

DEEPEN Ask children to write five number sentences based on one of the charts or diagrams in this section using the signs <, > or =.

ASSESSMENT CHECKPOINT Question **3** is key to this lesson. It will allow you to see whether children can solve problems associated with statistics, relating the information shown in one chart to how it would be shown in a different representation.

ANSWERS Answers for the **Practice** part of the lesson appear in the separate **Practice and Reflect answer guide**.

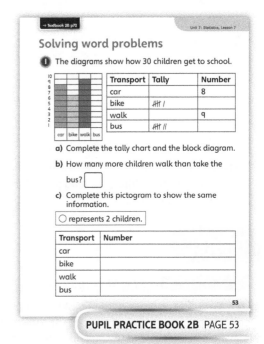

PUPIL PRACTICE BOOK 2B PAGE 53

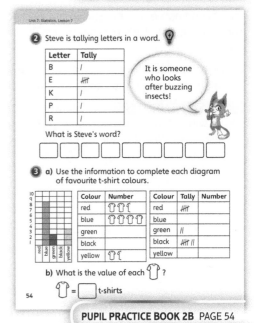

PUPIL PRACTICE BOOK 2B PAGE 54

Reflect

WAYS OF WORKING Independent thinking

IN FOCUS This question will get children thinking deeply about the different charts and diagrams. Listen carefully to children's answers and support them with their reasoning. An answer like, 'the pictograms are easier' will need more development. Ask children what they mean: *Easier to understand? Easier to draw? Easier to represent large numbers?* Put some key words or sentence starters on the board to help children structure answers.

ASSESSMENT CHECKPOINT This question assesses children's reasoning skills and whether they have grasped that all of the charts and diagrams have a different purpose.

ANSWERS Answers for the **Reflect** part of the lesson appear in the separate **Practice and Reflect answer guide**.

After the lesson ⏸

- Are all children ready to move on to the next unit?
- Is further intervention needed?
- Would a home learning statistics investigation deepen learning?

PUPIL PRACTICE BOOK 2B PAGE 55

End of unit check

Don't forget the *Power Maths* unit assessment grid on p26.

WAYS OF WORKING Group work – adult led

IN FOCUS All questions in the **End of unit check** will give you a good insight into which children can read and interpret information from a range of charts and diagrams.

Think!

WAYS OF WORKING Pair work or small groups

IN FOCUS The purpose of the **Think!** question is to find out whether children are secure enough to spot Ola's mistake. See if children can explain where she went wrong and if their explanations are confident.

The second part of the question requires children to read the pictogram and come up with their own questions. This will involve some deep thinking.

Children should use words such as: how many, same, equal, more than, less than, least, most, total and altogether.

ANSWERS AND COMMENTARY Children who have mastered this unit should be secure with interpreting data and explaining methods and answers. They will also be confident in solving problems involving charts and diagrams.

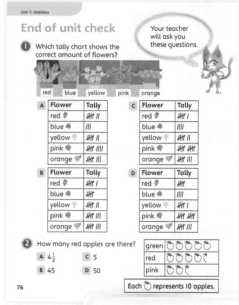

PUPIL TEXTBOOK 2B PAGE 76

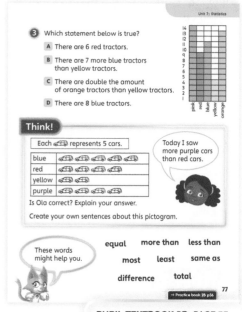

PUPIL TEXTBOOK 2B PAGE 77

Q	A	WRONG ANSWERS AND MISCONCEPTIONS	STRENGTHENING UNDERSTANDING
1	C	A suggests that the child is not secure with counting the tally marks. They may be miscounting or not counting the oblique.	Run intervention activities in which children construct tally charts from data. Particularly provide support when reaching '5' – the oblique. Challenge students to make pictograms and block charts from tally charts.
2	B	C indicates the child has rushed their answer based on a quick guess – without checking their answer.	
3	B	D suggests that children have not counted each block as 1. C might tell you that a child is not secure with counting and doubling numbers.	Practise counting tally chart and pictogram totals. Children could use counters or blocks to support them (and prevent miscounting). Move children on to pictograms in which a symbol represents two or ten items. This work will link closely with practising times tables.

My journal

Independent thinking

ANSWERS AND COMMENTARY

Children will need to realise that Ola is incorrect as the amounts are equal. They should make use of the vocabulary provided in the workbook to form their answer. An exemplary answer would be: Ola is incorrect because there are 4 red and 4 purple cars. This means the amounts are equal.

Children may need strengthening exercises such as reading the question in groups and discussing what it is asking.

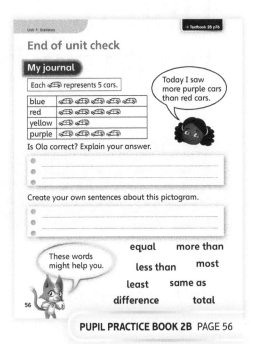

PUPIL PRACTICE BOOK 2B PAGE 56

Power check

WAYS OF WORKING Independent thinking

ASK

- *Why do you feel like that about pictograms?*
- *What was your main strength in this unit?*
- *Are there some charts or diagrams that you feel better about than others?*

Power puzzle

WAYS OF WORKING Pair work or small groups

IN FOCUS Children will need to use reasoning to work out how many of each fruit there are before they can complete the block diagram. If children do not know where to start, suggest they start with the two amounts they know and use them to work out how many pears there would be before focusing on the oranges. Add to check the total is correct, remembering to also check their answers against each sentence again.

ANSWERS AND COMMENTARY 5 pears, 7 oranges and 10 apples plus 3 bananas = 25 fruit

Children could use counters or cubes of different colours to represent the fruits but should not try to complete the block graph before they know how many of each fruit is needed. Children will need to use reasoning to reach the correct answers.

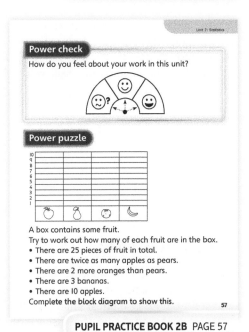

PUPIL PRACTICE BOOK 2B PAGE 57

After the unit ⏸

- How did the unit go?
- What lessons went well? Why did they go well?
- Did children depend on apparatus or support? Or did they get more secure as the unit progressed?

Strengthen and **Deepen** activities for this unit can be found in the *Power Maths* online subscription.

Unit 8
Length and height

Don't forget to watch the Unit 8 video!

Mastery Expert tip! "I keep records of the heights of children in my class by asking them to measure each other at the start of each term. We use the data to ask questions that revise the key vocabulary introduced in this unit, such as 'Who has grown most?' and 'Who is the tallest?'."

WHY THIS UNIT IS IMPORTANT

Length and height are familiar and useful ideas from daily life. Children will probably take an interest in measuring their own height and making comparisons with others' heights, and this can easily be extended to looking at heights and lengths more generally. This work also makes use of simple standard units and scales; reading a simple scale accurately is an important skill which will be useful in a wide range of settings.

WHERE THIS UNIT FITS

→ Unit 7: Statistics
→ **Unit 8: Length and height**
→ Unit 9: Properties of shapes

Before they start this unit, it is expected that children:
- have at least an informal understanding of the ideas of length and height
- can accurately manipulate simple apparatus such as multilink cubes, rulers and metre sticks and are familiar with some of the basic vocabulary that will be needed, such as 'how long?' and 'how high?'.

ASSESSING MASTERY

Children who master the work in this unit will be able to estimate, measure and compare the lengths or heights of a range of objects, using simple measuring equipment, such as rulers, metre sticks and tape measures, and appropriate standard units (centimetres or metres). Children will be aware of some of the common practical difficulties that arise when measuring, such as not starting at zero when using a ruler, or failing to deal with flexible objects consistently, and will know how to avoid these difficulties.

COMMON MISCONCEPTIONS	STRENGTHENING UNDERSTANDING	GOING DEEPER
Children may confuse metres and centimetres.	Provide plenty of practice in measuring and estimating lengths in order to build up children's understanding of the range of sizes over which metres and centimetres are appropriate units.	Children will benefit from developing a feel for the size of a range of objects. This will enable children to make quick estimates of lengths and heights in centimetres or metres without using measuring apparatus.
Children may struggle to read scales on rulers and metre sticks (including not aligning objects on zero or failing to compensate where this is not possible).	Measuring objects in centimetres and metres is a key skill that you should encourage children to practise repeatedly.	Measurement provides a simple but useful practical context for basic arithmetic, so make sure that children understand the connections between the scale on a ruler and the number line.

Unit 8: Length and height

WAYS OF WORKING

These pages provide an overview of key content in this unit, including the idea of using a ruler and the role of centimetres and metres, which are the standard units that children will use. Discuss these pages with children, questioning them to assess their familiarity with the main content and key language.

STRUCTURES AND REPRESENTATIONS

Bar model

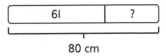

Number lines

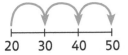

Rulers

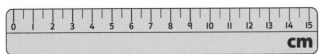

KEY LANGUAGE

There is some key language that children will need to know as part of the learning in this unit:

→ length, height
→ width, distance
→ long, longer, short, shorter
→ tall
→ metres (m), centimetres (cm)
→ order, compare
→ ruler, metre stick
→ measure
→ zero
→ greater than (>)
→ less than (<)
→ equal to (=)

PUPIL TEXTBOOK 2B PAGE 78

PUPIL TEXTBOOK 2B PAGE 79

Measuring in centimetres

Learning focus

In this lesson, children will use rulers to measure simple objects to the nearest centimetre.

Small steps

→ Previous step: Solving word problems
→ **This step: Measuring in centimetres**
→ Next step: Measuring in metres

NATIONAL CURRICULUM LINKS

Year 2 Measurement

Choose and use appropriate standard units to estimate and measure length/height in any direction (m/cm); mass (kg/g); temperature (°C); capacity (litres/ml) to the nearest appropriate unit, using rulers, scales, thermometers and measuring vessels.

ASSESSING MASTERY

Children can use a ruler marked in centimetres to measure the length (or height) of a range of simple objects to the nearest centimetre.

COMMON MISCONCEPTIONS

Children may align objects against the ruler incorrectly (typically aligning the end of the object against the 1 cm mark instead of the zero). Instead of simply reading the scale at the end of the object, children may also count in centimetres along the ruler starting from 1 cm and therefore will get the wrong result. Ask:
• *Where would you put the end of the object? How can you find the length without counting?*

STRENGTHENING UNDERSTANDING

Children who are counting or misaligning objects against the ruler could be given a set of objects of agreed length and asked to check the length using their measuring procedure. Start with a 1 cm cube and agree its length; then ask children to show you how they would measure it.

GOING DEEPER

This topic naturally leads to ideas of addition and subtraction. To deepen understanding of finding length, place a 6 cm pencil against a ruler so that one end of the pencil lines up with the 8 cm mark. Ask:
• *Where is the other end? Is there more than one possible answer?*

KEY LANGUAGE

In lesson: measure, centimetres, cm, length, ruler, exactly, long, tall, longer, shorter, longest

Other language to be used by the teacher: height, high

STRUCTURES AND REPRESENTATIONS

Rulers

RESOURCES

Mandatory: rulers (scale marked and labelled in centimetres)

Optional: a selection of objects to measure, including paper strips cut to a whole number of centimetres, interlocking centimetre cubes

 In the eTextbook of this lesson, you will find interactive links to a selection of teaching tools.

Before you teach ⏸

• Do children have a reasonable idea of how big a centimetre is?
• Can they use their fingers to show what a centimetre looks like?

Discover

WAYS OF WORKING Pair work

ASK

- *How many objects are the children measuring?*
- *How are they doing the measuring?*

IN FOCUS In question ❶, and the lesson as a whole, the focus is on making sense of the centimetre as a unit of length, and making sure that children understand the correct procedure for measuring simple objects using a ruler.

ANSWERS

Question ❶ a): The pencil is exactly 10 cm long.

Question ❶ b): The items that look half this size (the rubber and the paper clip) are 5 cm long.

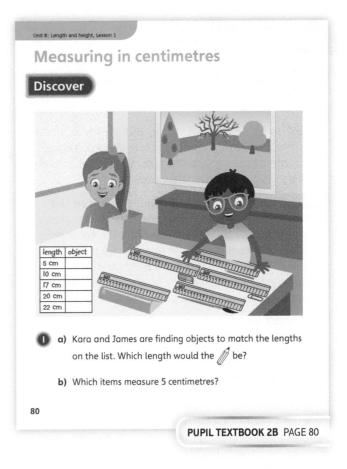

Measuring in centimetres

Discover

length	object
5 cm	
10 cm	
17 cm	
20 cm	
22 cm	

❶ a) Kara and James are finding objects to match the lengths on the list. Which length would the ✏ be?

b) Which items measure 5 centimetres?

80

PUPIL TEXTBOOK 2B PAGE 80

Share

WAYS OF WORKING Whole class teacher led

ASK

- Question ❶ a): *Look at the left end of the pencil. Which number did Ash line it up with?*
- Question ❶ a): *Why didn't Ash put the end of the pencil at one (the 1 cm mark)?*
- Question ❶ b): *How can you tell that the pencil case cannot be 5 cm long?*

IN FOCUS Question ❶ provides an opportunity to check that children are using the correct procedure for measuring, and that they have a good understanding of the relative sizes of objects. For example, the pencil case cannot be 5 cm long because it is longer than the pencil.

Share

a) *I am going to use a ruler to measure the length of the ✏.*

The ✏ is exactly 10 cm long.

b) The items that look half this size are 5 cm long.

The ▱ and the ✐ are 5 cm long.

81

PUPIL TEXTBOOK 2B PAGE 81

Think together

WAYS OF WORKING Whole class teacher led (I do, We do, You do)

ASK

- Question ❶ : *Why does Astrid say that she needs to count the centimetres? Do you need to count the centimetres?*
- *If you are measuring something yourself, is it better to do it Astrid's way? Is there a different way?*

IN FOCUS Before children tackle question ❶ , ensure they understand that each division on the ruler represents one centimetre, and that they know that the abbreviation 'cm' stands for 'centimetre'. Use question ❶ to establish the idea that when children are making their own measurements, they can decide how to align the object against the ruler, and it makes sense to start at zero.

Question ❸ extends the concept of length, establishing that it can be an intrinsic property of a flexible shape, rather than just the distance between the ends of string.

STRENGTHEN Interlocking centimetre cubes can be used to allow children to check the accuracy of their measurements for themselves, and to increase confidence: children can measure a 'stick' of known length (found by counting) and see that measuring gives the same result. It is important to move beyond cubes, however, as their use may encourage a reliance on counting rather than measurement.

DEEPEN To deepen understanding, ask: *How could Astrid work out how long the shape in question ❶ is without counting?* Encourage alternative explanations and methods; for example, visualising the two 'missing' cubes and then counting back 2 from 10, or just using known number facts (2 + 8 = 10).

ASSESSMENT CHECKPOINT Question ❷ allows you to check that children know how to measure objects accurately, and to assess their understanding of relative size and the associated vocabulary (longer and shorter).

ANSWERS

Question ❶ a): The pencil case is 20 cm long.

b): The tower is 8 cm tall.

Question ❷ : Any objects longer than 20 cm and shorter than 8 cm respectively, correctly measured and recorded.

Question ❸ : The second string is longer.

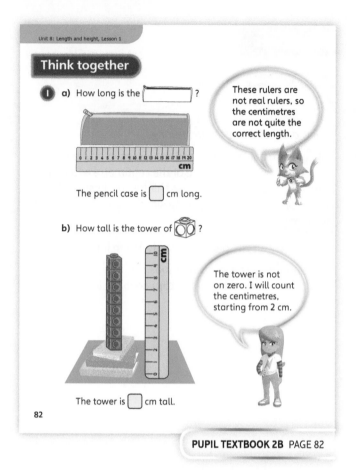

PUPIL TEXTBOOK 2B PAGE 82

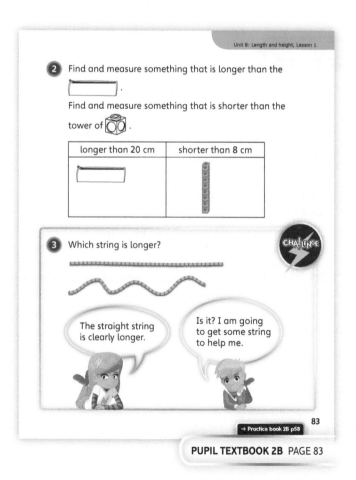

PUPIL TEXTBOOK 2B PAGE 83

Practice

WAYS OF WORKING Independent thinking

IN FOCUS Questions ① and ② provide further opportunities to revise some important vocabulary – 'longer than' and 'greater than'. Encourage children to answer questions orally, using complete sentences like: 'The twig is longer than the pinecone.' and 'The pinecone is shorter than the twig.'

STRENGTHEN Children may find it difficult to visualise lengths in centimetres. Give children strips of paper cut to the required lengths to support them in answering question ④. Ask children to find objects that are about the same length. Discuss how children can use the 10 cm strip to find something that measures less than 10 cm, and the 30 cm strip to find something that is longer than 30 cm.

DEEPEN Extend question ⑤ by asking, for example: *My stick is 9 cm long – if one end is at the 13 cm mark on the ruler, where could the other end be?*

ASSESSMENT CHECKPOINT Question ④ provides a further opportunity to check children's proficiency with the process of measurement, and their sense of the sizes of objects. Are children picking objects randomly, or do they have a reasonable idea of what an object with a length of, for example, 26 cm would look like?

ANSWERS Answers for the **Practice** part of the lesson appear in the separate **Practice and Reflect answer guide**.

Reflect

WAYS OF WORKING Pair work

IN FOCUS This simple **Reflect** activity can be used to summarise the key content of the lesson; the paired format makes the work self-checking, but it is important to make sure that both members of a pair are not making the same mistake.

ASSESSMENT CHECKPOINT Use this activity to check that all children are confident that they know how to use a ruler to measure an object to the nearest centimetre.

ANSWERS Answers for the **Reflect** part of the lesson appear in the separate **Practice and Reflect answer guide**.

After the lesson ⏸

- Are children able to use a ruler to measure a range of objects to the nearest centimetre?
- Do children have a reasonable idea (without measuring) of how long a range of familiar small objects are – for example, a pen, or a pencil case?

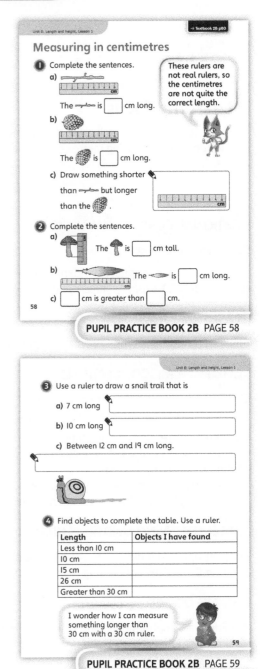

PUPIL PRACTICE BOOK 2B PAGE 58

PUPIL PRACTICE BOOK 2B PAGE 59

PUPIL PRACTICE BOOK 2B PAGE 60

Measuring in metres

Learning focus

In this lesson, children will estimate and measure a range of objects, using metres as a unit of measurement.

Small steps

→ Previous step: Measuring in centimetres
→ **This step: Measuring in metres**
→ Next step: Comparing lengths

NATIONAL CURRICULUM LINKS

Year 2 Measurement

Choose and use appropriate standard units to estimate and measure length/height in any direction (m/cm); mass (kg/g); temperature (°C); capacity (litres/ml) to the nearest appropriate unit, using rulers, scales, thermometers and measuring vessels.

ASSESSING MASTERY

Children can estimate, measure and compare lengths, using metres or centimetres as appropriate.

COMMON MISCONCEPTIONS

Children may find it difficult to remember which of the two units (m and cm) is which. Ask:
• *Who can remember what a centimetre looks like? Show me with your fingers.*

Children may also fail to understand that both units measure length, perhaps because centimetres are seen as marks on a scale to be read or counted, whereas metres are seen as complete objects (metre sticks). Emphasise the relationship between centimetres and metres. Ask:
• *I measured my pencil and wrote down the length, but I forgot the unit and just wrote '15'. What should it be – metres or centimetres? I would like to measure something quite big – such as this classroom. How long do you think that is?*

STRENGTHENING UNDERSTANDING

Children who find it difficult to visualise the size of large objects, such as the bus in the **Share** activity, will benefit from additional practice in measuring real objects using metre sticks.

GOING DEEPER

If children are confident enough to start converting between units, challenge them to answer questions such as: *How many centimetres make half a metre? How many metres does 500 cm make?*

KEY LANGUAGE

In lesson: measure, metre, m, long, height, width, tallest, distance, centimetres, cm, shorter, taller

Other language to be used by the teacher: estimate, compare, length, height, tall, side, short

STRUCTURES AND REPRESENTATIONS

Metre sticks, rulers

RESOURCES

Mandatory: metre sticks (or metre rulers), centimetre rulers

Optional: tape measures, and a range of objects to measure

 In the eTextbook of this lesson, you will find interactive links to a selection of teaching tools.

Before you teach ⏸

• Are children able to work confidently with centimetres?
• Are children ready for the idea that larger objects cannot be conveniently measured in centimetres?

Discover

ASK

- Question ① a): *How would you use the metre sticks to answer the question?*
- *Do you need to measure the length of the bus or the classroom or both?*

IN FOCUS In question ① b), encourage children to ignore practical issues, such as getting the bus through the classroom door, and focus on the comparative width and height of the bus and the room.

ANSWERS

Question ① a): Kara and Tariq must measure the length of the bus and the length of the classroom. If the classroom is longer then the length of the bus then the bus would fit.

Question ① b): Kara and Tariq also need to know the height and width of the classroom, and whether these measurements are more than the height and width of the bus.

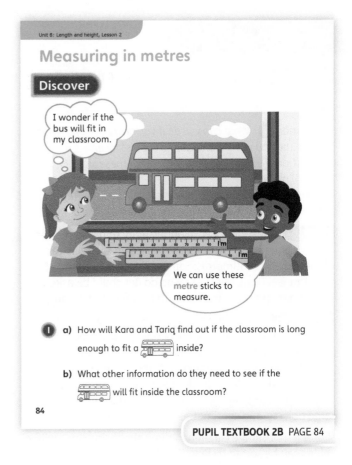

PUPIL TEXTBOOK 2B PAGE 84

Share

ASK

- *The children in the picture used metre sticks to measure their classroom. Would the bus fit there?*
- *What about our classroom? Would that bus fit in here? How do you know?*

IN FOCUS Question ① b) considers the height and width of the classroom and the bus. This is a good opportunity to reinforce vocabulary ('height', 'tall', 'width', and so on) and to do some estimation.

PUPIL TEXTBOOK 2B PAGE 85

Think together

WAYS OF WORKING Whole class teacher led (I do, We do, You do)

ASK

- Question ❶ : *What can you do if you only have one metre stick, and you want to measure a big distance?*
- Question ❷ : *Can you remember what these signs (<, > and =) mean?*
- Question ❷ : *A metre ruler is marked in centimetres. Will this help you to see how many centimetres make a metre?*

IN FOCUS Question ❷ is an opportunity to revise the use of the inequality signs, but also focuses on the relative size of metres and centimetres. Some children may already know that 1 m = 100 cm, but those who do not could be asked to look at a metre ruler (marked with centimetre divisions).

STRENGTHEN Allow children to practise estimating and measuring the size of a variety of objects and spaces within the school. Have a range of measuring equipment available, including metre sticks (unmarked), metre rulers (marked in centimetres), and large (reel-type) tape measures. Make sure children understand that metres are used for measuring large objects, and centimetres for smaller ones.

DEEPEN Encourage children to think about situations where things can be sorted by length without the need for precise measurement. Ask: *Suppose a zookeeper wanted to know which animals were more than one metre tall, and which ones were shorter? How could they do that? Would they actually need to measure the animals?*

ASSESSMENT CHECKPOINT As children become more experienced with estimating visually, assess whether they understand that it is possible to answer question ❸ without doing any precise measurement.

ANSWERS

Question ❶ a): No – unless the classroom has an unusually tall door.

Question ❶ b): This depends on the size of the school hall.

Question ❶ c): Again, this depends on your school building; you could ask some children to measure it.

Question ❷ a): 2 metres < 20 metres

Question ❷ b): 9 metres > 9 centimetres

Question ❷ c): 100 centimetres = 1 metre

Question ❸ : This answer depends on the height of the objects children find in the playground.

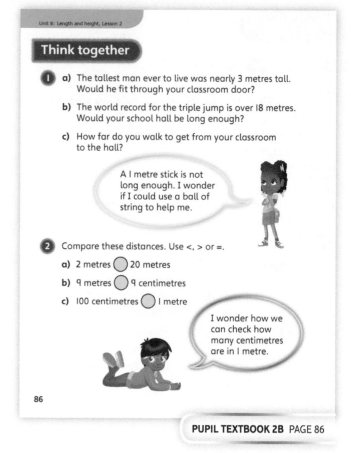

Think together

❶ a) The tallest man ever to live was nearly 3 metres tall. Would he fit through your classroom door?

b) The world record for the triple jump is over 18 metres. Would your school hall be long enough?

c) How far do you walk to get from your classroom to the hall?

A 1 metre stick is not long enough. I wonder if I could use a ball of string to help me.

❷ Compare these distances. Use <, > or =.

a) 2 metres ◯ 20 metres

b) 9 metres ◯ 9 centimetres

c) 100 centimetres ◯ 1 metre

I wonder how we can check how many centimetres are in 1 metre.

86

PUPIL TEXTBOOK 2B PAGE 86

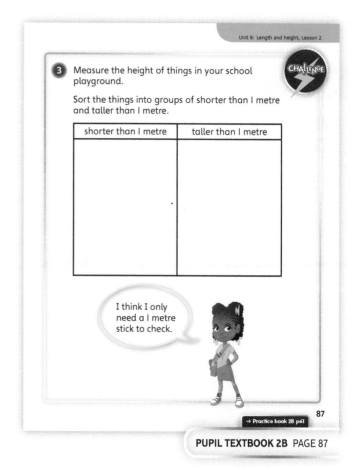

❸ Measure the height of things in your school playground.

Sort the things into groups of shorter than 1 metre and taller than 1 metre.

CHALLENGE

shorter than 1 metre	taller than 1 metre

I think I only need a 1 metre stick to check.

→ Practice book 2B p61

87

PUPIL TEXTBOOK 2B PAGE 87

Practice

WAYS OF WORKING Independent thinking

IN FOCUS Question ④ provides a good summary of children's understanding of the relative size of metres and centimetres. You could ask further questions of the same kind.

STRENGTHEN Children who confuse centimetres and metres could be given further practice in measuring large and small or tall and short objects, using a metre stick and a ruler marked in centimetres, respectively.

DEEPEN Ask children who tackle question ⑤ confidently to suggest objects with other particular lengths (or the lengths of particular objects). For example: *What animal might be 3 metres long? How long do you think a whale might be?*

ASSESSMENT CHECKPOINT Assess whether children understand the relative size of the units, and can choose the appropriate unit to estimate and measure a variety of objects.

ANSWERS Answers for the **Practice** part of the lesson appear in the separate **Practice and Reflect answer guide**.

Reflect

WAYS OF WORKING Independent thinking

IN FOCUS The **Reflect** part of the lesson requires children to list items they would measure with a metre stick and with a 30 cm ruler. Expect them to suggest a sensible range of objects for each measuring instrument. The metre stick examples should be clearly larger than a metre (for example, a car or a corridor), while the ruler examples should be less than 30 cm (for example, a pencil or a mobile phone).

ASSESSMENT CHECKPOINT Where children's suggestions are ambiguous (for example, the width of a desk could reasonably be measured with either instrument), ask what they would expect the measurement to be.

ANSWERS Answers for the **Reflect** part of the lesson appear in the separate **Practice and Reflect answer guide**.

After the lesson ⏸

- Are children confident using metres and centimetres to estimate and measure in daily routines?
- For example, can they answer questions such as: *How long is the lunch queue? How long are the tadpoles in the pond?*

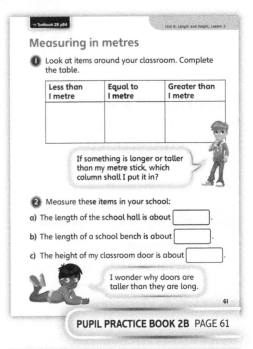

PUPIL PRACTICE BOOK 2B PAGE 61

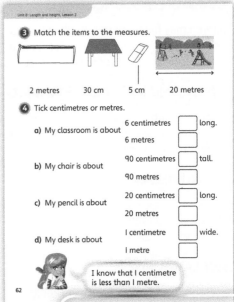

PUPIL PRACTICE BOOK 2B PAGE 62

PUPIL PRACTICE BOOK 2B PAGE 63

Comparing lengths

Learning focus

In this lesson, children will compare lengths measured in centimetres and metres.

Small steps

→ Previous step: Measuring in metres
→ **This step: Comparing lengths**
→ Next step: Ordering lengths

NATIONAL CURRICULUM LINKS

Year 2 Measurement

Compare and order lengths, mass, volume/capacity and record the results using >, < and = .

ASSESSING MASTERY

Children can compare lengths, including those measured in centimetres and metres, and write results using inequality signs.

COMMON MISCONCEPTIONS

Children may fail to appreciate the importance of place value when comparing numerical measurements. The use of the place value grid in this lesson is designed to address this misconception. Ask:
• *Which is longer, 35 cm or 53 cm? How do you know?*

STRENGTHENING UNDERSTANDING

Strengthen understanding of place value by asking questions such as: *Which is longer – 23 cm or 32 cm?* If children answer incorrectly, cut paper strips to each size to establish the correct answer, and then use the place value grid representation to justify the conclusion.

GOING DEEPER

Several of the exercises in this lesson involve completing inequality statements. Challenge children to explore the range of values that are valid. Ask:
• *How many different digits could go in this box?*

KEY LANGUAGE

In lesson: compare, <, >, =, cm, m, length, long, longest, difference, greater than, less than, tens, shortest, tall, taller, smaller

Other language to be used by the teacher: centimetres, metres, inequality, place value

STRUCTURES AND REPRESENTATIONS

Ruler, number line, place value grid

RESOURCES

Mandatory: Base 10 equipment

Optional: rulers, paper strips cut to particular lengths, place value grid, interlocking cubes

 In the eTextbook of this lesson, you will find interactive links to a selection of teaching tools.

Before you teach

• How will you support children who need more practice in comparing 2-digit numbers?

Discover

Unit 8: Length and height, Lesson 3

WAYS OF WORKING Pair work

ASK

- *What is in the display case? Why do you think the museum would put a ruler in with the bones?*
- *Why do you think scientists might measure the bones of ancient animals like this?*

IN FOCUS Question ➊ is designed to remind children of some key ideas: that they can measure an object by aligning it against a ruler, and that they do not necessarily need to measure two objects to decide which is the longer, as they may be able to line one object up against the other and see which is longer by direct comparison.

ANSWERS

Question ➊ a): The ▬▬▬ is 30 cm long.

Question ➊ b): The ▬▬▬▬▬ is longer than the ▬▬▬ .

Comparing lengths

Discover

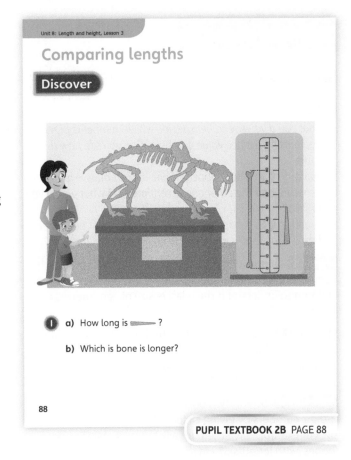

➊ a) How long is ▬▬▬ ?

   b) Which is bone is longer?

88

PUPIL TEXTBOOK 2B PAGE 88

Share

WAYS OF WORKING Whole class teacher led

ASK

- *Which of the bones is easier to measure?*
- *Question ➊ a): How did Flo measure the bone? How is that different from what Astrid did?*
- *Question ➊ b): How can the place value grid help you decide which of the numbers is bigger? Can you answer the question without using the place value grid?*

IN FOCUS Use the personalities of the characters to help explain their approaches to question ➊ a): Astrid boldly opens the cabinet so she can move the bone and align it with the start of the ruler, while Flo looks for a more creative approach. Ask children which approach they prefer.

In question ➊ b), the place value grid may help some children to compare the lengths.

Share

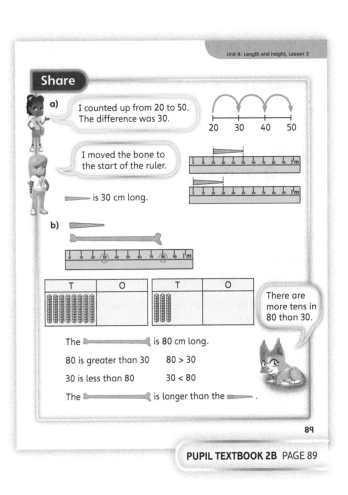

89

PUPIL TEXTBOOK 2B PAGE 89

117

Think together

WAYS OF WORKING Whole class teacher led (I do, We do, You do)

ASK

- *What could you use to help decide which number is bigger? Would using a place value grid help? Can you see how this works?*
- Question **2** : *What happens if one of the bones is measured in metres, and the other one in centimetres? What would you do then?*
- Question **2** : *'A bone measured in metres must be longer than a bone that is measured in centimetres.' Is this true?*

IN FOCUS In question **2** a) the place value grid makes the comparison of two numbers easier. Question **2** b) requires children to understand the relative size of centimetres and metres.

Question **3** requires children to find objects that are taller and smaller than 40 cm. They could choose to use a metre ruler (with markings at 1 cm or 10 cm intervals), or a strip of paper measuring 40 cm.

STRENGTHEN Strengthen understanding of comparing 2-digit numbers by giving children further examples to work on. For example, give them (or ask them to make) paper 'bones' with lengths 57 cm and 75 cm and ask them to decide which is longer; then challenge them to say how they could have answered the question without the 'bones'.

DEEPEN Challenge children to explain how they would represent a length like 2 metres in the place value grid. Show them how the grid can be extended to three columns, for hundreds, tens and ones.

ASSESSMENT CHECKPOINT Use question **2** to check that children understand the role of place value in comparing 2-digit numbers; the number with most tens is always bigger – if the tens are the same, compare the ones.

ANSWERS

Question **1** : 30 is less than 55

30 < 55

The ▭ (leg) bone is shorter.

Question **2** a): 75 cm > 57 cm

Question **2** b): 20 cm < 2 m

Question **2** c): 50 cm = 50 cm

Question **3** : Any list of three objects that meet each of the criteria.

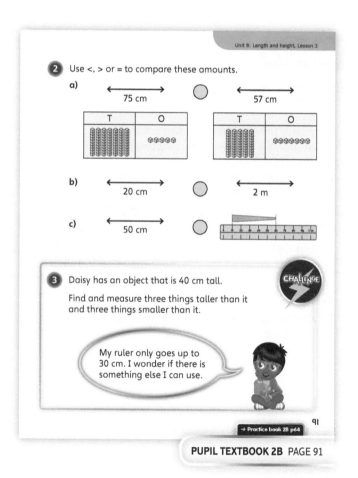

PUPIL TEXTBOOK 2B PAGE 90

PUPIL TEXTBOOK 2B PAGE 91

Practice

IN FOCUS Question ③ covers some of the key content of the lesson – children are expected to complete the inequality statements without using a place value grid. This should be straightforward, provided they understand that the tens digit is most significant in determining the value of a 2-digit number.

STRENGTHEN Children who find question ③ difficult should be encouraged to write the numbers in a place value grid, until they are more confident with the role of the tens digit in comparing numbers.

DEEPEN Challenge children to find more answers to question ④. For example, question ④ c) has many possible answers.

ASSESSMENT CHECKPOINT Use question ⑤ to check that children understand the importance of 'starting from zero' and of 'finding the difference' when measuring with a ruler.

ANSWERS Answers for the **Practice** part of the lesson appear in the separate **Practice and Reflect answer guide**.

Reflect

WAYS OF WORKING Pair work

IN FOCUS The **Reflect** part of the lesson will help you ensure that this lesson does not become a purely formal exercise in comparing numbers. While a sound knowledge of place value will be needed in some situations, this question provides an opportunity for children to measure two objects, and reinforces the idea that lengths can sometimes be compared without formal measurement and without using numbers.

ASSESSMENT CHECKPOINT Ask: *When can you compare lengths without doing any measuring or using any numbers?* Children who have mastered the ideas of this lesson should be able to explain that we can do this if it is possible to put the objects side by side. Some children may be able to explain that we can do this without having to move the objects, provided that we can line up a suitable third object (for example, a piece of string) against each of them in turn.

ANSWERS Answers for the **Reflect** part of the lesson appear in the separate **Practice and Reflect answer guide**.

After the lesson ⏸

- Did children understand all the concepts covered in this lesson, including understanding direct (side-by-side) comparison of lengths, and using place value to compare 2-digit numbers?
- Do you have a clear idea of where children who found the work difficult need more help?

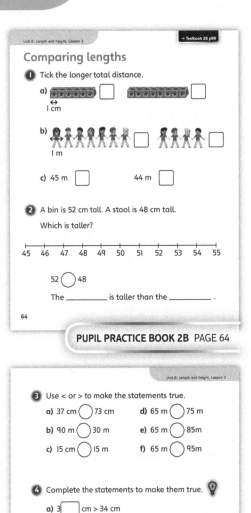

PUPIL PRACTICE BOOK 2B PAGE 64

PUPIL PRACTICE BOOK 2B PAGE 65

PUPIL PRACTICE BOOK 2B PAGE 66

Ordering lengths

Learning focus

In this lesson, children will order sets of lengths measured in centimetres or metres.

Small steps

→ Previous step: Comparing lengths
→ **This step: Ordering lengths**
→ Next step: Solving word problems – length

NATIONAL CURRICULUM LINKS

Year 2 Measurement

Compare and order lengths, mass, volume/capacity and record the results using >, < and = .

ASSESSING MASTERY

Children can put a small set of lengths, in metres or centimetres, into ascending or descending order.

COMMON MISCONCEPTIONS

Children may continue to have difficulty comparing 2-digit numbers. Give children who find it difficult to answer questions such as *Which number is bigger – 24 or 42?* place value charts to support them. Ask:
- *Which digit tells you which number is bigger?*

STRENGTHENING UNDERSTANDING

The step from comparing two numbers to ordering a set of three numbers may be difficult for some children. The number line provides a useful picture of what is required; encourage children to locate each number on the line, and then read them in order.

GOING DEEPER

Challenge children to put four or more lengths in order, or to order a set of lengths given in mixed units (centimetres and metres).

KEY LANGUAGE

In lesson: order, length, distance, metre, m, smallest, greatest, difference, longest, shortest, tens, ones, cm, greater, smaller, measure, height, compare

Other language to be used by the teacher: centimetre, ascending, descending

STRUCTURES AND REPRESENTATIONS

Number line, place value grid, column method

RESOURCES

Mandatory: Base 10 equipment, rulers (marked in centimetres), dice

Optional: interlocking centimetre cubes

 In the eTextbook of this lesson, you will find interactive links to a selection of teaching tools.

Before you teach

- Do children understand the idea of 'putting things in order'?
- Are there practical activities that could be used to demonstrate what is meant – for example, asking the class to line up in order of height?

Discover

WAYS OF WORKING Pair work

ASK

• Question **1** a): *What does 'order the three distances' mean? What would it mean if I asked you all to line up in order of height?*
• Question **1** b): *How could you work out the difference between the longest and shortest distance?*

IN FOCUS There is a lot of detail in this apparently simple activity. Children will need to make sense of equivalent sets of vocabulary ('smallest' and 'shortest', 'greatest' and 'longest'). Children will also need to understand what is meant by 'order the three distances', and to recall how to find the difference between two numbers.

ANSWERS

Question **1** a): From shortest to longest, the distances are 7 metres, 16 metres, 25 metres.

Question **1** b): The difference between the longest and shortest distance is 18 metres.

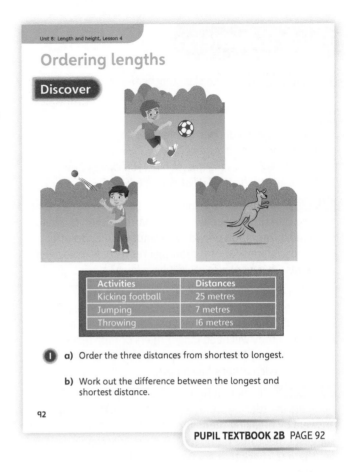

PUPIL TEXTBOOK 2B PAGE 92

Share

WAYS OF WORKING Whole class, teacher led

ASK

• Question **1** a): *Why did Flo make a model for each of the numbers? How do the models help her to put the numbers in order?*
• Question **1** a): *Astrid did it differently – she used place value grids. Can you tell which number each grid represents? How did the grids help Astrid to put the numbers in order?*
• Question **1** b): *How can you use this number line to find the difference between 7 and 25?*

IN FOCUS For question **1** b), the number line method is conceptually simple: put the smaller number at one end of the line, and the larger number at the other end – then find the difference between them. For children who are ready for a more formal approach, the place value grid and column subtraction show how the same result can be obtained by decomposition.

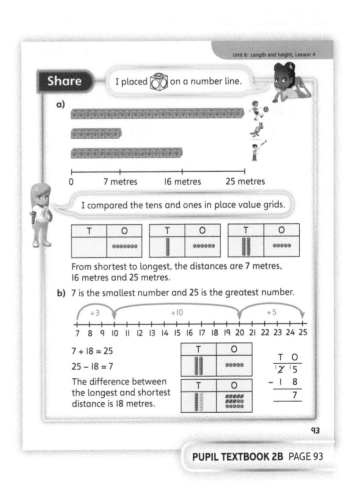

PUPIL TEXTBOOK 2B PAGE 93

121

Think together

Unit 8: Length and height, Lesson 4

WAYS OF WORKING Whole class teacher led (I do, We do, You do)

ASK

- Question **1** : *What does 'greatest' mean – is it the biggest distance or the smallest one?*
- Question **2** : *Does the question tell you exactly how far Martha kicked the ball? What does it tell you?*

IN FOCUS In question **2** , be careful to draw out the point that we cannot tell exactly how far Martha kicked the ball from the information provided. Prompt children to offer other possibilities. Say, for example: *Yes, it could have been 21 metres – but what else could it have been?*

Question **3** requires children to order some 'real' measurements. For measuring feet, children can use 30 cm rulers and can keep their shoes on. For measuring arms and hair length they will need longer rulers or tape measures. Supervision may be needed, especially when children are measuring each other's hair length.

STRENGTHEN If children find it difficult to put a set of three numbers in order, encourage them to check their suggested answers by breaking them into pairs. For example, if a child suggests that three numbers A, B, C are in ascending order, get them to check that A < B and then that B < C.

DEEPEN Challenge children to put sets of four or more numbers in order.

ASSESSMENT CHECKPOINT Assess whether children are able to sequence the numbers correctly (equentially along the number line), and check that they give the list of numbers in the right order (ascending or descending).

ANSWERS

Question **1** : 20 m, 12 m, 5 m

Question **2** : Martha could have kicked the football 21 m, 22 m, 23 m or 24 m.

Question **3** : A set of realistic measurements in ascending order.

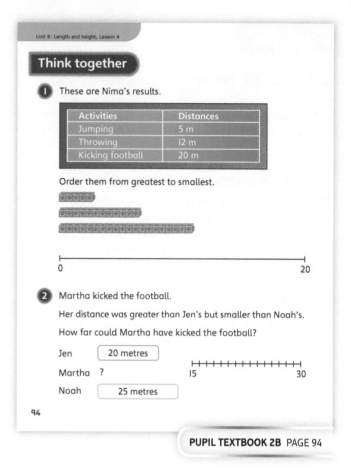

PUPIL TEXTBOOK 2B PAGE 94

PUPIL TEXTBOOK 2B PAGE 95

122

Practice

WAYS OF WORKING Independent thinking

IN FOCUS Question **4** provides an interesting and non-routine challenge. Children need to decide which of the three numbers is in the wrong place, and then find a number that could correctly go in that position. This can be done by pair-wise checking, but the exact logic of deciding which number needs to be changed is not trivial.

STRENGTHEN Ask children to locate the numbers on a number line. This may help them to find the correct answers, but should in any case provide useful diagnostic information.

DEEPEN Deepen understanding by extending question **5** and asking children to find a range of numbers for each box.

ASSESSMENT CHECKPOINT Question **3** summarises much of the key content of this lesson. Check that children can put each of these sets of numbers into order, with or without using a place value grid.

ANSWERS Answers for the **Practice** part of the lesson appear in the separate **Practice and Reflect answer guide**.

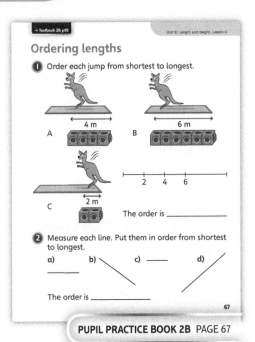

PUPIL PRACTICE BOOK 2B PAGE 67

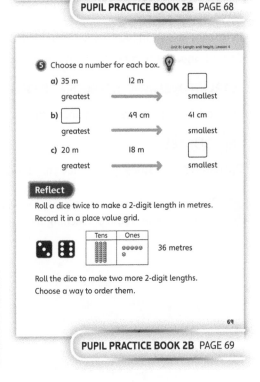

PUPIL PRACTICE BOOK 2B PAGE 68

Reflect

WAYS OF WORKING Pair work

IN FOCUS The **Reflect** part of the lesson requires children to roll a dice to make 2-digit numbers. Some of the sets of numbers generated will be easier to order than others. You could make a note of any interesting examples (for example, sets where the tens digit is repeated or the same number occurs twice) and ask other pairs of children to order them, or discuss them as a class.

ASSESSMENT CHECKPOINT Assess whether children understand that they need to look at the ones digit when comparing numbers with the same tens digit.

ANSWERS Answers for the **Reflect** part of the lesson appear in the separate **Practice and Reflect answer guide**.

After the lesson

- Are children confident in their use of the language used in this lesson – including 'greatest', 'smallest', and so on?
- Can children compare and order 2-digit numbers 'on sight'? Do children still need the help of a place value grid?

PUPIL PRACTICE BOOK 2B PAGE 69

Solving word problems – length

Learning focus

In this lesson, children will use a range of methods to solve word problems involving length and height.

Small steps

→ Previous step: Ordering lengths
→ **This step: Solving word problems – length**
→ Next step: Recognising 2D and 3D shapes

NATIONAL CURRICULUM LINKS

Year 2 Measurement

Solve problems with addition and subtraction using concrete objects and pictorial representations, including those involving numbers, quantities and measures.

ASSESSING MASTERY

Children can select and use appropriate techniques and representations to solve a range of problems involving length and height.

COMMON MISCONCEPTIONS

Some children may find the idea of conversion of length difficult; for example, they may not appreciate that the height of a tower of cubes is the same as the length of the tower when it is laid on its side; and they may not understand that the length of a piece of string remains the same as it is rearranged.

STRENGTHENING UNDERSTANDING

The structures and representations used in this lesson are designed to support children's reasoning and visualisation as they work on the problems. All the models are equally valid; for children who find this work difficult, try varying the representation to see whether another model is better understood.

GOING DEEPER

When working with lengths, bar modelling methods can result in a literal representation of the situation being modelled – a picture of some pieces of string can effectively become a bar model diagram. For more confident children, it may then be only a short step to 'the diagram in your head', where the modelling method becomes a tool for thinking rather than a diagram on paper.

KEY LANGUAGE

In lesson: length, in total, long, bar model, adding, column method, shorter, combined, smaller, difference

Other language to be used by the teacher: height, subtracting, tens, ones

STRUCTURES AND REPRESENTATIONS

Bar models, column method, number lines

RESOURCES

Optional: rulers, string, place value charts, Base 10 equipment, paper strips

 In the eTextbook of this lesson, you will find interactive links to a selection of teaching tools.

Before you teach ⏸

- Would children benefit from additional support, such as prepared paper strips to help them model the calculations, or place value charts to help carry them out?

Discover

WAYS OF WORKING Pair work

ASK

- *Look at the two pieces of string. Which one is longer?*
- *Question ❶ a): What do you need to work out when you are asked: 'How much string is there in total?'*
- *Question ❶ b): Where does the question say these two pieces of string came from?*

IN FOCUS Question ❶ is quite straightforward, but it is important to make sure that children understand what is required. Be careful with the language – note how the word 'string' refers both to the individual pieces ('my string, your string') and the material in general ('how much string'). This could lead to an error in children's thinking – they might think that the answer to question ❶ a) is 'two' – as in, 'there are two strings in total'.

ANSWERS

Question ❶ a): 27 + 34 = 61
There is 61 cm of string in total.

Question ❶ b): There is 19 cm of string left.

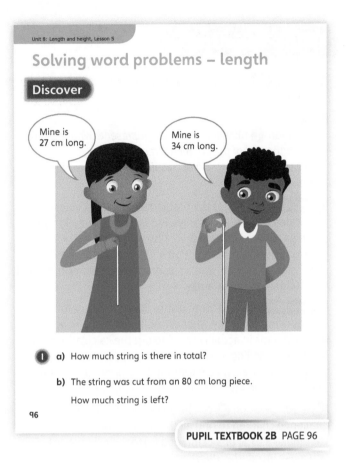

Share

WAYS OF WORKING Whole class, teacher led

ASK

- *Question ❶ a): Why did Ash draw this picture? Did any of you draw a picture like that?*
- *Question ❶ a): Look at the calculation that Astrid did. Who did it the same way? Did you get the same answer?*
- *Question ❶ b): What sort of calculation is needed to work out how much string is left? How do you know?*

IN FOCUS In both parts of the solution, a bar model is used to determine which calculation is needed. The calculation is then carried out using the column method for question ❶ a), and a number line for question ❶ b). Some children may benefit from using a number line to count on for question ❶ a); others may be confident enough to use the column method for both questions.

STRENGTHEN Children who are less confident with the column method may benefit from using a place value grid to help with the calculations.

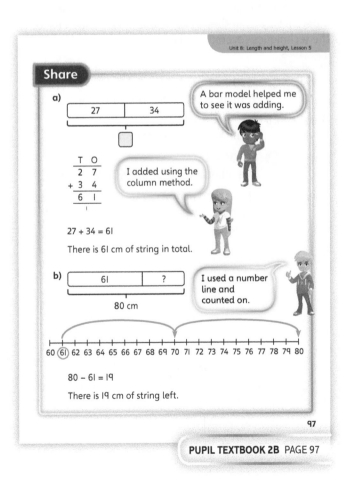

Think together

Whole class teacher led (I do, We do, You do)

ASK

- Question **1** b): *What does '9 cm' represent? What does the bar at the end of the bar model represent?*
- Question **2** : *What sort of calculation do you need to do to answer the question?*

IN FOCUS Notice that the problems here can reasonably be tackled in a variety of ways. For example, question **2** can be answered using either subtraction (45 – 30 = ?) or a 'trial addition' approach (? + 30 = 45). The important thing is that children should have a reasonably efficient approach of which they can make sense.

STRENGTHEN Help children distinguish between problems in modelling (deciding what calculations will be needed) and problems in actually carrying out the calculations. To support modelling, try using physical apparatus, such as paper strips or even actual string. To support calculation, use place value grids and Base 10 equipment.

DEEPEN Question **3** can be generalised quite easily; challenge children to find all the possible pairs of values that make a total of 34 cm. For a further challenge, ask: *Can you make up another question like this?*

ASSESSMENT CHECKPOINT Question **2** provides an opportunity to cover a lot of the key techniques and vocabulary – make sure that children understand the different ways that they could answer this question using the techniques covered in this lesson.

ANSWERS

Question **1** a): 65 – 49 = 16.
There is 16 cm of string left.

Question **1** b): 9 + 7 + 6 = 22.
The string was 22 cm long.

Question **2** : 45 - 30 = 15
The other piece of string is 15 cm long.

Question **3** : The second number is 14. Other examples could be any pair of numbers with a total of 34.

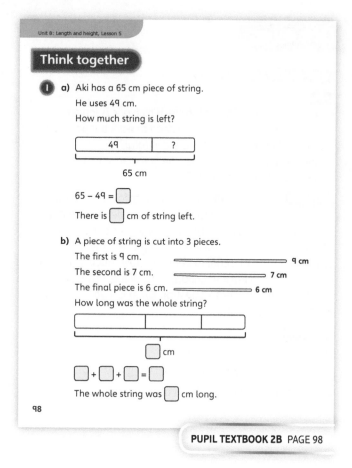

PUPIL TEXTBOOK 2B PAGE 98

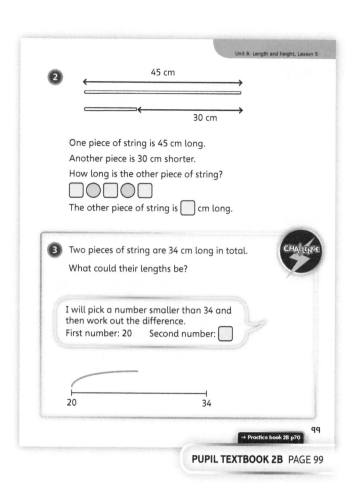

PUPIL TEXTBOOK 2B PAGE 99

Practice

IN FOCUS Question ② involves a substantial amount of reading and interpretation. It may be useful to talk through this question with children, and ask them what calculations will be needed at each stage, and how they will carry them out.

STRENGTHEN To help strengthen understanding, provide place value grids and Base 10 equipment for children who need additional support with the calculations.

DEEPEN Children who are confident in answering question ② could be challenged to write their own similar question, focusing on lengths.

ASSESSMENT CHECKPOINT Remember to distinguish between difficulties that arise at the modelling stage, and those that result from wrong calculations. Question ④ provides a good opportunity to check children's approaches and the thinking behind them. Ask: *Why did you choose to do this calculation? Can you draw a picture to show me?*

ANSWERS Answers for the **Practice** part of the lesson appear in the separate **Practice and Reflect answer guide**.

Reflect

IN FOCUS Some children may need prompting to help them explain the steps they used to answer the **Reflect** question. Challenge children to think of other ways they could have tackled the question.

ASSESSMENT CHECKPOINT Ask the class what strategies they used, both for modelling and for calculation. Check that all children have workable approaches for both aspects.

ANSWERS Answers for the **Reflect** part of the lesson appear in the separate **Practice and Reflect answer guide**.

After the lesson ⏸

- What modelling approaches are children using?
- What calculation approaches are being used? Are children using column methods accurately or are they relying on less efficient approaches, like counting?

Unit 8: Length and height, Lesson 5

→ Textbook 2B p96

Solving word problems – length

① a) Zara is 90 cm tall.

Her younger brother Ellis is 60 cm tall.

How much taller is Zara than Ellis?

Zara is ☐ cm taller than Ellis.

b) Zara's leg is 41 cm long.

Ellis's leg is 27 cm long.

How much shorter is Ellis's leg than Zara's leg?

Ellis's leg is ☐ cm shorter than Zara's leg.

70

PUPIL PRACTICE BOOK 2B PAGE 70

Unit 8: Length and height, Lesson 5

② a) If a badger is 70 cm long and a fox is 18 cm shorter, then the fox is ☐ cm long.

b) If a sheep is 96 cm tall and a dog is 28 cm shorter, then the dog is ☐ cm tall.

③ a) A 20 cm long strip of paper has been cut into two equal pieces.

Each piece of paper is ☐ cm long.

b) A strip of paper has been cut into four equal pieces. Each piece is 5 cm long.

The strip of paper was ☐ cm long.

71

PUPIL PRACTICE BOOK 2B PAGE 71

Unit 8: Length and height, Lesson 5

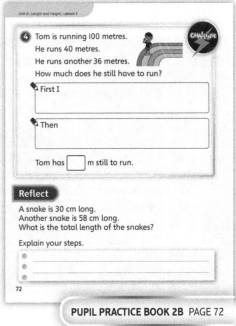

④ Tom is running 100 metres.

He runs 40 metres.

He runs another 36 metres.

How much does he still have to run?

First I

Then

Tom has ☐ m still to run.

Reflect

A snake is 30 cm long.
Another snake is 58 cm long.
What is the total length of the snakes?

Explain your steps.

72

PUPIL PRACTICE BOOK 2B PAGE 72

End of unit check

Don't forget the *Power Maths* unit assessment grid on p26.

WAYS OF WORKING Group work – adult led

IN FOCUS This **End of unit check** covers all of the main skills developed in the unit, including measuring with a ruler, choosing appropriate units and ordering and comparing lengths.

Think!

WAYS OF WORKING Pair work

IN FOCUS This activity focuses on the skill of reading a scale correctly.

Children could explain that the pencil is not properly positioned on the ruler because the end should be aligned with the zero on the scale.

Other children could explain how the length of the pencil can be calculated from the picture by treating the scale as a number line and finding the difference between 8 and 2: 8 – 2 = 6 cm.

ANSWERS AND COMMENTARY Children who master the work in this unit will be able to estimate, measure and compare the lengths or heights of a range of objects, using simple measuring equipment, such as rulers, metre sticks and tape measures, and appropriate standard units (centimetres or metres). Children will be aware of some of the common practical difficulties that arise when measuring, such as not starting at zero when using a ruler or failing to deal with flexible objects consistently, and will know how to avoid these difficulties.

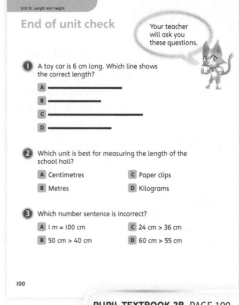

PUPIL TEXTBOOK 2B PAGE 100

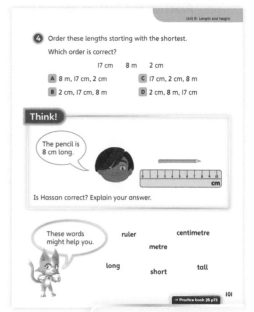

PUPIL TEXTBOOK 2B PAGE 101

Q	A	WRONG ANSWERS AND MISCONCEPTIONS	STRENGTHENING UNDERSTANDING
1	D	Any incorrect answer here might indicate that children are struggling with using a scale. Choosing A would suggest that children are aligning the start of the line with the 1 cm mark on the ruler.	The work in this unit involves a combination of mathematical knowledge and practical skills and experience. Make sure that children continue to get plenty of practical experience of estimating, measuring and comparing lengths using centimetres and metres as appropriate. Look for opportunities to build this kind of activity into other parts of the school calendar, such as in art or sports.
2	B	Choosing A would indicate that children are not aware of the relative sizes of centimetres and metres.	
3	C	Choosing A would indicate that children do not know that 100 cm makes 1 m.	
4	B	Choosing D shows that children have ignored the units and ordered the numbers.	

My journal

WAYS OF WORKING Independent thinking

ANSWERS AND COMMENTARY

Hassan is wrong because the end of the pencil is not on 0. If the pencil is moved so that the end is on 0, the other end would be on 6, which means that the pencil is 6 cm long.

Children who simply say that Hassan is correct do not appreciate the importance of starting from zero. Where children identify the mistake that Hassan has made, look for responses that go on to find the correct answer. These could describe a physical procedure, such as moving the pencil so that its end sits on 0, or may use the scale as a number line and calculate the difference between 8 and 2.

PUPIL PRACTICE BOOK 2B PAGE 73

Power check

WAYS OF WORKING Independent thinking

ASK

- *Were you able to measure the length and height of things accurately before the lesson? How do you feel about this now? Do you think that you are better at it?*

Power play

WAYS OF WORKING Pair work or small groups

IN FOCUS This activity provides an opportunity to use a range of physical resources to reinforce the idea of the length of one metre. Give each pair of children a metre stick and challenge them to assemble a range of resources from around the classroom that make a total approximate length of one metre.

ANSWERS AND COMMENTARY Once all pairs of children have successfully made at least one collection of objects with a total approximate length of one metre, ask everyone to leave their materials in place and encourage children to look each other's work. Ask: *Which pair got closest to a metre? Which pair used the most objects? Which pair used the fewest objects?*

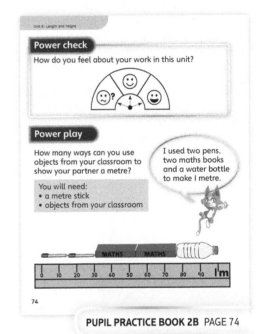

PUPIL PRACTICE BOOK 2B PAGE 74

After the unit ⏸

- Were children confident using the key language encountered in this unit?
- Did children become confident using a ruler to measure small objects in centimetres?
- Were children confident in choosing appropriate units (either metres or centimetres) to estimate heights and lengths or to measure a range of objects?

Strengthen and **Deepen** activities for this unit can be found in the *Power Maths* online subscription.

Unit 9
Properties of shapes

Mastery Expert tip! "There is a lot of topic-specific key language in this lesson. I found that displaying a list of this language in the classroom and encouraging children to contribute to it helped them to learn and understand the language so that they could use it during whole class and peer discussions."

Don't forget to watch the Unit 9 video!

WHY THIS UNIT IS IMPORTANT

This unit focuses on the properties of 2D and 3D shapes. Children will learn to describe and sort shapes based on the shapes' mathematical properties, using the correct terminology. Although this is the first unit covering geometry in Year 2, children have experience of recognising, naming, describing and sorting 2D and 3D shapes from Unit 5 in Year 1.

Children will also draw on their counting skills and their ability to compare and order numbers. In this unit, children will learn to describe and categorise shapes based on their number of sides, vertices, edges and faces.

WHERE THIS UNIT FITS

→ Unit 8: Length and height

→ **Unit 9: Properties of shapes**

→ Unit 10: Fractions

Children should already be able to recognise and name familiar 2D and 3D shapes. Children will be familiar with using the word 'face' to describe a flat surface of a 3D shape and they will be able to describe the shape of the faces. Children have also experienced identifying and describing repeating patterns using 2D and 3D shapes.

Before they start this unit, it is expected that children:

• know how to distinguish between 2D and 3D shapes
• understand that shapes are categorised based on specific properties
• know the names of common 2D and 3D shapes and some of their properties.

ASSESSING MASTERY

Children who have mastered this unit will be able to use key language (such as faces, edges and vertices) fluently when describing 2D and 3D shapes. Children will be able to sort shapes in different ways based on different mathematical properties and create both repeating and symmetrical patterns involving shapes of increasing complexity.

COMMON MISCONCEPTIONS	STRENGTHENING UNDERSTANDING	GOING DEEPER
Children may confuse key language, such as identifying edges as vertices.	Give children concrete 2D and 3D shapes to handle and practise counting the different properties. Encourage children to contribute to a classroom display of the definitions of the different terms.	Ask children to explore what happens to the number of faces, vertices, sides or edges when they join shapes together. Prompt children to look for patterns and to suggest explanations for what they observe.
Children may miscount the number of edges, vertices, faces or sides.	Give children dry-wipe markers and concrete 3D shapes so that children can mark off a specific property as they count it. Ask children to record the number of each property and add it to the classroom display so that they can refer to it in future.	

WAYS OF WORKING

Use these pages to introduce the unit and to prompt children to recall what they already know about 2D and 3D shapes. Focus on the key vocabulary and discuss the potential meanings of this vocabulary. This will indicate what children already know and expose any misconceptions that they may have about the properties of shapes.

STRUCTURES AND REPRESENTATIONS

Although there are no set mathematical structures and representations in this unit, 2D and 3D shapes should be used in this unit.

KEY LANGUAGE

There is some key language that children will need to know as part of the learning in this unit:

→ circle, semicircle

→ oval, triangle, square, rectangle, quadrilateral

→ polygon, pentagon, hexagon, octagon

→ sphere, hemisphere

→ cone, ovoid, cylinder

→ triangle-based pyramid, square-based pyramid, pentagon-based pyramid, hexagon-based pyramid

→ cube, cuboid

→ triangular prism, pentagonal prism, hexagonal prism

→ 2D, 3D

→ properties

→ side, vertex, vertices, edge, face

→ pattern

→ symmetry, symmetrical, line of symmetry

→ curved surface

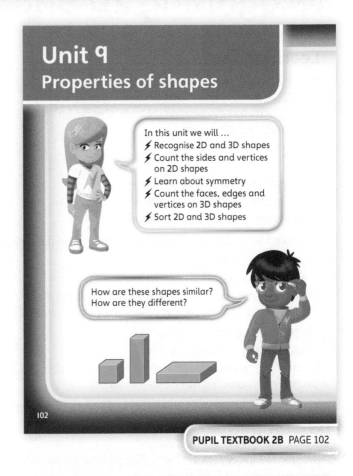

PUPIL TEXTBOOK 2B PAGE 102

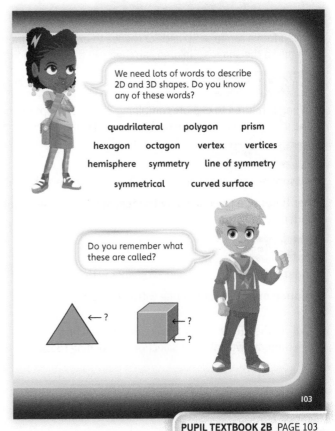

PUPIL TEXTBOOK 2B PAGE 103

Recognising 2D and 3D shapes

Learning focus

In this lesson, children will recognise and name 2D and 3D shapes and make links between them. They will begin to identify common features of different types of 2D and 3D shapes.

Small steps

→ Previous step: Solving word problems – length
→ **This step: Recognising 2D and 3D shapes**
→ Next step: Drawing 2D shapes

NATIONAL CURRICULUM LINKS

Year 2 Geometry – Properties of Shape

Compare and sort common 2D and 3D shapes and everyday objects.

ASSESSING MASTERY

Children can name and describe a range of 2D and 3D shapes, identifying what features determine the type of shape and any similarities and differences across different types of shapes. Children will begin to describe the faces of 3D shapes.

COMMON MISCONCEPTIONS

Children may misname a shape when its orientation changes. Hold up different shapes and rotate them. Ask:
• *How has it changed? Is it now a different shape?*

Children may apply names of 2D shapes to 3D shapes. Hold up a cube and ask:
• *What do you call this shape? What can you tell me about it?*

Hold up a square next to it and ask:
• *Are these the same? How are they different? What do you call these shapes?*

STRENGTHENING UNDERSTANDING

Give children a range of 2D and 3D shapes to explore and manipulate. Provide corresponding name labels that children have to match to the shapes. Children can then use these as a point of reference throughout the lesson.

GOING DEEPER

Challenge children to explore combining 2D or 3D shapes to create new shapes. Discuss how children know what type of shape it is so that they begin to think carefully about common features.

KEY LANGUAGE

In lesson: rectangle, square, quadrilateral, triangle, cuboid, 2D, 3D

Other language to be used by the teacher: right angle, cone, prism, polygons, pyramid, sphere, cube, oblong, cylinder, circle

RESOURCES

Mandatory: a range of 2D and 3D shapes with labels

Optional: materials for printing with 3D shapes

 In the eTextbook of this lesson, you will find interactive links to a selection of teaching tools.

Before you teach

• What do children already know about 2D and 3D shapes?
• How can you reinforce the vocabulary used in this lesson?
• How will you support children in identifying the key properties for classifying 2D and 3D shapes?

Discover

WAYS OF WORKING Pair work

ASK

- *What different shapes can you see?*
- *How did you know which shapes were squares?*
- *How is the square the same as or different from the oblong?*

IN FOCUS This part of the lesson reinforces the concept that size, colour and orientation are not important when naming a 2D shape. Identify misconceptions that children may have when naming a shape that has been rotated. For example, children may see the red square in the middle picture as a 'diamond'.

ANSWERS

Question ① a): This is Mia's picture.

Question ① b): This is Sunil's picture.

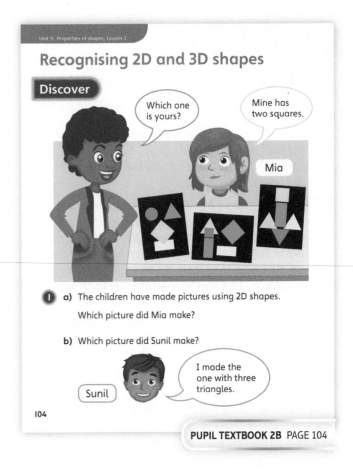

Recognising 2D and 3D shapes

Discover

Which one is yours?

Mine has two squares.

Mia

① a) The children have made pictures using 2D shapes.

Which picture did Mia make?

b) Which picture did Sunil make?

Sunil

I made the one with three triangles.

104

PUPIL TEXTBOOK 2B PAGE 104

Share

WAYS OF WORKING Whole class teacher led

ASK

- *How do the shapes differ?*
- *What features can we ignore when naming the shapes?*
- *What features are important when naming shapes?*

IN FOCUS Sparks' first comment introduces the idea that there is a family of shapes known as quadrilaterals. This may be the first time that children have come across this term, so it is important to ensure they understand what constitutes a quadrilateral.

Sparks also makes the distinction between the two types of quadrilateral in the pictures. Children may have the misconception that a square is not a rectangle. Explain to children that a rectangle has four sides with four right angles and that there are two types of quadrilateral in the pictures: a square rectangle and an oblong rectangle. Discuss how the shapes are different.

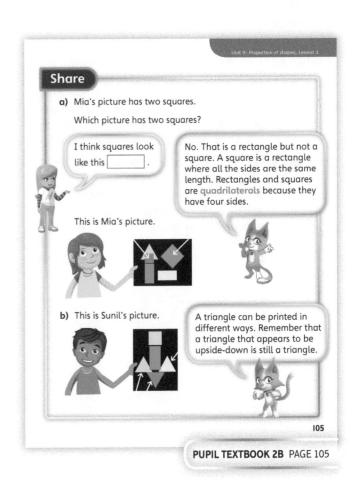

Share

a) Mia's picture has two squares.

Which picture has two squares?

I think squares look like this ☐ .

No. That is a rectangle but not a square. A square is a rectangle where all the sides are the same length. Rectangles and squares are quadrilaterals because they have four sides.

This is Mia's picture.

b) This is Sunil's picture.

A triangle can be printed in different ways. Remember that a triangle that appears to be upside-down is still a triangle.

105

PUPIL TEXTBOOK 2B PAGE 105

Think together

WAYS OF WORKING Whole class teacher led (I do, We do, You do)

ASK

- Question ❷ : *Is there more than one possibility for printing each shape? How can you be sure you have found them all?*
- Question ❸ : *What shapes can you use to draw a rectangle? What shapes can you not use?*

IN FOCUS Questions ❷ and ❸ prompt children to look at the faces of the 3D shapes. Although the term 'face' is not used, children are looking specifically at describing the types of faces they can see. Children will realise that different 3D shapes may share the same shaped face and that, as a result, there is more than one way to answer the questions.

STRENGTHEN Provide 3D shapes for children to draw around or print with in order to help them identify the shapes of different faces.

DEEPEN Ask children if they can create different 2D shapes by combining faces. For example, ask: *Can you create an oblong rectangle using just a cube? Can you use the triangle face of a pyramid to create a four-sided 2D shape?*

ASSESSMENT CHECKPOINT Question ❶ will show whether children can identify rectangles and whether they understand that squares are a special type of rectangle.

ANSWERS

Question ❶ : There are 7 rectangles in this picture (2 squares and 5 oblongs).

Question ❷ : The circle can be printed using the cylinder. The square can be printed using the cube, cuboid or square-based pyramid. The oblong can be printed using the cuboid or triangular prism. The triangle can be printed using the triangular prism or square-based pyramid.

Question ❸ : The cube can produce a square. The cuboid can produce a square or an oblong. The square-based pyramid can produce a square or a triangle. The triangular prism can produce a triangle or an oblong. The cone can produce a circle. The cylinder can produce a circle. The sphere cannot be used to produce a 2D shape.

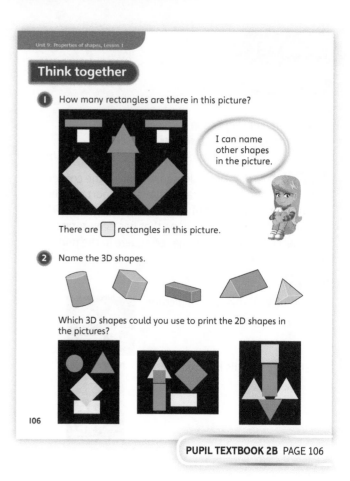

PUPIL TEXTBOOK 2B PAGE 106

PUPIL TEXTBOOK 2B PAGE 107

Practice

WAYS OF WORKING Pair work

IN FOCUS Question ④ requires children to reason about which child created which picture based on limited information. They have to read all the descriptions from the children in order to find a suitable starting point. The first child's comment may highlight if any children in your class have the misconception that a square is not a rectangle. The last two children's pictures are the easiest to identify as they clearly have only one possibility each. However, some children may think the ovals and semicircles in picture one are circles because of the curved side.

STRENGTHEN Provide children with a range of 2D and 3D shapes with name labels as prompts. For question ③, children could use the 3D shapes to draw around to help identify the shapes of the faces.

DEEPEN Ask children to create their own picture using 2D shapes. Children can describe their picture to a partner who then has to replicate it behind a screen. Children can then compare pictures to see how accurate they were in giving and following instructions.

ASSESSMENT CHECKPOINT Question ① will determine whether children are able to identify triangles and squares correctly, while question ② will determine whether children can identify cuboids, pyramids and spheres correctly. Question ③ will determine whether children can identify the shapes of the faces of a cylinder and a triangle-based pyramid (tetrahedron). Question ④ will determine whether children can correctly identify rectangles, triangles, circles and squares.

ANSWERS Answers for the **Practice** part of the lesson appear in the separate **Practice and Reflect answer guide**.

Reflect

WAYS OF WORKING Pair work

IN FOCUS This activity encourages children to identify 2D and 3D shapes in the real world. In order to do this, children have to focus on the shapes' mathematical properties rather than on their aesthetic or contextual characteristics. This activity could be turned into a game of 'I spy' where one child says the name of the shape they can see and the other child has to point to it.

ASSESSMENT CHECKPOINT This activity will determine whether children are able to identify and name a range of 2D and 3D shapes.

ANSWERS Answers for the **Reflect** part of the lesson appear in the separate **Practice and Reflect answer guide**.

After the lesson ⏸

- Are children confident naming 2D and 3D shapes?
- Are children beginning to use the mathematical properties when describing shapes?
- How can you display the shapes and vocabulary in the classroom in the next lesson to reinforce children's understanding?

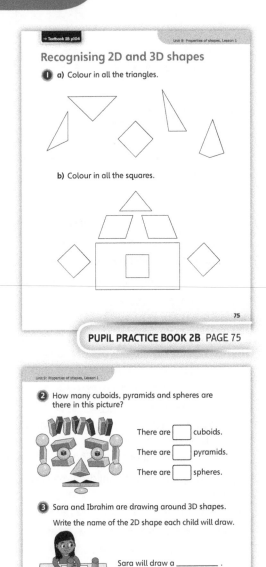

→ Textbook 2B p104   Unit 9: Properties of shapes, Lesson 1

Recognising 2D and 3D shapes

① a) Colour in all the triangles.

b) Colour in all the squares.

75

PUPIL PRACTICE BOOK 2B PAGE 75

Unit 9: Properties of shapes, Lesson 1

② How many cuboids, pyramids and spheres are there in this picture?

There are ☐ cuboids.

There are ☐ pyramids.

There are ☐ spheres.

③ Sara and Ibrahim are drawing around 3D shapes.

Write the name of the 2D shape each child will draw.

Sara will draw a _____ .

Ibrahim will draw a _____ .

76

PUPIL PRACTICE BOOK 2B PAGE 76

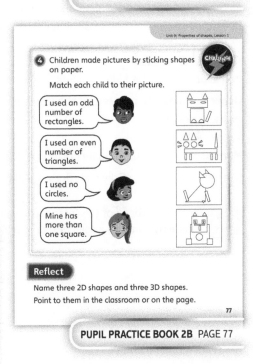

Unit 9: Properties of shapes, Lesson 1

④ Children made pictures by sticking shapes on paper.   CHALLENGE

Match each child to their picture.

I used an odd number of rectangles.

I used an even number of triangles.

I used no circles.

Mine has more than one square.

Reflect

Name three 2D shapes and three 3D shapes.

Point to them in the classroom or on the page.

77

PUPIL PRACTICE BOOK 2B PAGE 77

Drawing 2D shapes

Learning focus

In this lesson, children will apply what they have learned about the properties of shapes in order to accurately draw 2D shapes.

Small steps

→ Previous step: Recognising 2D and 3D shapes
→ **This step: Drawing 2D shapes**
→ Next step: Counting sides on 2D shapes

NATIONAL CURRICULUM LINKS

Year 2 Geometry – Properties of Shape

Identify and describe the properties of 2D shapes, including the number of sides and line symmetry in a vertical line.

ASSESSING MASTERY

Children can accurately draw triangles, squares and oblongs, identifying and including the properties of these shapes. They can create different types of triangle, recognising the need for three straight lines only, and different types of rectangle, recognising the need for four straight lines and four right angles.

COMMON MISCONCEPTIONS

When drawing triangles, children may not recognise irregular triangles as triangles. Show children an equilateral and a scalene triangle and ask:

• *What is the same about these shapes? What is different about them? Are they both triangles?*

When drawing rectangles, children may not realise the need for four right angles. Show children a rectangle and a trapezium and ask:

• *Are they both rectangles? What is the same about these shapes? What is different about them?*

STRENGTHENING UNDERSTANDING

Children may need to have shapes to draw around first. Ask children to place dots on the corners (children will be introduced to the term vertices in Lesson 4) so that they can see how the shape is formed. Children could then use art straws to recreate the shapes using sticky tack on the vertices. Not all 'rectangles' created in this way will have accurate right angles, so be on hand to discuss what makes a rectangle a special type of quadrilateral.

GOING DEEPER

Children could combine 2D shapes to create new ones. Ask children to explore joining squares or triangles to create rectangles and other quadrilaterals. Help children to notice that they can only make a true rectangle by joining two matching rectangles or two matching right-angled triangles.

KEY LANGUAGE

In lesson: 2D, square, sides, triangle, polygons, rectangle

Other language to be used by the teacher: oblong

RESOURCES

Mandatory: 2D shapes, square dotted paper, squared paper, plain paper, rulers

Optional: art straws, sticky tack, dry-wipe markers, isometric paper

 In the eTextbook of this lesson, you will find interactive links to a selection of teaching tools.

Before you teach

• Are children secure in recognising the properties of rectangles and triangles?
• How can you reinforce understanding of what is required for a square, oblong and rectangle?
• What resources and prompts could you use to support understanding?

Discover

WAYS OF WORKING Pair work

ASK

- *What shapes can you see? How do you know?*
- *Why are the girl's shapes not accurate?*
- *How would you draw a shape more accurately?*

IN FOCUS This part of the lesson highlights that an approximate representation of a 2D shape is not adequate. The shapes drawn do not have straight sides and they do not all join to create vertices. Children may see the top two shapes as squares, even though the sides are not of equal length. It is important to show that precision is needed in order to draw an accurate representation of a 2D shape.

ANSWERS

Question ❶ a): Children must draw a shape with four straight sides of the same length and with four right angles, using a ruler and squared paper.

Question ❶ b): Children must draw a shape with three straight sides and three vertices, using a ruler.

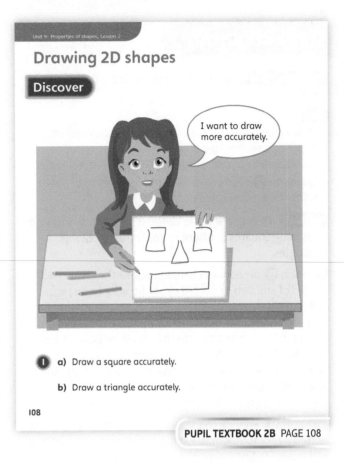

Drawing 2D shapes

Discover

I want to draw more accurately.

❶ a) Draw a square accurately.

b) Draw a triangle accurately.

108

PUPIL TEXTBOOK 2B PAGE 108

Share

WAYS OF WORKING Whole class teacher led

ASK

- *How do the squared paper and ruler help?*
- *Question ❶ a): How can you measure the sides of the square to ensure they are of equal length? How do you know your shape has four right angles?*
- *Question ❶ b): Is that the only way to draw a triangle?*

IN FOCUS This section introduces the term 'polygon'. Sparks' comment informs us that all sides of a polygon have to be straight. Children can now differentiate between those 2D shapes that are polygons and those that are not.

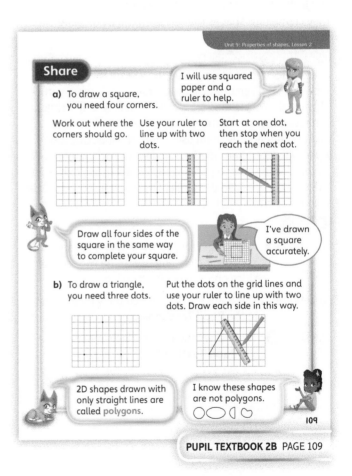

Share

I will use squared paper and a ruler to help.

a) To draw a square, you need four corners.

Work out where the corners should go.

Use your ruler to line up with two dots.

Start at one dot, then stop when you reach the next dot.

Draw all four sides of the square in the same way to complete your square.

I've drawn a square accurately.

b) To draw a triangle, you need three dots.

Put the dots on the grid lines and use your ruler to line up with two dots. Draw each side in this way.

2D shapes drawn with only straight lines are called **polygons**.

I know these shapes are not polygons.

109

PUPIL TEXTBOOK 2B PAGE 109

Think together

Whole class teacher led (I do, We do, You do)

ASK

- *Which paper makes it easier to draw polygons: squared paper or square dotted paper?*
- *Question ❶ : Is it possible to draw a different rectangle?*
- *Question ❷ : Can you draw any other types of triangles using the square dotted paper?*

IN FOCUS Question ❶ asks children to use their knowledge of drawing squares in **Share** to apply this to oblong rectangles.

Question ❸ b) requires children to draw the shapes without the aid of squared or dotted paper. In order to do this, children have to draw on their learning of measurement from Unit 8 in order to accurately measure the lengths of the sides. Be on hand to help children draw perpendicular sides for the rectangles, perhaps using a right-angled object. For the isosceles triangles, help children find the midpoint of the base and create a perpendicular line, so they can then find where the other equal sides meet.

STRENGTHEN Provide children with laminated squared and dotted paper for them to explore creating squares, oblongs and triangles. Encourage children to identify the shapes they have drawn and describe their properties.

DEEPEN Ask children to draw a square. Can they draw a single line to create two new shapes that are identical? Can they create new shapes that are identical by drawing two lines?

ASSESSMENT CHECKPOINT Question ❶ will determine whether children recognise the mathematical properties of a rectangle and can draw them accurately with some vertices already given. Question ❷ will determine whether children can recognise the mathematical properties of triangles and accurately copy them using dotted paper. Question ❸ a) will determine whether children can accurately copy shapes using squared paper. Question ❸ b) will determine whether children can use a ruler to accurately copy squares, rectangles and triangles.

ANSWERS

Question ❶ : A rectangle four squares by two squares; a square, or a rectangle with the two shorter sides one diagonal square long.

Question ❷ : The triangles should accurately match those in the **Pupil Textbook**.

Question ❸ : The shapes should accurately match those in the **Pupil Textbook**.

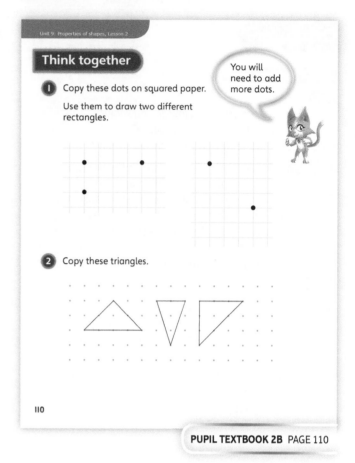

PUPIL TEXTBOOK 2B PAGE 110

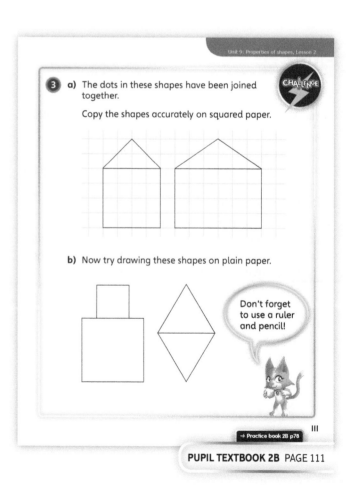

PUPIL TEXTBOOK 2B PAGE 111

Practice

WAYS OF WORKING Independent thinking

IN FOCUS Question ③ asks children to copy triangles without squared paper, so they are likely to need support getting the angles and distances accurate. Question ④ asks children to draw different squares. In order for the squares to be different, they have to be different sizes. Some children may think that positioning the square in a different place on the grid will create a different square. It is also possible to create different squares that are rotated from the horizontal. Some children may overlook these as they are used to squares being presented horizontally.

STRENGTHEN Provide 2D shapes as a reference for children. Distribute laminated versions of the problems so that children can attempt them using dry-wipe markers and can correct and adapt what they do easily.

DEEPEN Provide children with a similar version of question ④ but with isometric paper. Challenge children to create different triangles, rectangles and other quadrilaterals. If children say they have found a square, help them to check – it is more likely to be a rectangle!

ASSESSMENT CHECKPOINT Question ① will determine whether children are able to identify a polygon when presented with only the vertices. In question ②, children must add the final vertex in order to complete each rectangle. Question ③ will determine whether children are able to accurately measure and copy triangles. Question ④ will determine whether children are able to accurately draw squares of different sizes and orientations.

ANSWERS Answers for the **Practice** part of the lesson appear in the separate **Practice and Reflect answer guide**.

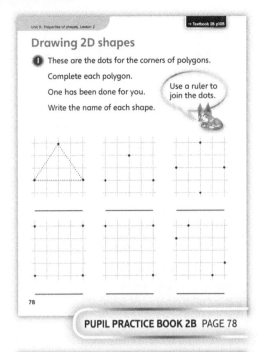

PUPIL PRACTICE BOOK 2B PAGE 78

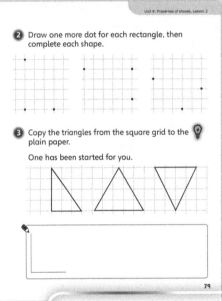

PUPIL PRACTICE BOOK 2B PAGE 79

Reflect

WAYS OF WORKING Pair work

IN FOCUS This section requires children to think carefully about how a shape is drawn in order to give clear instructions, which they can then try on a partner. The limited number of instructions prompts children to think about how to accurately locate each vertex of the shape.

ASSESSMENT CHECKPOINT This section will determine whether children are able to accurately identify the location of each vertex in relation to another.

ANSWERS Answers for the **Reflect** part of the lesson appear in the separate **Practice and Reflect answer guide**.

After the lesson ⏸

- Were children able to accurately draw the required shapes?
- Were children accurate in drawing the sides and angles of the shapes?
- What challenges did children face when drawing the shapes and how can you help them overcome those challenges?

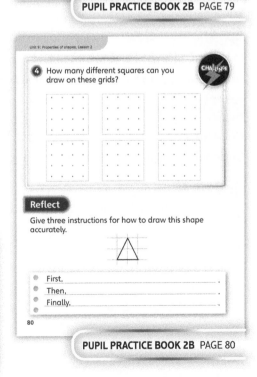

PUPIL PRACTICE BOOK 2B PAGE 80

Counting sides on 2D shapes

Learning focus

In this lesson, children will count the number of sides on 2D shapes and will learn to use this knowledge to categorise different shapes.

Small steps

→ Previous step: Drawing 2D shapes
→ **This step: Counting sides on 2D shapes**
→ Next step: Counting vertices on 2D shapes

NATIONAL CURRICULUM LINKS

Year 2 Geometry – Properties of Shape

Identify and describe the properties of 2D shapes, including the number of sides and line symmetry in a vertical line.

ASSESSING MASTERY

Children can identify how many sides a 2D shape has and can use this information to categorise the shape. Children will be able to name and sort irregular polygons by counting the number of sides.

COMMON MISCONCEPTIONS

Children may miscount the number of sides due to either being unsystematic in their approach to counting or losing track of where they started counting. Ask:

• *How will you ensure that you count all the sides only once?*

Children may misname shapes if they are irregular, particularly if one of the internal angles is a reflex angle. Show children some irregular polygons and ask:

• *What shape is this? How do you know? How many sides does it have?*

STRENGTHENING UNDERSTANDING

Provide a selection of regular and irregular 2D shapes. Work with children to sort them into sorting hoops by counting the number of sides. Children could mark which side they start with using a dry-wipe marker in order to aid their counting. Encourage children to touch or mark each side as they count it. Support children in writing labels for each group.

GOING DEEPER

Using pattern shapes, children explore what happens to the number of sides when they combine two of the same shape. Do they notice a pattern? Why do they think the number of sides changes the way that it does? Is it the same pattern for all the shapes? What happens if they combine two different shapes?

KEY LANGUAGE

In lesson: sides, 2D, corners, pentagon, hexagon, quadrilateral

Other language to be used by the teacher: triangle, square, oblong, rectangle, polygon

RESOURCES

Mandatory: regular and irregular 2D shapes, sorting hoops, pattern shapes, rulers

Optional: dry-wipe markers, sticks, art straws, sticky notes

 In the eTextbook of this lesson, you will find interactive links to a selection of teaching tools.

Before you teach

• Do children need support to reliably count the sides of 2D shapes?
• Are children secure in recognising different triangles, squares and oblongs?
• Where could you include practical activities in this lesson?

Discover

Pair work

ASK

- *Can you name any of the shapes?*
- *Can you order the shapes by number of sides? What do you notice?*
- *What shapes do you know that also have four sides?*

IN FOCUS This part of the lesson prompts children to focus on the property of 'number of sides'. Children may immediately recognise certain shapes, particularly regular polygons, without the need to count the sides. However, the number of sides of a 2D shape is a crucial element in determining the type of shape, especially when the shape is not instantly recognisable.

ANSWERS

Question ❶ a): Jess will use 5 different coloured pens.

Question ❶ b): No. Jess has enough pens for four of the shapes, but she does not have enough pens to draw the hexagon.

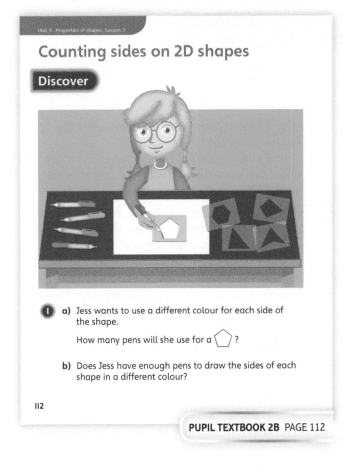

PUPIL TEXTBOOK 2B PAGE 112

Share

Whole class teacher led

ASK

- *Question ❶ a): Did you count the sides in the same way as Astrid? Why do you think she counted the sides in the way that she did?*
- *Question ❶ b): Look at the two shapes with four sides. How are they the same? How are they different?*

IN FOCUS This part of the lesson illustrates that the number of sides a shape has determines what type of shape it is. The illustrated shapes with numbered sides highlight how we can reliably count the number of sides by having a systematic approach. This section also introduces children to pentagons and hexagons.

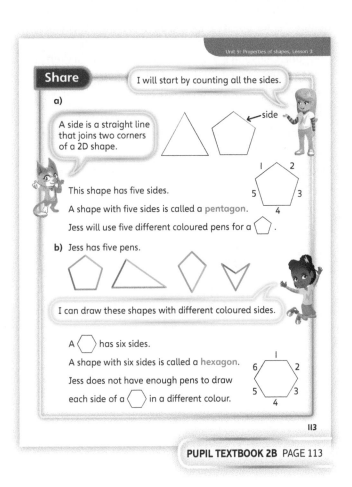

PUPIL TEXTBOOK 2B PAGE 113

Think together

WAYS OF WORKING Whole class teacher led (I do, We do, You do)

ASK

- Question ❶: *What different shapes can you see? How do you know what the shapes are?*
- Question ❷: *How would you sort the shapes into those with more than four sides and those with fewer than four sides?*
- Question ❸: *Did you find any shapes difficult to identify?*

IN FOCUS Question ❸ is a collection of irregular polygons. Children will not be able to immediately identify the shapes and will therefore have to count the sides in order to name them. The blue hexagon and the reflex kite both have reflex internal angles. Some children may find it challenging to identify all the sides in these shapes as they are used to shapes having only acute, right angle and obtuse internal angles.

STRENGTHEN Ask children to use sticks or straws to replicate the shapes in question ❷. Encourage children to make different triangles, quadrilaterals, pentagons and hexagons using the sticks or straws.

DEEPEN Ask children to walk around the classroom or school and label the different polygons they can see using sticky notes. See if they can find examples of triangles, quadrilaterals, pentagons and hexagons.

ASSESSMENT CHECKPOINT Question ❶ will determine whether children can identify both regular and irregular quadrilaterals. Question ❷ will determine whether children can accurately count the number of sides of different polygons. Question ❸ will determine whether children are able to correctly identify the type of polygon based on the number of sides.

ANSWERS

Question ❶ : The quadrilaterals are square, oblong, kite and reflex kite.

Question ❷ : The shapes have 3 sides, 4 sides, 5 sides and 5 sides respectively.

Question ❸ : From left to right, top to bottom, the number of sides are: 4, 3, 3, 5, 4, 6, 4, 4.

There are four quadrilaterals (the green, yellow and two pink shapes).

There is one pentagon (purple shape).

There is one hexagon (dark blue shape).

PUPIL TEXTBOOK 2B PAGE 114

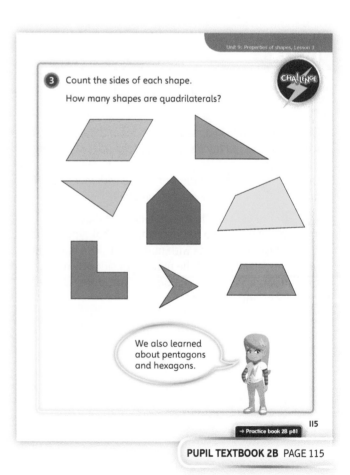

PUPIL TEXTBOOK 2B PAGE 115

142

Practice

WAYS OF WORKING Independent thinking

IN FOCUS Question ❹ relates properties of shapes to multiplication and division. These are word problems that require children to draw on their learning from Unit 5 and Unit 6. The main challenge here is identifying what operation is required in order to solve the problem. Using practical materials such as straws may help support children in understanding what they need to do in order to find the solution.

STRENGTHEN For question ❷, suggest that children mark each side as they count it and write the number of sides next to each shape.

Give children a laminated version of question ❸. They can then use dry-wipe pens to practise joining the vertices before completing the drawings in their books. For question ❹, provide straws so that children can carry out the task practically. If necessary, remind children of the learning they did in Unit 5 and Unit 6.

DEEPEN Give children an A4 piece of paper. Ask them to draw a number of lines randomly across the paper so that they intersect to make different types of polygons. They then have to colour all the triangles green, the quadrilaterals blue, the pentagons red and the hexagons yellow.

ASSESSMENT CHECKPOINT Question ❶ will determine whether children can correctly count the number of sides of different polygons with a familiar representation and name them. Question ❷ will determine whether children can count the sides and reason about unfamiliar irregular polygons. Question ❸ will determine whether children can draw sides to join vertices and count the number of sides. Question ❹ will determine whether children can apply their knowledge of 2D shapes, multiplication and division to solve problems.

ANSWERS Answers for the **Practice** part of the lesson appear in the separate **Practice and Reflect answer guide**.

Reflect

WAYS OF WORKING Pair work

IN FOCUS This section asks children to group the shapes by counting the number of sides and then justify their decisions. The irregular nature of the polygons forces children to physically count the sides. They have to be systematic in their counting to ensure it is reliable.

ASSESSMENT CHECKPOINT This section will determine whether children are able to count the number of sides accurately and whether they understand that polygons are categorised by how may sides they have.

ANSWERS Answers for the **Reflect** part of the lesson appear in the separate **Practice and Reflect answer guide**.

After the lesson ⏸

- Did children find it challenging to identify irregular and unfamiliar polygons?
- How successful were the practical opportunities that you provided for children?
- Are children secure in understanding that polygons are categorised by the number of sides?

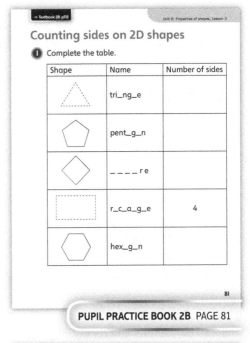

PUPIL PRACTICE BOOK 2B PAGE 81

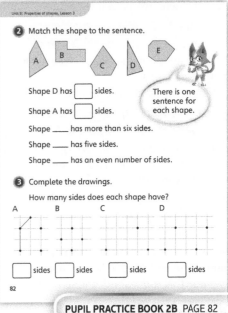

PUPIL PRACTICE BOOK 2B PAGE 82

PUPIL PRACTICE BOOK 2B PAGE 83

Counting vertices on 2D shapes

Learning focus

In this lesson, children will learn that vertices are points where two or more sides of a polygon meet. Children will learn that they can classify shapes by the number of vertices.

Small steps

→ Previous step: Counting sides on 2D shapes
→ **This step: Counting vertices on 2D shapes**
→ Next step: Finding lines of symmetry

NATIONAL CURRICULUM LINKS

Year 2 Geometry – Properties of Shape

Identify and describe the properties of 2D shapes, including the number of sides and line symmetry in a vertical line.

ASSESSING MASTERY

Children can identify and count the vertices of a variety of regular and irregular polygons. Children understand that the corner where two sides meet is called a vertex and that they can categorise shapes by the number of vertices.

COMMON MISCONCEPTIONS

Children may not identify a vertex if it is a reflex internal angle. Show children a quadrilateral with a reflex internal angle on a peg board and ask:

• *How many sides does this shape have? What is a vertex? How many vertices does this shape have?*

STRENGTHENING UNDERSTANDING

Take children outside with a large loop of string. Ask children to use their ankles to create vertices. Can they make a triangle, quadrilateral, pentagon and hexagon? Ask: *How many ankles are needed for each shape? How many sides does each shape have? How many vertices?*

GOING DEEPER

Using pattern shapes, ask children to explore what happens to the number of vertices when they combine two of the same shape. If children did this activity in the last lesson exploring the number of sides, can they predict what will happen to the number of vertices and justify their predictions? Do they notice a pattern? Why do they think the number of vertices changes the way that it does? Is it the same pattern for all the shapes? What happens if they combine two different shapes?

KEY LANGUAGE

In lesson: square, corners, **vertex**, **vertices**, triangle, hexagon, sides, pentagon

Other language to be used by the teacher: oblong, rectangle, quadrilateral, polygon

RESOURCES

Mandatory: string, pattern shapes, straws, a selection of regular and irregular 2D shapes

Optional: peg board, dry-wipe pen, isometric paper

 In the eTextbook of this lesson, you will find interactive links to a selection of teaching tools.

Before you teach

• Are children secure in identifying shapes by the number of sides?
• How can you display the vocabulary in this lesson for children to refer to?
• Where can you provide practical opportunities for children in this lesson?

Discover

WAYS OF WORKING Pair work

ASK

- *What do you notice about the part of the shape where the fingers are?*
- *What shapes can you make using four fingers?*

IN FOCUS This part of the lesson draws the focus from sides to vertices of polygons. By using their fingers, children create 'corners', or vertices. Discuss how two sides meet at each finger. Some children may begin to see the relationship between number of sides and number of vertices.

ANSWERS

Question ① a): Four fingers are needed to create a ▢.

Five fingers are needed to create a ⬠.

Question ① b): The only shape you can make with three fingers is a triangle.

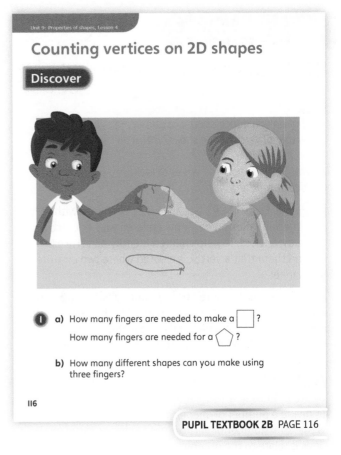

Share

WAYS OF WORKING Whole class teacher led

ASK

- *How can you make sure that you count all the vertices only once?*
- *How is this similar to what you did in the last lesson?*

IN FOCUS Sparks' comment introduces children to the terms 'vertex' and 'vertices'. Previously, children may have referred to vertices as corners. Emphasise that a vertex is created where two sides of a polygon meet.

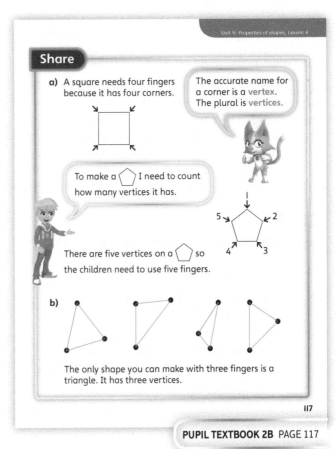

145

Think together

WAYS OF WORKING Whole class teacher led (I do, We do, You do)

ASK
- *What do you notice about the number of sides and the number of vertices of a shape? Is this always true? Why do you think that is?*
- *Which way do you find easier to identify a polygon? Counting sides or counting vertices?*

IN FOCUS Question ② has a number of shapes with at least one internal reflex angle. Some children may not recognise these as vertices. To help children identify all vertices, remind them that a vertex is created where two or more sides meet.

STRENGTHEN Get children to carry out questions ① and ② practically. This will help them to identify the vertices. When counting vertices in a pictorial representation of a polygon, encourage children to mark off the vertices as they count them.

DEEPEN Ask children to explore what polygons they can create by cutting a straight line from one vertex to another to divide a number of shapes into two new polygons. What is the total number of vertices of the shapes created? How does it relate to the number of vertices children started with? Why do they think that is? Can children predict the total number of vertices after cutting one line, based on the starting number of vertices? For example, say: *A square has four vertices. After cutting one line from one vertex to another, you create two triangles with a total of six vertices. This is two more than the original square. If I start with a hexagon and cut a line from a vertex to vertex to create two new polygons, will I have a total of eight vertices?*

ASSESSMENT CHECKPOINT Question ① will determine whether children can count the vertices of a variety of shapes. Question ② will determine whether children can identify all vertices of both regular and irregular polygons, including those with reflex internal angles. Question ③ will determine whether children can identify and count the sides and vertices of polygons and identify the relationship between them.

ANSWERS

Question ① : The oblong and kite have 4 vertices; the regular and irregular pentagons have 5 vertices; the hexagon has 6 vertices.

Question ② : From left to right and top to bottom, the numbers of vertices are: 6, 6, 6, 6, 5, 6.

Question ③ : Shape A has 6 sides and 6 vertices; shape B has 4 sides and 4 vertices; shape C has eight 8 sides and 8 vertices.

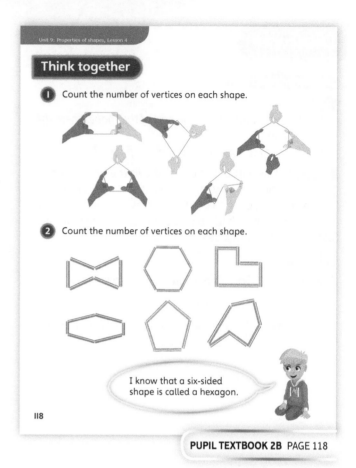

PUPIL TEXTBOOK 2B PAGE 118

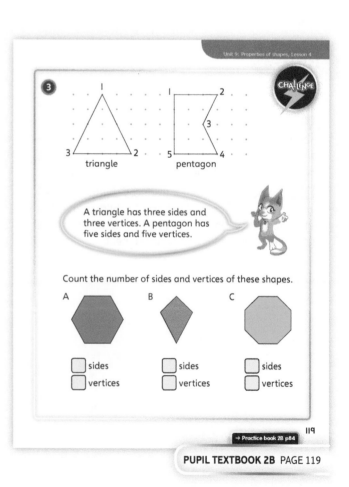

PUPIL TEXTBOOK 2B PAGE 119

Practice

IN FOCUS Question ❹ explores the misconception that when a polygon is drawn on square dotted paper, a vertex is created when a side touches a dot. Children must draw on their understanding that a vertex is created only when two or more sides meet, and cannot exist where only one side is present.

STRENGTHEN For questions ❶ and ❷, encourage children to mark off each vertex as they count it. For question ❸, have the corresponding 2D shapes available for children to refer to. Provide children with a laminated version of question ❺ and a dry-wipe pen so that they can practise, review and correct their responses before drawing them.

DEEPEN Provide children with isometric paper. Encourage them to create different quadrilaterals, pentagons and hexagons. See if children can create polygons with seven, eight and nine vertices.

ASSESSMENT CHECKPOINT Question ❶ will determine whether children can match polygons with the correct number of vertices. Question ❷ will determine whether children can correctly count the number of vertices in a polygon. Question ❸ will determine whether children can match the names of polygons to the correct number of vertices and sides. Question ❹ will determine whether children understand that a vertex is created where two sides of a polygon meet. Question ❺ will determine whether children can accurately draw polygons with a given number of vertices.

ANSWERS Answers for the **Practice** part of the lesson appear in the separate **Practice and Reflect answer guide**.

Reflect

IN FOCUS This section highlights the misconception that a vertex is not present where an internal angle in a polygon is reflex. Sparks' comment reminds children to think about where vertices are in order to identify them correctly. Children may struggle to articulate the differences between the two shapes. Support children by suggesting they think about the angles as turns. Tell children to imagine standing on the vertices facing a side. They then have to turn to face inside the shape and then continue turning until they end up facing the other side. Would they have to make more than a half turn on any of the vertices?

ASSESSMENT CHECKPOINT This section will determine whether children can correctly identify vertices even where there is an internal reflex angle.

ANSWERS Answers for the **Reflect** part of the lesson appear in the separate **Practice and Reflect answer guide**.

After the lesson ⏸

- Do children understand the definition of a vertex?
- Can children identify vertices even on unfamiliar irregular polygons?
- Do children understand the relationship between the number of vertices and the number of sides of polygons?

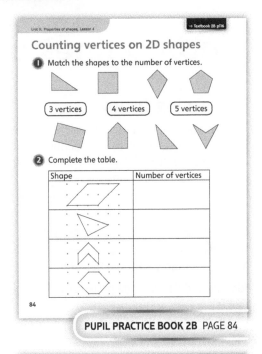

PUPIL PRACTICE BOOK 2B PAGE 84

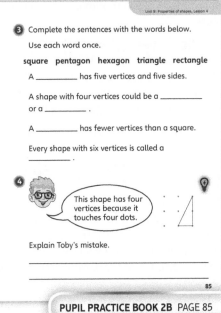

PUPIL PRACTICE BOOK 2B PAGE 85

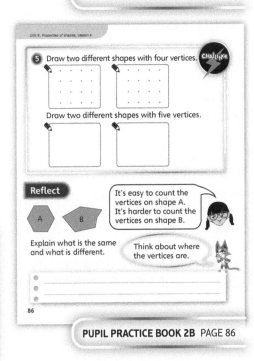

PUPIL PRACTICE BOOK 2B PAGE 86

Finding lines of symmetry

Learning focus

In this lesson, children will explore reflective symmetry. They will learn to identify shapes and images that have reflective symmetry and identify where the line of symmetry lies.

Small steps

→ Previous step: Counting vertices on 2D shapes
→ **This step: Finding lines of symmetry**
→ Next step: Sorting 2D shapes

NATIONAL CURRICULUM LINKS

Year 2 Geometry – Properties of Shape

Identify and describe the properties of 2D shapes, including the number of sides and line symmetry in a vertical line.

ASSESSING MASTERY

Children can identify lines of symmetry in images and shapes. Children can understand that the halves either side of the line of symmetry are mirror images of each other and they can identify what the symmetrical shape will be when only one half is shown.

COMMON MISCONCEPTIONS

Children may think that by drawing a line to halve a shape, you have found the line of symmetry, even if the two halves are not mirror images of each other. Show children an oblong and ask:
• *Is this symmetrical? Where is the line of symmetry?*

Now draw a line from corner to corner and ask:
• *Have I drawn the line of symmetry?*

STRENGTHENING UNDERSTANDING

A nice way to introduce reflective symmetry is to create symmetrical butterflies. Provide children with an outline of a butterfly that has a vertical line of symmetry. Children can then use paint of different colours and place blobs of paint on one side of the butterfly. They then fold it in half and smooth it down so that the paint is printed on the opposite side. When children open it up, they reveal a symmetrical pattern. Discuss how the colours match up when the butterfly is folded in half. You could compare these with pictures of actual butterflies and discuss the symmetrical patterns.

GOING DEEPER

Provide children with some Rangoli-style patterns. These usually have a number of lines of symmetry. Can children find them all? Children could try creating their own symmetrical patterns with more than one line of symmetry using peg boards or colouring in squared paper.

KEY LANGUAGE

In lesson: line of symmetry, symmetrical

Other language to be used by the teacher: symmetry, vertical, horizontal, reflective

RESOURCES

Mandatory: mirrors

Optional: peg boards, squared paper, paint, butterfly templates, butterfly pictures, tracing paper, paper cutouts of regular polygons

 In the eTextbook of this lesson, you will find interactive links to a selection of teaching tools.

Before you teach ⏸

• How will you explain reflective symmetry?
• How will you support children who may struggle to understand the concept of reflective symmetry?
• What resources and images could you have available to reinforce understanding of reflective symmetry?

Discover

Pair work

ASK

- *How did you know what the shape would be?*
- *What can you tell me about the two halves of the image? Are they the same?*

IN FOCUS This section asks children to visualise a symmetrical image when only half of it is presented. This introduces reflective symmetry as the idea that when the image is folded along the line of symmetry, the two halves match.

ANSWERS

Question ① a): The shape will look like a person when it is unfolded.

Question ① b): The shape will look like a heart when it is unfolded.

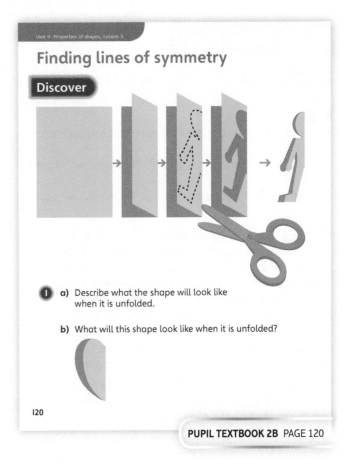

PUPIL TEXTBOOK 2B PAGE 120

Share

Whole class teacher led

ASK

- *Can you see anything in the room that has a line of symmetry?*
- *Can you think of any 2D shapes that have a line of symmetry?*

IN FOCUS Astrid's comment explains how a mirror can be used to test for lines of reflective symmetry. Provide some mirrors for children and ask them to try to find objects that have reflective symmetry.

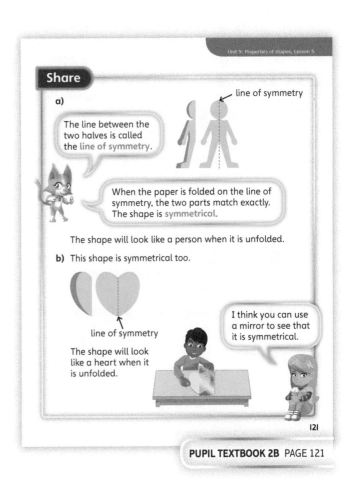

PUPIL TEXTBOOK 2B PAGE 121

Think together

Whole class teacher led (I do, We do, You do)

ASK

- Question **2**: *How can you work out where to draw each vertex?*
- Question **2**: *Can you identify what the shape will be before you draw it?*
- Question **3**: *Are there any shapes that do not have a line of symmetry?*

IN FOCUS Question **2** provides children with half a symmetrical image and asks them to complete it. This will highlight whether children understand that with reflective symmetry, each side of the line of symmetry is a mirror image of the other. The use of squared paper provides children with a reference when trying to complete the image, enabling them to count the number of squares from the line of symmetry to vertices of the shape. Children can check their responses with a mirror, as suggested by Astrid.

STRENGTHEN For question **2**, children could trace over the half shape using tracing paper and then flip the paper over in order to see how the second half should be positioned.

Provide children with paper cutout versions of the shapes in question **3**. Children can then fold them in half in order to identify the line of reflective symmetry.

DEEPEN When children have completed question **2**, ask them if any of the shapes have more than one line of symmetry. This will be true for the squares and oblongs. Provide children with paper cutouts of regular polygons. Can they identify all the lines of symmetry by folding them?

ASSESSMENT CHECKPOINT Question **1** will determine whether children can visualise the whole image when presented with only half. Question **2** will determine whether children can draw the missing half of a symmetrical 2D shape. Do children understand that the half they need to draw is a mirror image of the first half? Question **3** will determine whether children can identify lines of reflective symmetry in 2D shapes.

ANSWERS

Question **1** : Circle, star, smiley face, house.

Question **2** : Column 1: square, isosceles triangle, square, oblong; column 2: square, oblong, square, isosceles triangle.

Question **3** : From left to right, top to bottom: no, yes, no, yes, yes, no.

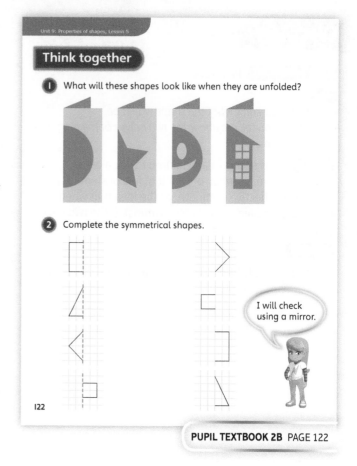

PUPIL TEXTBOOK 2B PAGE 122

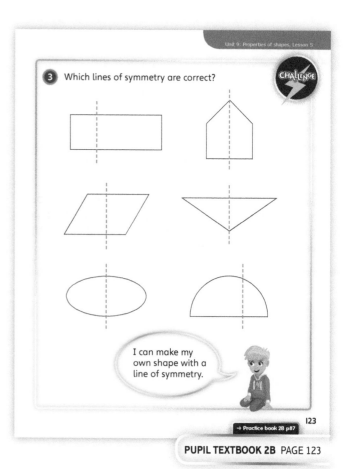

PUPIL TEXTBOOK 2B PAGE 123

Practice

WAYS OF WORKING Independent thinking

IN FOCUS Question **5** asks children to draw one half of a 2D quadrilateral shape that can be reflected to create the complete 2D shape. Children need to be able to identify reflective lines of symmetry, understand that the two halves of the shape are mirror images of each other along the line of symmetry and be able to visualise what the complete shape will look like.

STRENGTHEN For question **2**, provide children with tracing paper so that they can trace the first half and then flip the paper to identify where to position the second half. For question **4**, provide children with matching paper shapes. They can then fold them in half to identify the lines of symmetry, making sure that the two halves match when folded.

DEEPEN Provide children with peg boards or squared paper. Can children produce a pattern that has both vertical and horizontal lines of symmetry? What about a diagonal line of symmetry?

ASSESSMENT CHECKPOINT Use question **6** to assess children's understanding. Children should draw a shape with reflective symmetry, ensuring that the line of symmetry is drawn correctly.

ANSWERS Answers for the **Practice** part of the lesson appear in the separate **Practice and Reflect answer guide**.

Reflect

WAYS OF WORKING Pair work

IN FOCUS In this section, children will need to apply what they have learned from this lesson and the previous lesson. As the shape has fewer than five vertices, it can only be a quadrilateral or a triangle. Children have to think carefully about how they describe the shape; they should draw on what they have already learned about the properties of the shapes they draw.

ASSESSMENT CHECKPOINT This section will determine whether children are able to visualise shapes with reflective symmetry and whether they can use correct mathematical vocabulary to describe a given shape's properties.

ANSWERS Answers for the **Reflect** part of the lesson appear in the separate **Practice and Reflect answer guide**.

After the lesson

- Are children confident in identifying lines of reflective symmetry in 2D shapes?
- How does this build on the previous lessons on properties of shapes?
- What practical opportunities can you provide for children who may still not be secure in their understanding of reflective symmetry?

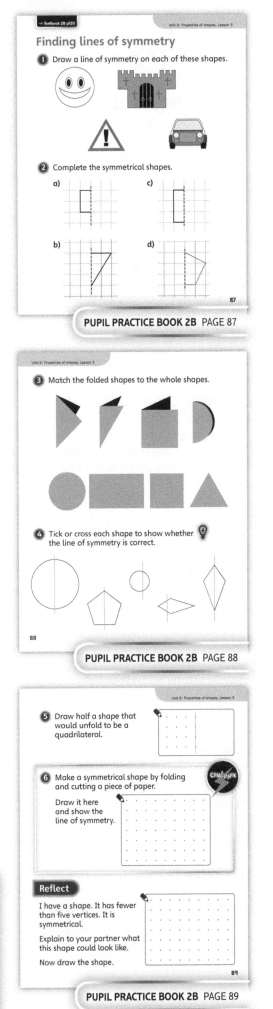

PUPIL PRACTICE BOOK 2B PAGE 87

PUPIL PRACTICE BOOK 2B PAGE 88

PUPIL PRACTICE BOOK 2B PAGE 89

Sorting 2D shapes

Learning focus

In this lesson, children will draw on their previous learning about properties of 2D shapes in order to sort polygons by different criteria. This will include focusing on number of sides, number of vertices and reflective symmetry.

Small steps

→ Previous step: Finding lines of symmetry
→ **This step: Sorting 2D shapes**
→ Next step: Making patterns with 2D shapes

NATIONAL CURRICULUM LINKS

Year 2 Geometry – Properties of Shape

Compare and sort common 2D and 3D shapes and everyday objects.

ASSESSING MASTERY

Children can sort 2D shapes based on a variety of given criteria. Children are also able to choose their own criteria to sort shapes based on the mathematical properties of each shape.

COMMON MISCONCEPTIONS

Children may be unsuccessful in counting the number of sides or vertices, particularly when the shape is irregular and has an internal reflex angle. Show children a variety of irregular polygons and ask:

- *How many sides does this shape have? How many vertices does this shape have? How can you make sure that you count them all correctly?*

Children may focus on properties such as colour rather than mathematical properties. Provide children with a variety of 2D shapes and ask them to sort them into groups. If they sort them by colour, ask:

- *Can you sort them a different way?*

STRENGTHENING UNDERSTANDING

Wherever possible, provide children with shapes and sorting hoops so that they can physically sort the shapes. To begin with, you may need to provide labels for the different groups before children start to write their own. Ensure that you encourage children to talk about their decisions as they sort the shapes.

GOING DEEPER

Provide children with shapes and sorting criteria where some shapes belong either in both groups or in neither. Ask them where they would place those shapes. Some children may be ready to sort shapes using a Carroll diagram in which each group is determined by two criteria.

KEY LANGUAGE

In lesson: most, vertices, more than, triangle, hexagon, **octagon**, greater than, polygon, 2D, side, circle, oval, semicircle, fewest, symmetry

Other language to be used by the teacher: vertex, symmetrical, square, oblong, rectangle, pentagon, less than, fewer than, odd, even, sort, group

RESOURCES

Mandatory: 2D shapes, sorting hoops, labels

 In the eTextbook of this lesson, you will find interactive links to a selection of teaching tools.

Before you teach ⏸

- Are children secure in identifying the properties of 2D shapes?
- How could you display the vocabulary used in this lesson for children to refer to?

Discover

Pair work

ASK

- *Why does the triangle not go in either box?*
- *How else could you sort the shapes?*

IN FOCUS This part of the lesson requires children to sort the shapes into two separately defined groups. The placement of the pentagon requires extra thought as it has 5 vertices and is stripy. Children may think it belongs in both groups if they do not realise that the second group does not include shapes with 5 vertices.

ANSWERS

Question ① a): The triangle will not go in either box.

Question ① b): The octagon has the most vertices.

Sorting 2D shapes

Discover

① a) Which shape will **not** go in either box?

b) Which shape has the most vertices?

124

PUPIL TEXTBOOK 2B PAGE 124

Share

Whole class teacher led

ASK

- *What else could you call the 'blue stripy' group so that the triangle can go into it as well?*
- *Is there a way of sorting all the shapes into three separate groups?*

IN FOCUS Question ① b) uses the sign '>', which children last came across in Unit 4. Can children write similar expressions to compare the number of vertices between other shapes? The ability to compare the number of sides or vertices between shapes is an important skill when sorting shapes.

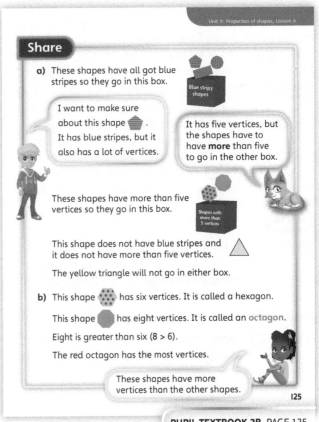

Share

a) These shapes have all got blue stripes so they go in this box.

I want to make sure about this shape 🔷. It has blue stripes, but it also has a lot of vertices.

It has five vertices, but the shapes have to have **more** than five to go in the other box.

These shapes have more than five vertices so they go in this box.

This shape does not have blue stripes and it does not have more than five vertices.

The yellow triangle will not go in either box.

b) This shape 🔵 has six vertices. It is called a hexagon.

This shape ⬡ has eight vertices. It is called an octagon.

Eight is greater than six (8 > 6).

The red octagon has the most vertices.

These shapes have more vertices than the other shapes.

125

PUPIL TEXTBOOK 2B PAGE 125

Think together

Whole class teacher led (I do, We do, You do)

ASK

- *What different properties can you look at when sorting shapes?*
- Question ❶: *Is there more than one way you could label the boxes?*
- Question ❸: *Can you sort them into two groups, three groups or four groups?*

IN FOCUS Question ❸ requires children to come up with their own criteria for sorting the shapes. As Sparks says, there are a number of different ways to sort them. Encourage children to come up with more than one solution and discuss them with a partner. Astrid talks about using symmetry to sort the shapes, drawing on the learning from the previous lesson. However, the quarter circle has a line of symmetry that may not be very obvious to children as it is not vertical.

STRENGTHEN Provide children with 2D shapes and sorting hoops so that they can physically sort the shapes. Begin by sorting by type of shape and then move towards sorting them by number of sides and vertices. Use the vocabulary 'more than', 'greater than', 'less than' and 'fewer than'.

DEEPEN Focus on Astrid's comment in question ❸. Provide children with a variety of shapes and some sorting hoops, and ask them to sort the shapes based on symmetry. Children will most likely begin by sorting them into two groups: 'Symmetrical' and 'Not symmetrical'. Ask children: *Can you have more than two groups?* Prompt children to sort shapes by how many lines of symmetry each one has. For example: 'No lines of symmetry', 'One line of symmetry' and 'More than one line of symmetry'.

ASSESSMENT CHECKPOINT Question ❶ will determine whether children can identify sorting criteria for shapes that have already been sorted. Question ❷ will determine whether children can identify and count the number of sides of irregular polygons and order them based on the number of sides. Question ❸ will determine whether children can identify different criteria for sorting shapes and then sort them accordingly.

ANSWERS

Question ❶ : There is more than one possible answer. An example would be 'Polygons with 3 sides', 'Polygons with more than 3 sides' and 'Not polygons'.

Question ❷ : A, D, E and F (same number of sides), C, B

Question ❸ : There is more than one possible way. An example would be '4 vertices' and 'Fewer than 4 vertices'.

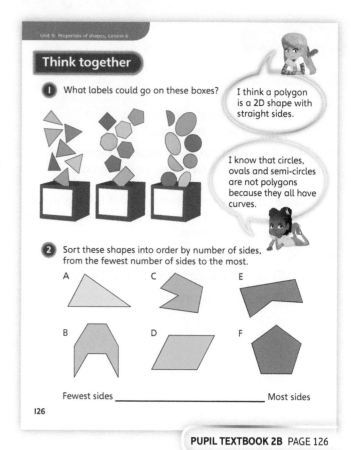

PUPIL TEXTBOOK 2B PAGE 126

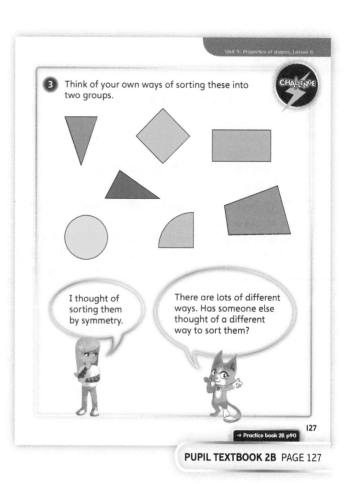

PUPIL TEXTBOOK 2B PAGE 127

Practice

WAYS OF WORKING Independent thinking

IN FOCUS Question ❹ asks children to identify shapes with odd and even numbers of vertices. This is a different way to sort by number of vertices from the ways children have encountered before. Children have to draw on their knowledge about odd and even numbers in order to solve this question. There are also several possible solutions. Ask children to think of as many different shapes that would fit in each group as possible.

STRENGTHEN Have 2D shapes available for children to manipulate and sort. When they are counting the vertices, it may help children to mark off each vertex as they count it. When determining criteria for sorting, ask children: *What is the same about the shapes? What is different about them?* This will help children to identify common properties that they can use as sorting criteria.

DEEPEN Provide children with two overlapping sorting hoops. Explain that in the space where the hoops overlap, shapes have to follow the rules for both groups. Provide children with a range of 2D shapes. Can they think of a way to sort the shapes so that there is at least one shape in the overlap?

ASSESSMENT CHECKPOINT Question ❶ will determine whether children can distinguish between polygons and non-polygons. Question ❷ will determine whether children can identify the number of vertices within a 2D shape and order the shapes accordingly. Question ❸ will determine whether children can identify possible criteria for how shapes have been sorted. Question ❹ will determine whether children can identify shapes with an odd number of vertices and shapes with an even number of vertices. Question ❺ will determine whether children can identify possible criteria for how shapes have been sorted and suggest other possible shapes that meet those criteria.

ANSWERS Answers for the **Practice** part of the lesson appear in the separate **Practice and Reflect answer guide**.

Reflect

WAYS OF WORKING Pair work

IN FOCUS This section requires children to think about how to sort the shapes into two groups of three. There are a number of ways to do this; these will most likely involve numbers of sides or vertices. Children should compare what criteria they used and whether or not different criteria resulted in different groupings.

ASSESSMENT CHECKPOINT Are children able to identify common properties between shapes? Can they select criteria that include some shapes but eliminate others? Do the criteria ensure that all shapes can be sorted into two equal groups of three (or four or five) shapes?

ANSWERS Answers for the **Reflect** part of the lesson appear in the separate **Practice and Reflect answer guide**.

After the lesson ⏸

- How secure are children with the vocabulary relating to sorting?
- Was the use of practical activities successful in supporting children whose understanding in this area needed strengthening?
- Were children able to apply their knowledge of the properties of 2D shapes in order to sort them?

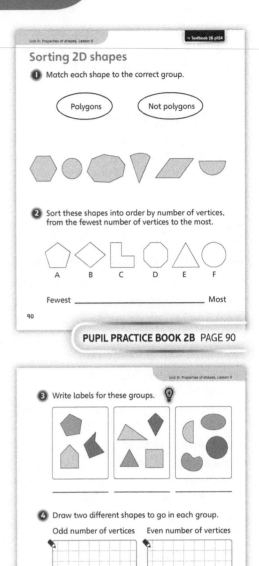

PUPIL PRACTICE BOOK 2B PAGE 90

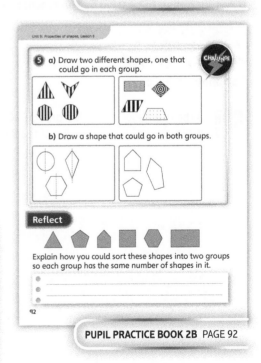

PUPIL PRACTICE BOOK 2B PAGE 91

PUPIL PRACTICE BOOK 2B PAGE 92

Making patterns with 2D shapes

Learning focus

In this lesson, children will identify patterns involving 2D shapes. By isolating the pattern core, children will be able to identify missing terms.

Small steps

→ Previous step: Sorting 2D shapes
→ **This step: Making patterns with 2D shapes**
→ Next step: Counting faces on 3D shapes

NATIONAL CURRICULUM LINKS

Year 2 Geometry – Properties of Shape

Order and arrange combinations of mathematical objects in patterns and sequences.

ASSESSING MASTERY

Children can identify the core of a pattern, using this to find missing terms and to make generalisations in order to find a given term, such as the 10th or 20th.

COMMON MISCONCEPTIONS

Children may struggle to identify the pattern core, particularly when a shape is repeated within the core. Ask:
• *What is the repeating part of the pattern? How many shapes are in the repeating part?*

STRENGTHENING UNDERSTANDING

Provide children with tracing paper. When they think they have identified the pattern core, ask them to trace over it and move their tracing across to test whether they have correctly identified the core.

Children may need time to create their own repeating patterns. Provide children with 2D shapes so they can use tracings of them to create a pattern. Ask children to highlight the pattern core.

GOING DEEPER

Ask children to create a repeating pattern of more than one row. Can they create a pattern that has a core both horizontally and vertically? Can they use this to predict what the 10th row will look like? How about the 100th?

KEY LANGUAGE

In lesson: pattern, repeating, triangle, circle

Other language to be used by the teacher: term, core, square, kite, pentagon, hexagon

RESOURCES

Mandatory: 2D shapes

Optional: tracing paper

 In the eTextbook of this lesson, you will find interactive links to a selection of teaching tools.

Before you teach

• Are children secure in identifying the 2D shapes that appear in this lesson?
• How will you support children as they explain their reasoning when identifying a given term within a pattern?

Discover

WAYS OF WORKING Pair work

ASK

- *What is the repeating part of the pattern?*
- Question ❶ a): *How do you know which shapes complete the pattern?*
- Question ❶ b): *How did you work out what the 20th term would be?*

IN FOCUS Question ❶ b) requires children to generalise in order to identify the 20th term in the pattern. Children need to reason that the even terms are always a circle and that 20 is an even number. Therefore, the 20th term must be a circle. Children have to draw on their knowledge of number as well as make careful observations about the pattern. Some children may begin by continuing the pattern to the 20th term. If this happens, support them by asking: *What shape appears at every even term? Can you use this to help you work out the 20th term?*

ANSWERS

Question ❶ a): C is the correct option to complete the pattern.

Question ❶ b): The 20th shape must be a circle.

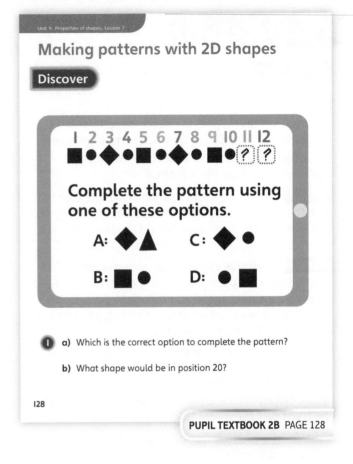

PUPIL TEXTBOOK 2B PAGE 128

Share

WAYS OF WORKING Whole class teacher led

ASK

- *Can you describe the pattern core?*
- *How many shapes are there in the pattern core?*
- *If you know that after every four shapes the pattern starts again, can you work out what the 41st term will be?*

IN FOCUS Question ❶ a) highlights how the repeating part, or pattern core, needs to be identified in order to work out what the missing shapes are. Isolating the pattern core is an important skill that enables children to not only describe the pattern but to make generalisations and find missing terms.

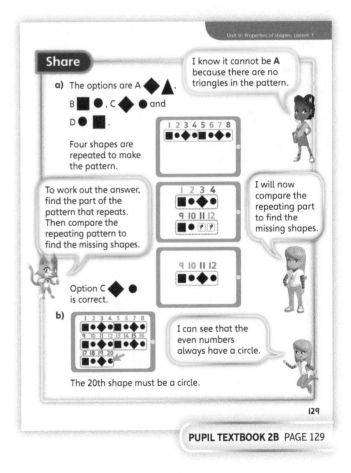

PUPIL TEXTBOOK 2B PAGE 129

Think together

Whole class teacher led (I do, We do, You do)

ASK

- *Can you identify the pattern core for the pattern?*
- Question ❶: *How did you work out the missing shapes?*
- Question ❸: *Can you use what you know about the patterns to work out the 30th term?*

IN FOCUS Question ❷ asks children to find the 15th term. Here the pattern has a core of 5 shapes. By identifying the core, children can then rationalise that any term that is a multiple of 5 will be the last shape in the pattern core.

STRENGTHEN Provide children with tracing paper so that they can trace the pattern cores. They can then use this to determine the missing shapes or continue the patterns. Discuss the shapes that are in the repeating part and how many shapes there are in the core.

DEEPEN Focus on question ❸ and ask children to work out the position of each shape. Ask children to choose one shape from the pattern. In what positions does that shape appear? When will it appear next? When will it appear for the 10th time? 20th time? 100th time?

ASSESSMENT CHECKPOINT Question ❶ will determine whether children can identify the pattern core and can identify the missing shapes in a pattern by using their knowledge of the pattern core. Question ❷ will determine whether children can use their knowledge of the pattern core to work out a given term. Question ❸ will determine whether children can use their knowledge of the pattern core to continue a pattern.

ANSWERS

Question ❶ : ▲ ▼

Question ❷ : ▲

Question ❸ a):

Question ❸ b):

Question ❸ c):

PUPIL TEXTBOOK 2B PAGE 130

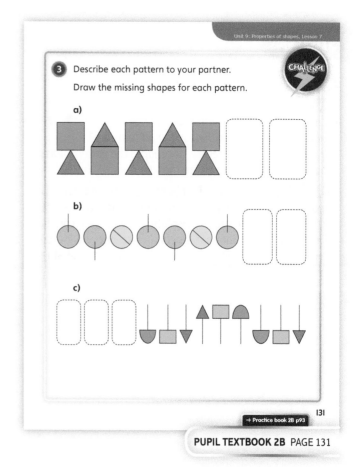

PUPIL TEXTBOOK 2B PAGE 131

Practice

WAYS OF WORKING Pair work

IN FOCUS Question **5** has patterns that work both horizontally and vertically. There is also no repeating part, so children will not be able to identify the pattern core. Instead, children will have to reason about how the shape changes as it goes from left to right as well as top to bottom in order to fill in the missing terms. In order to do this, they will have to look at completed rows and columns to identify the pattern. This is a different approach from what children have done before. Instead of asking children to identify the repeating part, ask them to describe how the shape changes as they go across and down.

STRENGTHEN Asking children to say the name of each shape as they look at the patterns from left to right can help them to identify the missing part. It may also help if an adult or a partner says the name of each shape so children can listen for the repeating part. Once the repeating part has been identified, ask children to circle the pattern core each time throughout the pattern to help them see it in isolation.

DEEPEN Extend question **5** by asking children to draw one more row and one more column. Can children explain why they chose the shapes they did? Did anyone come up with a different possibility? Can children try to convince a partner that their answer is correct?

ASSESSMENT CHECKPOINT Question **1** will determine whether children are able to identify the pattern core. Question **2** will determine whether children can identify the pattern core and use this to complete the pattern. Question **3** will determine whether children can rationalise about the pattern in order to work out the 10th and 20th term. Question **4** will determine whether children can identify the pattern core and use this to continue a pattern. Question **5** will determine whether children can identify how the shape changes in each column and thus complete the pattern.

ANSWERS Answers for the **Practice** part of the lesson appear in the separate **Practice and Reflect answer guide**.

Reflect

WAYS OF WORKING Pair work

IN FOCUS This question requires children to come up with their own pattern game. In order to do this, they need to have secure understanding of the concept of a pattern core and pose a problem with enough information that it can be solved. Children can choose how many shapes are missing, allowing them to make the problem simple or more challenging. Once they have finished designing their problem, they should test it out on their partner to see if it works.

ASSESSMENT CHECKPOINT Can children create a pattern with a repeating part? Can they identify the information needed to solve the problem?

ANSWERS Answers for the **Reflect** part of the lesson appear in the separate **Practice and Reflect answer guide**.

After the lesson ⏸

- Were children confident in identifying the pattern core?
- Were children secure in describing the pattern?
- Do children need further support in applying what they know about the pattern in order to identify missing terms?

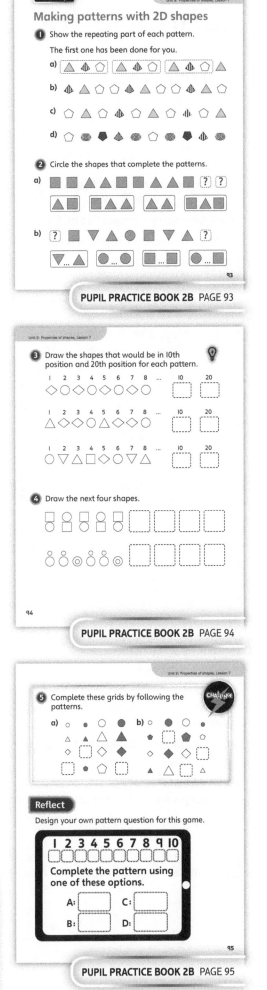

PUPIL PRACTICE BOOK 2B PAGE 93

PUPIL PRACTICE BOOK 2B PAGE 94

PUPIL PRACTICE BOOK 2B PAGE 95

Counting faces on 3D shapes

Learning focus

In this lesson, children will count and describe the faces of 3D shapes. They will learn that a curved surface on a 3D shape is not classed as a face.

Small steps

→ Previous step: Making patterns with 2D shapes
→ **This step: Counting faces on 3D shapes**
→ Next step: Counting edges on 3D shapes

NATIONAL CURRICULUM LINKS

Year 2 Geometry – Properties of Shape

Identify and describe the properties of 3D shapes, including the number of edges, vertices and faces.

ASSESSING MASTERY

Children can identify how many faces there are on a range of 3D shapes and are able to describe them based on their knowledge of 2D shapes.

COMMON MISCONCEPTIONS

Children may think that a curved surface is considered a face. Show children a cylinder and ask:
• *How many faces does this cylinder have? What 2D shapes can you get from printing with a cylinder?*

For some shapes, children may miscount the number of faces as they struggle to keep track of which ones they have counted. Show children a cuboid and ask:
• *How many faces does this cuboid have?*

Observe how children count the faces and whether they have a systematic approach.

STRENGTHENING UNDERSTANDING

Have some 3D shapes and different coloured paint. Ask children to paint each face a different colour and make a print of each face. Children can then label each 2D shape they have produced and count how many shapes they have made with their chosen 3D shape. This will help them to identify the number of faces and to describe them.

GOING DEEPER

Provide children with nets of familiar 3D shapes made with construction materials. Ask children to predict what they will make and then test their predictions by making the shape. Children could also challenge each other by placing a variety of 3D shapes in a feely bag. They take it in turns to feel a shape and describe its faces to their partner. Their partner then has to work out what the shape is.

KEY LANGUAGE

In lesson: 3D, 2D, face, flat, surface, cuboid, rectangle, square, square-based pyramid, triangle, cone, **hemisphere**, **curved surface**, sphere, circle

Other language to be used by the teacher: 3D shape, cube, cylinder, oblong, ovoid

RESOURCES

Mandatory: variety of 3D shapes, construction materials to create polyhedrons

Optional: paint of various colours

 In the eTextbook of this lesson, you will find interactive links to a selection of teaching tools.

Before you teach

• Are children secure in identifying the 2D shapes that occur in this lesson when describing faces?
• Can you provide the vocabulary needed for this lesson for children to refer to?
• What concrete apparatus can you provide for children in order to reinforce their learning?

Discover

ASK

- *How many faces can you see? How many faces are hidden?*
- *Can you think of another shape that has six faces?*
- *How do you know what shape each face is?*

IN FOCUS Question ① a) requires children to visualise the shape in order to identify the number of faces. Some children may struggle with this and could benefit from having a cuboid so that they could count each face physically. Encourage children to see that each face that is visible has a similar shaped face opposite it.

ANSWERS

Question ① a): Ben will need 6 different colours.

Question ① b): The shape of each face is a rectangle.

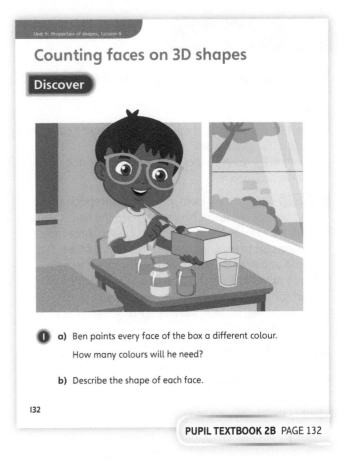

Unit 9: Properties of shapes, Lesson 8

Counting faces on 3D shapes

Discover

① **a)** Ben paints every face of the box a different colour. How many colours will he need?

b) Describe the shape of each face.

132

PUPIL TEXTBOOK 2B PAGE 132

Share

WAYS OF WORKING Whole class teacher led

ASK

- *Question ① a): Is Sparks' first comment always true?*
- *Do you know of any other shapes that have rectangular faces (square or oblong)?*
- *How did you make sure that you counted all the faces correctly?*

IN FOCUS Being able to describe what type of faces a 3D shape has is an essential part of describing its properties. Two different 3D shapes can have the same number of faces, so describing the shape of each face enables children to distinguish between them. For example, a triangular prism and a square-based pyramid both have five faces. However, the prism has two triangular faces and three rectangular faces, whereas the pyramid has one square face and four triangular faces.

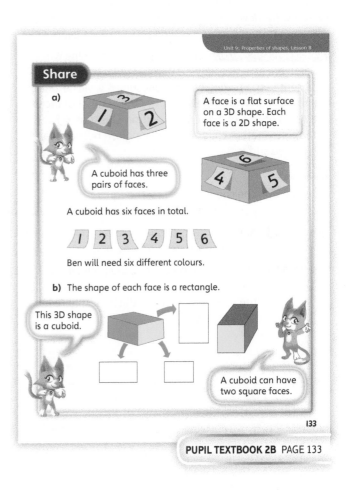

Share

a)

A face is a flat surface on a 3D shape. Each face is a 2D shape.

A cuboid has three pairs of faces.

A cuboid has six faces in total.

1 2 3 4 5 6

Ben will need six different colours.

b) The shape of each face is a rectangle.

This 3D shape is a cuboid.

A cuboid can have two square faces.

133

PUPIL TEXTBOOK 2B PAGE 133

Think together

Think together

WAYS OF WORKING Whole class teacher led (I do, We do, You do)

ASK

- Question ② : *What faces will you need to make a cube? How about a triangular prism?*
- Question ③ : *What shapes could you use to print a square, a triangle and a circle?*

IN FOCUS Question ③ looks at the misconception that a curved surface is a face. Children may see the hemisphere as having two faces or the cylinder as having three faces. It is important to explain that, by definition, a face is flat. Thinking about whether they can print with it can help children to make the distinction between a face and a curved surface. It is important to ensure that children use the term 'curved surface' when describing the types of shape in this question.

STRENGTHEN Provide children with 3D shapes that they can manipulate. Encourage them to mark off each face to help them count the faces reliably. Provide children with paint and paper so that they can print with the 3D shapes to help identify the shapes of the faces.

DEEPEN Ask children to think about combining two different 3D shapes so that the faces fit together exactly. What would happen to the total number of faces? For example, place a square-based pyramid on top of a cube to make a new 3D shape. Ask: *How many faces did you have to start with? How many faces are there now? Can you explain why the total number of faces changes the way that it does?*

ASSESSMENT CHECKPOINT Question ① will determine whether children are able to count the number of faces on a pictorial representation of a polyhedron. Question ② will determine whether children are able to identify the number of faces and types of face of a given polyhedron. Question ③ will determine whether children can distinguish between faces and curved surfaces.

ANSWERS

Question ① : The cube has 6 faces; the square-based pyramid has 5 faces; the cuboid has 6 faces.

Question ② : Anna will need 1 square face and 4 triangular faces. She will need 5 faces in total.

Question ③ : The sphere has no faces; the cylinder has 2 circular faces; the cone has 1 circular face; the ovoid has no faces; the hemisphere has 1 circular face.

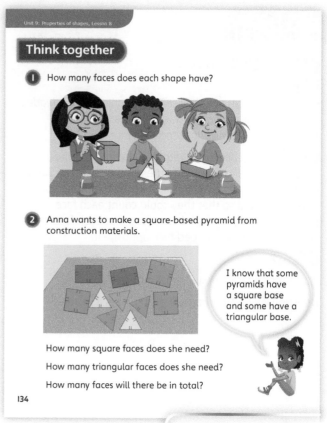

PUPIL TEXTBOOK 2B PAGE 134

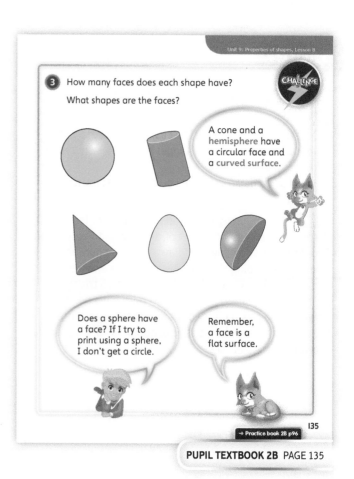

PUPIL TEXTBOOK 2B PAGE 135

Practice

Independent thinking

IN FOCUS Question **5** requires children to apply their understanding of multiplication and division as well as their knowledge of 3D shapes in order to solve the problem. In question **5** a), children have to calculate 5 x 6. They could do this by repeated addition or by drawing on their multiplication facts. In question **5** b), they have to calculate 8 ÷ 4 and then identify the shape with two faces.

STRENGTHEN Before children start, provide them with concrete representations of the 3D shapes in this section. Begin by getting children to match name labels to the shapes, then prompt them to count the faces and write down how many faces each shape has. Finally, support children in identifying the shape of each face. They could then use their notes as a reference point when answering the questions.

DEEPEN Ask children to set up a 3D shape shop. Provide them with a range of 3D shapes to sell. They have to price the shapes following these rules: curved surfaces cost 2p; triangular faces cost 5p; square and oblong faces cost 10p and circular faces cost 20p. Can they work out the total cost of each shape?

ASSESSMENT CHECKPOINT Question **1** will determine whether children can name 3D shapes and correctly identify how many faces they have. Question **2** will determine whether children can identify the number of faces and the shapes of the faces of a variety of polyhedrons. Question **3** will determine whether children can apply their learning from this lesson to find the combined total of a number of 3D shapes. Question **4** will determine whether children can distinguish between faces and curved surfaces. Question **5** will determine whether children can apply their understanding of multiplication, division and properties of 3D shapes to solve a problem.

ANSWERS Answers for the **Practice** part of the lesson appear in the separate **Practice and Reflect answer guide**.

Reflect

Pair work

IN FOCUS This part of the lesson requires children to visualise a 3D shape, then describe its faces. Children need to have a secure understanding of what they have learned in this lesson in order to do this. This could be extended by asking children to think of a shape and describe it to their partner. Their partner then has to work out what the shape is.

ASSESSMENT CHECKPOINT This section will determine whether children can correctly count and name the faces of a 3D shape without having a pictorial or concrete representation.

ANSWERS Answers for the **Reflect** part of the lesson appear in the separate **Practice and Reflect answer guide**.

After the lesson ⏸

- How can you further support children who were not secure in identifying the number of faces on a given 3D shape?
- Could children create a display of the properties of 3D shapes that can be added to over the next two lessons?

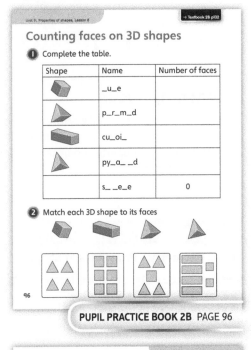

PUPIL PRACTICE BOOK 2B PAGE 96

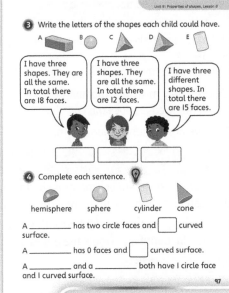

PUPIL PRACTICE BOOK 2B PAGE 97

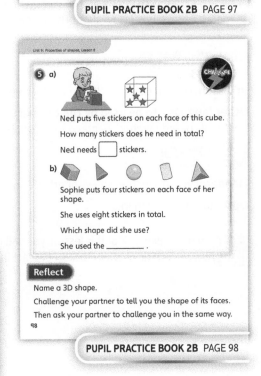

PUPIL PRACTICE BOOK 2B PAGE 98

Counting edges on 3D shapes

Learning focus

In this lesson, children will identify edges of a 3D shape as the line where two faces meet. They will learn to use the property of number of edges to describe 3D shapes.

Small steps

→ Previous step: Counting faces on 3D shapes
→ **This step: Counting edges on 3D shapes**
→ Next step: Counting vertices on 3D shapes

NATIONAL CURRICULUM LINKS

Year 2 Geometry – Properties of Shape

Identify and describe the properties of 3D shapes, including the number of edges, vertices and faces.

ASSESSING MASTERY

Children can identify and count the edges of 3D shapes and use this knowledge when comparing and describing 3D shapes.

COMMON MISCONCEPTIONS

Children may make the mistake of thinking the point where a face meets a curved surface is an edge. Give children a cylinder and ask:

• *How many edges does this cylinder have?*

Children may miscount the number of edges on 3D shapes. Provide children with a cube and ask:
• *How many edges does this cube have?*

Observe how children count them.

STRENGTHENING UNDERSTANDING

Using concrete 3D shapes, prompt children to mark off the edges with a dry-wipe marker as they count them. Discuss how they can be systematic in the way they count the edges.

Where possible, provide children with straws to make the 3D shapes. As each straw represents an edge, this will support children in identifying where the edges are on a 3D shape.

GOING DEEPER

Provide children with straws and challenge them to make shapes with different numbers of edges. Can children make a 3D shape with two edges? How about three, four or five edges? Why? What different number of edges can they use to make 3D shapes?

KEY LANGUAGE

In lesson: cube, face, edge, 3D, prism, triangular prism, pyramid

Other language to be used by the teacher: 3D shape, cuboid, triangle-based pyramid, square-based pyramid, pentagon-based pyramid, pentagonal prism, hexagonal prism

RESOURCES

Mandatory: construction straws or art straws, 3D shapes

Optional: dry-wipe marker

 In the eTextbook of this lesson, you will find interactive links to a selection of teaching tools.

Before you teach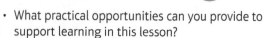

• What practical opportunities can you provide to support learning in this lesson?
• How can you link learning from the last lesson to this lesson?
• How will you reinforce the new vocabulary in this lesson?

Discover

ASK

- *Can you describe the faces of the cube?*
- *How many straws are needed to make two cubes? What about three cubes?*

IN FOCUS Question **1** b) highlights how, if the type of shape does not change, then the number of faces and edges remains the same regardless of the size of the shape. Some children may want to count the edges of all the cubes in this problem as they may not see that the number of edges is constant as the size of the shape changes. Use this as an opportunity to reinforce that all cubes have 12 edges. This is one of the properties of a cube.

ANSWERS

Question **1** a): Hassan needs 12 straws.

Question **1** b): Each cube has 6 square faces and 12 edges, and this fact stays the same. The size of all the faces changes, and the length of all the edges changes.

Counting edges on 3D shapes

Discover

Look at my bubble!

Molly   Bob   Hassan

1 a) Hassan wants to make his own ▭. How many ▐ does he need?

b) There are three different ▭: small, medium and large.

What stays the same and what changes?

136

PUPIL TEXTBOOK 2B PAGE 136

Share

ASK

- *What other shape has 12 edges?*
- *How would you describe what an edge is?*
- *How can you be sure that you have counted all the edges only once?*

IN FOCUS Question **1** a) defines an edge. Children need to understand that an edge is only created where two faces meet. This is a good opportunity to allow children to make a cube from straws so that they can see how each straw they use represents an edge. This will provide a practical context for children to refer back to when identifying edges on 3D shapes.

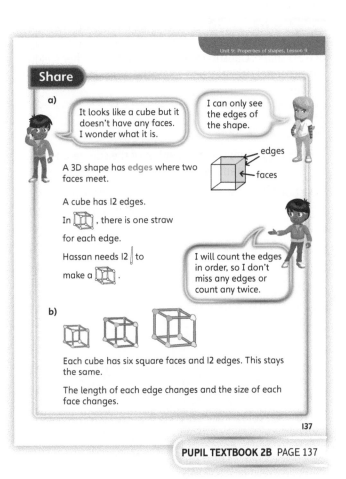

Share

a) It looks like a cube but it doesn't have any faces. I wonder what it is.

I can only see the edges of the shape.

A 3D shape has **edges** where two faces meet.

edges
faces

A cube has 12 edges.

In ▭, there is one straw for each edge.

Hassan needs 12 ▐ to make a ▭.

I will count the edges in order, so I don't miss any edges or count any twice.

b) Each cube has six square faces and 12 edges. This stays the same.

The length of each edge changes and the size of each face changes.

137

PUPIL TEXTBOOK 2B PAGE 137

Think together

Whole class teacher led (I do, We do, You do)

ASK

- Question **2**: *Can you put the shapes in order from the fewest edges to the most?*
- Question **2**: *Can you describe the faces of the different shapes?*
- Question **2**: *If the triangular prism and the square-based pyramid have the same number of faces, why don't they have the same number of edges?*

IN FOCUS Question **3** asks children to investigate the relationship between the number of faces and the number of edges of 3D shapes. For all polyhedrons, there will be more edges than faces. However, this is not the case for hemispheres and cylinders, which do not have any edges.

STRENGTHEN For questions **1** and **2**, provide children with concrete representations of the shapes. Children can then physically count the edges. Encourage children to mark off the edges with a dry-wipe marker so that they can keep track of which edges they have counted.

DEEPEN Ask children to make a cube and a square-based pyramid with straws. Tell them to place the pyramid on top of the cube so that the square face of the pyramid sits exactly on a square face of the cube. What has happened to the total number of edges? Can children explain why that is? What happens if they join two other shapes in a similar way?

ASSESSMENT CHECKPOINT Questions **1** and **2** will determine whether children can accurately count the number of edges of a 3D shape. Question **3** will determine whether children can accurately identify and count the faces and edges of 3D shapes.

ANSWERS

Question **1** : 6, 12, 9

Question **2** : Sam can make either of the square-based pyramids.

Question **3** : All 3D shapes with flat faces have more edges than faces. Cylinders and hemispheres do not.

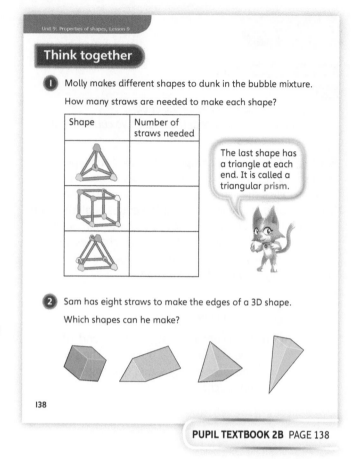

PUPIL TEXTBOOK 2B PAGE 138

PUPIL TEXTBOOK 2B PAGE 139

166

Practice

WAYS OF WORKING Pair work

IN FOCUS Question **5** requires children to apply their multiplication and division knowledge and what they have learned about edges of 3D shapes in order to find the solution. Children have to first identify how many edges each shape has, then determine the calculation that is needed. For question **5** a), children have to calculate 5 × 6 and for question **5** b), they have to calculate 50 ÷ 10.

STRENGTHEN Ask children to help contribute towards the class display of 3D shapes. Present some shapes and ask children to count the number of faces and edges for each. Children then label each shape accordingly. Display this so that children are able to refer to it when answering the questions.

DEEPEN Extend question **4** by asking children to explore the relationship between the number of sides of the end face and the number of edges on the prism. For example, a triangle has 3 sides and a triangular prism has 9 edges; a pentagon has 5 sides and a pentagonal prism has 15 edges. Can children see a relationship? Can they explain it?

ASSESSMENT CHECKPOINT Question **1** will determine whether children can accurately count the number of edges for different 3D shapes. Question **2** will determine whether children can count and compare the number of edges for different polyhedrons. Question **3** will determine whether children can accurately identify and count the number of faces and edges for different polyhedrons. Question **4** will determine whether children can accurately identify and count the number of edges for unfamiliar polyhedrons. Question **5** will determine whether children can apply their learning of properties of 3D shapes and multiplication and division in order to solve problems.

ANSWERS Answers for the **Practice** part of the lesson appear in the separate **Practice and Reflect answer guide**.

Reflect

WAYS OF WORKING Pair work

IN FOCUS This section asks children to think carefully about the definition of face and edge for 3D shapes. By explaining the distinction between the two to a partner, children help to secure their understanding of the concepts.

ASSESSMENT CHECKPOINT This section will determine whether children are secure in their understanding of what edges and faces are in relation to 3D shapes.

ANSWERS Answers for the **Reflect** part of the lesson appear in the separate **Practice and Reflect answer guide**.

After the lesson

- Did children confuse faces and edges? If so, how can you further support them?
- Were children able to apply their learning from the previous lesson?
- Were the practical opportunities successful in reinforcing children's understanding of the properties of 3D shapes?

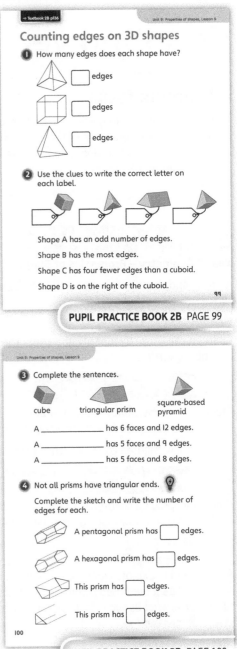

PUPIL PRACTICE BOOK 2B PAGE 99

PUPIL PRACTICE BOOK 2B PAGE 100

PUPIL PRACTICE BOOK 2B PAGE 101

Counting vertices on 3D shapes

Learning focus

In this lesson, children will learn that vertices on a 3D shape are where three or more edges meet. They will then use this knowledge to help describe the properties of 3D shapes.

Small steps

→ Previous step: Counting edges on 3D shapes
→ **This step: Counting vertices on 3D shapes**
→ Next step: Sorting 3D shapes

NATIONAL CURRICULUM LINKS

Year 2 Geometry – Properties of Shape

Identify and describe the properties of 3D shapes, including the number of edges, vertices and faces.

ASSESSING MASTERY

Children can correctly identify and count the vertices of a variety of 3D shapes. They can describe and compare shapes by the number of vertices.

COMMON MISCONCEPTIONS

Children may miscount the number of vertices or they may confuse vertices with edges. Show a cube and ask:
• *How many faces does this cube have? How many edges does this cube have? How many vertices?*

Observe how children count. Are they being systematic? Are they counting the correct property?

STRENGTHENING UNDERSTANDING

If possible, provide children with marshmallows and straws so that they can have a go at making their own 3D shapes. They could then count how many marshmallows they have used to determine how many vertices there are.

GOING DEEPER

Ask children to explore what happens to the number of vertices when two different shapes are combined. For example:
A cube and a square-based pyramid have a total of 13 vertices. If you place the pyramid on top of the cube so that the square faces match, what happens to the number of vertices? Can you explain it? What about if you combine two other shapes?

KEY LANGUAGE

In lesson: triangle-based pyramid, vertex, vertices

Other language to be used by the teacher: face, edge, 3D shapes, square-based pyramid, pentagon-based pyramid, hexagon-based pyramid, cube, cuboid, triangular prism, pentagonal prism, hexagonal prism, cone, cylinder, sphere, hemisphere, circle, triangle, square, oblong, rectangle, pentagon, hexagon, curved surface

RESOURCES

Mandatory: 3D shapes

Optional: marshmallows, straws

 In the eTextbook of this lesson, you will find interactive links to a selection of teaching tools.

Before you teach ⏸

• What resources can you provide to help secure children's understanding of properties of 3D shapes?

Discover

WAYS OF WORKING Pair work

ASK

- *How many sticks are there in each marshmallow?*
- *What part of the shape do the sticks represent?*

IN FOCUS This section draws children's attention to another property of 3D shapes. Using marshmallows to join the edges of the 3D shape makes the vertices easier to identify. It also helps to communicate the idea that vertices are where the edges meet.

ANSWERS

Question ❶ a): Eve needs 4 ⬭ for this pyramid.

Question ❶ b): Eve needs 1 more ⬭ for △

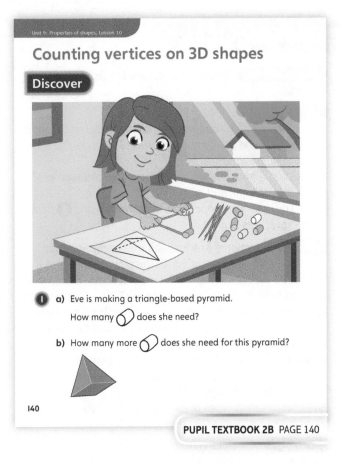

Counting vertices on 3D shapes

Discover

❶ **a)** Eve is making a triangle-based pyramid.
How many ⬭ does she need?

b) How many more ⬭ does she need for this pyramid?

140

PUPIL TEXTBOOK 2B PAGE 140

Share

WAYS OF WORKING Whole class teacher led

ASK

- *How would you describe a vertex?*
- *How many marshmallows would Eve need if she made a cube instead of a square-based pyramid?*
- *Can you explain why the square-based pyramid has one more marshmallow than the triangle-based pyramid?*

IN FOCUS Question ❶ a) explains to children that the marshmallows represent the vertices of the shape. Children need to be secure in the distinction between edges and vertices and how the vertices are created. It is important that the correct terminology is used as some children may call the vertices 'corners'. Encourage children to use the correct vocabulary to avoid confusion or misinterpretation.

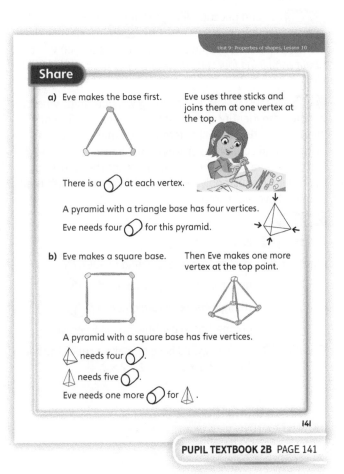

Share

a) Eve makes the base first.   Eve uses three sticks and joins them at one vertex at the top.

There is a ⬭ at each vertex.

A pyramid with a triangle base has four vertices.

Eve needs four ⬭ for this pyramid.

b) Eve makes a square base.   Then Eve makes one more vertex at the top point.

A pyramid with a square base has five vertices.

△ needs four ⬭.

△ needs five ⬭.

Eve needs one more ⬭ for △.

141

PUPIL TEXTBOOK 2B PAGE 141

Think together

WAYS OF WORKING Whole class teacher led (I do, We do, You do)

ASK

- Question **2**: *Can you see a relationship between the shape of the base and the number of vertices? What do you think that relationship is?*
- Question **2**: *Are there always more edges than vertices? Why do you think that is?*
- *Can you order the shapes from questions* **1** *and* **2** *from fewest vertices to most?*

IN FOCUS Question **3** tackles the misconception that vertices are always protruding. In the picture, there are a total of 21 vertices, some of which are concave, not convex (back to front 8 + 9 + 4, left to right 6 + 7 + 4 + 4, or bottom to top 6 + 4 + 7 + 4). By definition, a vertex is created where three or more edges meet, so children should be counting these concave vertices as well. Some children may think, incorrectly, that a vertex is created where two cubes join together. In order to find a solution to this question, children need to recognise that a cuboid has eight vertices and that different types of cuboids can be made using the eight cubes.

STRENGTHEN Ask children to create their own versions of the shapes in questions **1** and **2** using marshmallows and straws. Children can then use these shapes to physically count the number of vertices on each shape.

DEEPEN Extend question **3** by asking children: *What is the greatest number of vertices you can create by combining three cubes?* (12) *What is the fewest number of vertices?* (8) *What about combining four cubes?* (16 and 8) *Or five cubes* (20 and 8)?

ASSESSMENT CHECKPOINT Question **1** will determine whether children can identify and count the vertices of different 3D shapes. Question **2** will determine whether children can visualise and count the vertices of 3D shapes. Question **3** will determine whether children can count the vertices of unfamiliar irregular polyhedrons and if they recognise that cuboids have eight vertices.

ANSWERS

Question **1** : 8, 4, 8

Question **2** : Pentagon-based pyramid needs 6 ⬭;
hexagon-based pyramid needs 7 ⬭;
triangle-based pyramid needs 4 ⬭;
oblong-based pyramid needs 5 vertices.

Question **3** : Yes, she would have to make a cuboid either 1 × 1 × 8, 1 × 2 × 4 or 2 × 2 × 2.

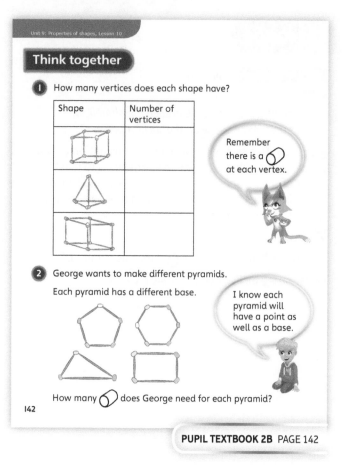

PUPIL TEXTBOOK 2B PAGE 142

PUPIL TEXTBOOK 2B PAGE 143

Practice

Pair work

IN FOCUS Question **5** combines the three types of properties of 3D shapes that children have learned to identify in the last three lessons. It encourages children to look for patterns between the number of faces, edges and vertices of different types of pyramids, as well as the relationship between faces, edges and vertices.

STRENGTHEN Provide children with 3D shapes that correspond to those in the questions to enable them to physically count the vertices. This will support them in answering the questions.

DEEPEN Provide children with a range of polyhedrons and ask them to count and write down the number of faces, edges and vertices of each shape. They could create a simple table to do this. Ask: *Can you see any link between the number of faces, edges and vertices that is true for all the shapes? What about if you start by adding the number of faces and vertices together? What happens if you now subtract the number of edges?*

Children should discover that **faces + vertices – edges = 2**.
Ask: *Is this the same for all the shapes?*

ASSESSMENT CHECKPOINT Questions **1** and **2** will determine whether children can correctly identify and count the number of vertices of 3D shapes. Question **3** will determine whether children can compare and group shapes based on their number of vertices. Question **4** will determine whether children can apply their knowledge of vertices, addition, subtraction, multiplication and division in order to find solutions. Question **5** will determine whether children are able to identify the number of faces, edges and vertices of 3D shapes.

ANSWERS Answers for the **Practice** part of the lesson appear in the separate **Practice and Reflect answer guide**.

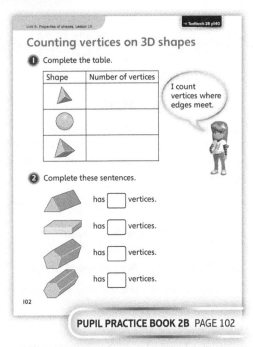

PUPIL PRACTICE BOOK 2B PAGE 102

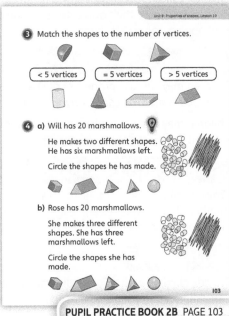

PUPIL PRACTICE BOOK 2B PAGE 103

Reflect

Group work

IN FOCUS This section requires children to visualise and either recall or count the number of vertices on a 3D shape. Children should start to remember how many vertices there are on familiar shapes such as cuboids and pyramids.

ASSESSMENT CHECKPOINT This section will determine whether children can recall or visualise the number of vertices on familiar 3D shapes.

ANSWERS Answers for the **Reflect** part of the lesson appear in the separate **Practice and Reflect answer guide**.

After the lesson ⏸

- Were children secure on the distinction between faces, edges and vertices?
- Are children able to describe 3D shapes by the number of faces, vertices and edges?
- Is there opportunity to display the definitions and properties of 3D shapes to reinforce learning?

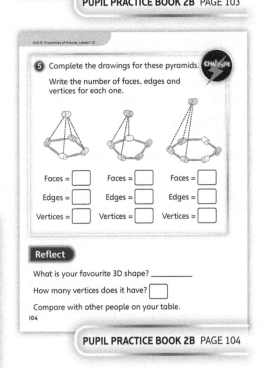

PUPIL PRACTICE BOOK 2B PAGE 104

Sorting 3D shapes

Learning focus

In this lesson, children will sort 3D shapes based on their properties. Children will have to apply their learning from the previous three lessons about 3D shapes.

Small steps

→ Previous step: Counting vertices on 3D shapes
→ **This step: Sorting 3D shapes**
→ Next step: Making patterns with 3D shapes

NATIONAL CURRICULUM LINKS

Year 2 Geometry – Properties of Shape

Compare and sort common 2D and 3D shapes and everyday objects.

ASSESSING MASTERY

Children can sort 3D shapes based on given criteria, identifying similarities and differences in the properties of shapes in order to choose their own criteria for sorting 3D shapes. Children will be able to use groups (sets), both separate and overlapping, to sort 3D shapes.

COMMON MISCONCEPTIONS

Children may confuse properties of shapes, such as mistaking edges for vertices. Give children a 3D shape and ask:
• *Can you point to an edge? A vertex? A face?*

Children may make the mistake of describing a curved surface as a face. Hold up a cylinder and ask:
• *How many faces does this shape have?*

STRENGTHENING UNDERSTANDING

Provide children with a range of 3D shapes and sorting hoops. Discuss the properties of each shape and note down the number of faces, vertices and edges for each. Children can then work in pairs to sort the shapes into two or more groups. Ask children to label each group and then compare with another pair to see if they sorted the shapes in a different way.

GOING DEEPER

Provide children with a Carroll diagram, with the headings 'Pyramid', 'Prism', 'Six or fewer vertices' and 'More than six vertices'. Can children think of a shape to go in each group?

KEY LANGUAGE

In lesson: faces, pyramid, cuboid, sphere, curved surface, pentagon, edges, 2D

Other language to be used by the teacher: 3D shapes, groups, overlapping groups, vertex, vertices, hemisphere, triangle-based pyramid, square-based pyramid, pentagon-based pyramid, hexagon-based pyramid, cube, triangular prism, pentagonal prism, cylinder, cone, circle, oblong, rectangle

RESOURCES

Mandatory: 3D shapes, sorting hoops

 In the eTextbook of this lesson, you will find interactive links to a selection of teaching tools.

Before you teach ⏸

• Do children still need support when identifying properties of 3D shapes?
• How will you encourage children to explain their reasoning with regard to sorting 3D shapes?
• How will you make the links to the previous lessons clear?

Discover

WAYS OF WORKING Pair work

ASK

- *What is a pyramid?*
- *Which shapes do you find tricky to sort?*
- *Why do you think they put the cone in the wrong group?*

IN FOCUS Question ① a) requires children to look carefully at the shapes and determine whether they meet the criteria for the group in which they are placed. The cone looks similar to a pyramid as it has an apex, so some children may think that it is in the correct group. However, it is not a polyhedron; it has a curved surface and therefore is not a pyramid.

Some of the shapes have a different orientation from how they are usually presented and this may confuse some children. Tell children to look carefully at each shape to count the faces. Having corresponding concrete shapes may help some children.

ANSWERS

Question ① a): ⬭, △ and ◣ are in the wrong groups.
They belong in the 'Other' group as they are not pyramids and they do not have six faces.

Question ① b): A pentagon-based pyramid could go in both groups as it is a pyramid and has six faces.

Sorting 3D shapes

Discover

① a) Which shapes are in the wrong place?

b) Can you think of a different shape that could go in both the 'Six faces' group and the 'Pyramids' group?

144

PUPIL TEXTBOOK 2B PAGE 144

Share

WAYS OF WORKING Whole class teacher led

ASK

- *What group could you have for the cone and sphere? Can you think of another shape that would go in this group?*
- *What could you rename the 'Six faces' group so that the triangular prism could go into it as well as the cuboids?*
- *Can you think of a different way of sorting the shapes?*

IN FOCUS Question ① b) introduces the idea of overlapping (intersecting) groups. In order for a shape to go in the intersection, it has to meet the criteria for both the groups. Some children often struggle to place an item if it belongs in more than one group, so it is important to show how this can sometimes occur.

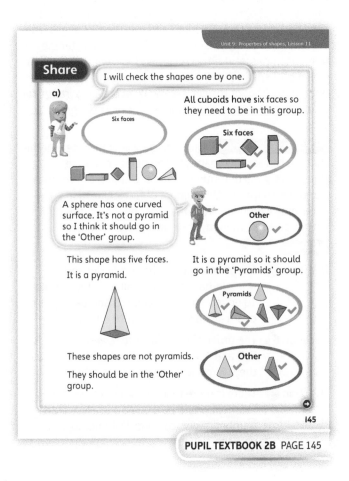

Share

I will check the shapes one by one.

a) All cuboids have six faces so they need to be in this group.

Six faces

A sphere has one curved surface. It's not a pyramid so I think it should go in the 'Other' group.

This shape has five faces. It is a pyramid.

It is a pyramid so it should go in the 'Pyramids' group.

These shapes are not pyramids. They should be in the 'Other' group.

145

PUPIL TEXTBOOK 2B PAGE 145

Think together

WAYS OF WORKING Whole class teacher led (I do, We do, You do)

ASK

- Question **1**: *Could you sort these in a similar way but by number of faces?*
- Question **2**: *Would the order be the same if it was number of edges or vertices?*
- Question **3**: *Can you think of more than one way of sorting them?*

IN FOCUS Question **3** presents children with 3D shapes as everyday objects. First, children have to look beyond the real-life context and focus on the mathematical properties. Flo helps children by giving them a criterion for one of the groups. Children then have to decide on how to sort the remaining shapes into two groups. There is more than one possible solution to this and it would be valuable to ask children to share and justify how they sorted the shapes.

STRENGTHEN Provide children with concrete representations of the shapes in questions **1** and **2** to help them count the edges and faces so that they can physically sort and order them. Encourage them to talk about their thinking as they do it and to explain their decisions.

DEEPEN Look at question **1** and ask children: *What would happen if the groups were '< 12 edges' and '> 12 edges'?* After children have had time to think and discuss, ask them where they would put the cuboids. Some children may think that cuboids are in both groups, but a shape cannot have both more than 12 edges and less than 12 edges. The cuboids need to be outside the circles. Draw a rectangle that encompasses the two circles and ask where the cuboids would go. Explain that the cuboids belong in the rectangle, but not in either of the circles. Ask: *What are you sorting? You are sorting 3D shapes, so you can call the universal group '3D shapes'.*

ASSESSMENT CHECKPOINT Question **1** will determine whether children can sort 3D shapes by the number of edges. Question **2** will determine whether children can compare and order shapes by the number of faces. Question **3** will determine whether children can identify properties of 3D shapes and sort them by their own chosen criteria.

ANSWERS

Question **1** : The sphere, hemisphere, cylinder and triangle-based pyramid all have fewer than 10 edges. The cube, cuboids and pentagonal prism all have more than 10 edges.

Question **2** : The order of most faces to fewest faces is B, E, D and A, C. The order would be the same if they were sorted by edges or vertices.

Question **3** : There is more than one way to solve this. An example would be 'Curved surfaces', 'Odd number of vertices' and 'Even number of vertices'.

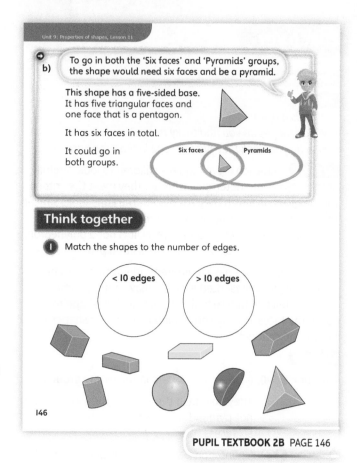

PUPIL TEXTBOOK 2B PAGE 146

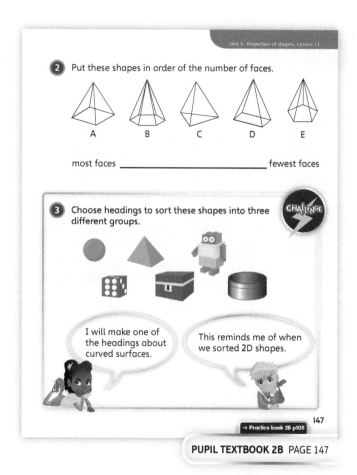

PUPIL TEXTBOOK 2B PAGE 147

174

Practice

WAYS OF WORKING Pair work

IN FOCUS Question ❹ requires children to choose their own criteria for sorting the shapes into two groups. There are a number of possible solutions to this question, so it could be a good opportunity to ask children to explain their reasoning and justify their decisions. Ask children to challenge themselves. The most straightforward solution would be a 'true' or 'not true' approach, such as 'curved surface' and 'no curved surface'. But children could try a 'less than' or 'more than' approach and consider the number of vertices, edges or faces.

STRENGTHEN If children are finding it difficult to sort 3D shapes, provide them with a variety of concrete 3D shapes and ask them to select all shapes with a given property. For example, ask: *Can you find all the shapes with a circular face? How about shapes with a curved surface?* You could then extend this by secretly choosing a property and selecting all those shapes that match it and then asking children: *What do all these shapes have in common?* Children could then carry out the same activity in pairs.

DEEPEN Extend question ❹ by asking children to sort the shapes so that at least one shape has to go in the overlap between the groups. Could children sort them into three groups, with at least one shape belonging to all three groups? For example, 'Has a triangular face', 'Has a rectangular face', 'Has fewer than eight vertices'.

ASSESSMENT CHECKPOINT Question ❶ will determine whether children can identify shapes that do not match a given criterion. Questions ❷ and question ❸ will determine whether children can identify shapes that meet more than one criterion. Question ❹ will determine whether children can devise their own criteria for sorting 3D shapes. Question ❺ will determine whether children can compare and order 3D shapes by the number of vertices and edges.

ANSWERS Answers for the **Practice** part of the lesson appear in the separate **Practice and Reflect answer guide**.

Reflect

WAYS OF WORKING Pair work

IN FOCUS This question prompts children to think of more than one way to sort the shapes. In order to do this, they have to consider more than one type of property. The added challenge of having two in each group means that children have to think carefully about the shapes' similarities and differences.

ASSESSMENT CHECKPOINT This section will determine whether children can identify similarities and differences between 3D shapes and whether they can sort them in more than one way by considering different types of properties.

ANSWERS Answers for the **Reflect** part of the lesson appear in the separate **Practice and Reflect answer guide**.

After the lesson ⏸

- Did the discussions between children help them to reason more deeply about properties of 3D shapes?
- Did any children struggle due to gaps in their understanding of properties of 3D shapes?

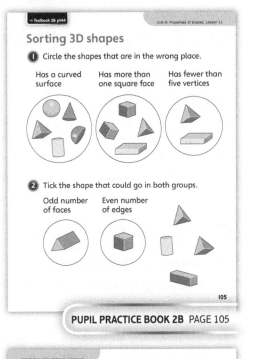

PUPIL PRACTICE BOOK 2B PAGE 105

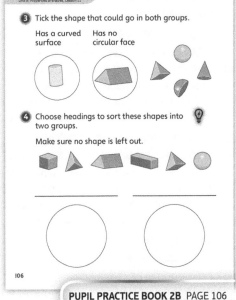

PUPIL PRACTICE BOOK 2B PAGE 106

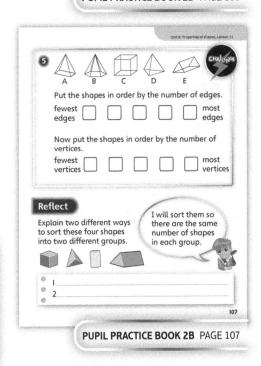

PUPIL PRACTICE BOOK 2B PAGE 107

Making patterns with 3D shapes

Learning focus

In this lesson, children will make symmetrical patterns with 3D shapes. They will use what they know about symmetrical patterns to identify missing shapes and create their own.

Small steps

→ Previous step: Sorting 3D shapes
→ **This step: Making patterns with 3D shapes**
→ Next step: Understanding whole and parts

NATIONAL CURRICULUM LINKS

Year 2 Geometry – Properties of Shape

Order and arrange combinations of mathematical objects in patterns and sequences.

ASSESSING MASTERY

Children can identify the symmetry in patterns and use this to find missing shapes. Children can create their own symmetrical patterns from a given set of 3D shapes and apply their knowledge of properties of 3D shapes when designing their own patterns.

COMMON MISCONCEPTIONS

Children may assume that the pattern is a repeating pattern when there is no repeating core. Children may try to repeat the whole sequence of shapes in order to create a repeating pattern or reverse the mirror image so that the pattern repeats. Show children a symmetrical pattern made from 3D shapes and ask:
• *Can you name all the shapes? Are there any parts of the pattern that repeat?*

STRENGTHENING UNDERSTANDING

Allow children to create their own symmetrical patterns with 3D shapes. Start with a single shape for the centre of the pattern, then tell children to pick up two of the same shape, one in each hand. Next, tell them to place these shapes on either side of the centre shape. Repeat this process of placing two identical shapes on either side to create a symmetrical pattern. Working from the centre out, ask children to point and name each shape.

GOING DEEPER

Ask children to explore making a symmetrical pattern with 3D shapes that has both a vertical and horizontal line of symmetry. How will children go about doing this? Where will they start? How can they ensure that their pattern has horizontal and vertical symmetry?

KEY LANGUAGE

In lesson: 3D, symmetrical, cylinder, repeating pattern

Other language to be used by the teacher: sphere, cone, triangle-based pyramid, square-based pyramid, cube, cuboid, faces, edges, vertices, symmetry, vertical, horizontal, reflective

RESOURCES

Mandatory: 3D shapes, mirrors

 In the eTextbook of this lesson, you will find interactive links to a selection of teaching tools.

Before you teach ⏸

- Are children secure in naming the 3D shapes in this lesson?
- How can you make links from this lesson to children's learning in Lessons 5 and 7?
- How will you promote discussions of thinking and strategies when children complete and create patterns?

Discover

Unit 9: Properties of shapes, Lesson 12

WAYS OF WORKING Pair work

ASK

- Question **1** a): *Which shape is not repeated in the pattern?*
- Question **1** a): *Are you able to continue the pattern?*
- Question **1** b): *Which shape is there only one of? How can this help you?*

IN FOCUS Question **1** a) asks children to identify the pattern in the sequence of shapes. There is no repeating core in the pattern and this may puzzle children as they have looked at repeating patterns in Lesson 5 of this unit. Children may try to repeat the whole sequence or think that the repeating core is cube, cylinder, pyramid. Ask children to look at the centre shape first and work out from both sides rather than starting from the end if they struggle to see the pattern.

ANSWERS

Question **1** a): It is a symmetrical pattern with the line of symmetry running down the centre of the blue cuboid.

Question **1** b): The cylinder has to be in the centre, with two identical shapes either side and the final two identical shapes at either end.

Making patterns with 3D shapes

Discover

1 a) Describe the pattern of 3D shapes.

b) Create the same sort of pattern using these shapes.

148

PUPIL TEXTBOOK 2B PAGE 148

Share

WAYS OF WORKING Whole class teacher led

ASK

- Question **1** a): *Could you rearrange these shapes and still have a symmetrical pattern?*
- Question **1** a): *If you removed the centre cuboid would it still be symmetrical?*
- Question **1** b): *How many different ways are there to do this?*
- Question **1** b): *Why do you think symmetrical patterns start with the middle shape?*

IN FOCUS Question **1** b) shows children how a symmetrical pattern can be created. By starting in the middle, symmetry can be assured by placing identical shapes either side. Although in the pictures the characters place the spheres next to the cylinder, they could have placed the cubes or the cones next to the cylinder. This can lead to a discussion about there being more than one possibility and how children could find all the possibilities.

Share

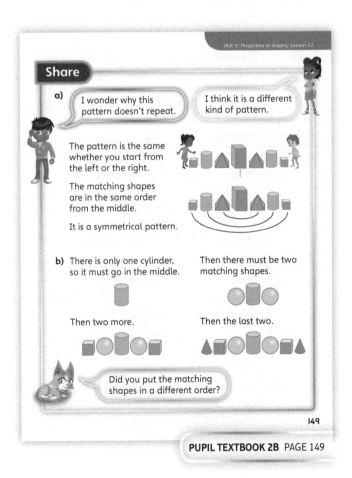

a) I wonder why this pattern doesn't repeat.

I think it is a different kind of pattern.

The pattern is the same whether you start from the left or the right.

The matching shapes are in the same order from the middle.

It is a symmetrical pattern.

b) There is only one cylinder, so it must go in the middle.

Then there must be two matching shapes.

Then two more.

Then the last two.

Did you put the matching shapes in a different order?

149

PUPIL TEXTBOOK 2B PAGE 149

Think together

Think together

WAYS OF WORKING Whole class teacher led (I do, We do, You do)

ASK

- Question ❶: *Which shape will you look at first?*
- Question ❷: *Which shape or shapes will you start with?*
- Question ❷: *Is your pattern different from your partner's pattern? Explain to your partner why you chose to do it your way.*
- Question ❸: *Is it possible to use these shapes to create a pattern that is repeating and symmetrical?*

IN FOCUS Question ❸ requires children to design their own symmetrical pattern. Children have to choose how many of each shape they have. They could have one shape in the centre or two identical shapes, so the line of reflective symmetry runs between them. This question allows children to explore different ways of creating symmetrical patterns. This question also draws on children's learning from Lesson 5 by asking them to create a repeating pattern. This helps children understand the distinction between repeating and symmetrical patterns.

STRENGTHEN Provide children with a mirror for question ❶ so that they can use it to identify what shapes are missing. If they struggle to find the line of reflective symmetry, this can be drawn for them.

For questions ❷ and ❸, provide children with the corresponding 3D shapes or pictures of the shapes so that they can explore arranging them. Children can then use a mirror to test whether their design is symmetrical.

DEEPEN Extend question ❷ by asking children to find as many ways as they can to use the shapes to create a symmetrical pattern. Can they work systematically to ensure that they have them all? Get them to check their solutions with a partner to see if they have missed any out.

ASSESSMENT CHECKPOINT Question ❶ will determine whether children can identify missing shapes in a symmetrical pattern. Question ❷ will determine whether children can create a symmetrical pattern with given shapes. Question ❸ will determine whether children can design their own symmetrical patterns and whether they understand the difference between symmetrical and repeating patterns.

ANSWERS

Question ❶ : In the first pattern, the missing shapes are cube and sphere. In the second pattern, the missing shapes are sphere and cube.

Question ❷ : There are various solutions to this problem. Check children's answers to ensure the patterns are symmetrical.

Question ❸ : There are various solutions to this problem. Check children's answers to ensure they have created both a symmetrical and a repeating pattern.

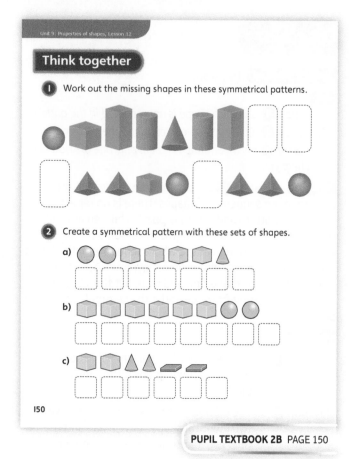

PUPIL TEXTBOOK 2B PAGE 150

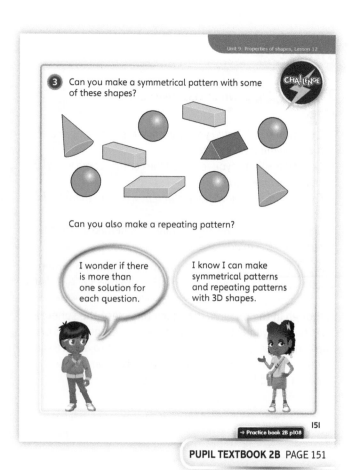

PUPIL TEXTBOOK 2B PAGE 151

178

Practice

WAYS OF WORKING Pair work

IN FOCUS Question **5** requires children to apply what they have learned about properties of shape in order to find the solution. As there are to be only three shapes, two of them have to be the same. Children must think of a shape, count the faces, edges or vertices and double it. They then subtract this from the total number of faces, edges and vertices in order to identify the centre shape. This is a multi-step problem that requires a high level of reasoning. Therefore, children will benefit from working in pairs or small groups to promote discussion and help them find the solution.

STRENGTHEN Provide children with mirrors to identify missing shapes and to check their own symmetrical patterns. Where possible, provide children with 3D shapes so that they can manipulate them and easily adapt their ideas.

DEEPEN Provide children with a range of cutouts of 3D shapes. Children work in pairs. Each child takes it in turn to add two identical shapes to create a joint symmetrical pattern. Each time they add two shapes, they count the number of faces, edges and vertices, and add that number to the running total for the pattern. The first pair to reach or pass 100 wins. This can be further extended by asking children to create a pattern that has both a vertical and a horizontal line of reflective symmetry.

ASSESSMENT CHECKPOINT Question **1** will determine whether children can identify missing shapes from a symmetrical pattern. Questions **2** and **3** will determine whether children can create their own symmetrical patterns from given 3D shapes. Question **4** will determine whether children can create their own symmetrical patterns, devise their own problems and identify patterns to find missing shapes. Question **5** will determine whether children can carry out multi-step problems involving shape by applying their understanding of properties of shape and symmetrical patterns.

ANSWERS Answers for the **Practice** part of the lesson appear in the separate **Practice and Reflect answer guide**.

Reflect

WAYS OF WORKING Pair work

IN FOCUS This question tests children's understanding of symmetrical and repeating patterns. In order for children to give a concise and accurate explanation of the difference, they need to be secure in their understanding. Ask children to discuss and compose their answer to this problem with a partner and to use a whiteboard so that they can edit and improve their answer before writing it in their practice books.

ASSESSMENT CHECKPOINT This section will determine whether children have a secure understanding of what constitutes a repeating pattern and a symmetrical pattern and what the differences are between them.

ANSWERS Answers for the **Reflect** part of the lesson appear in the separate **Practice and Reflect answer guide**.

After the lesson ⏸

- Were children able to use their knowledge of the names and properties of 3D shapes fluently in this lesson?
- How confident were children in identifying, completing and creating symmetrical patterns?

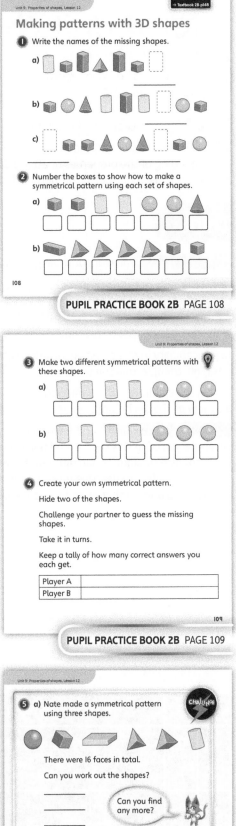

PUPIL PRACTICE BOOK 2B PAGE 108

PUPIL PRACTICE BOOK 2B PAGE 109

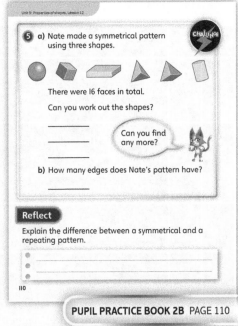

PUPIL PRACTICE BOOK 2B PAGE 110

End of unit check

Don't forget the *Power Maths* unit assessment grid on p26.

WAYS OF WORKING Group work – adult led

IN FOCUS This end of unit check requires children to draw on their understanding of the properties of 2D and 3D shapes and how shapes are categorised based on specific properties that they share.

Think!

WAYS OF WORKING Pair work or small groups

IN FOCUS This question requires children to apply their understanding of the vertices of 2D shapes in order to solve the problem. By working with a partner, children can discuss and justify their strategies. Provide children with squares of paper to encourage a 'trial and improve' approach.

Key vocabulary in this question includes: vertices, sides, pentagon, hexagon, triangle, quadrilateral.

Encourage children to think through or discuss the number of vertices for a variety of shapes before writing their answer in **My journal**.

ANSWERS AND COMMENTARY Children will be able to recognise the key vocabulary used in this section and reliably count each property. Children can recognise similarities and differences between shapes and use the correct vocabulary to describe these. Children will confidently name a variety of 2D and 3D shapes and recognise patterns involving shapes.

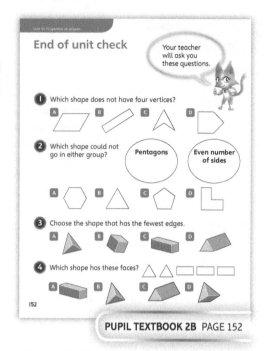

PUPIL TEXTBOOK 2B PAGE 152

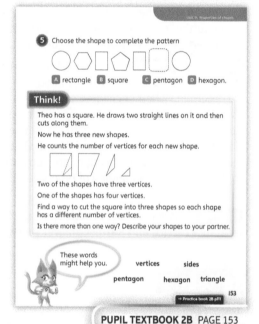

PUPIL TEXTBOOK 2B PAGE 153

Q	A	WRONG ANSWERS AND MISCONCEPTIONS	STRENGTHENING UNDERSTANDING
1	D	A, B or C suggests that children have miscounted or do not understand the meaning of 'vertices'. C may also suggest that children did not include the concave vertex.	Provide children with concrete 2D and 3D shapes so that they can practise recognising and counting the different properties. Children can also use dry-wipe markers to mark off properties as they count them.
2	B	A suggests that children have miscounted or do not understand the meaning of 'even'. C suggests that children have miscounted or do not recognise a pentagon. D suggests that children have miscounted or have not recognised all sides.	
3	A	B, C or D suggests that children have miscounted or do not understand the meaning of 'edges'.	
4	C	A, B or D suggests that children do not recognise the shapes of faces.	
5	D	A, B or C suggests that children do not recognise the names of 2D shapes or have failed to recognise the symmetrical pattern.	

My journal

WAYS OF WORKING Independent thinking

ANSWERS AND COMMENTARY

If children cut off one of the square's corners, they produce a pentagon and a triangle. Children could then cut off a corner from the triangle to create a smaller triangle, a quadrilateral and a pentagon.

Alternatively, children could cut the square from side to side to produce two quadrilaterals. By cutting a corner off from either quadrilateral, children will end up with a pentagon, a quadrilateral and a triangle.

Provide children with squares of paper so that they can physically cut the square and then reassemble it so that they can see where the cut lines are. Encourage children to count the sides or vertices and then refer to a classroom display of the properties of shape to help children identify the shapes they have created.

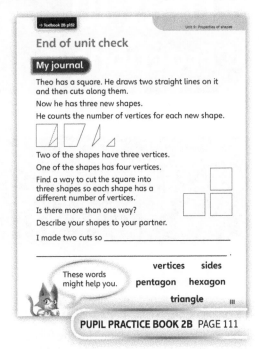

PUPIL PRACTICE BOOK 2B PAGE 111

Power check

WAYS OF WORKING Independent thinking

ASK

- *Do you think you are better at naming and describing 2D shapes and 3D shapes than before?*
- *Do you think you can sort shapes in different ways?*

Power puzzle

WAYS OF WORKING Pair work or small groups

IN FOCUS Use this **Power puzzle** to assess whether children are able to identify and create different types of cuboid. Working in pairs will encourage children to work collaboratively to find all the solutions.

ANSWERS AND COMMENTARY With 24 cubes, children could create a 1 × 1 × 24 cuboid, a 1 × 2 × 12 cuboid, a 1 × 3 × 8 cuboid, a 1 × 4 × 6 cuboid, a 2 × 2 × 6 cuboid or a 2 × 3 × 4 cuboid. In order to find all the possibilities, children need to understand that cuboids need to have six faces and that the faces can be square or oblong.

With 27 cubes, children can create a 1 × 1 × 27 cuboid, a 1 × 3 × 9 cuboid or a 3 × 3 × 3 cuboid. To find all 3, children need to understand that a cube is a special type of cuboid.

If children are unsuccessful in identifying all the cuboids, or if they create shapes that are not cuboids, provide opportunities for them to create their own cuboids using a range of construction equipment, straws and multilink cubes. Encourage children to produce a range of cuboids, including cubes, and to check the shapes they make against the key mathematical properties.

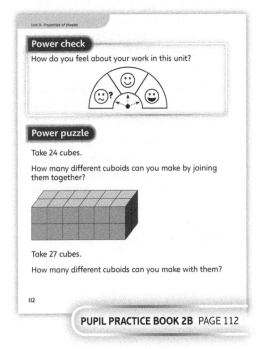

PUPIL PRACTICE BOOK 2B PAGE 112

After the unit ⏸

- Were children able to use the key vocabulary accurately, fluently and confidently when naming, sorting and describing 2D and 3D shapes?
- Can you find opportunities to reinforce this learning in other areas of the curriculum?

Strengthen and **Deepen** activities for this unit can be found in the *Power Maths* online subscription.

Unit 10
Fractions

Mastery Expert tip! "There were plenty of physical resources in the classroom that I could use to model equals in fractions, which allowed children to make links between what they saw on the page and real-life objects. Every time a lesson showed an image or shape split into equal parts, I would show children a physical object that also represents it, such as the window, an egg box or a pack of pencils."

Don't forget to watch the Unit 10 video!

WHY THIS UNIT IS IMPORTANT

This unit introduces fractions for the first time. It builds on children's knowledge of equal parts, which they have come across in previous units about multiplication and division. This unit also exposes children to equal parts in a range of contexts, including shape, numbers, measurements and money.

Within this unit, children will be introduced to fraction-specific key language such as numerator and denominator and will be able to explain what each word means in context.

At first, children will deal with unit fractions where the numerator is always one, focusing on halves, thirds and quarters. Children will then move onto non-unit fractions and learn about the equivalence between them, particularly between $\frac{1}{2}$ and $\frac{2}{4}$. Children will practise counting up in quarters and halves on a number line, including crossing through whole number barriers.

WHERE THIS UNIT FITS

→ Unit 9: Properties of shapes

→ **Unit 10: Fractions**

→ Unit 11: Position and direction

This unit builds on children's knowledge of sharing and grouping in division, asking children to divide a whole into equal parts and learn that the equal parts have given names. Children also learn to halve shapes by folding them or cutting them in two. Children can find a fraction of an amount using the previous strategy of sharing objects into equal groups but can now name these parts, such as by saying that $\frac{1}{2}$ of 6 is 3.

Before they start this unit, it is expected that children:

• know how to split an amount into equal parts by sharing or grouping

• understand that the same whole can have a different number of equal parts (building upon Unit 6)

• know what ÷ means.

ASSESSING MASTERY

Children who have mastered this unit will be able to explain what each part of a fraction represents. Children will be able to relate fractions to different contexts where there are equal parts and will be able to find a unit and non-unit fraction of a number, shape, measurement or time. Children will be able to recognise equivalent fractions and explain the relationship between the numerator and denominator in equivalent fractions. Children will also be able to work out a whole from a non-unit fraction using a bar model.

COMMON MISCONCEPTIONS	STRENGTHENING UNDERSTANDING	GOING DEEPER
Children may think that more parts always means a greater amount.	Fold a strip of paper into equal parts, label the parts and then fold them into equal parts again. Count up how many equal pieces there are now and count the whole again.	Show children a shape that has been halved and then each half halved again in a different way. Discuss whether each of the parts still represents $\frac{1}{4}$, even though they may be different shapes.
Children may think that it is only possible to count in whole numbers and not in fractions.	Demonstrate that there are lots of ways of making one half of a square. Give children pieces of squared paper and encourage them to investigate this.	Give children a whole number, such as 12, and ask them to make as many different equal parts as they can. Investigate which whole numbers allow children to make the most equal parts.

Unit 10: Fractions

Use these pages to introduce the unit. Use the characters to discuss concepts and phrases that children have heard before. For example, children were introduced to the concept of equal parts when learning about division.

STRUCTURES AND REPRESENTATIONS

Fraction number line: This model will help children recognise patterns when counting in fractions and will help them to practise counting up or down in halves.

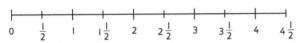

Part whole model: This model has been used before and is now used to show the partition of a mixed number. For example, $2\frac{1}{2}$ is partitioned into 2 and $\frac{1}{2}$.

KEY LANGUAGE

There is some key language that children will need to know as part of the learning in this unit:

→ fraction
→ half ($\frac{1}{2}$), quarter ($\frac{1}{4}$), third ($\frac{1}{3}$)
→ whole
→ part, equal part
→ numerator, denominator
→ fraction bar
→ unit fraction, non-unit fraction
→ equivalent
→ three-quarters ($\frac{3}{4}$)
→ equal
→ divided by (÷)
→ odd, even
→ share
→ pattern

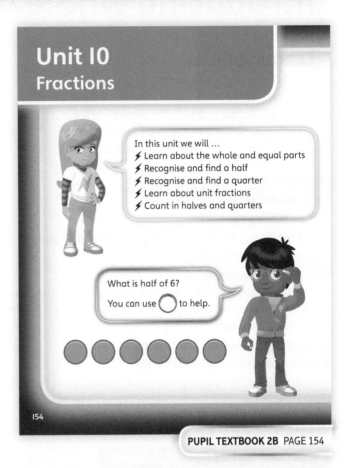

PUPIL TEXTBOOK 2B PAGE 154

PUPIL TEXTBOOK 2B PAGE 155

Introducing whole and parts

Learning focus

In this lesson, children will talk about the difference between a whole and a part in different contexts. Children will match parts to the correct wholes and fill in sentence scaffolds to match parts and wholes.

Small steps

→ Previous step: Making patterns with 3D shapes
→ **This step: Introducing whole and parts**
→ Next step: Making equal parts

NATIONAL CURRICULUM LINKS

Year 2 Number – Fractions

Recognise, find and name a half as one of two equal parts of an object, shape or quantity (year 1).

ASSESSING MASTERY

Children can imagine what the whole could be if they are given one part. Children understand that there can be many wholes and many parts within each whole and they can find multiple parts of one whole, understanding each time that the whole has not changed.

COMMON MISCONCEPTIONS

Children may believe that a whole needs to be something very big or that a part has to be something very small. Expose children to lots of different examples, such as wholes that are different shapes and sizes and parts that are big as well as small. Ask:

• *Does a whole or part have to be a certain size? Does the size matter?*

STRENGTHENING UNDERSTANDING

A number of objects in the classroom can represent a whole and can be taken apart into different parts. For example, a pencil case is a whole and holds a number of small objects that can be different parts. Ask children to find their own physical examples of wholes and parts in the classroom, guiding them towards understanding that the part is always smaller than the whole and the whole is always bigger than the part.

GOING DEEPER

Challenge children to zoom in on or zoom out of a whole or a part so that each object becomes both a whole and a part. For example, a book can be part of a book shelf (the whole) and the whole, with a page becoming the part.

KEY LANGUAGE

In lesson: whole, equal, part, how many?, different

Other language to be used by the teacher: split

STRUCTURES AND REPRESENTATIONS

Part-whole model

RESOURCES

Mandatory: sentence scaffolds

Optional: objects in the classroom, such as pencil cases, that contain multiple parts

 In the eTextbook of this lesson, you will find interactive links to a selection of teaching tools.

Before you teach ⏸

• Are children confident with the words 'whole' and 'part' in relation to number?
• What curriculum links could make this lesson more tangible?

Discover

Pair work

ASK

- Question ❶ a): *What is the whole?*
- *Is the number of parts the same as the number of continents?*
- *Could you split up the whole in any other way?*

IN FOCUS The world map should be familiar to children so it is a good starting point for working out parts. If children struggle with continent names, use familiar places such as their home and school. This allows children themselves to also be part of the whole.

ANSWERS

Question ❶ a): The world is the whole. The continents are the parts.

Question ❶ b): There are seven continents, so there are seven parts.

Introducing whole and parts

Discover

There are seven continents.

Europe
Asia
North America
South America
Africa
Australia
Antarctica

❶ a) Complete the sentences.

The _____ is the whole.

The _____ are the parts.

world

continents

b) How many parts are there?

156

PUPIL TEXTBOOK 2B PAGE 156

Share

Whole class teacher led

ASK

- Question ❶ a): *Does the whole change because it has different parts?*
- Question ❶ a): *Can the whole have lots of different parts?*
- Question ❶ b): *What important word does Ash say? Do you think the parts are equal?*

IN FOCUS Astrid says that lots of different sentences can be made using the words whole and parts. How many different sentences can children make using these words? Now bring children's attention to what Ash says and see whether they can spot the important word, 'equal'. Refer to the images to encourage children to compare the different parts and see whether they are equal.

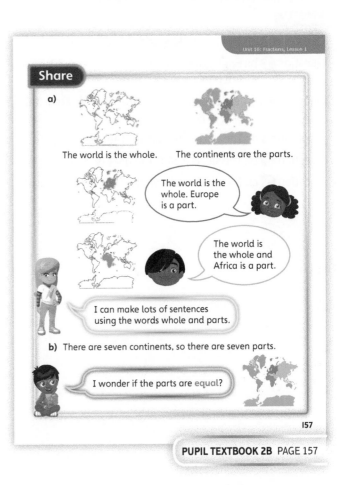

Share

a)

The world is the whole.   The continents are the parts.

The world is the whole. Europe is a part.

The world is the whole and Africa is a part.

I can make lots of sentences using the words whole and parts.

b) There are seven continents, so there are seven parts.

I wonder if the parts are equal?

157

PUPIL TEXTBOOK 2B PAGE 157

Think together

WAYS OF WORKING Whole class teacher led (I do, We do, You do)

ASK

• *Does the whole change when you identify a different part?*
• *Can you think of any more parts?*

IN FOCUS In question ❶ , children can cross out each country as they say its name in each sentence. Encourage them to do the same when answering question ❷ .

Question ❸ arranges the parts and wholes in different orders so that the first sentence is not necessarily the sentence about the whole. This requires children to look closely and work out whether each object is a part or a whole.

STRENGTHEN Ask children to think of different parts for each object in question ❸ . Can they name other parts of the duck, boat and pizza?

DEEPEN Encourage children to take a whole and create a new sentence where that whole is now a part of a new whole. For example, the elephant is the part and the zoo is the whole.

ASSESSMENT CHECKPOINT When reading the sentence scaffolds, can children instantly identify the whole or do they have to work it out? Are children confident in their ability to label each object a whole or a part, even when the order of the sentence scaffold has changed?

ANSWERS

Question ❶ a): The United Kingdom is the whole.

Question ❶ b): England/Scotland/Northern Ireland/Wales is a part.

Question ❷ : The elephant is the whole. The trunk/ear/tail/tusk/eye is a part.

Question ❸ a): The duck is the whole. The beak is a part.

Question ❸ b): The sail is a part. The boat is the whole.

Question ❸ c): The pizza is the whole. The cheese is a part.

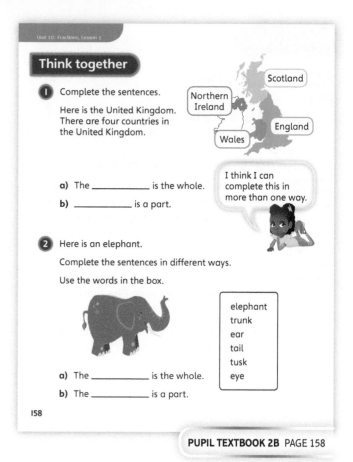

PUPIL TEXTBOOK 2B PAGE 158

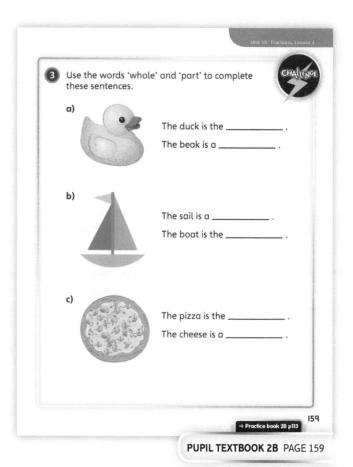

PUPIL TEXTBOOK 2B PAGE 159

Practice

WAYS OF WORKING Independent thinking

IN FOCUS The sentence scaffolds in question ❸ contain the written names of the objects or the words 'part' and 'whole' in different orders. Children must read and understand each sentence carefully to identify the word that would complete the sentence.

Question ❺ is the first question to present children with a part rather than the whole. It requires children to imagine the whole rather than identify a part.

STRENGTHEN Ask children to use the sentence scaffolds they have heard in the lesson to explain which objects in question ❶ they are linking together and whether each object is the whole or a part. Ask children to write the whole and the part in different orders when answering question ❹ so that they have to identify each part for themselves rather than relying on the order in which parts and wholes usually appear.

DEEPEN Take the objects in question ❹ and ask children what the whole would be if the flower or the swing was a part. For example, the flower would be a part if a field was the whole. Expand this further by discussing the fact that a petal would be a part of both the flower and the field.

ASSESSMENT CHECKPOINT Do children choose the truck in question ❷ as the whole in both instances? Do they make up an inaccurate set of statements because they are just trying to fill the blank, such as 'The light is the whole, the window is a part'?

Do children think of the window in question ❺ as a part or do they try to follow the pattern of previous questions and think of it as a whole? Do they answer with legitimate wholes or do they try to think of possible parts of the window?

ANSWERS Answers for the **Practice** part of the lesson appear in the separate **Practice and Reflect answer guide**.

Reflect

WAYS OF WORKING Pair work

IN FOCUS Children choose objects found in the classroom to make sentences using the words part and whole, with the freedom to choose an object of their choice.

ASSESSMENT CHECKPOINT Do children put their objects in the correct order when describing them as part or whole in relation to each other? Do children understand that a part must be smaller than the whole they have chosen? Equally, if they decide that an object is a part, do they understand that the whole must be bigger?

ANSWERS Answers for the **Reflect** part of the lesson appear in the separate **Practice and Reflect answer guide**.

After the lesson ⏸

- Were children confident with the relationship between a part and a whole across a range of contexts?
- Could children think of both a part and a whole from a given object?
- Did children show any awareness of parts being unequal or equal, such as commenting on the relative size of different parts of the same whole?

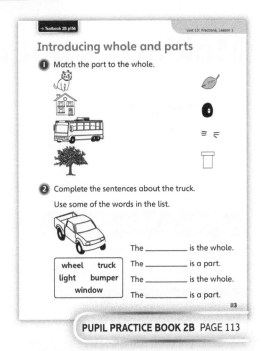

PUPIL PRACTICE BOOK 2B PAGE 113

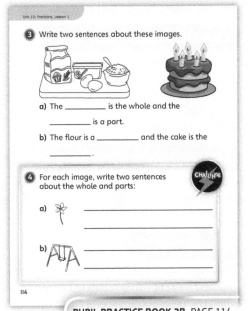

PUPIL PRACTICE BOOK 2B PAGE 114

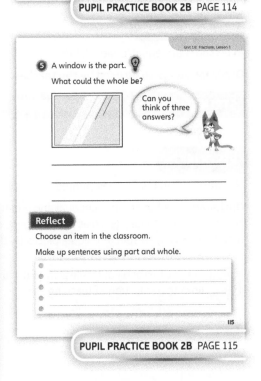

PUPIL PRACTICE BOOK 2B PAGE 115

187

Making equal parts

Learning focus

In this lesson, children will identify equal parts of a whole in different contexts including shape, quantity, volume and money.

Small steps

→ Previous step: Introducing whole and parts
→ **This step: Making equal parts**
→ Next step: Recognising a half ($\frac{1}{2}$)

NATIONAL CURRICULUM LINKS

Year 2 Number – Fractions

Recognise, find and name a half as one of two equal parts of an object, shape or quantity (year 1).

ASSESSING MASTERY

Children can associate the act of splitting a whole into equal parts with being fair and understand that the parts need to be the same. Children can recognise when parts of a variety of objects, shapes and volumes are unequal, can explain why and can rearrange unequal parts to make them equal parts.

COMMON MISCONCEPTIONS

When there is the same number of objects in each part but each object has a different value, children may believe that the parts are equal. For example, if there are three parts, each of which is one different value of coin, children may say that these parts are equal because there is one coin in each part. However, the coins have different values, which makes them unequal parts. Ask:

• *What is each group worth?*

STRENGTHENING UNDERSTANDING

Use real-life objects in the classroom to split equally between children. Ask children to think of times when a whole has to be split into equal parts to be fair, such as sharing out a pack of pens amongst the class or a packet of sweets with other children.

GOING DEEPER

When splitting an object into equal parts where the parts are not clear (perhaps because they are different shapes), ask children how they might check that all the parts are equal. For example, how would children cut a banana into equal pieces when the ends of the banana are different shapes to the middle? How would they check that the parts are equal?

KEY LANGUAGE

In lesson: part, equal, unequal, fair, fairly, differently, divide, odd one out, equal parts

Other language to be used by the teacher: whole, split, exactly

STRUCTURES AND REPRESENTATIONS

2D shapes

RESOURCES

Mandatory: multilink cubes, printed 2D shapes for children to fold into parts

Optional: a cake to cut into unequal and equal parts, objects that are easy to split equally (such as packs of pens or pencils), objects that are less easy to split into equal pieces (such as a banana)

 In the eTextbook of this lesson, you will find interactive links to a selection of teaching tools.

Before you teach

• Where might children have come across the concept of fair before? Did they discuss it when learning division?
• Are children confident with what the word equal means when talking about numbers from previous units?

Discover

WAYS OF WORKING Pair work

ASK

- Question ❶ a): *Why is it not fair? Who has more? Who has less?*
- Question ❶ b): *If you divided the cake for four children, would the slices be the same as the boy's slice or the girl's slice?*

IN FOCUS Explain that each child has a piece of cake but that one child does not look happy. Guide children to conclude that it is not fair because the children have different amounts of cake.

ANSWERS

Question ❶ a): It is not fair because one of the parts is bigger than the other. They could have split the cake into two equal parts.

Question ❶ b): The cake has been cut into four equal parts. Each child will get the same size piece.

Share

WAYS OF WORKING Whole class teacher led

ASK

- Question ❶ a): *Do the pieces of cake look the same?*
- Question ❶ b): *Do these pieces of cake look the same as each other or different to each other?*
- Question ❶ a) and ❶ b): *Are any of the parts bigger than the others?*

IN FOCUS Dexter explains that the pieces of cake in question ❶ a) are not equal. The next picture then shows the whole split into two equal parts to be shared equally between two children. The picture in question ❶ b) shows the whole split into four equal parts to be shared equally between four children. Bring in a cake or use circular pieces of paper to represent the cake.

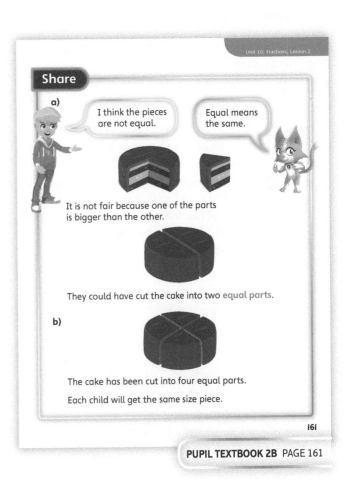

Think together

Whole class teacher led (I do, We do, You do)

ASK

- Question **1** : *Do all of the parts look the same or different? What makes them equal?*
- Question **1** : *How many parts has each been split into?*
- Question **1** : *Have all of the shapes been split?*

IN FOCUS Question **1** shows a variety of pictures and contexts that have been divided. Children need to work out which shapes have parts that are all the same.

Question **2** requires children to explain which picture is the odd one out based on the criterion of having equal parts.

STRENGTHEN In question **1** , B and C are the same shape split differently so children can compare them if they are unsure. You could print the shapes out so that children can fold them into the constituent parts to check whether the parts are the same or not.

DEEPEN Question **3** is a *Challenge* question, so provide children with physical resources to model it. For example, if one multilink cube represents one child, cubes can be put into three unequal piles to represent the children in the boats.

ASSESSMENT CHECKPOINT In question **1** , do children understand the idea of equal parts in shapes, volumes, money, and so on? Does F confuse them because each hand contains the same number of coins but they have different values? Do children want to use rulers to check whether E has been split into parts that have the same length and width?

ANSWERS

Question **1** : B and E show equal parts.

Question **2** : The odd one out is A because the children have not been split equally between the two carriages.

Question **3** : Children could make equal groups by moving one child from C to B to make three equal groups of two children or by moving one child from B to A to make two equal groups of three children.

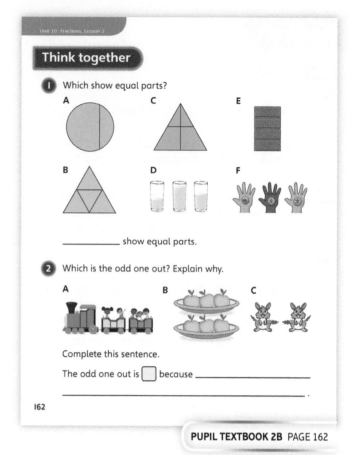

PUPIL TEXTBOOK 2B PAGE 162

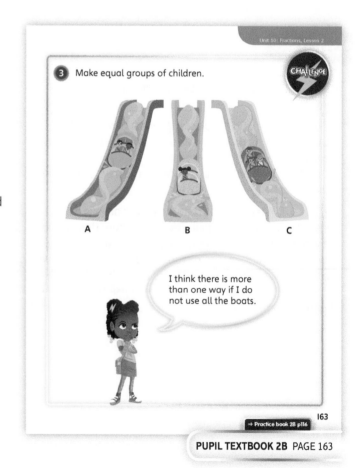

PUPIL TEXTBOOK 2B PAGE 163

Practice

WAYS OF WORKING Independent thinking

IN FOCUS Question ❶ requires children to count how many equal parts each whole has been split into.

Questions ❷ and ❸ ask children to decide whether the food and shapes have been split into equal or unequal parts.

Question ❹ asks children to rearrange unequal parts into equal parts. This can be modelled using multilink cubes, as suggested by Flo.

STRENGTHEN When children are answering question ❹ , ask them to articulate what the whole is and how many equal groups they will split the whole into. Ask how they would share out 12 cubes if they were using a sharing strategy. When children have worked out that there should be three cubes in each group, can they recreate the unequal arrangement in question ❹ and rearrange them in order to have three cubes in each group? Can they arrange them into groups of six cubes?

DEEPEN Question ❺ requires children to fold pieces of paper into equal and unequal parts. Can they do this with pieces of paper that are a variety of shapes and sizes? Refer to what Ash says and ask children whether they can do this in more than one way.

ASSESSMENT CHECKPOINT Question ❸ provides a circle that has been split into two equal parts with a diagonal line. Does this confuse children because they are more familiar with a circle split into two equal parts vertically?

When answering question ❺ , do children have a strategy for folding the pieces of paper exactly in half, such as by measuring the length of each side?

ANSWERS Answers for the **Practice** part of the lesson appear in the separate **Practice and Reflect answer guide**.

Reflect

WAYS OF WORKING Independent thinking

IN FOCUS The loaf of bread has been split into two unequal parts. This is easier to explain than a loaf split into three unequal parts because the uneven edges would have provided more ambiguity. Children must either agree or disagree with the statement that the parts are equal and explain why.

ASSESSMENT CHECKPOINT When explaining, do children give a reason why one part is more or less than the other? Do they identify a way to split the loaf equally, such as by measuring it?

ANSWERS Answers for the **Reflect** part of the lesson appear in the separate **Practice and Reflect answer guide**.

After the lesson ⏸

- Were children confident when splitting a range of objects into equal parts?
- Could children spot when parts were unequal and suggest how to arrange them to make them equal?
- Did children show any awareness of the names of equal parts, such as half?

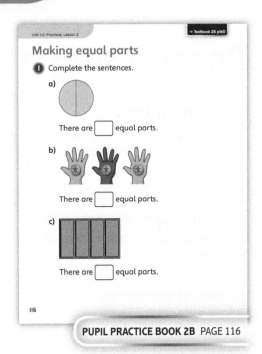

PUPIL PRACTICE BOOK 2B PAGE 116

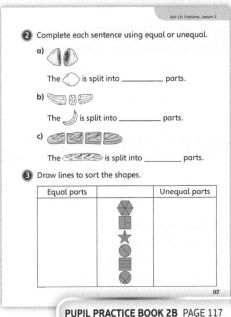

PUPIL PRACTICE BOOK 2B PAGE 117

PUPIL PRACTICE BOOK 2B PAGE 118

Recognising a half ($\frac{1}{2}$)

Learning focus

In this lesson, children will identify which objects have been split into two equal parts. They will be introduced to $\frac{1}{2}$ as a written fraction with a numerator and a denominator.

Small steps

→ Previous step: Making equal parts
→ **This step: Recognising a half ($\frac{1}{2}$)**
→ Next step: Finding a half

NATIONAL CURRICULUM LINKS

Year 2 Number – Fractions

Recognise, find and name a half as one of two equal parts of an object, shape or quantity (year 1).

ASSESSING MASTERY

Children can explain what the 1 and 2 represent in one half written as a fraction and can understand that it represents one whole divided into two equal parts in a range of contexts. Children can link finding one half of a shape to finding a line of symmetry.

COMMON MISCONCEPTIONS

Children may associate a shape that has been split into two equal parts with $\frac{1}{2}$ when it actually represents $\frac{2}{2}$. Show children that each part in the whole represents $\frac{1}{2}$. For example, you could label each part of a shape one half and label the whole shape one whole. Ask:

• *Where can you see $\frac{1}{2}$? What is the whole?*

STRENGTHENING UNDERSTANDING

When splitting a shape into two equal parts, have a mirror available so children can check either part. In addition, encourage children to experiment with folding cut-out shapes in half. Provide children with tracing paper or baking paper so they can trace one half of the shape and turn it over to check that the other half is the same.

GOING DEEPER

There are many contexts in which to find one half, such as half a distance to a place, half the weight of an object, half the height of a person, half of a bath full of water. Give children the opportunity to explore finding one half in as many contexts as possible so that they do not think that finding a half is only ever related to shapes, numbers or numbers of objects.

KEY LANGUAGE

In lesson: $\frac{1}{2}$, fraction, denominator, numerator, fraction bar, diagram, equal parts, half, halves, share equally, divide

Other language to be used by the teacher: whole, symmetrical, the same, line of symmetry, middle

STRUCTURES AND REPRESENTATIONS

3D shapes, 2D shapes

RESOURCES

Mandatory: 2D shapes printed out to be folded into equal and unequal parts, multilink cubes, a large printed and labelled $\frac{1}{2}$ as shown in the **Share** part of the lesson

Optional: mirrors, tracing paper, cardboard cylinders

 In the eTextbook of this lesson, you will find interactive links to a selection of teaching tools.

Before you teach ⏸

- Do children know the meaning of the word half in the context of halving and doubling numbers?
- Could you place a big display explaining $\frac{1}{2}$ in the classroom for children to refer to?

Discover

WAYS OF WORKING Pair work

ASK

- Question **1** b): *What makes the diagrams show one half?*
- Question **1** b): *Why do some of the diagrams not show one half?*

IN FOCUS Question **1** provides a variety of pictures to prompt children to recognise and identify one half. Children may be able to recognise some halves more easily than others, such as the multilink cubes, because they may have experience of sharing out this familiar physical resource.

ANSWERS

Question **1** a): $\frac{1}{2}$ means one part of two equal parts.

Question **1** b):

Halves	Not halves
☆	(cylinder)
(circle)	(triangle)
(cubes)	(cubes)

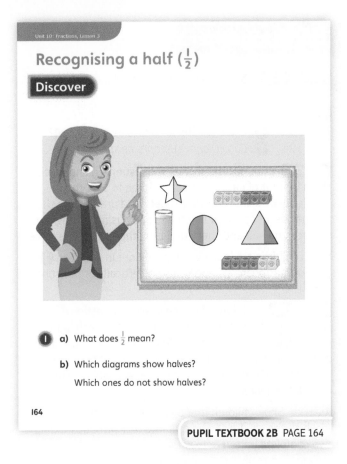

Recognising a half ($\frac{1}{2}$)

Discover

1 a) What does $\frac{1}{2}$ mean?

b) Which diagrams show halves?
Which ones do not show halves?

164

PUPIL TEXTBOOK 2B PAGE 164

Share

WAYS OF WORKING Whole class teacher led

ASK

- Question **1** a): *What does the 1 represent in $\frac{1}{2}$? What does the 2 represent in $\frac{1}{2}$?*
- Question **1** b): *Where can you see two equal parts in these diagrams?*

IN FOCUS Explain that the fraction bar is like the line in ÷ and means divide by. Question **1** b) highlights what a half is by also showing what a half is not in three different contexts. Encourage children to label each part $\frac{1}{2}$ to avoid confusion with the whole. Each half of the circle is $\frac{1}{2}$, whereas the circle is a whole.

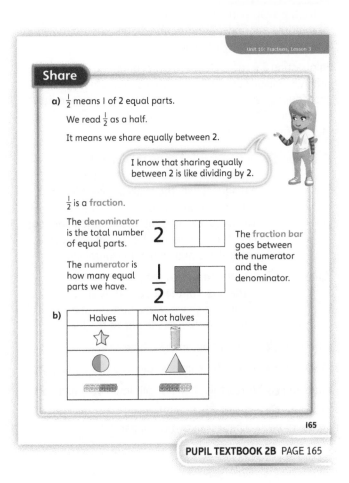

Share

a) $\frac{1}{2}$ means 1 of 2 equal parts.

We read $\frac{1}{2}$ as a half.

It means we share equally between 2.

I know that sharing equally between 2 is like dividing by 2.

$\frac{1}{2}$ is a fraction.

The denominator is the total number of equal parts.

The numerator is how many equal parts we have.

The fraction bar goes between the numerator and the denominator.

b)

Halves	Not halves
☆	(cylinder)
(circle)	(triangle)
(cubes)	(cubes)

165

PUPIL TEXTBOOK 2B PAGE 165

Think together

WAYS OF WORKING Whole class teacher led (I do, We do, You do)

ASK

- Question ❶ : *Can any of these shapes be split in half?*
- Question ❶ : *Can 2D and 3D shapes be split in half?*

IN FOCUS Print out the shapes in question ❶ and place them in front of each child. Ask children to split them physically by using a mirror to check and draw where the two halves meet, by folding them, or by using tracing paper to trace one half and check that the other side is the same.

When children are looking at the cylinder in question ❶ , provide cardboard cylinders to split vertically or horizontally in half.

STRENGTHEN If children find the shape in question ❸ b) confusing, represent each part of the square with light- and dark-coloured multilink cubes. Show children that, as long as there are two dark cubes and two light cubes, it does not matter which way they are rearranged when forming a complete square.

DEEPEN Show children that there are plenty of other ways in which the square can be split into half without shading two complete parts. For example, each quarter could be halved diagonally to create a pattern of triangles or the whole square could be halved by a diagonal line.

ASSESSMENT CHECKPOINT What method do children use to halve the shapes in question ❶ ? Do they show awareness of multiple methods? Are they able to find multiple ways of splitting the rectangle in half?

In question ❸ , do children appear confident that there are still two halves despite the fact that the whole is split up into four equal parts? Can they circle each of the two halves in question ❸ a)?

ANSWERS

Question ❶ : The rectangle can be split in half with a vertical line, with a horizontal line and with a diagonal line. The oval can be split in half with a horizontal line and with a vertical line. The arrow can be split in half with a horizontal line. The cylinder can be split in half with a vertical line and with a horizontal line.

Question ❷ a): Children should shade one half of the triangle. For the square, they should first split the shape with a horizontal or vertical line and then shade one of the halves.

Question ❷ b): The whole shape will be a circle.

Question ❸ a): Yes, this shape is split into two equal parts.

Question ❸ b): Yes, this shape is split into two equal parts.

Question ❸ c): There are four other ways you can split this shape into two equal parts.

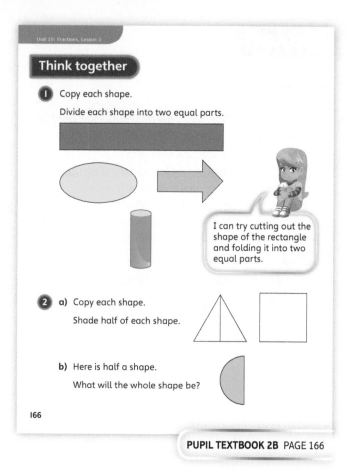

PUPIL TEXTBOOK 2B PAGE 166

PUPIL TEXTBOOK 2B PAGE 167

Practice

→ Textbook 2B p164

WAYS OF WORKING Independent thinking

IN FOCUS Question **2** gives children one whole and asks them to shade in $\frac{1}{2}$ of each shape. Questions **2** b) and **2** d) do not include a line to indicate halves, but children can add one themselves.

Question **3** gives children shapes that represent one half and asks them to draw one whole. Children can use tracing paper to help them visualise what the whole could look like. Prompt further thought by referring to what Ash says.

STRENGTHEN Cut the shapes in question **5** out of paper and give them to children. Provide tracing paper for children to check whether each part is the same by rotating the tracing paper to fit one half over the other. Point out that they need to be a perfect match.

DEEPEN If children are confident working out whether the shapes in question **5** are divided into half, do they still agree that the shape is shaded in half if further lines are added? For example, do children change their answers if each L shape is split into two separate rectangles?

ASSESSMENT CHECKPOINT Do children draw the other half of the shapes in question **3** so that they are symmetrical or do they draw the other half anywhere on the page next to the first half?

When answering question **5**, do children associate splitting in half with dividing symmetrically and do they think that parts are unequal if they are in different orientations?

ANSWERS Answers for the **Practice** part of the lesson appear in the separate **Practice and Reflect answer guide**.

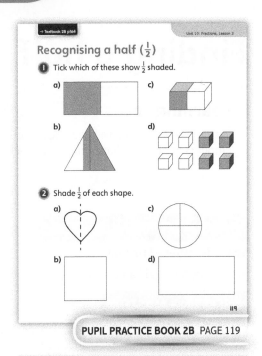

PUPIL PRACTICE BOOK 2B PAGE 119

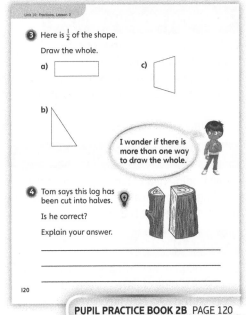

PUPIL PRACTICE BOOK 2B PAGE 120

Reflect

WAYS OF WORKING Pair work

IN FOCUS Children are presented with different shapes and they must decide whether they can be split in half or not. Children have already come across halved circles, but the hexagon may seem confusing because children are not as familiar with hexagons and the multiple lines of symmetry could confuse them.

ASSESSMENT CHECKPOINT Do children instantly spot that the third shape cannot easily be halved or do they need to use a physical resource to check this? Do children see that there are multiple ways of halving the hexagon? What physical resources do children use to help them?

ANSWERS Answers for the **Reflect** part of the lesson appear in the separate **Practice and Reflect answer guide**.

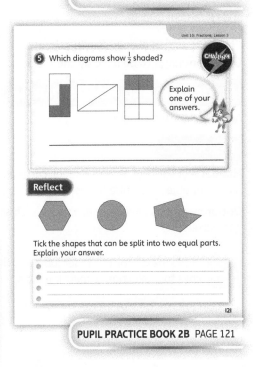

PUPIL PRACTICE BOOK 2B PAGE 121

After the lesson ⏸

- Could children explain what 1 and 2 represent in $\frac{1}{2}$?
- Did children understand that there is more than one way to split regular shapes?
- Did children relate any part of the lesson to halving numbers?

Finding a half

Learning focus

In this lesson, children will find one half of different amounts of objects, shapes and numbers.

Small steps

→ Previous step: Recognising a half ($\frac{1}{2}$)
→ **This step: Finding a half**
→ Next step: Recognising a quarter ($\frac{1}{4}$)

NATIONAL CURRICULUM LINKS

Year 2 Number – Fractions

Recognise, find and name a half as one of two equal parts of an object, shape or quantity (year 1).

ASSESSING MASTERY

Children can find one half of numbers of objects up to 20. Children can fill in sentence scaffolds stating that '$\frac{1}{2}$ of ___ is ___', sometimes filling in the $\frac{1}{2}$ for themselves too. Children should be able to also link this with dividing by 2 and times-table facts.

COMMON MISCONCEPTIONS

Children may struggle to split a group of objects in half when the objects are scattered on the page rather than arranged in neat rows. Encourage children to develop a strategy, such as first counting how many objects there are in the whole, representing each object with cubes and rearranging them into neat groups, or circling one object and leaving one object alternately. Children may also lose track of the original whole number and may not check that their two groups are equal. Ask:

• *How many objects have you circled or crossed out? How many have you not circled or crossed out? Are the numbers the same?*

STRENGTHENING UNDERSTANDING

When finding half of a number, encourage children to represent the number using physical resources, such as cubes. When splitting the physical resources into halves by adding one to each stack, children will find that their stacks of cubes will be the same height at the end.

GOING DEEPER

Some children may be able to spot that half of an odd number is possible if you include $\frac{1}{2}$ in the answer. For example, half of 7 is $3\frac{1}{2}$. Guide children to spot this in contexts such as splitting seven squares in half, and to understand the difference between this and splitting seven children in half.

KEY LANGUAGE

In lesson: split, equal parts, same as, odd number

Other language to be used by the teacher: numerator, denominator, symmetrical, the same, line of symmetry, middle

STRUCTURES AND REPRESENTATIONS

Arrays, cubes and counters

RESOURCES

Mandatory: squared paper, multilink cubes and counters to represent objects, sorting hoops

Optional: groups of classroom objects, such as pencils and erasers

 In the eTextbook of this lesson, you will find interactive links to a selection of teaching tools.

Before you teach

• Were children confident when splitting a square with more than two parts into half in the previous lesson?
• How will you build on children's previous strategies of finding a half?
• Do children understand what odd and even numbers are?

Discover

WAYS OF WORKING Pair work

ASK

- Question **1** a): *How many players are there?*
- Question **1** a): *What strategy could you use to split these players into two teams?*
- Question **1** b): *If another player joins the group, how many players are there now?*

IN FOCUS Emphasise the word 'equal' and ask children to explain what this means. Do children know half of 12 already as a number fact or do they have to use a sharing technique to find it out?

When another player joins the group, point out that now there is an odd number of players and explain that they cannot be split into two equal teams. Embed this by letting children try to share 13 multilink cubes equally.

ANSWERS

Question **1** a): $\frac{1}{2}$ of 12 is 6.

There are six players in each team.

Question **1** b): 13 is an odd number. The teams cannot be equal. We need two more each time for the teams to be equal.

Finding a half

Discover

1 a) Make two equal teams.

b) Another player joins. Can the teams still be equal? Explain your answer.

168

PUPIL TEXTBOOK 2B PAGE 168

Share

WAYS OF WORKING Whole class teacher led

ASK

- Question **1** a): *What does it mean to have equal teams?*
- Question **1** b): *What is an odd number?*
- Question **1** b): *Dexter asks if it is possible to split an odd number into equal parts. Can you do this with an odd number of cubes? Why not?*

IN FOCUS This part of the lesson gives children a pictorial representation of even numbers up to 12 split into two teams. There is the same number of players in both the teams in each row. Splitting 12 into two groups can be modelled by sharing 12 multilink cubes into two different sorting hoops. Ash asks if this is the same as 12 ÷ 2. Can children make this link for themselves or do you have to explain it to them?

Share

a) There are 12 players.

They need to be in two equal teams.

Team A   Team B

You can share the players one at a time.

There are 6 players in each team.

$\frac{1}{2}$ of 12 is 6.

Is that the same as 12 ÷ 2 = 6?

b) 13 is an odd number.

Can I split an odd number into two equal parts?

The teams cannot be equal.

We need two more each time for the teams to be equal.

169

PUPIL TEXTBOOK 2B PAGE 169

Think together

Whole class teacher led (I do, We do, You do)

ASK

- *How many groups do you have to share between if you are finding $\frac{1}{2}$?*
- *Question ❶ : Are the numbers of bees in each box equal?*

IN FOCUS Question ❶ provides pictures of objects for children to find $\frac{1}{2}$ of. Question ❶ a) shows eight bees which need to be shared equally into two boxes. Encourage children to cross out one bee each time a bee is shared, as Astrid suggests, for both questions ❶ a) and ❶ b). Can children see how to halve the amounts pictorially rather than sharing objects out like in question ❶?

STRENGTHEN Encourage children to use a wide variety of physical resources to demonstrate halving 6 or 10. Question ❷ a) requires children to halve a pictorial representation of six pencils, so ask children whether they can also do this physically with a range of other objects such as six marbles or books. This will reinforce the number fact in a range of contexts.

DEEPEN Questions ❶ a) and ❷ a) require children to find half of 8 and half of 6. Ask children whether they can halve the halves. Do children instinctively know that 4 can be halved again but that 3 cannot be halved again because 4 is even and 3 is odd? What is the largest number of times that children can repeatedly halve a number?

ASSESSMENT CHECKPOINT In question ❸ , can children identify the original whole in each example and put it in the correct place in the sentence scaffold?

The shape in question ❸ b) can be split in half by splitting the columns into two groups or splitting the rows into two groups. However, the same strategy cannot be applied to question ❸ a) as there is an unequal number of rows. Do children split the shape vertically into two groups of two columns or do they split it horizontally into two groups of $1\frac{1}{2}$ rows?

ANSWERS

Question ❶ a): $\frac{1}{2}$ of 8 is 4.

Question ❶ b): $\frac{1}{2}$ of 14 is 7.

Question ❷ a): $\frac{1}{2}$ of 6 is 3.

Question ❷ b): $\frac{1}{2}$ of 10 is 5.

Question ❸ a): $\frac{1}{2}$ of 12 = 6.

Question ❸ b): $\frac{1}{2}$ of 16 = 8.

PUPIL TEXTBOOK 2B PAGE 170

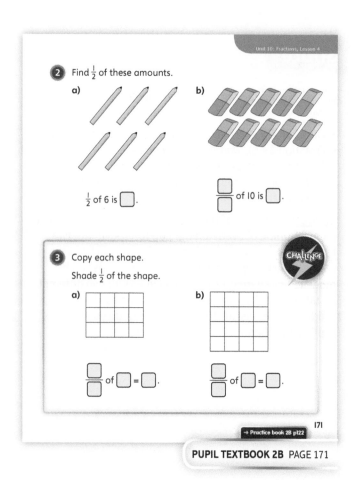

PUPIL TEXTBOOK 2B PAGE 171

Practice

WAYS OF WORKING Independent thinking

IN FOCUS Questions ❶, ❷ and ❸ ask children to find half the number of objects or squares and record it in the sentence scaffolds.

Question ❹ requires children to work out $\frac{1}{2}$ of each number in the left-hand column in order to match it to the correct number in the right-hand column.

Question ❺ provides an odd number for children to share and asks them to explain why they cannot do this equally.

Question ❻ presents an amount as one half of an unknown whole rather than presenting the whole itself. This differs to what children have seen so far in this lesson.

STRENGTHEN Ask children to cut the arrays in question ❷ out of squared paper. Children could fold them in different ways to find a half. Encourage children to rearrange the squares in question ❷ a) so that they look more like the array in question ❷ b), guiding them to realise that the array in question ❷ a) is half the array in question ❷ b).

DEEPEN Provide children with more questions similar to question ❻ a), giving one half rather than one whole, and ask children about their strategy each time. Do children realise that they are doubling the given number? Ask: *Is it possible to halve all numbers? Is it possible to double all numbers? Can all numbers be both a half and a whole?*

ASSESSMENT CHECKPOINT Look for words such as odd, even, fair or equal in children's answers to question ❺. Are children aware there will be an odd one out so it is not possible to split the sweets into two equal parts? Do they attempt to split the leftover sweet in half?

In question ❻, are children able to take what they have learned about halving and apply it to the process of doubling a half to find a whole? Do they count forwards 7 from 7 or can they recall a previously learned fact to identify the whole?

ANSWERS Answers for the **Practice** part of the lesson appear in the separate **Practice and Reflect answer guide**.

Reflect

WAYS OF WORKING Pair work

IN FOCUS This question allows children to talk through their preferred strategy for halving numbers, so give them the opportunity to discuss with a partner and draw it or model it using physical resources. Select two or three different strategies and show them to the class. Ask: *What is the same about these strategies? What is different? Which would you find more helpful?*

ASSESSMENT CHECKPOINT Listen to children's explanations to each other about how to halve 16. What drawings or models do they use? Do they use the word equal in their explanation?

ANSWERS Answers for the **Reflect** part of the lesson appear in the separate **Practice and Reflect answer guide**.

After the lesson ⏸

- Did children show any awareness of the link between the numbers in this lesson and the 2 times-table and related division facts?
- Did children struggle to find a whole from a half?
- Were children confident that odd numbers cannot be halved because there is always one left over?

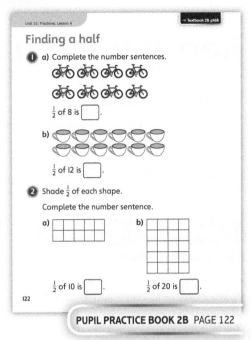

PUPIL PRACTICE BOOK 2B PAGE 122

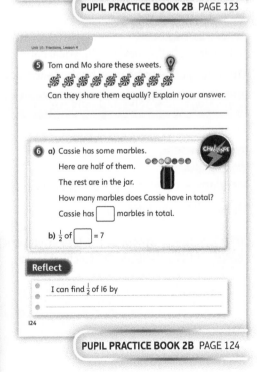

PUPIL PRACTICE BOOK 2B PAGE 123

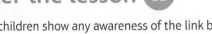

PUPIL PRACTICE BOOK 2B PAGE 124

Recognising a quarter ($\frac{1}{4}$)

Learning focus

In this lesson, children will recognise shapes that have been split into four equal parts and see $\frac{1}{4}$ shown as part of a distance around a whole track. Children will draw what a whole looks like from $\frac{1}{4}$.

Small steps

→ Previous step: Finding a half
→ **This step: Recognising a quarter ($\frac{1}{4}$)**
→ Next step: Finding a quarter

NATIONAL CURRICULUM LINKS

Year 2 Number – Fractions

- Recognise, find and name a quarter as one of four equal parts of an object, shape or quantity (year 1).
- Recognise, find, name and write fractions $\frac{1}{3}$, $\frac{1}{4}$, $\frac{2}{4}$ and $\frac{3}{4}$ of a length, shape, set of objects or quantity.

ASSESSING MASTERY

Children can recognise that $\frac{1}{4}$ is less than $\frac{1}{2}$, recognise different shapes that have been correctly or incorrectly split into four equal parts and shade $\frac{1}{4}$ of different shapes. Children can recreate what a whole looks like based on what a $\frac{1}{4}$ looks like.

COMMON MISCONCEPTIONS

Sometimes children may believe that a shape cannot be split into four equal parts if the equal parts have different orientations to the original shape. Drawing around the parts on tracing paper and turning the tracing paper will help. Ask:
- *Does it matter which way round the part is or is it still an equal part?*
- *Does it matter if the quarters look different?*

STRENGTHENING UNDERSTANDING

Give children pieces of paper to fold into quarters. Demonstrate that there are two ways of doing this: children can fold the piece of paper in half and then half again or they can fold the piece of paper in half, unfold it so that it is flat and then fold it in half again in a different way.

GOING DEEPER

Help children recognise that $\frac{1}{4}$ is half of $\frac{1}{2}$ by showing them two identical squares and explaining that this is half of the original shape. Ask them to shade in $\frac{1}{4}$ of the original shape. Do they realise that one square needs to be shaded because the original shape would have been made up of four squares?

KEY LANGUAGE

In lesson: $\frac{1}{4}$, half, $\frac{1}{2}$, how much?, equal parts, quarters, compare, split, square, triangle

Other language to be used by the teacher: whole, half of a half

STRUCTURES AND REPRESENTATIONS

2D shapes

RESOURCES

Mandatory: counters, squared paper, rulers, printed 2D shapes, such as ovals, to fold

Optional: tracing paper

 In the eTextbook of this lesson, you will find interactive links to a selection of teaching tools.

Before you teach

- How will you recap the meaning of numerator and denominator before starting this lesson?
- Could you change your classroom display of fractions to show $\frac{1}{4}$ and clearly display a representation of four equal parts for children to refer to?

Discover

WAYS OF WORKING Pair work

ASK

- *How many runners are taking part in the race?*
- *How far will each runner have to go?*
- *Where would halfway around the track be? Is that further than one runner has to run?*

IN FOCUS This question introduces $\frac{1}{4}$ as part of a distance around a whole track. Each runner represents $\frac{1}{4}$ of the distance to be run. Children can discuss what running $\frac{1}{4}$ of the track would look like and how far the runner would have to go. You could introduce this race as a relay race where runners take over from each other at different points on the track rather than starting from the same place.

ANSWERS

Question ❶ a): Runner A has gone too far because the other runners must each run less than $\frac{1}{2}$ of the track.

Question ❶ b): Each runner must run $\frac{1}{4}$ of the running track to make it equal.

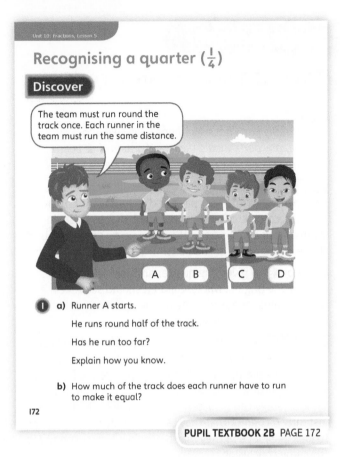

Share

WAYS OF WORKING Whole class teacher led

ASK

- Question ❶ a): *Where does runner A start?*
- *What shape is the running track? Can this be split up equally?*

IN FOCUS Give children an oval piece of paper to help them understand. Ask children to fold the oval in half and then in half again so they can see where to place counters. Remind children that the counters represent the points where a different runner starts. Children can use different coloured pens to draw a line around the edge showing how far each runner runs. Folding up the oval also demonstrates that each runner runs the same distance. When using a ruler to split the oval into four equal parts, use the folds as a guide. Alternatively, children could go outside or to the hall to do this practically, by running around a circuit. The circuit does not have to be oval – children just need to be able to run around the inside of the hall and stop at the $\frac{1}{4}$, $\frac{1}{2}$ and $\frac{3}{4}$ points.

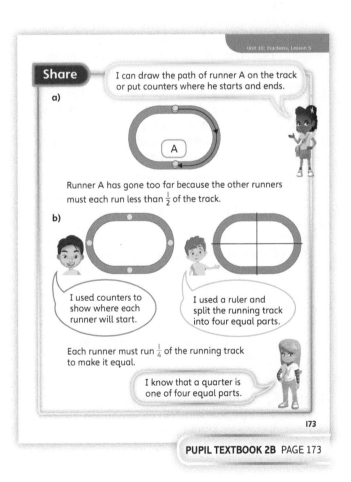

Think together

WAYS OF WORKING Whole class teacher led (I do, We do, You do)

ASK

- *How many parts has each shape been split into?*
- *How many parts should there be if a shape has been split into quarters?*

IN FOCUS Questions ❶ and ❷ show different shapes that have been split into four parts in different ways. Children should recognise quarters of different shapes by seeing them as four equal parts rather than being distracted by the shape of the whole or the parts.

Question ❸ a) gives one quarter and asks children to identify the original whole. Children should see that the original whole needs to contain four squares and that only one shape matches this requirement.

STRENGTHEN When answering question ❶ , children can recreate the sandwiches by folding or cutting up large squares of squared paper. Encourage children to find other ways of splitting the paper, such as into four columns. The same strategy can be used for question ❷ . Children may instantly recognise that they cannot evenly fold their paper to look like Joey's or they may try to do it before coming to the same conclusion.

DEEPEN Question ❸ b) asks children if they can draw a different shape that the single square could have come from. Children can draw as many different wholes as they can think of using one square quarter as a base for their drawings. Children could use tracing paper to help recreate different orientations of four squares and may even try turning the squares so that they appear diagonally.

ASSESSMENT CHECKPOINT In question ❶ , do children recognise that Kath's and Rob's sandwiches have been split into quarters in different but equally correct ways? Can children articulate which line in Lena's sandwich needs to be moved so that there are equal parts?

In question ❸ a), do children misunderstand the question and split the square into four parts because they believe that the part is actually the whole?

ANSWERS

Question ❶ : Kath's sandwich and Rob's sandwich have been cut into quarters because they are each split into four equal parts.

Question ❷ : Fred is correct because Fred and Joey have both split their table in half horizontally but Joey did not split those halves into equal halves.

Question ❸ a): The $\frac{1}{4}$ is from shape C.

Question ❸ b): Answers will vary but should be made up of a whole with four equal squares.

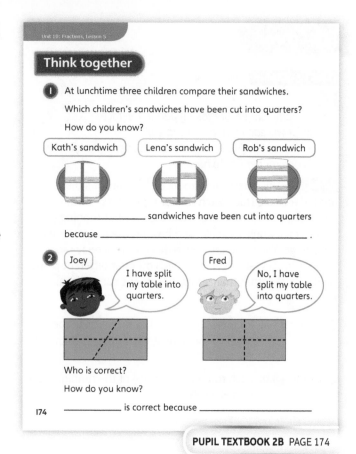

PUPIL TEXTBOOK 2B PAGE 174

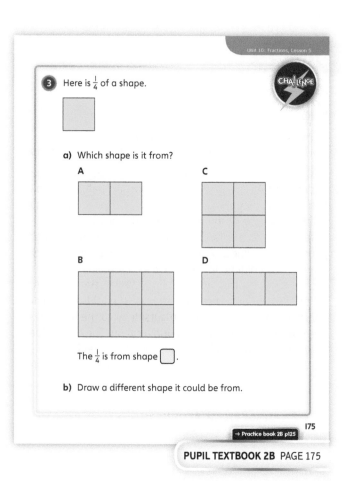

PUPIL TEXTBOOK 2B PAGE 175

Practice

IN FOCUS Question **2** simply asks children to shade $\frac{1}{4}$ of each shape, but some of the shapes are not straightforward. For example, the blank circle provides no guidelines, requiring children to split it into quarters. The other circle has been split into eight equal parts, requiring children to recognise that two parts make one quarter.

Dan has split the stick of rock in question **4** into halves, not quarters. Can children explain this using the phrase equal parts? Children might be able to suggest that Dan can split the stick of rock into quarters by halving the halves.

STRENGTHEN When they are drawing the wholes in question **3**, encourage children to use tracing paper.

Demonstrate how to split one of the blank diagonally orientated squares in question **5** into triangles by drawing a horizontal line and vertical line. Give children the opportunity to explore and discuss this.

DEEPEN To challenge children who are confident answering question **3**, split up the square in question **3** a) into two triangles which, together, represent $\frac{1}{4}$. Ask children to recreate the whole using these two triangles as one quarter. The triangles do not have to be arranged to make a square and can be in different orientations. This requires children to work out that eight triangles are needed.

ASSESSMENT CHECKPOINT Are children confident that each part of the rectangle in question **2** shows $\frac{1}{4}$ even though the quarters look different? Can children explain why they do or do not think that they are quarters? When drawing a whole from the quarter circle in question **3** b), are children aware that the whole is a circle or do they draw four separate quarter circles next to each other?

ANSWERS Answers for the **Practice** part of the lesson appear in the separate **Practice and Reflect answer guide**.

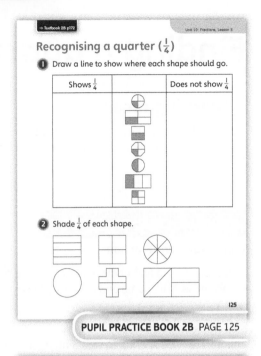

PUPIL PRACTICE BOOK 2B PAGE 125

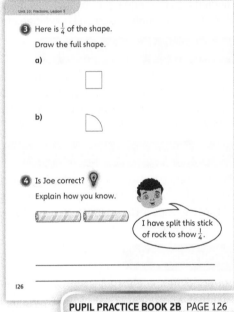

PUPIL PRACTICE BOOK 2B PAGE 126

Reflect

IN FOCUS This part of the lesson presents different shapes that may or may not be capable of being split into quarters. Some shapes can be halved accurately but cannot be halved again. Some shapes allow this to be done in multiple ways, such as the hexagon.

ASSESSMENT CHECKPOINT Do children immediately spot that the irregular shapes cannot be split into quarters? Do they think that shapes that can be halved must also be capable of being quartered?

ANSWERS Answers for the **Reflect** part of the lesson appear in the separate **Practice and Reflect answer guide**.

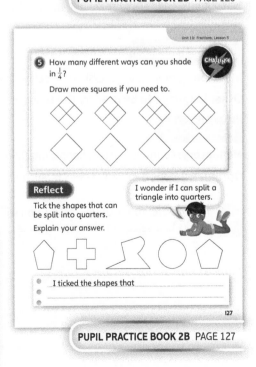

PUPIL PRACTICE BOOK 2B PAGE 127

After the lesson

- Were children able to relate their understanding of the role of 1 and 2 in $\frac{1}{2}$ to the role of 1 and 4 in $\frac{1}{4}$?
- Did children understand $\frac{1}{4}$ as a distance?
- Did children know that, when finding $\frac{1}{4}$ of a sheet of paper, they could fold it in half and then fold in half again?

Finding a quarter

Learning focus

In this lesson, children will find one quarter of different amounts by sharing them into four equal groups.

Small steps

→ Previous step: Recognising a quarter ($\frac{1}{4}$)
→ **This step: Finding a quarter**
→ Next step: Unit fractions

NATIONAL CURRICULUM LINKS

Year 2 Number – Fractions

- Recognise, find and name a quarter as one of four equal parts of an object, shape or quantity (year 1).
- Recognise, find, name and write fractions $\frac{1}{3}$, $\frac{1}{4}$, $\frac{2}{4}$ and $\frac{3}{4}$ of a length, shape, set of objects or quantity.

ASSESSING MASTERY

Children can use sharing to split a number of objects into four equal groups and can recognise when a number cannot be divided into four equal groups and how much greater it needs to be in order to be divided into four. Children can work out the value of a whole based on knowledge of the value of one quarter.

COMMON MISCONCEPTIONS

So far, children have mainly seen quarters of objects that have been split into four parts and may associate $\frac{1}{4}$ as being one object split into four parts. They may find it confusing to be presented with multiple objects that either need to be split into quarters or are one quarter of a whole. Relate the number of objects to being one group of four groups. Ask:
- *How many groups do you share these objects into in order to split them into quarters?*

STRENGTHENING UNDERSTANDING

Relate sharing between four to sharing between two and ask: *What are the similarities between these?* Do children see that dividing by four could be achieved by dividing into two groups, as when finding one half, and then further dividing each of those groups into two more groups? Model this by sharing out different amounts of counters and reinforcing the link between $\frac{1}{2}$ and $\frac{1}{4}$.

GOING DEEPER

Some children might spot that quartering certain numbers will give you a whole number and one additional fraction. For example, when sharing out 13 multilink cubes, there will be one leftover cube. Children may say that the leftover cube can be split into quarters to share out among the other four groups. Model this using 2D squares to show the leftover cube being split into four equal parts.

KEY LANGUAGE

In lesson: $\frac{1}{4}$, quarters, share/sharing, split, equal groups, how many, same, equally, number sentence

Other language to be used by the teacher: divide/divided, whole, equal part, four parts

RESOURCES

Mandatory: counters, sorting hoops, multilink cubes

Optional: groups of multiple objects, such as pencils, sweets or erasers

 In the eTextbook of this lesson, you will find interactive links to a selection of teaching tools.

Before you teach 🕛

- Do children understand that $\frac{1}{4}$ means one of four equal parts?
- Are children confident in sharing a number of objects into two groups to find $\frac{1}{2}$?
- How can you encourage children to say a quarter rather than a fourth?

Discover

ASK

- Question **1** b): *If the counters are to be shared fairly, does each child have to have the same number of counters?*
- Question **1** b): *What fraction of the whole will each child receive?*

IN FOCUS You may want to ask four children to come up to the front of the classroom to represent the children in the picture and share out 12 counters to model the question.

ANSWERS

Question **1** a): The counters can be split into four equal groups.

Question **1** b): Each child will get three counters.

PUPIL TEXTBOOK 2B PAGE 176

Share

ASK

- Question **1** a): *How many equal groups have the counters been split into?*
- Question **1** a): *Is splitting the counters into four equal groups the same as splitting them into quarters?*
- Question **1** b): *How would you write the fraction of the whole number of counters that each child has been given?*

IN FOCUS Hand out the counters at random and ask children whether they think this is fair or unfair. Discuss whether there is a fair way to hand them out. Then refer to what Astrid says and model handing out the counters to the children one by one, without missing out any of the children, until there are no counters left. Keep referring to the fact that each child has the same number of counters before you give out any more counters.

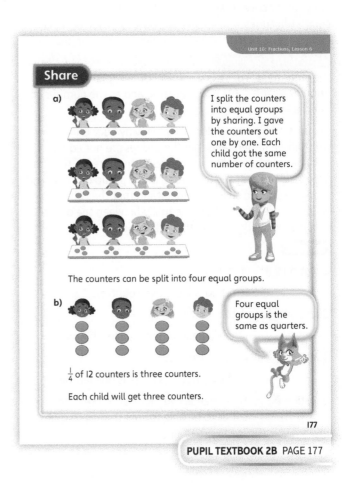

PUPIL TEXTBOOK 2B PAGE 177

Think together

Whole class teacher led (I do, We do, You do)

ASK

- Question ❶ : *How many counters are there in total?*
- Question ❶ : *How many children are you sharing between?*
- Question ❶ : *Does this number match the numerator or the denominator?*

IN FOCUS Questions ❶ and ❷ require children to share objects in order to find $\frac{1}{4}$ of different numbers. The groups have been represented by different objects and the sentence scaffolds for finding $\frac{1}{4}$ are given.

In question ❸ a), children will find that there is one left over when trying to share 13 cubes between four groups. Encourage children not to put this leftover cube into one of the groups but to leave it outside the groups.

STRENGTHEN For each question, ask children to count out the number of objects that they need using counters or cubes. Ask children to draw four circles to represent the number of groups into which they are going to split the cubes. This will model children's working and will help them to fill in the sentence scaffolds.

DEEPEN Question ❸ b) asks how many more cubes Harry needs to be able to split them into quarters. Ash wonders if there is more than one answer, so refer to this and ask children to find as many different possibilities as they can. They will discover that they need to add two cubes, six cubes, ten cubes, and so on to be able to divide by 4. Ask: *Can you see a pattern in those numbers? Why might that be?*

ASSESSMENT CHECKPOINT In question ❷ , there are two 4s in the statement '$\frac{1}{4}$ of 16 is 4'. Can children explain what the number 4 represents in the fraction and as the number of pencils in each pot?

In question ❸ , can children explain why Lucy is incorrect? Do children understand that the groups are not equal? Lucy has got four cubes in one group and three in the other groups. If she split the last group into a group of three, and a single cube, do children understand that the cube that is left over cannot be shared equally between the other groups? Do children make that distinction?

ANSWERS

Question ❶ : $\frac{1}{4}$ of 20 is 5.

　　　　　Each child will get five counters.

Question ❷ : $\frac{1}{4}$ of 16 is 4.

　　　　　There will be four pencils in each pot.

Question ❸ a): Lucy is incorrect.

　　　　　$\frac{1}{4}$ of 13 is not 3 as there is one left over.

Question ❸ b): Harry needs two more, six more or ten more cubes to be able to split them into quarters.

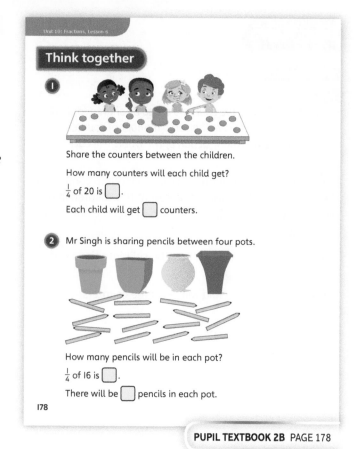

Think together

❶ Share the counters between the children.

How many counters will each child get?

$\frac{1}{4}$ of 20 is ☐.

Each child will get ☐ counters.

❷ Mr Singh is sharing pencils between four pots.

How many pencils will be in each pot?

$\frac{1}{4}$ of 16 is ☐.

There will be ☐ pencils in each pot.

178

PUPIL TEXTBOOK 2B PAGE 178

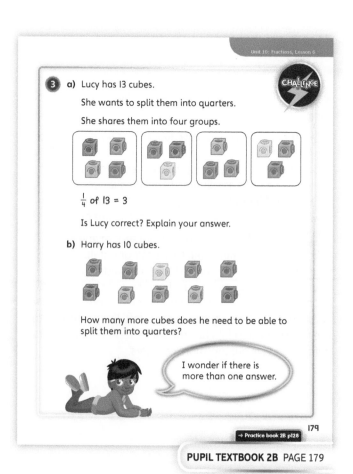

CHALLENGE

❸ a) Lucy has 13 cubes.

She wants to split them into quarters.

She shares them into four groups.

$\frac{1}{4}$ of 13 = 3

Is Lucy correct? Explain your answer.

b) Harry has 10 cubes.

How many more cubes does he need to be able to split them into quarters?

I wonder if there is more than one answer.

→ Practice book 2B p128

179

PUPIL TEXTBOOK 2B PAGE 179

Practice

IN FOCUS Questions ❶, ❷ and ❸ ask children to share out even numbers. Completing the sentence scaffold to identify $\frac{1}{4}$ of 24 in Question ❹, on the other hand, shows objects that have already been split into four equal groups. Children are asked to work out the original whole and complete the whole sentence scaffold.

Question ❺ gives half of a number and asks children to work out $\frac{1}{4}$. The half is also shown as six counters and the outline of the other half of the total number of counters is given to support children. Some children may start to realise that to find a quarter they find half of one half.

STRENGTHEN Question ❸ b) asks children to work out $\frac{1}{4}$ of 40 using a picture of 40 stars. Provide children with a 100 square that has been cut off at 40. Children could then fold the cut-off 100 square into four equal rows and see that each row ends in a multiple of 10.

DEEPEN Give children different numbers as $\frac{1}{4}$ without providing four parts that represent the whole. Ask children to draw four parts for themselves and put the provided $\frac{1}{4}$ in one of them. This may help children to spot an efficient method of working out the whole, such as doubling and doubling again or multiplying by 4.

ASSESSMENT CHECKPOINT In question ❹, do children count each individual sweet or do they count the number of sweets in one bag and multiply this number by 4? Do children fill in the blank scaffold correctly?

In question ❺, are children confident in the relationship between $\frac{1}{2}$ and $\frac{1}{4}$ so that they can work out one from the other?

Are children able to work out the whole from $\frac{1}{4}$ and understand the difference between 4 as the number of counters in one group and 4 as the number of groups in question ❻?

ANSWERS Answers for the **Practice** part of the lesson appear in the separate **Practice and Reflect answer guide**.

Reflect

IN FOCUS Children could complete the **Reflect** part of the lesson individually or with a partner. Children will soon come across numbers that cannot be divided into four groups. Ask children to predict which numbers might and might not be able to be shared equally between four groups.

ASSESSMENT CHECKPOINT Children might predict that all even numbers can be divided by 4. Can children modify this prediction based on attempts to divide 10 or 14 by 4? Are children able to link the numbers that can be divided by 4 to the 4 times-table?

ANSWERS Answers for the **Reflect** part of the lesson appear in the separate **Practice and Reflect answer guide**.

After the lesson ⏸

- Are children able to see a number both as a whole that can be divided into 4 and as a quarter of a number that needs to be multiplied by 4 to identify the whole?
- Are children secure in understanding that the 4 in $\frac{1}{4}$ means divided by 4?
- Do children call a quarter a fourth?

PUPIL PRACTICE BOOK 2B PAGE 128

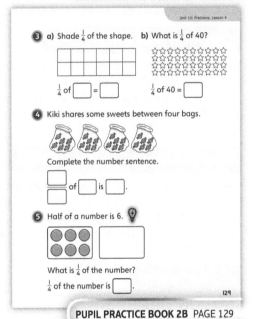

PUPIL PRACTICE BOOK 2B PAGE 129

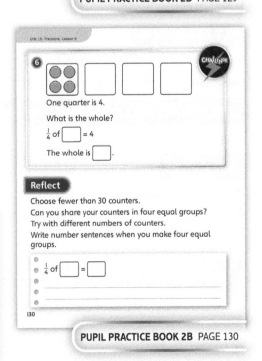

PUPIL PRACTICE BOOK 2B PAGE 130

Unit fractions

Learning focus

In this lesson, children will be introduced to the term unit fractions and will learn to recognise $\frac{1}{2}$, $\frac{1}{4}$ and $\frac{1}{3}$ of different shapes and amounts.

Small steps

→ Previous step: Finding a quarter
→ **This step: Unit fractions**
→ Next step: Understanding other fractions

NATIONAL CURRICULUM LINKS

Year 2 Number – Fractions

Recognise, find, name and write fractions $\frac{1}{3}$, $\frac{1}{4}$, $\frac{2}{4}$ and $\frac{3}{4}$ of a length, shape, set of objects or quantity.

ASSESSING MASTERY

Children can recognise a shape that has been divided into two, three or four equal parts as being divided into halves, thirds or quarters. Children can label one part of a divided whole with the name of the correct fraction and can work out unit fractions of an amount. Children can also find $\frac{1}{3}$ of an amount.

COMMON MISCONCEPTIONS

Children might believe that you can work one fraction out if you know another, when in fact they cannot simply use knowledge of $\frac{1}{4}$ and $\frac{1}{2}$ to work out what $\frac{1}{3}$ could be. Children may also think that because 2 + 1 = 3, it is possible to add a half to make a third. Similarly, children may think that because 4 – 1 = 3, it is possible to take away a quarter to make a third. Show each of these fractions on a fraction wall to demonstrate them alongside each other. Ask:
• *What does the 3 in $\frac{1}{3}$ represent?*

STRENGTHENING UNDERSTANDING

Use physical resources to model the questions and activities in this unit. Cubes can be used to represent the colours of different parts of each flag. This will help children who are struggling to accommodate the different unit fractions with which they are working. For example, if a flag is split up into different-coloured thirds, demonstrate this using three multilink cubes of different colours. This will help children to work out how each flag has been divided and to recognise the denominator as the number of cubes.

GOING DEEPER

Children could design their own flags according to specific unit fraction instructions. Ask: *Can you draw a flag with $\frac{1}{3}$ green/ $\frac{1}{4}$ red/$\frac{1}{2}$ blue?*

KEY LANGUAGE

In lesson: fraction, same, different, equal parts, numerator, denominator, **third, unit fraction,** $\frac{1}{2}$, $\frac{1}{3}$, $\frac{1}{4}$

Other language to be used by the teacher: whole, part, parts, divide, divided

STRUCTURES AND REPRESENTATIONS

Array, 2D shapes

RESOURCES

Mandatory: multilink cubes, counters

Optional: printed flag outlines for children to split into equal parts, squared paper, sorting hoops

 In the eTextbook of this lesson, you will find interactive links to a selection of teaching tools.

Before you teach ⏸

• Do children understand that the 1 in $\frac{1}{2}$ and $\frac{1}{4}$ represents having one part of a whole divided into that number of parts?
• Do you think children would be able to find $\frac{1}{2}$ and $\frac{1}{4}$ of the same number and know how many groups to share the same total into?

Discover

Pair work

ASK

• Question ❶ b): *How many parts are the flags of Chad and Germany split into? Are they equal parts?*

• Question ❶ b): *How do you think you would write that as a fraction?*

IN FOCUS This part of the lesson introduces the concept of $\frac{1}{3}$. Children should spot the flags that are split into halves ($\frac{1}{2}$) and quarters ($\frac{1}{4}$). Can children use this information to work out what fraction the other flags have been split into?

ANSWERS

Question ❶ a): Each stripe of ▭ is $\frac{1}{2}$ of the flag.

Each stripe of ▮▮ is $\frac{1}{3}$ of the flag.

Question ❶ b): Each flag is split into equal parts. The number of equal parts is different.

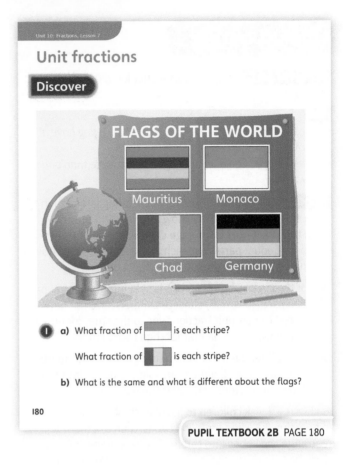

Unit fractions

Discover

FLAGS OF THE WORLD

Mauritius   Monaco

Chad   Germany

❶ a) What fraction of ▭ is each stripe?

What fraction of ▮▮ is each stripe?

b) What is the same and what is different about the flags?

180

PUPIL TEXTBOOK 2B PAGE 180

Share

Whole class teacher led

ASK

• Question ❶ a): *What is the new number of equal parts that some of these flags have been divided into?*

• Question ❶ b): *What is a unit fraction?*

• Question ❶ b): *What is the same in unit fractions? What is different?*

IN FOCUS Children should recognise that the flags are split into equal parts despite the orientation of the parts. Explain that $\frac{1}{3}$ is called 'one third' and ask children to repeat this several times. Relate $\frac{1}{3}$ to the flags that have been split into three horizontal or three vertical parts. Explain what a unit fraction is while drawing children's attention to the unit fractions written under each flag. Children may also talk about the colours being different and the flags being the same shape. This is all fine to discuss and completely valid.

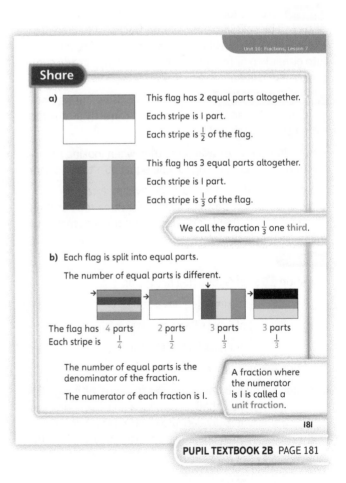

Share

a)   This flag has 2 equal parts altogether.
Each stripe is 1 part.
Each stripe is $\frac{1}{2}$ of the flag.

This flag has 3 equal parts altogether.
Each stripe is 1 part.
Each stripe is $\frac{1}{3}$ of the flag.

We call the fraction $\frac{1}{3}$ one third.

b) Each flag is split into equal parts.
The number of equal parts is different.

| The flag has | 4 parts | 2 parts | 3 parts | 3 parts |
| Each stripe is | $\frac{1}{4}$ | $\frac{1}{2}$ | $\frac{1}{3}$ | $\frac{1}{3}$ |

The number of equal parts is the denominator of the fraction.

The numerator of each fraction is 1.

A fraction where the numerator is 1 is called a unit fraction.

181

PUPIL TEXTBOOK 2B PAGE 181

Think together

Whole class teacher led (I do, We do, You do)

ASK

- Question **①** : *How many equal parts in each flag have a star?*
- Question **②** : *Can a unit fraction refer to more than one equal part?*

IN FOCUS Discuss what fraction of each flag in question **①** has a star. How do children know and what do they have to do to work it out? Encourage children to look for the number of equal parts that each flag has been split into and see that the star is in one of those equal parts.

One of the circles in question **②** is split into four equal parts with two parts (one half) shaded. Children have not been introduced to non-unit fractions yet so they may identify the circle as showing one half rather than two quarters.

Question **③** requires children to find $\frac{1}{3}$ of different numbers presented as arrays. Children can split the arrays into three equal rows or columns and count the number in each.

STRENGTHEN Ask children to make each of the arrays in question **③** using multilink cubes, then ask them to rearrange the cubes into three piles. Encourage children to go back to the image and circle the equal parts in the arrays to represent how they arranged the cubes into three equal piles.

DEEPEN In question **③** , ask children whether the first array of six can be split into another unit fraction. Children can experiment with putting the cubes representing this array into either two or four equal piles. They may already spot that half of 6 is 3.

ASSESSMENT CHECKPOINT Are children confident using one third in context and are they saying it correctly as one third rather than one three?

Do children show an awareness that, when looking for unit fractions, they are looking for one equal part that is shaded?

What strategy do children use for dividing arrays into three equal parts? Do children look for three rows or three columns to help them or do they count three as they go along and circle them?

ANSWERS

Question **①** : $\frac{1}{3}$ of Gaby's flag has a star.

$\frac{1}{4}$ of Tim's flag has a star.

$\frac{1}{2}$ of Anya's flag has a star.

$\frac{1}{3}$ of Milo's flag has a star.

Question **②** a): From left to right: $\frac{1}{3}, \frac{1}{4}, \frac{1}{2}, \frac{1}{3}$.

Question **②** b): A, B and D are unit fractions. Although C is half shaded, it is not a unit fraction because it is divided into quarters and has more than one equal part (two quarters) shaded.

Question **③** : $\frac{1}{3}$ of 6 = 2

$\frac{1}{3}$ of 9 = 3

$\frac{1}{3}$ of 15 = 5

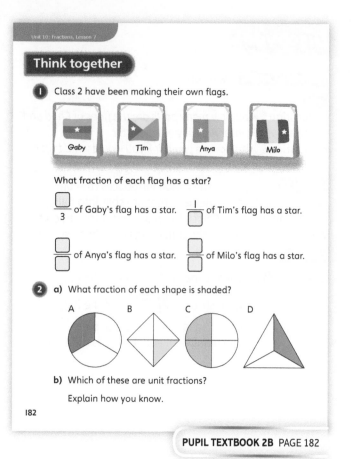

PUPIL TEXTBOOK 2B PAGE 182

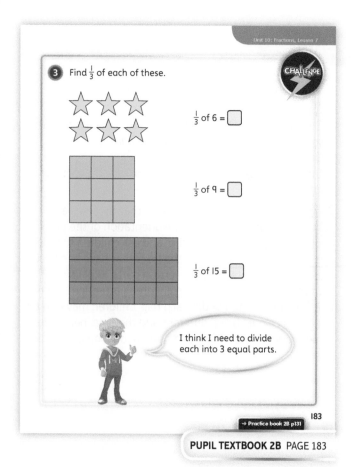

PUPIL TEXTBOOK 2B PAGE 183

Practice

WAYS OF WORKING Independent thinking

IN FOCUS Questions ❶ and ❸ help children understand what a unit fraction is. Children see it as one part shaded out of equal parts.

Questions ❷, ❹ and ❻ specifically focus on $\frac{1}{3}$ as this is a new fraction introduced in this lesson.

In question ❺, children are given a unit fraction and have to find the whole, while question ❼ requires children to work out different unit fractions from the same whole. Use multilink cubes to represent sweets being placed in two, three and four piles.

STRENGTHEN Ask children to model the chairs in question ❻ using physical resources such as cubes, splitting the total number of cubes into three lines of four cubes. For question ❼, do children know to start with 12 cubes each time? Can they explain that, when working out $\frac{1}{2}$, they need to use two sorting hoops?

DEEPEN If children are confident finding $\frac{1}{2}$, $\frac{1}{3}$ and $\frac{1}{4}$ of 12 in question ❼, ask them to do this for another number, such as 24. Can children see why the numbers 12 and 24 have been chosen?

ASSESSMENT CHECKPOINT Do children understand that unit fractions are represented by only one shaded part? Are they confused by the fully shaded triangle in question ❸?

Do children recognise the shape in question ❺ a) as being part of a circle? Do children know how many rectangles to draw in question ❺ b) or do they draw the whole as though the part is a quarter rather than a third?

What strategies do children use to work out $\frac{1}{3}$ of 12 chairs in question ❻?

ANSWERS Answers for the **Practice** part of the lesson appear in the separate **Practice and Reflect answer guide**.

Reflect

WAYS OF WORKING Whole class

IN FOCUS Children choose their own unit fraction to represent as a flag by dividing the flag equally and then colouring one equal part yellow. Squared paper will help with this, or flag scaffolds divided into two, three or four equal parts. Compare flags showing different unit fractions. Ask: *What is the same about these flags? What is different?*

ASSESSMENT CHECKPOINT Are children able to explain that one equal part in each flag is yellow and that this is a unit fraction? Have some children decided to split their flag into three equal parts? Can they explain what one third is?

ANSWERS Answers for the **Reflect** part of the lesson appear in the separate **Practice and Reflect answer guide**.

After the lesson ⏸

- Are children confident that a unit fraction means one part shaded and are not confused when equivalent fractions such as $\frac{2}{4}$ are shown?
- Were children able to relate their knowledge of equal parts of quarters and halves to thirds?
- Do children think there is a relationship between thirds and halves and between thirds and quarters or do they see them as distinct and separate fractions?

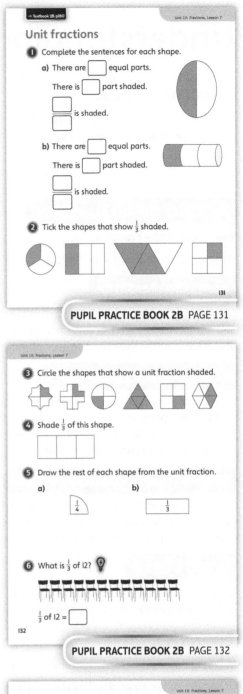

PUPIL PRACTICE BOOK 2B PAGE 131

PUPIL PRACTICE BOOK 2B PAGE 132

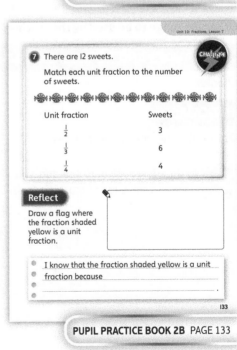

PUPIL PRACTICE BOOK 2B PAGE 133

Understanding other fractions

Learning focus

In this lesson, children will be introduced to non-unit fractions (fractions in which the numerator is not 1).

Small steps

→ Previous step: Unit fractions
→ **This step: Understanding other fractions**
→ Next step: $\frac{1}{2}$ and $\frac{2}{4}$

NATIONAL CURRICULUM LINKS

Year 2 Number – Fractions

Write simple fractions, for example, $\frac{1}{2}$ of 6 = 3, and recognise the equivalence of $\frac{2}{4}$ and $\frac{1}{2}$.

ASSESSING MASTERY

Children can recognise non-unit fractions and distinguish between these and unit fractions, and can explain the denominator and numerator of each fraction. Children can write the non-unit fractions they see in a picture and can draw their own non-unit fraction when they see it written numerically.

COMMON MISCONCEPTIONS

Children may mix up the meaning of the numerator and the denominator. For example, children may think that $\frac{3}{4}$ means having three parts and then get confused when they try to shade four parts. When seeing a number greater than one shaded for the first time, children may also take that to mean that the number of equal parts has increased. Ask:
• *How many equal parts are there? Does that change if you shade more parts?*

STRENGTHENING UNDERSTANDING

Use physical resources to represent a whole divided into three or four equal parts and count up to a whole in that fraction by moving each of the equal parts in turn while counting $\frac{1}{4}$, $\frac{2}{4}$, $\frac{3}{4}$ and so on. Ask children questions about what happens to the denominator and numerator each time you move a part.

GOING DEEPER

Once children have practised counting up in unit fractions, do they recognise that $\frac{2}{2}$ or $\frac{3}{3}$ or $\frac{4}{4}$ is the same as one whole? Give children a scenario such as a cake split into quarters that were all eaten. Ask them to write the fraction that has been eaten.

KEY LANGUAGE

In lesson: non-unit fraction, numerator, denominator, equal parts, greater than, true, false

Other language to be used by the teacher: unit fraction

STRUCTURES AND REPRESENTATIONS

Counters

RESOURCES

Optional: counters, multilink cubes

 In the eTextbook of this lesson, you will find interactive links to a selection of teaching tools.

Before you teach

• Could children explain a numerator and a denominator when studying unit fractions in the previous lesson?
• Were children confident drawing a unit fraction from seeing it written down in numbers in the previous lesson?

Discover

WAYS OF WORKING Pair work

ASK

- Question ❶ a): *How many children are there altogether?*
- Question ❶ b): *What is the denominator of Ola's kite? How many equal parts does that mean it is split into?*
- Question ❶ b): *Will Ola's kite be a little bit red or almost all red?*

IN FOCUS This picture portrays non-unit fractions for the first time. In question ❶ a), children know how many children there are in the picture and will understand that they are the equal parts, so they will write three as the denominator. Children may be able to label each child as $\frac{1}{3}$ and say that there are three of them, but they may not know the proper non-unit fraction name. Similarly, for the kite, children may recognise that there should be four equal parts of the kite but not know how to represent the 3 in $\frac{3}{4}$. Try to avoid giving too much guidance: see what children do for a kite showing $\frac{3}{4}$ shaded. You might want to provide a rhombus for the kite for children to split up.

ANSWERS

Question ❶ a): $\frac{2}{3}$ of the children are girls.

Question ❶ b): Ola's kite has four equal parts, three of which are red, so it is $\frac{3}{4}$ red.

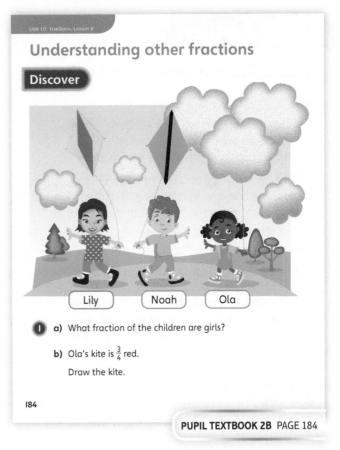

Understanding other fractions

Discover

Lily   Noah   Ola

❶ a) What fraction of the children are girls?

b) Ola's kite is $\frac{3}{4}$ red.
Draw the kite.

184

PUPIL TEXTBOOK 2B PAGE 184

Share

WAYS OF WORKING Whole class teacher led

ASK

- *How many equal parts are there altogether?*
- *How many parts do you have?*
- *Is this different to what you have learned before?*

IN FOCUS Questions ❶ a) and ❶ b) give a step-by-step explanation for each non-unit fraction and recap denominators at the same time. This is the first time children have met non-unit fractions, so they will need help with the reading. Explain that $\frac{2}{3}$ is read as two thirds and $\frac{3}{4}$ is read as three quarters. Ask children to label each child and each section of the kite with its unit fraction name and then circle how many they have. Explain that the total number of children or parts has not changed but that the number of each one you have has changed. Once you have explained and discussed each example, refer to what Sparks says and ask: *What do you notice about the numerator in non-unit fractions?*

STRENGTHEN The 3 in these examples has different roles. In question ❶ a), it is the number of equal parts (the number of children). In question ❶ b), it is the number of parts of the kite that are red. Point this out to children and discuss the distinction with them.

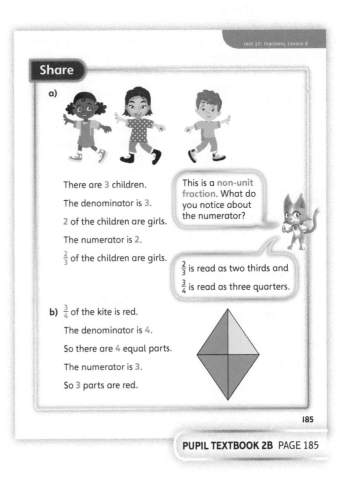

Share

a)

There are 3 children.
The denominator is 3.
2 of the children are girls.
The numerator is 2.
$\frac{2}{3}$ of the children are girls.

This is a non-unit fraction. What do you notice about the numerator?

$\frac{2}{3}$ is read as two thirds and $\frac{3}{4}$ is read as three quarters.

b) $\frac{3}{4}$ of the kite is red.
The denominator is 4.
So there are 4 equal parts.
The numerator is 3.
So 3 parts are red.

185

PUPIL TEXTBOOK 2B PAGE 185

Think together

Whole class teacher led (I do, We do, You do)

ASK

- *How many equal parts has each kite been split into?*
- *Is the same amount of each kite shaded?*
- *Do unit fractions always have one part shaded?*

IN FOCUS Question **1** asks children to fill in the sentence scaffolds for a non-unit fraction, requiring them to make the link to the numbers in the sentence that form the fraction.

Question **2** requires children to distinguish between a unit fraction and a non-unit fraction.

Question **3** a) may cause confusion as there are five equal parts, which children have not seen before. This question also demonstrates a common mistake that children may make because the number of one type of fruit (two apples) is over the number of the other type of fruit (three bananas). Encourage children to see the apples and the bananas as equal parts of a collective whole.

STRENGTHEN Ask children to repeat the sentence scaffolds in question **1** with the different contexts from question **3**. For example, question **3** b) would be phrased as, 'The group is made up of four equal parts. The denominator is 4. Three of the children are boys. The numerator is 3. $\frac{3}{4}$ of the children are boys.'

DEEPEN Refer to what Ash says about non-unit fractions being greater than unit fractions with the same denominator. If children immediately spot that this is true, can they say how much greater a non-unit fraction is than a unit fraction? Do they spot a pattern in the numerators depending on what the denominator is?

ASSESSMENT CHECKPOINT Do children use their knowledge about numerators from this and previous lessons to distinguish between unit and non-unit fractions? Are children able to apply previous knowledge and know that the denominator in question **3** a) should be 5 even if they do not know the fraction name?

ANSWERS

Question **1** : The denominator is 3. The numerator is 2. $\frac{2}{3}$ of the kite is yellow.

Question **2** a): A and D show $\frac{3}{4}$ shaded.

Question **2** b): C and E have unit fractions shaded.

Question **2** c): A, B and D have non-unit fractions shaded.

Question **3** a): False.

Question **3** b): True.

Question **3** c): True.

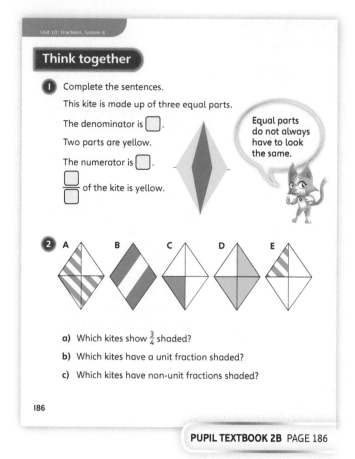

PUPIL TEXTBOOK 2B PAGE 186

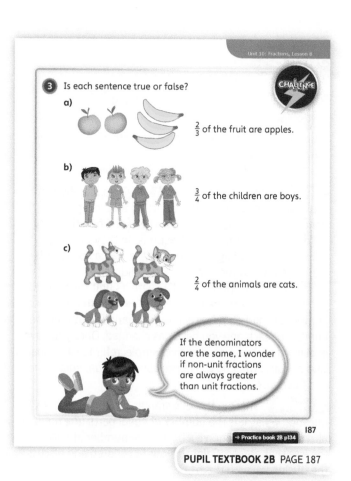

PUPIL TEXTBOOK 2B PAGE 187

Practice

WAYS OF WORKING Independent thinking

IN FOCUS Question ❶ asks children to fill in the sentence scaffolds, just as they did in the **Think together** part of the lesson, but this time using counters instead of kites.

Question ❷ asks children to match up fractions, which requires them to write down what fraction each shape represents and to visualise what each written fraction looks like as a shape.

Questions ❷ and ❸ allow children to show an understanding of what non-unit fractions are by having to match the shape to the relevant fraction and then having to shade in or circle the non-unit fraction.

Question ❺ asks children to write both the unit and the non-unit fractions that they see. Put this into real terms by referring to shaded and unshaded parts.

STRENGTHEN To help children explain their answer to question ❹, ask them to draw or make their own representation of what is shown in the picture. Encourage children to label each part to help them see that 3 should be the numerator because there are three shaded counters.

DEEPEN If children have successfully shaded or circled the non-unit fraction in question ❸, ask them whether they can work out what fraction is not circled or shaded.

ASSESSMENT CHECKPOINT Seeing $\frac{1}{3}$ in question ❹ is a common mistake. This is because there are three shaded parts, which children can misinterpret as the number of equal parts. Are children able to spot that this is a mistake and explain why? Can children articulate why 3 has been mistakenly identified as the number of equal parts?

ANSWERS Answers for the **Practice** part of the lesson appear in the separate **Practice and Reflect answer guide**.

Reflect

WAYS OF WORKING Pair work

IN FOCUS Write the words 'numerator', 'denominator' and 'equal parts' on the board for children to use when explaining why they have circled the fractions that they have circled. No pictorial representation is given, requiring children to look closely at the numbers and apply what they have learned to the written fraction.

ASSESSMENT CHECKPOINT Can children instantly recognise unit fractions by looking at the numerator or do they still look at the denominator? Which fraction do children pick to draw? Do children draw a model or an image that they have seen previously or are they able to create one for themselves? In their explanation, do children refer to the numerator when explaining why their chosen fraction is a non-unit fraction?

ANSWERS Answers for the **Reflect** part of the lesson appear in the separate **Practice and Reflect answer guide**.

After the lesson ⏸

- Were children confident in the distinction between unit and non-unit fractions and why there is a difference in the numerators?
- Were children easily able to include thirds in their thinking in this lesson or were thirds still too unfamiliar?

PUPIL PRACTICE BOOK 2B PAGE 134

PUPIL PRACTICE BOOK 2B PAGE 135

PUPIL PRACTICE BOOK 2B PAGE 136

$\frac{1}{2}$ and $\frac{2}{4}$

Learning focus

In this lesson, children will learn that $\frac{1}{2}$ and $\frac{2}{4}$ are equivalent fractions. Children will prove this using physical resources and different numbers of objects.

Small steps

→ Previous step: Understanding other fractions

→ **This step: $\frac{1}{2}$ and $\frac{2}{4}$**

→ Next step: Finding $\frac{3}{4}$

NATIONAL CURRICULUM LINKS

Year 2 Number – Fractions

Write simple fractions, for example, $\frac{1}{2}$ of 6 = 3, and recognise the equivalence of $\frac{2}{4}$ and $\frac{1}{2}$.

ASSESSING MASTERY

Children can recognise that $\frac{1}{2}$ and $\frac{2}{4}$ are equivalent in a range of contexts, such as shapes, pieces of paper and counters. Children can draw $\frac{1}{2}$ and $\frac{2}{4}$ using the same whole, can explain the similarities and differences between them and understand why the numerators and denominators are different while having the same value within each context.

COMMON MISCONCEPTIONS

Children may initially think that $\frac{2}{4}$ is more than $\frac{1}{2}$ because both numbers in $\frac{2}{4}$ are bigger. Break down each fraction and model them by folding one piece of paper in half and then folding one of the halves in two, showing that one half is the same as two quarters. This will show children that the only visual difference is that $\frac{2}{4}$ has an additional line through the middle. Ask:
- *Does each side of paper take up more space or less space than the other? Do bigger numbers mean a bigger fraction of the whole?*

STRENGTHENING UNDERSTANDING

There are lots of practical contexts to help children compare these fractions. For example, fractions of length can be modelled by using a metre stick and putting sticky notes at intervals of $\frac{1}{2}$ and $\frac{2}{4}$ and comparing how tall each fraction is.

GOING DEEPER

This picture demonstrates the equivalence between $\frac{1}{2}$ and $\frac{2}{4}$. The shape has been divided into half and then each half split into a different half to show very different-looking quarters. Ask: *If you cut up two of the quarters and placed them on the other half, would they take up the same amount of space as the other two quarters?*

KEY LANGUAGE

In lesson: equivalent, fraction, half, halves, same, quarter, different, bar model

Other language to be used by the teacher: numerator, denominator, split in, into

STRUCTURES AND REPRESENTATIONS

Part-whole model, bar model

RESOURCES

Mandatory: multilink cubes, counters, pieces of paper for folding, colouring pencils

Optional: metre sticks, any objects in the classroom that can be used to demonstrate $\frac{1}{2}$ and $\frac{2}{4}$ such as pencil pots, resource trays, reading book baskets or file dividers.

 In the eTextbook of this lesson, you will find interactive links to a selection of teaching tools.

Before you teach

- Have children shown any awareness of equivalence in fractions before this lesson?
- Are children able to find half of a number? Do they understand that this means dividing the number by 2?

Discover

$\frac{1}{2}$ and $\frac{2}{4}$

Discover

WAYS OF WORKING Pair work

ASK

- Question **1** a): *When you fold the paper in half and then in half again, how many parts have you folded it into?*
- Question **1** b): *Do you get the same fraction when folding a different-shaped piece of paper?*

IN FOCUS As children follow the instructions in the picture, ask them to explain what fraction the piece of paper is being split into each time they fold it. Are they aware that you make a quarter by folding a half in half? Ask children to compare the halves and quarters that they have created. Do they spot that the half they have coloured in is the same amount of space as $\frac{2}{4}$? Give children pieces of paper cut into the shapes shown in question **1** b) so that children can investigate this using the same technique.

ANSWERS

Question **1** a): When the paper is folded in half and two quarters are shaded, $\frac{1}{2}$ of the paper is shaded. $\frac{1}{2}$ and $\frac{2}{4}$ are equivalent. Therefore, $\frac{2}{4}$ and $\frac{1}{2}$ are the same size.

Question **1** b): It is the same with other shapes.

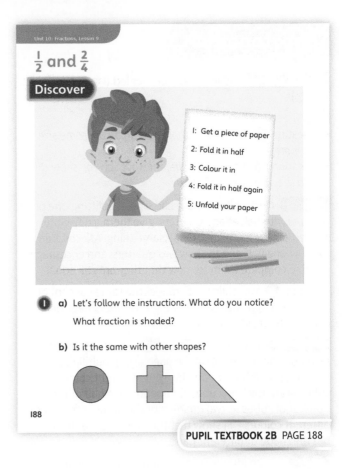

1 a) Let's follow the instructions. What do you notice? What fraction is shaded?

b) Is it the same with other shapes?

188

PUPIL TEXTBOOK 2B PAGE 188

Share

WAYS OF WORKING Whole class teacher led

ASK

- Question **1** a): *Do one half and two quarters take up the same amount of space when laid on top of each other?*
- Question **1** b): *There is more than one way to fold the cross. Is there more than one way to fold the piece of paper from question **1** a) into halves and quarters?*
- Question **1** b): *Would $\frac{1}{2}$ of the circle be equivalent to $\frac{2}{4}$ of the cross?*

IN FOCUS Using the pieces of paper that children folded and coloured in question **1** a), introduce the word equivalent. Ask: *Is one half equivalent to one quarter?* Encourage children to check this by cutting out their two quarters and laying them on top of the other half, as Astrid suggests. Ask children to demonstrate that this works for the other shapes. Do children understand that they need to use a circular piece of paper to find a fraction of a whole circle?

Children may not realise that the triangle can be halved twice to make quarters: you have to fold it vertex-to-vertex twice. Can children draw how the triangle looks after two vertex-to-vertex folds?

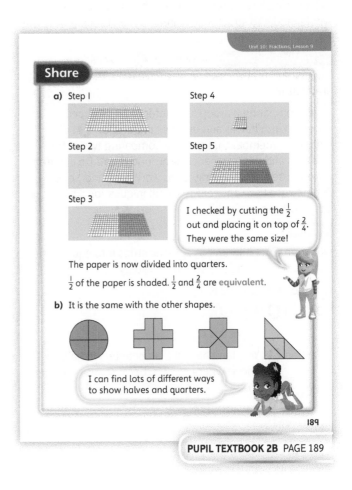

Share

a) Step 1   Step 4

Step 2   Step 5

Step 3

I checked by cutting the $\frac{1}{2}$ out and placing it on top of $\frac{2}{4}$. They were the same size!

The paper is now divided into quarters. $\frac{1}{2}$ of the paper is shaded. $\frac{1}{2}$ and $\frac{2}{4}$ are equivalent.

b) It is the same with the other shapes.

I can find lots of different ways to show halves and quarters.

189

PUPIL TEXTBOOK 2B PAGE 189

Think together

WAYS OF WORKING Whole class teacher led (I do, We do, You do)

ASK

- Question **1** : *Does each whole have to be the same size to compare?*
- Question **1** : *How many different ways can you show this with the same piece of paper?*

IN FOCUS Once children have had a go at splitting one piece of paper into halves and quarters, give them a different shaped piece of paper to do the same thing. Ask children to show one half and to show two quarters, and encourage them to compare them to show that they are still equal.

Question **2** asks children to model the same concept of equivalence but with counters. Eight counters have been circled into halves and quarters.

STRENGTHEN In questions **2** and **3**, encourage children to recreate what is shown on the page using multilink cubes, showing the different parts by using different coloured cubes or by stacking cubes. Comparing one half of the number of cubes to two quarters of the number of cubes in different colours will show that the amounts are the same but are made of different parts.

DEEPEN Ask children to use the numbers and pictorial representations in questions **2** and **3** to draw their own bar model with labelled parts, showing each half being split in half to make quarters. Demonstrate this first on a part-whole model to structure children's understanding of where each number comes from.

ASSESSMENT CHECKPOINT In question **1**, do children understand that the two wholes have to be the same size to start with?

When comparing a group of counters that has been arranged into halves and quarters in question **2**, do children remember that they are comparing two of the quarters and put another circle around them? Do children have to use a sharing strategy to work out $\frac{1}{2}$ and $\frac{1}{4}$ of 8? Do they use their answer for $\frac{1}{2}$ to fill in question **2** b) or do they work it out afresh?

ANSWERS

Question **1** : Children can split the strips into equal parts using any sensible strategy.

Question **2** a): $\frac{1}{2}$ of 8 is 4.

Question **2** b): $\frac{1}{4}$ of 8 is 2.

$\frac{2}{4}$ of 8 is 4.

Question **3** : Yes. Tami has split her counters in half, which shows what $\frac{2}{4}$ of 12 is, because $\frac{2}{4}$ is equivalent to $\frac{1}{2}$.

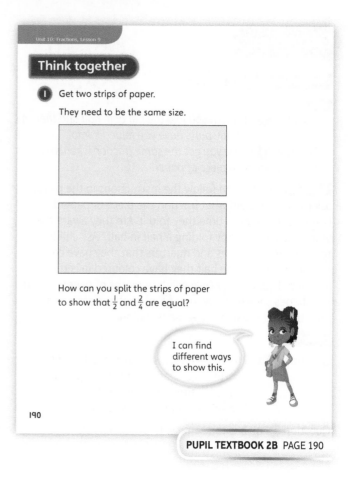

PUPIL TEXTBOOK 2B PAGE 190

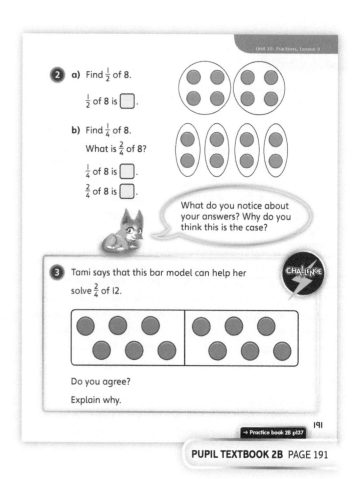

PUPIL TEXTBOOK 2B PAGE 191

Practice

WAYS OF WORKING Independent thinking

IN FOCUS Question ③ requires children to reason about the size of different fractions and to work out which ones are equivalent. Encourage children to use the pictures to help them decide. Refer to what Astrid says about using the image of $\frac{1}{2}$ as a benchmark: less than and greater than a $\frac{1}{2}$.

Question ⑤ asks children to work with fractions of numbers and investigate which numbers can be divided into halves and quarters. Encourage children to model this using cubes. It may help children to put cubes into a large part-whole model.

STRENGTHEN Encourage children to circle one half of the cherries in question ④. They have done this with a shape and this question asks them to practise with a quantity. Do children conclude that, as long as 10 cherries are circled, this is one half of 20?

DEEPEN For children who are confident that $\frac{1}{2}$ is equal to $\frac{2}{4}$ give them a $\frac{1}{4}$ and see if they can work out a half. For example, $\frac{1}{4}$ is 5. What is a $\frac{1}{2}$?

Some children may find the whole first (20), then halve it to get a half (10). Children may then see that they can simply double $\frac{1}{4}$ to get a $\frac{1}{2}$.

ASSESSMENT CHECKPOINT In question ②, do children colour in two cubes for $\frac{1}{2}$ or do they colour in one cube because the numerator is 1? Do they colour in the same cubes as they shaded for $\frac{2}{4}$ or do they use a count one, leave one strategy?

In question ④, how do children work out $\frac{1}{2}$ and $\frac{2}{4}$ of 20? Do they share out cubes; do they use a circle one, leave one strategy; or do they simply know it as a number fact?

Do children spot the link between the 4 times-table and numbers that can be divided into quarters?

ANSWERS Answers for the **Practice** part of the lesson appear in the separate **Practice and Reflect answer guide**.

Reflect

WAYS OF WORKING Whole class

IN FOCUS Children choose their own method to demonstrate equivalence between $\frac{1}{2}$ and $\frac{2}{4}$. They can fold paper, cut paper, stack cubes, and so on. Ensure that, whichever method they choose, children label each part and clearly show how one half has been halved again.

ASSESSMENT CHECKPOINT Listen for the words that children use in their explanation, such as the words 'equivalent' or 'equivalence' or references to the numerator and denominator. Do children understand that the whole has to be the same each time in order to compare the fractions?

ANSWERS Answers for the **Reflect** part of the lesson appear in the separate **Practice and Reflect answer guide**.

After the lesson ⏸

- Did children mention the relationship between the numerator and denominator in these equivalent fractions?
- Did children show that they understood one quarter as half of a half? Did children apply this to working out one quarter of a number?
- Did children understand that wholes have to be the same for the fractions to be equivalent?

219

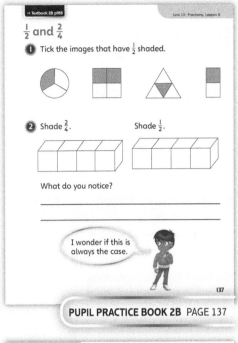

PUPIL PRACTICE BOOK 2B PAGE 137

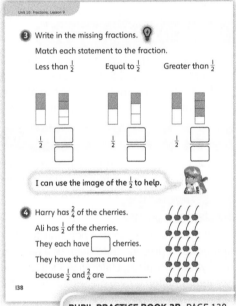

PUPIL PRACTICE BOOK 2B PAGE 138

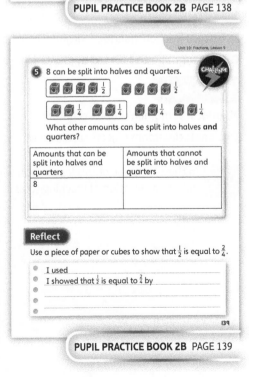

PUPIL PRACTICE BOOK 2B PAGE 139

Finding $\frac{3}{4}$

Learning focus

In this lesson, children will work out unit and non-unit fractions of numbers up to 20.

Small steps

→ Previous step: $\frac{1}{2}$ and $\frac{2}{4}$

→ **This step: Finding $\frac{3}{4}$**

→ Next step: Understanding a whole

NATIONAL CURRICULUM LINKS

Year 2 Number – Fractions

Recognise, find, name and write fractions $\frac{1}{3}$, $\frac{1}{4}$, $\frac{2}{4}$ and $\frac{3}{4}$ of a length, shape, set of objects or quantity.

ASSESSING MASTERY

Children can work out $\frac{1}{4}$ of a number and use this information to work out $\frac{3}{4}$. Children can understand that the number they are dividing by is the denominator of the fraction they are trying to find and can work out the whole from a non-unit fraction such as $\frac{3}{4}$.

COMMON MISCONCEPTIONS

The scaffolds in this lesson guide children through the process of working out a non-unit fraction step-by-step, but they may still become confused as to what each number in the fraction represents and what to do with it. Children might think that to get from $\frac{1}{4}$ to $\frac{3}{4}$ they multiply both the numerator and the denominator by 3 and get $\frac{3}{12}$. Ask:
• *These are all quarters. Does that change when you have more quarters?*

STRENGTHENING UNDERSTANDING

Provide physical resources such as paint brushes and pots so that children can model the questions. Share out the resources in quarters and ask children to count how many there are in three quarters.

GOING DEEPER

Working out a whole from a non-unit fraction requires strong conceptual understanding of what the denominator and the numerator represent. Give children a number that represents a non-unit fraction, for example $\frac{3}{4}$. With the help of pictures or physical resources, children will see that they divide that fraction by 3 in order to find one equal part because the non-unit fraction only represents three parts. Show children that they just have to add one of those parts to find the whole.

KEY LANGUAGE

In lesson: fraction, quarter, $\frac{3}{4}$, divided, equal parts, share, how many, half, whole, unit fraction, non-unit fraction

Other language to be used by the teacher: numerator, denominator

RESOURCES

Mandatory: multilink cubes, counters

Optional: classroom objects such as pots and paintbrushes or pencils and pencil cases

In the eTextbook of this lesson, you will find interactive links to a selection of teaching tools.

Before you teach

• Did children understand fractions when the numerator was greater than 1 in the previous lesson?
• Do children have a strategy for working out a fraction of a number, such as sharing physical resources, or do they rely on times-table knowledge?

Discover

Finding $\frac{3}{4}$

Discover

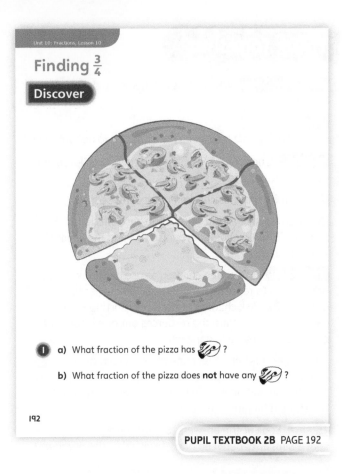

WAYS OF WORKING Pair work

ASK

- *How many equal pieces has the pizza been split into?*
- *How many equal pieces have mushrooms on?*
- *What is the same and what is different about the answers?*
- *Are there the same amount of mushrooms on each part?*

IN FOCUS This picture is a reminder of unit and non-unit fractions. First, the questions require children to work out that the pizza has been divided into four equal parts (quarters). Show children that three of those equal parts have mushrooms on and that this is represented as $\frac{3}{4}$.

ANSWERS

Question ❶ a): $\frac{3}{4}$ of the pizza has .

Question ❶ b): $\frac{1}{4}$ of the pizza does not have any .

❶ a) What fraction of the pizza has ?

b) What fraction of the pizza does **not** have any ?

192

Share

Share

WAYS OF WORKING Whole class teacher led

ASK

- *What is the same and what is different about the fractions in questions ❶ a) and ❶ b)?*
- *Why does the numerator change?*

IN FOCUS When both fractions have been written up, work together with the whole class to compare them. Refer to what Sparks says about $\frac{3}{4}$ being a non-unit fraction. Ask children to explain what a non-unit fraction is and where they might have seen one before.

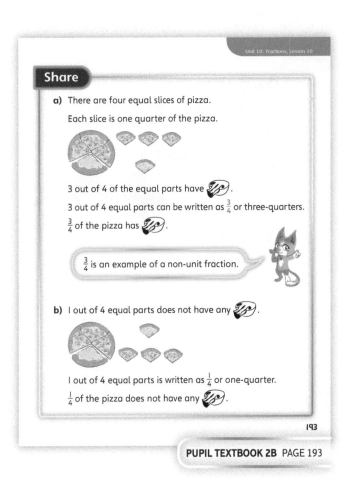

a) There are four equal slices of pizza.

Each slice is one quarter of the pizza.

3 out of 4 of the equal parts have .

3 out of 4 equal parts can be written as $\frac{3}{4}$ or three-quarters.

$\frac{3}{4}$ of the pizza has .

$\frac{3}{4}$ is an example of a non-unit fraction.

b) 1 out of 4 equal parts does not have any .

1 out of 4 equal parts is written as $\frac{1}{4}$ or one-quarter.

$\frac{1}{4}$ of the pizza does not have any .

193

Think together

WAYS OF WORKING Whole class teacher led (I do, We do, You do)

ASK

• *Does each whole have to be the same size to be compared?*

IN FOCUS Question ❶ is scaffolded to help children work out $\frac{3}{4}$ of a quantity.

Question ❷ requires children to recognise $\frac{3}{4}$.

Question ❸ shows that $\frac{1}{2}$ and a further $\frac{1}{4}$ shaded makes $\frac{3}{4}$ shaded. Children should recognise this and may split the $\frac{1}{2}$ into quarters.

STRENGTHEN Encourage children to use multilink cubes or counters to represent the slices of pizza shared in question ❶. Ask children to draw four sorting hoops, label each circle $\frac{1}{4}$ and share the resources out one by one into the circles until they have none left.

Encourage children to recreate the square in question ❸ by folding a piece of paper. When they fold the paper in half and then in half again, the folds will show them how to split the shaded half into quarters.

DEEPEN Look at the answers to question ❶. Do children spot a similarity between or pattern within the numbers?

ASSESSMENT CHECKPOINT Do children use the answer to question ❶ a), which they know to be $\frac{1}{4}$, to help them to work out $\frac{3}{4}$ in question ❶ b)? Do children work out $\frac{3}{4}$ another way, such as by sharing physical resources into four equal groups and counting the number of resources in three of the groups?

ANSWERS

Question ❶ a): $\frac{1}{4}$ of 8 = 2

He gives 2  to one person.

Question ❶ b): $\frac{3}{4}$ of 8 = 6

He gives 6  to three people.

Question ❷:

Question ❸: $\frac{3}{4}$ is shaded.

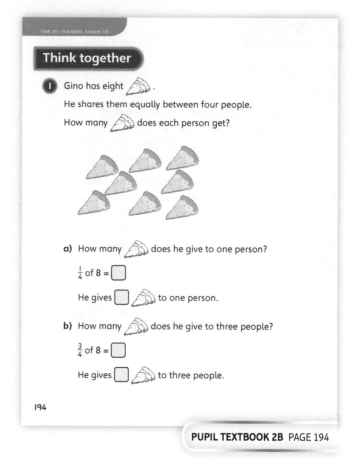

PUPIL TEXTBOOK 2B PAGE 194

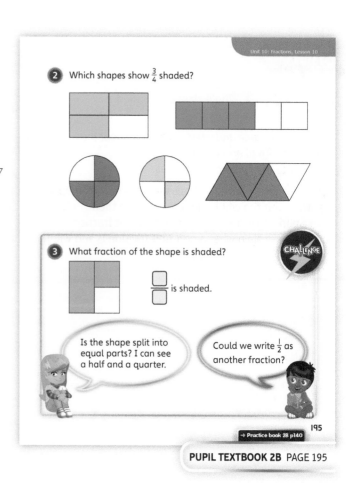

PUPIL TEXTBOOK 2B PAGE 195

Practice

WAYS OF WORKING Independent thinking

IN FOCUS The shapes in question ❶ have been split into different numbers of equal parts for children to shade $\frac{3}{4}$ of. The triangle has been split into four parts, which is a familiar representation for quarters, but the rectangle has been split into eight parts, requiring children to see that a column of two squares is one of four equal parts.

Questions ❷ , ❸ and ❹ ask children to work out $\frac{1}{4}$ and $\frac{3}{4}$ of different numbers. The questions provide no specific sentence scaffolds prompting children to identify the numerator and the denominator, so you may need to guide children to explain what each number in the fraction represents.

STRENGTHEN Question ❺ tells children that $\frac{3}{4}$ is 9 and shows a picture demonstrating this, and then asks them to identify $\frac{1}{4}$ and the whole. One of the quarters is empty, so ask children how they know the number of counters that should fill that quarter. Now cover the whole picture. How can children represent 9 as $\frac{3}{4}$ for themselves? Encourage them to draw four circles, share nine counters among three of the circles and draw a question mark in the last circle.

DEEPEN Give children a number such as 15 that cannot be divided into 4 and ask them to try to split that number of cubes into four equal groups. How do children cope when they reach the point when they do not have enough to continue sharing? Do children try to split the leftover cubes into halves and share those out equally? Guide children to make a link between the 4 times-table and the process of dividing by 4.

ASSESSMENT CHECKPOINT Question ❹ does not provide a picture as a prompt or a guide. Do children need to draw 20 dots in order to help them work out $\frac{3}{4}$?

ANSWERS Answers for the **Practice** part of the lesson appear in the separate **Practice and Reflect answer guide**.

Reflect

WAYS OF WORKING Whole class

IN FOCUS Ask children to refer to the word list to help them form answers in their own words. Highlight the differences between the words by giving a false statement and asking children to agree or disagree with it. For example: *Non-unit fractions always have a 1 as the numerator. Unit fractions can only be a whole divided by 2. One half is not a unit fraction.*

ASSESSMENT CHECKPOINT Which words from the word list do children choose to use in their answers? Do children struggle more to explain similarities or differences between unit fractions and non-unit fractions? Can children come up with other examples of non-unit fractions?

ANSWERS Answers for the **Reflect** part of the lesson appear in the separate **Practice and Reflect answer guide**.

After the lesson ⏸

- Were children able to find $\frac{1}{4}$ of an amount that has more than four equal parts?
- Did children require a pictorial representation to help them work out a fraction? Did they draw one for themselves if no pictorial representations were provided?
- Did children remember that $\frac{1}{2}$ is equivalent to $\frac{2}{4}$ from the previous lesson and use this to help them in this lesson?

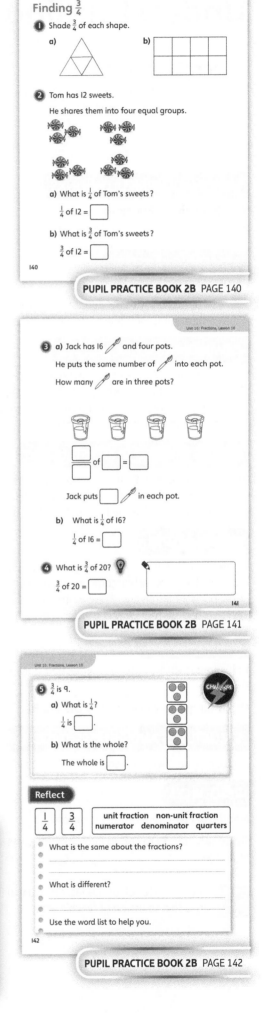

PUPIL PRACTICE BOOK 2B PAGE 140

PUPIL PRACTICE BOOK 2B PAGE 141

PUPIL PRACTICE BOOK 2B PAGE 142

Understanding a whole

Learning focus

In this lesson, children will learn about non-unit fractions becoming one whole.

Small steps

→ Previous step: Finding $\frac{3}{4}$

→ **This step: Understanding a whole**

→ Next step: Understanding whole and parts

NATIONAL CURRICULUM LINKS

Year 2 Number – Fractions

Recognise, find, name and write fractions $\frac{1}{3}$, $\frac{1}{4}$, $\frac{2}{4}$ and $\frac{3}{4}$ of a length, shape, set of objects or quantity.

ASSESSING MASTERY

Children can recognise a whole by seeing whether the numerator and denominator are the same and can understand that a whole as a fraction with the same numerator and denominator can represent the same whole as another fraction made up of a different number of equal parts. Children can fill in missing number sentence scaffolds in order to make one whole.

COMMON MISCONCEPTIONS

When comparing fractions that make one whole, such as $\frac{3}{3}$ and $\frac{4}{4}$, children may think that the whole has to look different. They may think that the whole that has been split into quarters has to be bigger because there are more parts. Show children two different wholes that are the same size but have been split into different parts. Ask:

• *Are the wholes the same size? What is different about them? Does one have to be bigger than the other?*

STRENGTHENING UNDERSTANDING

Part-whole models split into fractions are a useful model to demonstrate one whole being split into multiple parts. They can be shown as a whole with multiple equal parts. Alternatively, they can show the whole partitioned into a unit fraction and non-unit fraction, with the non-unit fraction further partitioned into its unit fractions.

GOING DEEPER

There are multiple ways of making and drawing one whole. Ask children to complete the sentence scaffold 1 = ? as many times as they can, with accompanying drawings. The whole can change each time as well as using a different number of equal parts. Children could also write the same number sentences using real-world contexts, such as a cake that is divided into quarters, all four of which are eaten, meaning that the whole cake is gone.

KEY LANGUAGE

In lesson: fraction, different, same, half, halves, whole, equals, quarters, numerator, denominator, diagram, number sentence, thirds

Other language to be used by the teacher: non-unit fraction, split, equal parts, unit fraction, equivalent

STRUCTURES AND REPRESENTATIONS

2D shapes, part-whole model

RESOURCES

Mandatory: multilink cubes, counters

Optional: objects to cut up into different parts such as cakes or oranges

 In the eTextbook of this lesson, you will find interactive links to a selection of teaching tools.

Before you teach ⏸

• Were children confident with equivalence when comparing $\frac{1}{2}$ and $\frac{2}{4}$ in Lesson 9? Could they apply this understanding of equivalence to $\frac{3}{3}$ and $\frac{4}{4}$?

• Were children confident when answering missing number sentence scaffolds in other units?

Discover

Understanding a whole

Discover

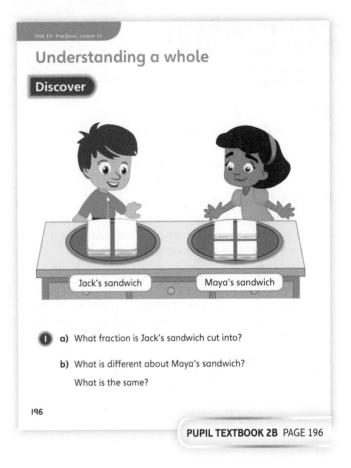

WAYS OF WORKING Pair work

ASK

- *Are the sandwiches different sizes?*
- *What is different about the sandwiches?*
- *Does Jack have more than Maya? Does Maya have more than Jack?*

IN FOCUS Encourage children to look carefully at the sandwiches in the picture and talk about what the sandwiches look like. Ask children to articulate how many equal pieces each sandwich has been split into. The sandwiches are the same whole but have been split into halves and quarters. One sandwich is made up of more equal parts but both sandwiches are the same overall whole.

ANSWERS

Question ❶ a): Jack's sandwich is cut into halves.

Question ❶ b): Maya's sandwich is cut into quarters.

Jack and Maya's sandwiches are the same size and therefore the wholes are the same size.

❶ a) What fraction is Jack's sandwich cut into?

 b) What is different about Maya's sandwich? What is the same?

196

PUPIL TEXTBOOK 2B PAGE 196

Share

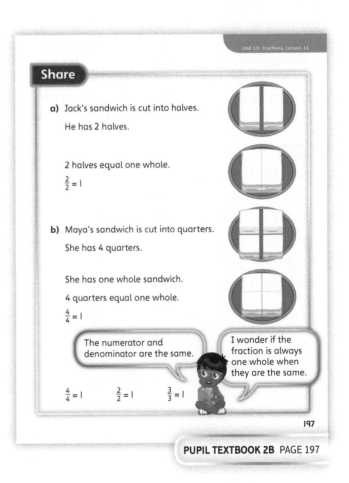

WAYS OF WORKING Whole class teacher led

ASK

- *Does each fraction show one whole sandwich?*
- *What is the same about the two fractions? What is different?*

IN FOCUS This part of the lesson explains how many different parts each sandwich has been cut into and introduces non-unit fractions where the numerator is the same as the denominator. Ash wonders if the fraction is always one whole when the numerator and denominator are the same. Ask children to look at the examples given to decide whether this is correct.

Share

a) Jack's sandwich is cut into halves.

 He has 2 halves.

 2 halves equal one whole.
 $\frac{2}{2} = 1$

b) Maya's sandwich is cut into quarters.

 She has 4 quarters.

 She has one whole sandwich.
 4 quarters equal one whole.
 $\frac{4}{4} = 1$

 The numerator and denominator are the same.

 I wonder if the fraction is always one whole when they are the same.

 $\frac{4}{4} = 1$ $\frac{2}{2} = 1$ $\frac{3}{3} = 1$

197

PUPIL TEXTBOOK 2B PAGE 197

Think together

Whole class teacher led (I do, We do, You do)

ASK

- Question ❶ : *What do you notice about the denominator in each of the fractions?*
- Question ❷ : *How do you know which fractions show one whole without drawing or making them?*

IN FOCUS Question ❶ requires children to work through the pictures and write the shaded fraction of each shape. The question guides children to point out that the last image with all the parts shaded is one whole.

In question ❸ , children complete a missing number sentence scaffold by writing the fraction that would make a whole. Children can use the accompanying pictures to help them, by assigning the parts of each shape to the different parts of the missing number sentence scaffold.

STRENGTHEN There are multiple ways to fill in the missing number sentence scaffolds in question ❸ . For example, question ❸ b) can make two different number sentences: $\frac{1}{3} + \frac{2}{3}$ and $\frac{2}{3} + \frac{1}{3}$. If children have physical resources to model the fractions they are working with, can they group the resources differently each time to model the parts that they are adding?

DEEPEN Building on work that children have done in previous lessons, can they add fractions to make one whole where the denominators are different? For example, $\frac{1}{2} + \frac{2}{4} = 1$.

ASSESSMENT CHECKPOINT In question ❷ , do children draw or make each fraction before deciding whether it is one whole or do they recognise a whole from the fact that the numerator and denominator are the same?

In question ❸ , do children know that the denominators have to be the same in order to add them to make the same whole?

ANSWERS

Question ❶ : A is $\frac{1}{4}$, B is $\frac{2}{4}$, C is $\frac{3}{4}$, D is $\frac{4}{4}$.

           D has the whole shaded.

Question ❷ : $\frac{3}{3}$, $\frac{2}{2}$ and $\frac{4}{4}$ are equal to one whole.

Question ❸ a): $\frac{1}{2} + \frac{1}{2} = 1$

Question ❸ b): $\frac{1}{3} + \frac{2}{3} = 1$

Question ❸ c): $\frac{3}{4} + \frac{1}{4} = 1$

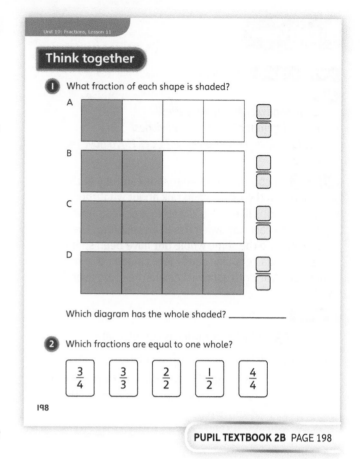

PUPIL TEXTBOOK 2B PAGE 198

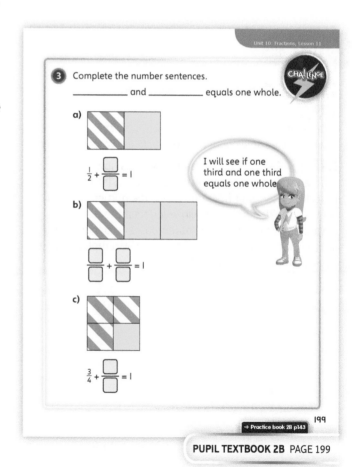

PUPIL TEXTBOOK 2B PAGE 199

Practice

WAYS OF WORKING Independent thinking

IN FOCUS In question ③, children look for the correct number of shaded parts to make a whole.

Question ④ asks children to make one whole by writing a non-unit fraction and a unit fraction based on the pictures. Children write the answer with the same numerator and denominator and see that this is equal to 1.

Refer children to what Flo asks and guide them to conclude that the missing fraction in question ⑤ c) can be written as $\frac{1}{2}$ or $\frac{2}{4}$.

STRENGTHEN Use different physical resources to model the different wholes in question ②. Ask: *What objects in the classroom can be split into two halves, three thirds or four quarters? Does the whole need to be different each time or can it be the same?*

DEEPEN Question ⑥ requires children to understand that they have to start with the same whole but split it into different numbers of equal parts so that each child can have the same amount of cake. Ask children to draw a picture to represent this question and check that they have drawn two wholes that are the same size rather than five parts that are the same size. Ask the same question with the addition of a child eating four equal parts while eating the same amount of cake as Jemima and Sam.

ASSESSMENT CHECKPOINT In question ①, do children label each equal part on the image to help them fill in the box?

In question ④, do children rely on the pictures to work out what fractions to add together or are they aware of the pattern of numerators making the same total as the denominator?

ANSWERS Answers for the **Practice** part of the lesson appear in the separate **Practice and Reflect answer guide**.

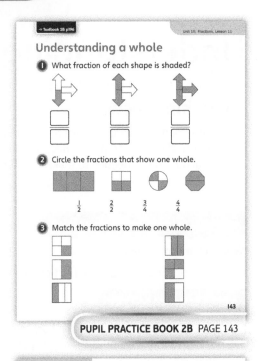

PUPIL PRACTICE BOOK 2B PAGE 143

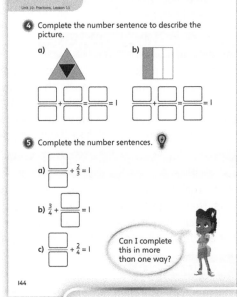

PUPIL PRACTICE BOOK 2B PAGE 144

Reflect

WAYS OF WORKING Independent thinking

IN FOCUS Encourage children to think about this question and explanation for themselves. Ask children to write down fractions with the same numerator and denominator, so that they can use them either to prove their opinion or to help inform their mathematical opinion.

ASSESSMENT CHECKPOINT Do children automatically know the answer or do they have to draw fractions to check? Are they able to explain why the numerators and denominators have to be the same for the fraction to equal one whole? Do they attempt to write other fractions that make one whole based on this knowledge, such as $\frac{5}{5}$ or $\frac{6}{6}$, even if they do not know the names of these fractions?

ANSWERS Answers for the **Reflect** part of the lesson appear in the separate **Practice and Reflect answer guide**.

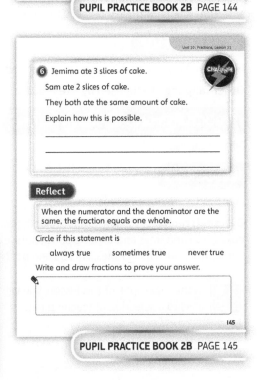

PUPIL PRACTICE BOOK 2B PAGE 145

After the lesson ⏸

- Did children recognise a whole as a written fraction?
- Did children represent wholes that were the same but that were split into different parts?
- Did children understand the relationship between the numerator and the denominator in a whole and explain why they are the same?

Understanding whole and parts

Learning focus

In this lesson, children will learn to write numbers that are made of whole and parts. Children will also write the fraction that is needed to make another whole.

Small steps

→ Previous step: Understanding a whole
→ **This step: Understanding whole and parts**
→ Next step: Counting in halves

NATIONAL CURRICULUM LINKS

Year 2 Number – Fractions

Recognise, find, name and write fractions $\frac{1}{3}$, $\frac{1}{4}$, $\frac{2}{4}$ and $\frac{3}{4}$ of a length, shape, set of objects or quantity.

ASSESSING MASTERY

Children can understand and write whole numbers and fractions together based on a picture and understand that wholes can be divided into the number of equal parts of the fraction, such as a whole also being $\frac{3}{3}$. Children can work out what fraction to add in order to make the next whole and can use the part-whole model to partition a mixed number into its whole and parts.

COMMON MISCONCEPTIONS

Children may find it difficult to count forwards from a whole number and a fraction to the next whole number. The presence of the whole number may confuse children as they may think that this number is related to the fraction, such as dividing $4\frac{2}{3}$ into quarters because there are four wholes. A picture of the parts that they need to add will help children to see how many parts are missing and what the whole has been divided into. Ask:

• *Draw the fraction that you have. How many parts have you divided the whole into? How many parts are missing?*

STRENGTHENING UNDERSTANDING

Model the ideas in this unit using objects that contain a set amount, such as egg boxes, ice cube trays or divided pencil pots. These objects can be cut up or arranged so that they have two, three or four parts. Smaller objects, such as marbles or erasers, can be placed within them to represent the numerator of the fraction. For example, cut a six-egg egg box in half and put one marble into one of the halves to represent $\frac{1}{3}$.

GOING DEEPER

If children are confident putting wholes and fractions into the part-whole models, can they write all of the different addition and subtraction number sentences that they can see around them like they have done in previous units on number?

KEY LANGUAGE

In lesson: how many?, fraction, whole, part, altogether, share, equally

Other language to be used by the teacher: mixed number, array, part-whole model

STRUCTURES AND REPRESENTATIONS

Part-whole model

RESOURCES

Mandatory: multilink cubes

Optional: containers to represent denominators, such as egg boxes, ice cube trays and divided pencil pots; objects to represent numerators, such as marbles, erasers and pencils

 In the eTextbook of this lesson, you will find interactive links to a selection of teaching tools.

Before you teach

• Were children confident that a fraction with the same numerator and denominator represents one whole in the previous lesson?
• Do children understand that one whole can represent different things in different contexts?

Discover

WAYS OF WORKING Pair work

ASK

- Question **1** a): *What fraction does each piece of chocolate represent?*
- Question **1** b): *How many of those pieces make up a whole chocolate bar?*

IN FOCUS Discuss whether the chocolate bars in the picture are all the same and all complete. Guide children to decide that four squares of chocolate make up one whole bar, then ask them to tell you how many whole bars of chocolate there are and how many pieces are left over.

ANSWERS

Question **1** a): There are three whole chocolate bars and three parts. There are 3 and $\frac{3}{4}$ chocolate bars.

Question **1** b): Another $\frac{1}{4}$ is needed to make four whole chocolate bars.

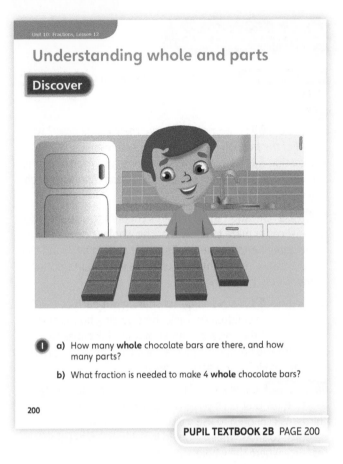

Understanding whole and parts

Discover

1 a) How many **whole** chocolate bars are there, and how many parts?

b) What fraction is needed to make 4 **whole** chocolate bars?

200

PUPIL TEXTBOOK 2B PAGE 200

Share

WAYS OF WORKING Whole class teacher led

ASK

- Question **1** a): *How do you know what the denominator should be for the three pieces?*
- Question **1** b): *How many more of those pieces need to be added in order to make one whole?*

IN FOCUS Three chocolate bars, each divided into four equal parts, are shown next to the sentence explaining that they are wholes. The three other equal pieces are shown to be $\frac{3}{4}$ of one whole bar. Explain to children that these three pieces do not form a whole chocolate bar so must be represented as a fraction.

ASSESSMENT CHECKPOINT Do children want to use 3 as the denominator for the three leftover pieces? If they do, they are treating the three leftover pieces as a whole that has been divided into three equal parts rather than as three parts of a bigger whole.

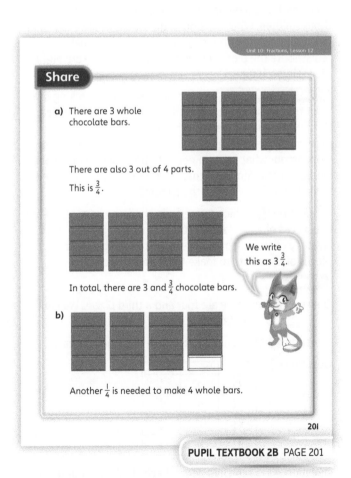

Share

a) There are 3 whole chocolate bars.

There are also 3 out of 4 parts.
This is $\frac{3}{4}$.

We write this as 3 $\frac{3}{4}$.

In total, there are 3 and $\frac{3}{4}$ chocolate bars.

b)

Another $\frac{1}{4}$ is needed to make 4 whole bars.

201

PUPIL TEXTBOOK 2B PAGE 201

Think together

Whole class teacher led (I do, We do, You do)

ASK

- Question **1** : *How many slices are there in one pizza? What part of the fraction does this number represent?*
- Question **1** : *How many more slices do you need to add to the leftover slice to make one whole pizza? What does each slice represent?*

IN FOCUS Question **1** a) requires children to visualise the other slices of pizza to know that the whole is divided into three equal parts, so the denominator should be 3, and that the extra slice represents one of those equal parts, so the numerator is 1.

In question **3** , Astrid suggests sharing out each bar, which would involve children drawing three sorting hoops and counting out the correct number of multilink cubes to represent the number of pieces each child gets. Discuss the benefits of Flo's alternative suggestion.

STRENGTHEN Label each of the pizza slices in question **1** as $\frac{1}{3}$ to show that each pizza is one whole made up of three thirds. Ask children to use a visually different physical resource to show what $4\frac{1}{3}$ would look like, such as using a resource where the whole is not a circle.

DEEPEN After working through question **3** , show children an array of 4 × 6 chocolate pieces and ask how many pieces each child would get if the chocolate was shared between three children. What fraction of the whole would each child get? Children will either share out the pieces equally or redistribute the pieces in the array so that there are eight pieces in each group.

ASSESSMENT CHECKPOINT In question **1** , when working out what fraction is represented by the leftover slice of pizza, do children know to refer to the whole pizza in order to determine the number of equal parts in the whole? When working out what fraction needs to be added to make one whole, do children know that the denominator will be the same before they look at the picture?

In question **3** , which strategy do children use to share out the pieces of chocolate? Do they immediately use a division strategy of sharing or are they able to manipulate the pieces of chocolate to make three columns of 4?

ANSWERS

Question **1** a): There are four and a third pizzas. We can write this as $4\frac{1}{3}$.

Question **1** b): $\frac{2}{3}$ is needed to make five whole pizzas.

Question **2** :

	Wholes	Part
$2\frac{1}{2}$	2	$\frac{1}{2}$
$7\frac{3}{4}$	7	$\frac{3}{4}$
$5\frac{1}{4}$	5	$\frac{1}{4}$
$9\frac{3}{4}$	9	$\frac{3}{4}$

Question **3** : Each child gets $\frac{1}{3}$. Each child gets four pieces of chocolate.

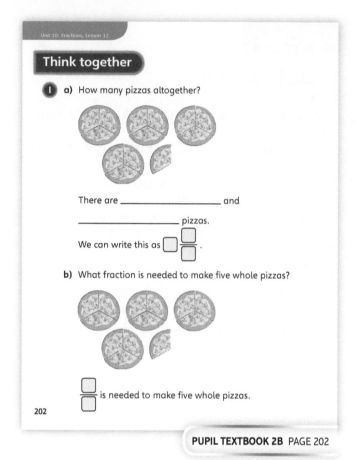

Think together

1 a) How many pizzas altogether?

There are _____ and

_____ pizzas.

We can write this as ☐ ☐/☐ .

b) What fraction is needed to make five whole pizzas?

☐/☐ is needed to make five whole pizzas.

202

PUPIL TEXTBOOK 2B PAGE 202

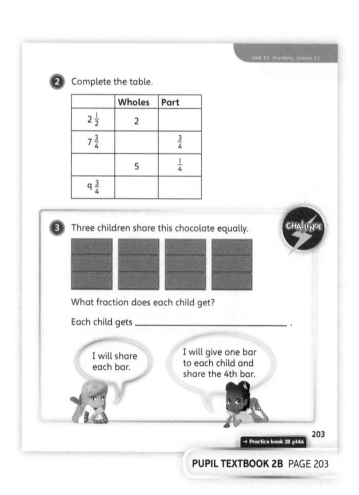

2 Complete the table.

	Wholes	Part
$2\frac{1}{2}$	2	
$7\frac{3}{4}$		$\frac{3}{4}$
	5	$\frac{1}{4}$
$9\frac{3}{4}$		

3 Three children share this chocolate equally.

CHALLENGE

What fraction does each child get?

Each child gets _____ .

I will share each bar.

I will give one bar to each child and share the 4th bar.

→ Practice book 2B p146

203

PUPIL TEXTBOOK 2B PAGE 203

Practice

PUPIL PRACTICE BOOK 2B PAGE 146

WAYS OF WORKING Independent thinking

IN FOCUS Question ① requires children to count up the parts that form one whole and then to work out the fraction that is left over. The apples in question ① a) are obviously grouped into wholes of four slices each. In question ① b), it is less obvious that the cake left over has been split into quarters and that three quarters of the last cake is left over.

Question ③ gives different representations of $2\frac{1}{4}$ and asks children to circle the correct representations. The quarters are different shapes and sizes but all represent $\frac{1}{4}$ of the whole.

Question ⑤ involves splitting $2\frac{1}{2}$ into two parts. Guide children to split the $\frac{2}{4}$ into two separate quarters.

STRENGTHEN In question ⑥, the part-whole model can be completed in different ways because $\frac{1}{2}$ is equivalent to $\frac{2}{4}$. Use physical resources to model six wholes and two quarters. Children should be able to write $6\frac{1}{2}$ and $6\frac{2}{4}$ based on what they have already learned.

DEEPEN Can children count the number of halves in total, using physical resources to help them, and write it down or say it aloud? If children can do that, do they notice a pattern between the number of halves and the number of wholes? Can they discuss why they think that might be?

ASSESSMENT CHECKPOINT Do children split up the wholes and fractions with ease in the part-whole models in question ② or do they get confused about how to separate them?

ANSWERS Answers for the **Practice** part of the lesson appear in the separate **Practice and Reflect answer guide**.

PUPIL PRACTICE BOOK 2B PAGE 147

Reflect

WAYS OF WORKING Pair work

IN FOCUS This open-ended question asks children to come up with and draw a whole and part of their own. If children are unsure, suggest objects that they could draw, such as apples, pizzas or chocolate bars. Ask children to compare their work with a partner and discuss what is similar or different about their pictures.

ASSESSMENT CHECKPOINT Do children's drawings match their written fractions? Are all of their wholes the same size or do they look different? Have children drawn the outline of the other parts in their fraction to show what the whole has been divided into? Do children accurately draw the part of their whole based on the size of their original whole?

ANSWERS Answers for the **Reflect** part of the lesson appear in the separate **Practice and Reflect answer guide**.

After the lesson ⏸

- Did children understand what is meant by a whole number and a fraction?
- Did children recognise a mixture of whole numbers and fractions? Were they able to draw this?
- Did children work out the fraction that needed to be added to make one whole and understand that it had to have the same denominator?

PUPIL PRACTICE BOOK 2B PAGE 148

Counting in halves

Learning focus

In this lesson, children will count forwards and backwards in halves with the aid of a number line.

Small steps

→ Previous step: Understanding whole and parts
→ **This step: Counting in halves**
→ Next step: Counting in quarters

NATIONAL CURRICULUM LINKS

Year 2 Non-statutory guidance

Pupils should count in fractions up to 10, starting from any number.

ASSESSING MASTERY

Children can count forwards and backwards in halves up to and down from 10. They can match fractions of wholes and halves on the number line and fill in an incomplete number line with intervals of one half.

COMMON MISCONCEPTIONS

When counting backwards in halves, children may also count backwards one whole as well as one half. For example, they may count backwards from $3\frac{1}{2}$ to 2 or $2\frac{1}{2}$. Model this on a number line and by using physical resources representing halves that children can take away each time they count backwards. Ask:
• *When counting backwards in halves, when does the whole go down?*

STRENGTHENING UNDERSTANDING

Counting forwards and backwards in halves on a metre stick or a displayed number line will help children to rehearse the pattern of halves going forwards and backwards. To embed conceptual understanding, provide pictures of wholes and halves going up like a staircase along the number line.

GOING DEEPER

If children are confident counting forwards and backwards in halves from 0 to 10, can they do the same starting from one quarter? The intervals on the counting stick will be the same but will land on different numbers. Can children pick up the pattern of one quarter and three quarters instead of wholes and halves? Can children explain why they will never say one whole when counting forwards in halves from one quarter?

KEY LANGUAGE

In lesson: halves, whole, parts, count up, count down, total, number line, next, last, how many, values, pattern

Other language to be used by the teacher: intervals, skip count, even, odd

STRUCTURES AND REPRESENTATIONS

Number line

RESOURCES

Mandatory: blank number lines, counting sticks or metre sticks, different coloured highlighters

Optional: physical resources to represent halves such as a halved apple, a halved circle or a halved chocolate bar

 In the eTextbook of this lesson, you will find interactive links to a selection of teaching tools.

Before you teach

• Can children recall facts such as $\frac{1}{2} = \frac{2}{4}$ or $\frac{4}{4} =$ one whole?
• Are children confident when skip counting in whole numbers?

Discover

Counting in halves

Discover

WAYS OF WORKING Pair work

ASK

- Question ① a): *How many apples is each child holding?*
- Question ① b): *How many children represent one apple?*

IN FOCUS Can children count in halves to work out how many whole apples are in the picture? If children know that $\frac{2}{2}$ is one whole, you can lead them to the conclusion that two children make one whole apple.

ANSWERS

Question ① a):

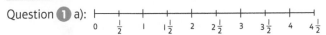

Question ① b): There are four whole apples. There is also $\frac{1}{2}$ an apple. There are $4\frac{1}{2}$ apples in total.

① **a)** Count in halves to see how many apples there are.

b) How many whole apples are there?

How many extra parts?

204

PUPIL TEXTBOOK 2B PAGE 204

Share

WAYS OF WORKING Whole class teacher led

ASK

- Question ① a): *Do you notice a pattern when counting forwards in halves?*
- Question ① a): *What words get repeated? Why is that?*

IN FOCUS Use a counting stick or metre stick to count how many apples each child has. Pictures can be added to the counting stick or on the board to make it clear when there is a half apple and when there is a whole apple.

Share

a)

$\frac{1}{2}$; 1; 1 and $\frac{1}{2}$; 2; 2 and $\frac{1}{2}$ ...

b) There are four whole apples.

There is also $\frac{1}{2}$ an apple.

There are $4\frac{1}{2}$ apples in total.

205

PUPIL TEXTBOOK 2B PAGE 205

Think together

Whole class teacher led (I do, We do, You do)

ASK

- Question ❶ *What will be the next point on the number line? How do you know?*
- Question ❶ *Could you count up in halves starting with a different number?*
- Question ❸ *Is there a similar pattern when counting backwards in halves as there is when counting forwards in halves?*

IN FOCUS Model question ❸ a) using a marked number line. Use a different coloured highlighter to represent Noah and Di. Mark in both colours starting at either end of the number line and jumping towards the centre to show what number Noah and Di would both say together. Repeat with new number lines starting from 8 and 7 for questions ❸ b) and ❸ c).

STRENGTHEN Create a number line with intervals of halves. Ask children to skip count forwards and backwards. Cover up different parts of the number line and ask children to skip count, calling out the covered numbers as children count. Keep changing the starting number from which children count forwards or backwards.

DEEPEN Provide a blank number line with every whole number marked by a longer line as in question ❷. Ask children to take turns to write a whole or a whole and a half in the middle of the number line. Ask children what number will be either side of it and how they know. Further extend this question by asking: *How many jumps to get to ___?*

ASSESSMENT CHECKPOINT When marking numbers on the number lines in questions ❶ and ❷, do children have to mark all of the values in order to do this? Do children count forwards from 0 for each value or do they count on from intervals that they have already marked?

Do children struggle more when counting backwards in halves than when counting forwards? Do they skip count backwards by one whole as well as one half?

In question ❸, do children spot that half of an even number is a whole number and half of an odd number always has a half?

ANSWERS

Question ❶ a): The next number will be 2.

Question ❶ b): The last number is 5.

Question ❷:

Question ❸ a): They will say $4\frac{1}{2}$ together.

Question ❸ b): 4

Question ❸ c): $3\frac{1}{2}$

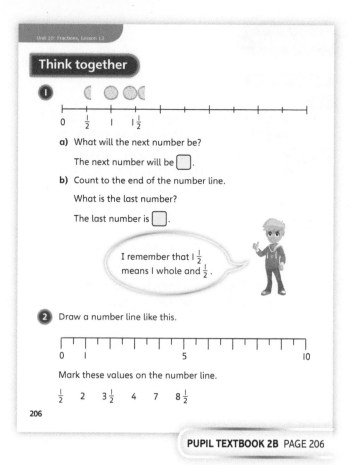

PUPIL TEXTBOOK 2B PAGE 206

PUPIL TEXTBOOK 2B PAGE 207

Practice

Independent thinking

IN FOCUS Question **1** asks children to complete the sentence scaffolds with the whole and fraction shown in the picture and then circle the number that comes next. Question **1** a) prompts the answer as the outline of the next half is shown, whereas question **1** b) requires children to visualise the outline of the next half of a shape.

Question **3** requires children to draw their own pictorial representation of the number. Do children attempt to draw the half in proportion to the whole? Prompt them to think about how they could represent 0. Some children may want to draw an outline, whereas others may prefer to leave it blank.

STRENGTHEN Children have partly drawn counting up in halves using sweets as a prompt. Can they draw their own number line, drawing a different pictorial representation to represent each half and whole? It could be a different shape, such as an apple, or it could be a length model that gets taller each time, perhaps using a pencil as a benchmark.

DEEPEN Question **5** can be completed alongside a number line marked with half intervals. If children are confident counting forwards and backwards in halves, ask what is $1\frac{1}{2}$ after or before a certain number, such as: *What is $1\frac{1}{2}$ after 4? What is $1\frac{1}{2}$ before 4?* Vary the starting number so that children work from either whole numbers or numbers with a half.

ASSESSMENT CHECKPOINT In question **1**, do children automatically know that the next number is 2 or do they have to shade in the blank half in the picture to check? Question **1** b) does not provide a shape to shade in, requiring children to either draw it themselves or visualise it to work out what comes next.

In questions **2** b) and c), do children count backwards to fill in missing values higher up on the number line?

If children draw a picture to represent 0 in question **3**, do they draw an outline of one whole sweet or of one half sweet?

ANSWERS Answers for the **Practice** part of the lesson appear in the separate **Practice and Reflect answer guide**.

Reflect

Pair work

IN FOCUS This part of the lesson asks children to explain in their own words how to count on one half from a whole number. Encourage children to refer to the number line when explaining or to draw their own model to illustrate their explanation.

ASSESSMENT CHECKPOINT Do children use jumps on a number line to explain their thinking or do they draw a series of boxes that have been halved with a dotted line down the middle? Are children confident that the next number will have the same whole number because not enough has been added to cross over to the next whole number?

ANSWERS Answers for the **Reflect** part of the lesson appear in the separate **Practice and Reflect answer guide**.

After the lesson ⏸

- Did children become familiar with the pattern of counting up in halves?
- Could children fill out a blank number line in halves?
- Were children able to count backwards as well as forwards in halves?

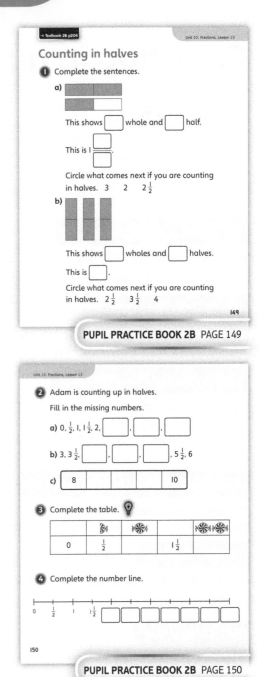

PUPIL PRACTICE BOOK 2B PAGE 149

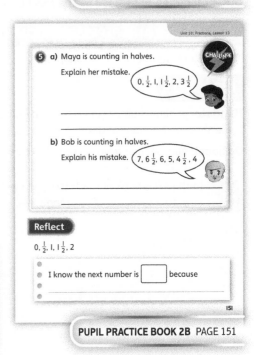

PUPIL PRACTICE BOOK 2B PAGE 150

PUPIL PRACTICE BOOK 2B PAGE 151

Counting in quarters

Learning focus

In this lesson, children will learn how to count in quarters. Children will work out how many quarters are needed to make one whole.

Small steps

→ Previous step: Counting in halves
→ **This step: Counting in quarters**
→ Next step: Describing movement

NATIONAL CURRICULUM LINKS

Year 2 Non-statutory guidance

Pupils should count in fractions up to 10, starting from any number.

ASSESSING MASTERY

Children can count in quarters and know when to say the next whole rather than $\frac{4}{4}$. Children can put written fractions in order starting from 0 and can work out how many wholes there are from a number of quarters.

COMMON MISCONCEPTIONS

Children may struggle to make the transition from $\frac{3}{4}$ to the next whole when counting forwards in quarters. This may be particularly challenging when the whole numbers are 3 or 4 because they match the numbers in $\frac{3}{4}$. Provide a number line with whole numbers written on it and intervals of 4 in between each whole number to help children start to make this transition.

STRENGTHENING UNDERSTANDING

If you displayed a number line counting up in halves during the previous lesson, use the same number line and mark on extra intervals for $\frac{1}{4}$ and $\frac{3}{4}$. This will reinforce equivalence between $\frac{1}{2}$ and $\frac{2}{4}$.

GOING DEEPER

When counting forwards in quarters, can children say $\frac{1}{2}$ instead of $\frac{2}{4}$, so that they say $\frac{1}{4}, \frac{1}{2}, \frac{3}{4}$, 1 rather than $\frac{1}{4}, \frac{2}{4}, \frac{3}{4}$, 1? If children can do this, are they able to count forwards in quarters from any given number with $\frac{1}{2}$, such as $3\frac{1}{2}$?

KEY LANGUAGE

In lesson: quarters, whole, number line, part, in total, how many?

Other language to be used by the teacher: fraction, intervals, counting forwards, equivalence

STRUCTURES AND REPRESENTATIONS

Number line, number track, 2D shapes

RESOURCES

Mandatory: blank number lines, filled-in number lines showing wholes and four intervals between each whole, number cards showing fractions and whole numbers

Optional: number line from Lesson 13 showing halves, amended to show quarters as well

 In the eTextbook of this lesson, you will find interactive links to a selection of teaching tools.

Before you teach ⏸

- Did children have any difficulty counting forwards in halves in the previous lesson?
- Are children confident that $\frac{4}{4}$ makes one whole?

Discover

Pair work

ASK

- Question ❶ a): *How many quarter circles are there?*
- Question ❶ b): *How would you show how many quarter circles there are in one whole?*

IN FOCUS The picture shows a lot of quarter circles all jumbled up so it is not obvious where the original wholes are. When children count the quarter circles, do they count them individually or do they call them quarters?

ANSWERS

Question ❶ a): There are five whole circles and one quarter in total.

Question ❶ b): We need to add $\frac{3}{4}$ to make a whole (or $\frac{4}{4}$).

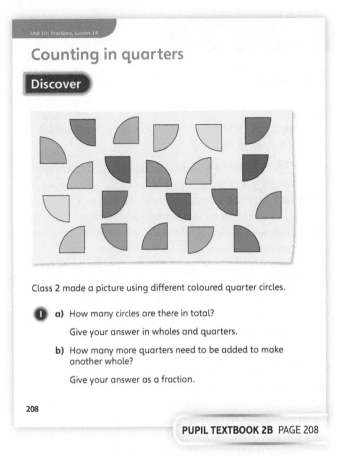

Counting in quarters

Discover

Class 2 made a picture using different coloured quarter circles.

❶ a) How many circles are there in total?

Give your answer in wholes and quarters.

b) How many more quarters need to be added to make another whole?

Give your answer as a fraction.

208

PUPIL TEXTBOOK 2B PAGE 208

Share

Whole class teacher led

ASK

- Question ❶ a): *Do each of the quarter circles match the fractions on the number line?*
- Question ❶ a): *Why have some quarter circles been labelled as whole numbers if you are counting up in quarters?*

IN FOCUS The quarter circles have all been labelled with quarters going from left to right. There is also a corresponding number line underneath the picture to match each quarter circle and check that nothing is missing. The quarters have been rearranged to make it clear how many wholes there are and how many quarter circles are left over.

In question ❶ b), Flo points out that only the last quarter circle left over is needed when working out how many quarter circles to add in order to make a whole.

Share

a) I counted each quarter and when I got to $\frac{4}{4}$ I knew it was a whole. I also used a number line to help me.

I put the four quarter circles together to make a whole.

There are 5 whole circles and one quarter in total.

209

PUPIL TEXTBOOK 2B PAGE 209

Think together

WAYS OF WORKING Whole class teacher led (I do, We do, You do)

ASK

• Question **1** : *What could these quarters of watermelon look like if they were rearranged?*

IN FOCUS Question **2** shows fraction cards that children are asked to put in order. The quarter circle fractions in the **Share** part of the lesson were already in order, so this extends what children have learned and requires them to apply their knowledge of where the whole numbers go in the sequence.

STRENGTHEN Print the fraction cards in question **2** so children can physically move them around. Prepare an empty number line to put them onto. Flo suggests ordering them in another way to prompt children to try ordering the cards from largest to smallest on the number line.

DEEPEN Question **3** can be reworded so that Jack starts with a certain number of whole chocolate bars, which can be marked on the number line, and he eats $\frac{1}{4}$ each day for nine days. This will require children to count backwards by nine quarters to see how much chocolate Jack has left. Vary the starting numbers so that children count backwards from whole numbers and from numbers with quarters.

ASSESSMENT CHECKPOINT In question **1** , what strategy do children use to group together four quarters of watermelon into one whole?

In question **2** , do children automatically put 0 first when ordering the fractions?

In question **3** , do children understand that each jump and interval on the number line is worth $\frac{1}{4}$?

ANSWERS

Question **1** a): $5\frac{3}{4}$ watermelons were eaten in total.

Question **1** b): $\frac{1}{4}$ needs to be added to make another whole.

Question **2** : $0, \frac{1}{4}, \frac{2}{4}, \frac{3}{4}, 1, 1\frac{1}{4}, 1\frac{2}{4}, 1\frac{3}{4}, 2, 2\frac{1}{4}, 2\frac{2}{4}, 2\frac{3}{4}, 3$

Question **3** : Jack will eat 2 whole bars over nine days. He will also eat another quarter of a bar.

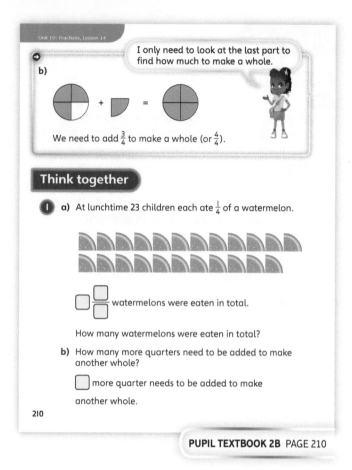

PUPIL TEXTBOOK 2B PAGE 210

PUPIL TEXTBOOK 2B PAGE 211

Practice

Independent thinking

IN FOCUS In question **5**, provide a blank number line to support children when counting forwards in quarters. Ask children to decide their starting point and encourage them to mark enough intervals between each whole number. Discuss the fact that this is a subtraction calculation, which means that children will jump backwards along the number line.

STRENGTHEN When children have answered questions **2** and **3**, ask them to create a giant number line of quarters from 0 all the way to 10. This could be done individually or as part of a class project to be displayed in the classroom. Every time a new whole number is reached, this can be represented by using a different colour to write with.

DEEPEN Children who are confident can create their own number line for question **5**. Their number line should display equally spaced intervals and the correct number of intervals to show five wholes. Can children write a calculation to match the word problem? Do they know how to represent ten quarters? Do they write this as a fraction, as a written word or as whole numbers and quarters left over?

ASSESSMENT CHECKPOINT In question **1**, do children label each quarter or do they circle around four quarters each time and see what is left over? Do children give their answer as the number of quarters they have counted rather than as a whole number?

Do children count backwards from any numbers when filling in the missing numbers in questions **2** and **3**?

In question **5**, do children understand that they are jumping backwards or do they try to jump forwards? If children have drawn a number line, do they fill in all of the intervals first by counting forwards in order to help them when jumping backwards?

ANSWERS Answers for the **Practice** part of the lesson appear in the separate **Practice and Reflect answer guide**.

Reflect

Independent thinking

IN FOCUS The **Reflect** part of the lesson requires children to apply what they know about making their own sequences of quarters to fill in the number sentence. Encourage children to indicate in their explanation whether the numbers are getting bigger or smaller and whether the whole needs to go up or down.

ASSESSMENT CHECKPOINT Do children initially spot that the sequence goes up in quarters? Do they mention that the next number could be $1\frac{1}{2}$ as well as $1\frac{2}{4}$?

ANSWERS Answers for the **Reflect** part of the lesson appear in the separate **Practice and Reflect answer guide**.

After the lesson

- Were children able to count backwards as well as forwards in quarters?
- Did children successfully go up or down to the next whole rather than having to write it as a number of quarters?
- Did children show awareness of the equivalence of quarters and halves?

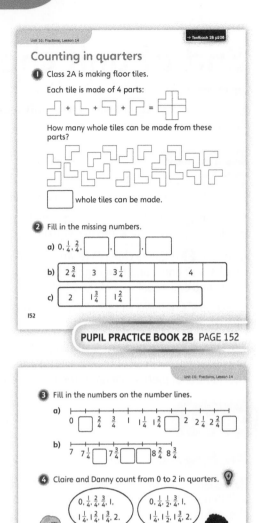

PUPIL PRACTICE BOOK 2B PAGE 152

PUPIL PRACTICE BOOK 2B PAGE 153

PUPIL PRACTICE BOOK 2B PAGE 154

End of unit check

Don't forget the *Power Maths* unit assessment grid on p26.

WAYS OF WORKING Group work – adult led

IN FOCUS Question ① requires children to identify which shape has been split into three equal parts with one part shaded.

Question ② focuses on calculating half of a number, reinforcing that children need to share 8 into two equal parts.

Question ③ requires children to work out the relationship between the numbers 12 and 4 and to recognise that these numbers represent the whole and one equal part of the whole.

Question ④ requires children to find an equivalent non-unit fraction to the unit fraction $\frac{1}{2}$.

Question ⑤ tests children's knowledge of non-unit fractions. The fact that the denominator in all of the fractions is 4 requires children to correctly link the number of pieces that are eaten to the numerator.

Think!

WAYS OF WORKING Pair work

IN FOCUS This task shows different unit and non-unit fractions. Ensure that children can read them out, can sort them into categories using words from the word bank and can understand what each fraction represents.

Children sort fractions creatively, revising the key concepts covered in this unit: denominators as equal parts, equivalent fractions, fractions making one whole, unit and non-unit fractions, and so on.

Children can come up with their own categories and sort the fractions under the correct headings. Get children to check other pairs' categories.

Encourage children to come up with one sentence to describe each of their categories before writing their answer in **My journal**. For example, 'On this side, all of the fractions have the denominator 4 because they have all been divided into four equal parts'.

ANSWERS AND COMMENTARY To show mastery, children will be able to see a number as both being a whole and a part. For example, if the number 8 is the whole, 4 would be $\frac{1}{2}$. If 8 is $\frac{1}{2}$, 16 would be the whole. Assess if children can go further and say what the whole would be if 8 were $\frac{1}{3}$ or $\frac{1}{4}$. Show this on a set of bar models, each split into equal parts representing 8.

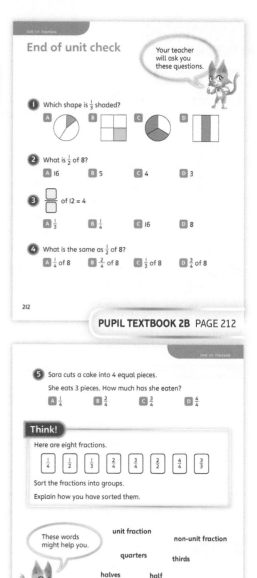

PUPIL TEXTBOOK 2B PAGE 212

PUPIL TEXTBOOK 2B PAGE 213

Q	A	WRONG ANSWERS AND MISCONCEPTIONS	STRENGTHENING UNDERSTANDING
1	D	A has been split into three parts but the parts are not equal. Children who choose A do not understand the concept of equal parts.	For question 2 to 5, cubes or counters can be used to physically represent each question. These resources can be arranged on paper so that children can draw around them to represent the whole and the equal parts. Each part can be labelled with the correct fraction name, such as $\frac{1}{4}$.
2	C	Children may mistakenly think that 8 is $\frac{1}{2}$ and choose A.	
3	A	Children may think that B is correct because $\frac{1}{4}$ has a 4 in it and the equal part is 4. Encourage children to see that 4 is one of three equal parts of 12, perhaps by using times-table facts.	
4	B	Children may choose A or C because they recognise that the numerator (1) is the same as in $\frac{1}{2}$.	
5	C	Children may choose $\frac{1}{4}$ because they relate the fact that the cake is split into four equal pieces to each piece being one quarter.	

My journal

ANSWERS AND COMMENTARY

This task allows children to write about one of the chosen categories by which they have sorted fractions. Children will have rehearsed this with their partner in **Think!** and now are asked to write this in their own words. Encourage children to strengthen their explanation by drawing bar models or pictures of what each category represents, such as drawing one shaded whole to illustrate the category 'fractions that make one whole'.

If children are struggling to articulate a pattern, give them sentence scaffolds such as 'all of the denominators are the same / different' or 'these fractions all make the same / a different amount'.

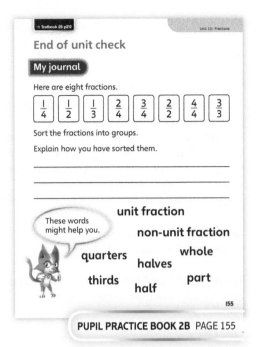

PUPIL PRACTICE BOOK 2B PAGE 155

Power check

WAYS OF WORKING Independent thinking

ASK

- *Do you think you could use physical resources to show that something has been divided into equal parts?*
- *Are you confident that you could draw a fraction?*
- *Could you draw the same fraction in different ways?*

Power play

WAYS OF WORKING Pair work

IN FOCUS This game gives children the opportunity to practise recognising, writing and drawing a fraction. It asks them to recognise fractions from shapes as well as from the numerator and denominator. Assess whether children can work together in pairs to decide what whole to start with when drawing a fraction.

ANSWERS AND COMMENTARY Children may say fractions incorrectly and read out the numbers they see, such as reading out $\frac{3}{4}$ as 'three fours'.

When writing down equivalent fractions, children may write $\frac{1}{2}$ when identifying two quarters. Does their partner realise what they have done and can they explain why they have done it?

With fractions such as $\frac{4}{4}$, children may draw one whole and shade it in without indicating that it is split into four equal parts. Can children see why they must split it into four equal parts in order to show that it does not represent another fraction, such as $\frac{3}{3}$ or $\frac{2}{2}$?

PUPIL PRACTICE BOOK 2B PAGE 156

After the unit ⏸

- Could children recognise fractions in a range of contexts?
- Did children confidently spot equivalent fractions when written down or did they require a visual image to see the equivalence?
- Were children able to make any generalisations about patterns that they spotted between the numerator and denominator in equivalent fractions or in fractions that made one whole?

Strengthen and **Deepen** activities for this unit can be found in the *Power Maths* online subscription.

Published by Pearson Education Limited, 80 Strand, London, WC2R 0RL.

www.pearsonschools.co.uk

Text © Pearson Education Limited 2017
Edited by Pearson, Little Grey Cells Publishing Services and Haremi Ltd
Designed and typeset by Kamae Design
Original illustrations © Pearson Education Limited 2017
Illustrated by Laura Arias, Nigel Dobbyn, Adam Linley and Nadene Naude at Beehive Illustration;
Emily Skinner at Graham-Cameron Illustration; Paul Higgins at Hunter Higgins Illustrations; Kamae; and Andy 327 at KJA.
Cover design by Pearson Education Ltd
Back cover illustration © Will Overton at Advocate Art and Nadene Naude at Beehive Illustration.

Series Editor: Tony Staneff
Consultant: Professor Liu Jian

The rights of Tony Staneff, David Board, Natasha Dolling, Julia Hayes, Derek Huby and Neil Jarrett to be identified as authors of this work have been asserted by them in accordance with the Copyright, Designs and Patents Act 1988.

First published 2017

20 19 18
10 9 8 7 6 5 4 3 2

British Library Cataloguing in Publication Data
A catalogue record for this book is available from the British Library

ISBN 978 0 435 18979 2

Printed in the UK by Ashford Colour Press

www.activelearnprimary.co.uk

Note from the publisher
Pearson has robust editorial processes, including answer and fact checks, to ensure the accuracy of the content in this publication, and every effort is made to ensure this publication is free of errors. We are, however, only human, and occasionally errors do occur. Pearson is not liable for any misunderstandings that arise as a result of errors in this publication, but it is our priority to ensure that the content is accurate. If you spot an error, please do contact us at resourcescorrections@pearson.com so we can make sure it is corrected.